What's on the CD

W9-CSX-161

The CD included with this second edition of the *A+: DOS/Windows Study Guide* contains a valuable software tool that will help you prepare for the A+ Core Module exam. An installation interface is designed to run automatically when you place the CD in your Windows 95 or Windows NT 4 or later machine. If it doesn't run automatically, you can access and install the files on the CD through a user-friendly graphical interface by running the **CLICKME.EXE** file located in the root directory.

Minimum System Requirements:
486/100MHz, 16MB RAM, 2× CD-ROM, SoundBlaster-compatible soundcard, 640×480 256-color display, Windows 95/NT 4 or later.

A+ Core Module Test Prep Program

Test your knowledge with this custom program that contains the review questions found in the *A+: DOS/Windows Study Guide.* You can choose to test yourself chapter by chapter or randomly. Click the Install Study Guide button on the autorun CD interface screen to install the test prep program on your hard disk, or run the **SETUP.EXE** program from the CD's StudyGuide folder.

Once installation is complete, you can run the program by choosing the A+ DOS/Windows Study Guide program icon in the Programs folder of your Start menu.

Please consult the **README.TXT** file located in the root directory for more detailed information on the CD contents.

During installation of the test engine, you may be prompted to allow the program to update certain system files. The files referred to are Microsoft DLL files and should not pose a threat to your system; however, as a precaution you may wish to back up your system files prior to installing this program. In some instances, you may need to reboot your computer before the new files can take effect. After rebooting, you will need to reaccess the CD interface before completing the program installation.

A+: DOS/Windows Study Guide

A+: DOS¨/Windows¨ Study Guide

Second Edition

David Groth

SYBEX®

San Francisco • Paris • Düsseldorf • Soest

Associate Publisher: Guy Hart-Davis
Contracts and Licensing Manager: Kristine Plachy
Acquisitions & Developmental Editor: Neil Edde
Editor: Brenda Frink
Technical Editor: Jon Hansen
Book Designers: Catalin Dulfu, Patrick Dintino,
Kris Warrenburg, Maureen Forys
Electronic Publishing Specialist: Kris Warrenburg
Production Coordinator: Blythe Woolston
Indexer: Ted Laux
Companion CD: Ginger Warner
Cover Designer: Design Site
Cover Illustrator: Design Site

Screen reproductions produced with Collage Complete.

Collage Complete is a trademark of Inner Media Inc.

SYBEX is a registered trademark of SYBEX Inc.

TRADEMARKS: SYBEX has attempted throughout this book
to distinguish proprietary trademarks from descriptive terms
by following the capitalization style used by the manufacturer.

The CD Interface music is from GIRA Sound AURIA Music
Library © GIRA Sound 1996.

The author and publisher have made their best efforts to prepare this book, and the content is based upon final release
software whenever possible. Portions of the manuscript may
be based upon pre-release versions supplied by software man-
ufacturer(s). The author and the publisher make no representation or warranties of any kind with regard to the
completeness or accuracy of the contents herein and accept no
liability of any kind including but not limited to performance,
merchantability, fitness for any particular purpose, or any
losses or damages of any kind caused or alleged to be caused
directly or indirectly from this book.

First edition copyright ©1998 SYBEX Inc.
Copyright ©1998 SYBEX Inc., 1151 Marina Village Parkway,
Alameda, CA 94501. World rights reserved. No part of this
publication may be stored in a retrieval system, transmitted,
or reproduced in any way, including but not limited to photo-
copy, photograph, magnetic or other record, without the prior
agreement and written permission of the publisher.

Library of Congress Card Number: 98-85953
ISBN: 0-7821-2351-1

Manufactured in the United States of America

10 9 8 7

Software License Agreement: Terms and Conditions

The media and/or any online materials accompanying this book that are available now or in the future contain programs and/or text files (the "Software") to be used in connection with the book. SYBEX hereby grants to you a license to use the Software, subject to the terms that follow. Your purchase, acceptance, or use of the Software will constitute your acceptance of such terms.

The Software compilation is the property of SYBEX unless otherwise indicated and is protected by copyright to SYBEX or other copyright owner(s) as indicated in the media files (the "Owner(s)"). You are hereby granted a single-user license to use the Software for your personal, noncommercial use only. You may not reproduce, sell, distribute, publish, circulate, or commercially exploit the Software, or any portion thereof, without the written consent of SYBEX and the specific copyright owner(s) of any component software included on this media.

In the event that the Software or components include specific license requirements or end-user agreements, statements of condition, disclaimers, limitations or warranties ("End-User License"), those End-User Licenses supersede the terms and conditions herein as to that particular Software component. Your purchase, acceptance, or use of the Software will constitute your acceptance of such End-User Licenses.

By purchase, use or acceptance of the Software you further agree to comply with all export laws and regulations of the United States as such laws and regulations may exist from time to time.

Software Support

Components of the supplemental Software and any offers associated with them may be supported by the specific Owner(s) of that material but they are not supported by SYBEX. Information regarding any available support may be obtained from the Owner(s) using the information provided in the appropriate read.me files or listed elsewhere on the media.

Should the manufacturer(s) or other Owner(s) cease to offer support or decline to honor any offer, SYBEX bears no responsibility. This notice concerning support for the Software is provided for your information only. SYBEX is not the agent or principal of the Owner(s), and SYBEX is in no way responsible for providing any support for the Software, nor is it liable or responsible for any support provided, or not provided, by the Owner(s).

Warranty

SYBEX warrants the enclosed media to be free of physical defects for a period of ninety (90) days after purchase. The Software is not available from SYBEX in any other form or media than that enclosed herein or posted to www.sybex.com. If you discover a defect in the media during this warranty period, you may obtain a replacement of identical format at no charge by sending the defective media, postage prepaid, with proof of purchase to:

SYBEX Inc.
Customer Service Department
1151 Marina Village Parkway
Alameda, CA 94501
(510) 523-8233
Fax: (510) 523-2373
e-mail: info@sybex.com
web: http://www.sybex.com

After the 90-day period, you can obtain replacement media of identical format by sending us the defective disk, proof of purchase, and a check or money order for $10, payable to SYBEX.

Disclaimer

SYBEX makes no warranty or representation, either expressed or implied, with respect to the Software or its contents, quality, performance, merchantability, or fitness for a particular purpose. In no event will SYBEX, its distributors, or dealers be liable to you or any other party for direct, indirect, special, incidental, consequential, or other damages arising out of the use of or inability to use the Software or its contents even if advised of the possibility of such damage. In the event that the Software includes an online update feature, SYBEX further disclaims any obligation to provide this feature for any specific duration other than the initial posting.

The exclusion of implied warranties is not permitted by some states. Therefore, the above exclusion may not apply to you. This warranty provides you with specific legal rights; there may be other rights that you may have that vary from state to state. The pricing of the book with the Software by SYBEX reflects the allocation of risk and limitations on liability contained in this agreement of Terms and Conditions.

Shareware Distribution

This Software may contain various programs that are distributed as shareware. Copyright laws apply to both shareware and ordinary commercial software, and the copyright Owner(s) retains all rights. If you try a shareware program and continue using it, you are expected to register it. Individual programs differ on details of trial periods, registration, and payment. Please observe the requirements stated in appropriate files.

Copy Protection

The Software in whole or in part may or may not be copy-protected or encrypted. However, in all cases, reselling or redistributing these files without authorization is expressly forbidden except as specifically provided for by the Owner(s) therein.

Dedicated to my wife Linda
and to the geek in all of us

ACKNOWLEDGMENTS

I've never known how a movie star feels when accepting an Academy Award, until now. I'm not saying this book is an award-winning book, but who knows? There are so many people to thank, and so little space. I'll begin by thanking my wife. She tirelessly edited the glossary, listened to my rants about the books, and gave me a "swift kick" when and where I needed it.

Then there's my Dad, who always told me that "You've gotta do what you've gotta do." Thanks, Dad. And Mom, for encouraging me to do whatever I wanted to, as long as I did the "have to"s first.

My contributing writer, Ray Mosely, made my life easier with his tireless work and patience.

Neil Edde and Brenda Frink, my editors, have turned my chicken scratchings into a professional study guide. I can't thank them enough, for without them, I would not be writing these acknowledgments. Many thanks also to Jon Hansen for double-checking the technical accuracy and relevance of the materials, and to Kris Warrenburg and Blythe Woolston for taking all the pieces and turning them into a good looking book.

Finally, I would like to thank you, the reader, for purchasing this book. I firmly believe that the A+ Study Guides are the best study guides available today for the A+ certification exams. I hope that you get out of this one as much as I put into it.

CONTENTS AT A GLANCE

TABLE OF CONTENTS

5 Operating System Configuration   235

INTRODUCTION: THE A+ CERTIFICATION PROCESS

All computer experts in the world today started out knowing nothing about computers. They started with the question "How do I...?" Perhaps they found the answer in a book or a magazine or from a friend. Little by little, they found out more about their computer until they felt comfortable enough to add new hardware to their computer.

Their first attempts may not have been successful. But they learned from those first attempts. They realized where they went wrong; and the next time they tried, they succeeded. During more successes and more failures they developed critical thinking skills.

This process is how computer service technicians are born. One of the most valuable skills a service technician has is the ability to troubleshoot problems. To do so, he or she needs to be able to think critically. When there is a problem, service technicians must rely on their critical thinking abilities and their background knowledge to fix the problem.

What Is A+ Certification?

A+ is a certification program designed to quantify the level of critical thinking skills and general industry knowledge demanded of computer service technicians. It was developed by the Computer Technology Industry Association (CompTIA) to provide an industry-wide recognition of those service technicians who have attained a high level of knowledge.

The A+ program was created to be a wide-ranging certification involving products from many vendors. In any situation, if computer service is needed, an A+ certified technician should be able to solve the problem.

Why Should You Get A+ Certified?

There are several good reasons to get your A+ Certification. The CompTIA "Candidate's Information" packet lists five major benefits:

- It demonstrates proof of professional achievement.

- It increases your marketability.

- It provides greater opportunity for advancement in your field.

- It is increasingly found as a requirement for some kinds of advanced training.

- It raises customer confidence in you and your company's services.

Provides Proof of Professional Achievement

A+ certification is quickly becoming a status symbol in the computer service industry. Organizations that contain members of the computer service industry are recognizing the benefits of A+ certification and are pushing for their members to become certified. And more people every day are putting the A+ Certified Technician emblem on their business cards.

Increases Your Marketability

A+ certification makes an individual more marketable to a potential employer. Also, that individual may be able to receive a higher base salary because the employer won't have to spend as much money on vendor-specific training.

What Is an AASC?

More service companies are becoming A+ Authorized Service Centers (AASCs). This means that over 50 percent of the technicians employed by that service center are A+ certified. At the time of the writing of this book, there are over 1,400 A+ Authorized Service Centers in the world. Because customers and vendors alike recognize that AASCs employ the most qualified service technicians, an AASC will get more business than a non-authorized service center. Also, because service centers want to reach the AASC level, they will give preference in hiring to a candidate who is A+ certified.

Provides Opportunity for Advancement

Most raises and advancement are based on performance. A+ certified employees work faster and more efficiently, thus making them more productive. The more productive an employee is, the more money they will make for their company. And of course, the more money they make for the company, the more valuable they will be to the company. If an employee is A+ certified, their chances of getting promoted will be greater.

Fulfills Training Requirements

A+ certification is recognized by most major computer hardware vendors, including (but not limited to) IBM, Hewlett-Packard, Apple, and Compaq. Some of these vendors will apply A+ certification toward prerequisites in their own respective certification programs. For example, an A+ certified technician is automatically given credit towards HP laser printer certification without having to take prerequisite classes and tests. This benefit reduces training costs for employers.

Raises Customer Confidence

As the A+ moniker becomes well-known among computer owners, more of them realize that the A+ technician is more qualified to work on their computer equipment than a non-certified technician is.

How to Get A+ Certified

A+ Certification is available to anyone who wishes to pay the registration fees. You don't have to work for any particular company. It's not a secret society. It is, however, an elite group. In order to become A+ certified you must do two things:

- Pass the A+ certification *Core* exam (the focus of my other study guide, also published by Sybex).

- Pass one of the A+ certification *Operating System Specialty* exams (the focus of this book is the DOS/Windows module; if you wish, you can take the Macintosh module in addition to or instead of the DOS/Windows module).

You don't have to take both exams at the same time; you have ninety days from the time you pass one test to pass the second.

The exams are administered by Sylvan Prometric and can be taken at any Sylvan Prometric Testing Center, with locations throughout the US. Arrangements can also be made for testing in Canada, the UK, and Australia. If you pass both exams, you will get a certificate in the mail from the CompTIA saying that you have passed, as well as a lapel pin and business card.

To register for the tests, call Sylvan at (800) 77-MICRO. You'll be asked for your name, Social Security number (an optional number may be assigned if you don't wish to provide SSN), mailing address, phone number, employer, when and where (i.e., at which Sylvan testing center) you want to take the test, and your credit card number (arrangement for payment must be made at the time of registration).

NOTE   Although you can save money by arranging to take more than one test at the same seating, there are no other discounts—for example, if you have to take a test more than once in order to get a passing grade, you have to pay both times.

It is possible to pass these tests without any reference materials but only if you already have the knowledge and experience that come from reading about and working with personal computers. Even experienced service people, however, tend to have what you might call a 20/80 situation with their computer knowledge—they may use 20 percent of their knowledge and skills 80 percent of the time and have to rely on manuals or guesswork or phone calls for the rest. By covering all the topics that are tested by the exam, this book can help you to refresh your memory concerning knowledge that until now you might have only seldom used. (It can also serve to fill in gaps that, let's admit, you may have tried to cover up for quite some time.) Further, by treating all the issues that the exam covers, i.e., problems you may run into in the arenas of PC service and support, this book can serve as a general field guide, one that you may want to keep with you as you go about your work.

NOTE In addition to reading the book, you might consider practicing these objectives through an internship program. (After all, all theory and no practice make for a poor technician.)

DOS/Windows Module Objectives

The following are the areas in which you must be proficient in order to pass the A+ DOS/Windows Module exam:

Domain 1.0: Function, Structure Operation and File Management

This domain requires knowledge of DOS, Windows 3.*x*, and Windows 95 operating systems in terms of functions and structure, for managing files and directories, and running programs. It also includes navigating through the operating system from DOS command line prompts and Windows procedures for accessing and retrieving information.

1.1 Identify the operating system's functions, structure, and major system files.

1.2 Identify ways to navigate the operating system and how to get to needed technical information.

1.3 Identify basic concepts and procedures for creating, viewing and managing files and directories, including procedures for changing file attributes and the ramifications of changes (for example, security issues).

1.4 Identify the procedures for basic disk management.

Domain 2.0: Memory Management

This domain requires knowledge of the types of memory used by DOS and Windows, and the potential for memory address conflicts.

2.1 Differentiate between types of memory.

2.2 Identify typical memory conflict problems and how to optimize memory use.

Domain 3.0: Installation, Configuration and Upgrading

This domain requires knowledge of installing, configuring and upgrading DOS, Windows 3.*x*, and Windows 95. This includes knowledge of system boot sequences.

3.1 Identify the procedures for installing DOS, Windows 3.x, and Windows 95, and for bringing the software to a basic operational level.

3.2 Identify steps to perform an operating system upgrade.

3.3 Identify the basic system boot sequences, and alternative ways to boot the system software, including the steps to create an emergency boot disk with utilities installed.

3.4 Identify procedures for loading/adding device drivers and the necessary software for certain devices.

3.5 Identify the procedures for changing options, configuring, and using the Windows printing subsystem.

3.6 Identify the procedures for installing and launching typical Windows and non-Windows applications.

Domain 4.0: Diagnosing and Troubleshooting

This domain requires the ability to apply knowledge to diagnose and troubleshoot common problems relating to DOS, Windows 3.*x*, and Windows 95. This includes understanding normal operation and symptoms relating to common problems.

4.1 Recognize and interpret the meaning of common error codes and startup messages from the boot sequence, and identify steps to correct the problems.

4.2 Recognize Windows-specific printing problems and identify the procedures for correcting them.

4.3 Recognize common problems and determine how to resolve them.

4.4 Identify concepts relating to viruses and virus types—their danger, their symptoms, sources of viruses, how they infect, how to protect against them, and how to identify and remove them.

Domain 5.0: Networks

This domain requires knowledge of network capabilities of DOS and Windows and how to connect to networks, including what the Internet is about, its capabilities, basic concepts relating to Internet access, and generic procedures for system setup.

5.1 Identify the networking capabilities of DOS and Windows including procedures for connecting to the network.

5.2 Identify concepts and capabilities relating to the Internet and basic procedures for setting up a system for Internet access.

Tips for Taking the A+ Exams

Here are some general tips for taking your exam successfully:

- Arrive early at the exam center so you can relax and review your study materials, particularly tables and lists of exam-related information.

- Read the questions carefully. Don't be tempted to jump to an early conclusion. Make sure you know *exactly* what the question is asking.

- Don't leave any unanswered questions. Unanswered questions are scored against you.

- When answering multiple-choice questions you're not sure about, use a process of elimination to get rid of the obviously incorrect questions first. This will improve your odds if you need to make an educated guess.

- Because the hard questions will eat up the most time, save them for last. You can move forward and backward through the exam.

How to Use This Book

This book has been written to provide you with the knowledge you need to pass the A+ certification exams. It has been written at a medium technical level. You should already be familiar with the concept of what a PC is and its basic function. The material in this book will hopefully "fill in the gaps" in your knowledge. I would recommend reading the review questions at the end of the chapter to gauge your level of knowledge of the subject. If you pass (greater than 80%), move on to the next chapter. If not, read the chapter, then re-take the review questions. Hopefully your score will increase.

Good Luck!

For the latest pricing on the exams and updates to the registration procedures, call the phone number listed earlier in this introduction. If you have further questions about the scope of the exams or about related CompTIA programs, refer to the CompTIA Web site at `http://www.comptia.org/`.

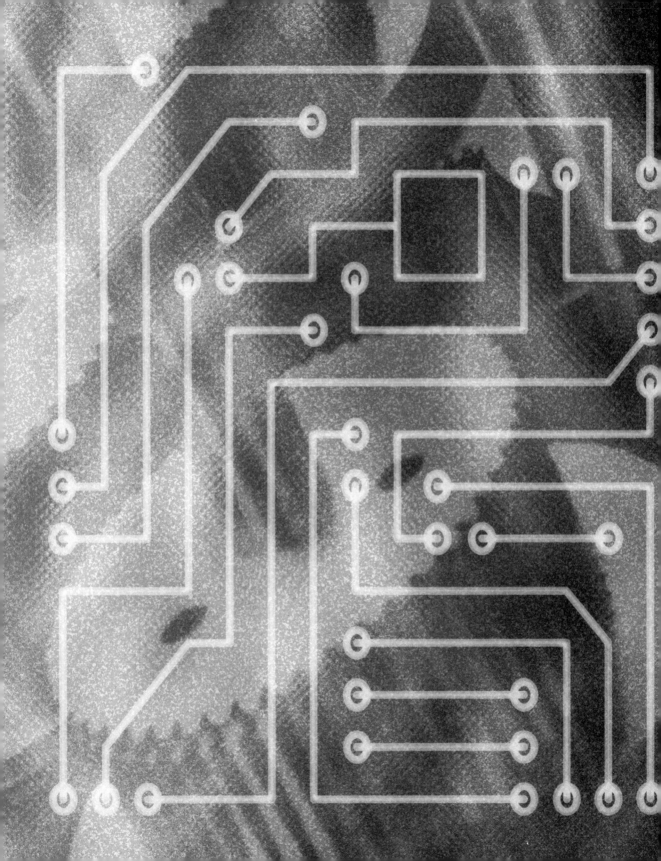

CHAPTER
ONE

1

A Brief History of Computer Operating Systems

The role of the computer has changed drastically over the course of its history. It has gone from table-making to the complex demands of the world today, including computer graphics and Internet access. This chapter takes a step back in time to map the directions the personal computer has taken, looking specifically at the following important developments in Intel platform PC operating systems:

- CP/M

- MS-DOS and PC-DOS

- Windows Interfaces to DOS

- Windows 95/98 and NT

- OS/2

- High-End Operating Systems

The foundation of computer software is the *operating system* (abbreviated *OS*). Operating system software gives users an interface so they can enter commands to their computers. The interface communicates with the computers' hardware to execute the users' commands. It offers commands for controlling disk and file management, device management, and memory management.

NOTE   By offering these commands, operating systems provide a consistent environment in which other software such as word processors and spreadsheets can execute commands. Rather than accessing devices and memory themselves, the programs simply request that the OS do it for them. This arrangement saves substantially on software overhead, as much of the executable code is "shared"—meaning that it is used by multiple programs. These programs are called *applications*, and they generally run only on the OS for which they were written.

In order to understand the emergence of modern graphical operating systems, you should know about the technologies that led to our present systems and about the critical relationship between hardware and software. Graphics, speed, GUI interfaces, and multiple programs running concurrently are all made possible by software designers taking full advantage of the hardware for which they are designing their software.

This chapter will introduce a few of the major operating systems of the past twenty years and will briefly describe how they work. These are not the only operating systems out there but are simply the ones that were accepted by a large enough segment of the PC market to become *de facto* standards. As you read about these different software products, try to think about the ways they differ from one another and the reasons they were designed in the fashion they were. By knowing the options available on the Intel platform, you can better decide which operating system will work best in a particular situation and can therefore be better prepared to recommend a particular OS to your customers. We will be discussing these operating systems in roughly chronological order.

CP/M

The *Control Program for Microcomputer* (CP/M) is an operating system you may never have heard of because it is not in use on modern PCs. This OS was written in 1973 by Gary Kildall using Kildall's PL/M programming language and initially ran on the Intel 8008. It was later ported to the 8080 chip and was in many ways very similar in function to DOS. As a matter of fact, it looks quite similar to DOS, as you can see in Figure 1.1.

FIGURE 1.1:

A typical CP/M
command line

```
Z80 C>SUBMIT AUTOEXEC.Z80
Z80 C>set_bdos min
Z80 C>set_cpmecho off
Z80 C>set_cpmlist lpt1
Z80 C>set_cpmpun com1
Z80 C>set_cpmrdr com1
Z80 C>set_cpu z80
Z80 C>set_fake off
Z80 C>set_illop fault
Z80 C>set_iobase 400
Z80 C>set_mask on
Z80 C>set_source z80
Z80 C>set_term h19
Z80 C>set_vars on
Z80 C>coldboot
Z80 C>
Z80 C>
```

The similarities between CP/M and DOS are underscored by the following bit of computer folklore, which, despite questionable authenticity, has become well known in the industry:

In 1981, IBM decided to begin marketing machines to the home user and the small office. They decided that for reasons of time and efficiency they would simply license an operating system rather than develop and support one of their own. To that end, they scheduled a meeting with Gary Kildall. The IBM representative arrived for the meeting at Kildall's house; but Gary wasn't there, he was out flying his plane. After an unsuccessful meeting with Kildall's wife and lawyer, the IBM rep left without an OS. Not long after, IBM found a different system, entering into a contract with Bill Gates (Microsoft) and licensing DOS.

Kildall says that this story is not accurate and in fact claims that Bill Gates was the first to tell the apocryphal story. One way or the other, the fact remains that Kildall's OS lost a huge opportunity. At the time that IBM allegedly came calling, CP/M was in fact the industry standard for low-cost computers on the Intel platform.

Within a few years of losing the IBM contract, it was nothing but a memory.

NOTE   For more information on CP/M, check out the Caldera CP/M Web site at `http://www.caldera.com/dos/html/legacyindex.html`. This page includes information about CP/M, sources for software, and links to several other CP/M sites.

MS-DOS and PC-DOS

In the 1980s or early 1990s, the operating system that shipped with most PCs was some version of the *Disk Operating System* (DOS) created by Microsoft: *MS-DOS*. (There are a number of manufacturers of DOS, but most of them produce similar versions—they differ only in syntax and a few utilities. The important differences between DOSes are to be found from one chronological version to the next.)

NOTE   A *version* is a particular revision of a piece of software, normally described by a number, which tells you how new the product is in relation to other versions of the product. MS-DOS, for instance, is currently in its sixth major version. Major revisions are distinguished from minor ones in this manner: DOS 5.0 to 6.0 was a major revision, while 6.0 to 6.2 was a minor revision. This way of marking changes is now relatively standard in marking changes in other OS and application software. Additionally, very minor revisions are indicated with an additional decimal point. Upgrading from DOS version 6.21 to 6.22 involved only a few new files, but it was still an upgrade.

In next section, you will look at the origins of DOS and the way it has evolved, version by version, over time. In the following chapters, you'll examine the commands and syntax of the DOS OS, as you will need a very strong knowledge of this operating system before taking the A+ exam.

The Origins of DOS

As noted, the story behind MS-DOS is one of the most often told of all computer fables. But the intrigue goes further than the mystery of why Gary Kildall missed his meeting with IBM. As noted, Microsoft contracted with IBM to write the operating system for their new Intel-based microcomputer project. Although Bill Gates and his partner Paul Allen were both experienced programmers, they had gained their success through the creation of programming languages, not operating systems.

Gates and Allen had created the BASIC language in 1976 and had also released versions of COBOL and FORTRAN for Intel-based machines. However, they had never created an operating system from scratch, which is exactly what they promised to do for IBM. Gates and Allen also took active roles as consultants on the type of hardware that should be used, and Gates was instrumental in IBM's decision to go with the 8086 chip, rather than the cheaper (and less powerful) 8080 processor IBM had originally planned. Microsoft also argued that the machine should have 64KB of memory, rather than the 16KB that IBM initially had thought would be sufficient.

In an interesting twist, just as Seattle-based Microsoft was finishing up a very secretive deal with IBM, Tim Patterson of Seattle Computer Products began writing an operating system specifically for use with the 8086-based computer. Patterson was dissatisfied with how long it was taking for an x86 version of CP/M to be released, so he named his operating system *Quick-and-Dirty Disk Operating System (QDOS)*, and showed it to Microsoft even as they were in the middle of talks with IBM. Paul Allen soon contracted with Seattle Computer Products to purchase QDOS, for sale to an unnamed client (IBM, of course). The purchase price of around $100,000 bought Microsoft an operating system, and a few months later Patterson followed his operating system: he quit SCP and took a job with Gates and Allen. Microsoft acquired all rights to QDOS and renamed it MS-DOS.

From there, MS-DOS was modified for use with the new IBM mini-computer, and in the fall of 1981, IBM announced the IBM 5150 PC Personal Computer. The 5150 had a 4.77MHz Intel 8088 CPU, 64KB RAM, 40KB ROM, one 5.25-inch floppy drive, color graphics capability, and an OS called *PC-DOS 1.0*. PC-DOS, of course, was simply IBM's moniker for the MS-DOS they were licensing from Microsoft.

NOTE   Before the PC, most computers were sold as kits. This meant that the customer had to assemble the machine, install the OS, etc. IBM debuted the PC as a machine that anyone could use, because it was "ready to go" right out of the box.

As noted above, IBM PCs shipped with a version of MS-DOS called PC-DOS. But Gates and Allen had contracted to allow IBM to *use* their operating system, rather than allowing IBM to *buy* it outright. Moreover, IBM had not been granted any type of exclusivity over DOS, hence Microsoft was also able to license versions of DOS to other companies, allowing the creation of what were originally called "IBM clone" machines. These machines ran on the same Intel chip as the IBM PC and used a similar version of the operating system. Because this allowed for any number of companies to make hardware that was roughly compatible with that of other vendors, software companies could begin to create and market programs for a wider and wider market. These programs were not dependent upon proprietary technology other than the Intel chip set and the Microsoft operating system that formed the nucleus of these computers. From 1981 on, the future of the personal computer was to be largely determined by the increasingly powerful processors created by Intel and the increasingly sophisticated operating systems Microsoft wrote to take advantage of Intel's enhancements.

The remainder of this chapter will deal with the evolution of the MS-DOS operating system and will examine the major changes in microcomputer architecture and standards that are reflected in each revision. Smaller revisions—1.0 to 1.1, 6.0 to 6.1—are not enumerated, but their changes are included in the overall enhancements made to the overall version.

You will notice as you read about and use DOS that most of the versions of this operating system are very similar, as the OS proved to be very stable in its original design. Although various enhancements or features may or may not be available to you depending on the version you are using, in a general sense you can trust that if you learn one version, you can probably use any of them.

MS-DOS 1

The original version of DOS was, to put it mildly, a "no-frills" operating system. It had no provisions for networking, did not include any sort of graphical shell program, and had limited ability to manage system resources. The good news was that most of these features would have been too complex for the hardware that version 1.0 was designed for anyway, so no one really noticed.

NOTE   PC-DOS and MS-DOS were very similar, differing mainly in the fact that PC-DOS was specific to IBM machines, while MS-DOS was sold on clone microcomputers. They generally share version numbers: version *x*.1 of PC-DOS should have most of the same enhancements as version *x*.1 of MS-DOS. There are, of course, some technical differences, which I will discuss in Chapter 2.

Approximately a year after the release of DOS 1.0, a revision—DOS 1.1—added support for double-sided 320KB floppy drives. Double-sided disks were important, as they effectively doubled the machine's storage and retrieval capacity. It is difficult to grasp this concept today, when a one- or two-gigabyte hard drive is standard on most new desktop machines, but in 1981 internal hard drives were neither easily available nor supported by DOS. Users generally had only a single 5.25" drive, so the OS, any programs the users wanted to run, and any data they wanted to retrieve all had to be accessed through the 5.25" floppies, each of which stored a maximum of either 320 KB or 640 KB depending on whether it was single- or double-sided. For comparison, consider that you would need more than 1,600 double-sided 640KB floppies to store a single gigabyte of information.

DOS 1.25 followed soon after 1.1 and was designed to be sold with "clone" (non-IBM) hardware. Any machine that could run DOS 1.25 could lay claim to at least some level of "IBM compatibility."

MS-DOS 2

In early 1983, IBM introduced the IBM PC XT. The XT featured a 10MB hard drive, a serial interface, and three additional expansion slots. It also had 128 KB of RAM and a 360KB floppy drive (40 KB more capacity than that of single-sided floppies on the previous PC). Users of this new PC needed an operating system that would allow them to take advantage of this new hardware, and Microsoft did not disappoint them.

The XT shipped with MS-DOS 2.0, a revision of the DOS operating system that had to be redone almost from the ground up. It closely fit the machine it was built for, and it supported 10 MB hard drives and the new 360 KB floppy disks. It also introduced the hierarchical "tree" structure to the DOS file system. The PC Jr., which was one of IBM's first real microcomputer failures, used PC-DOS 2.1.

MS-DOS 3

With DOS 3.0, released in summer 1984, Microsoft continued to include additional DOS features and to support more powerful hardware. DOS 3.0 supported hard drives larger than 10MB, as well as enhanced graphics formats. Three revisions—3.1, 3.2 and 3.3— provided additional innovations. The IBM PC AT was the first machine shipped with DOS 3. It had 256 KB of RAM, an Intel 80286 processor (6 MHz!), and a 1.2MB 5.25" floppy drive. A 20MB hard drive and color video card were also available.

Version 3.1 was notable because it featured the first DOS support for networking. The IBM PC Network was a simple Local Area Network structure that was similar to today's workgroup networks.

NOTE   A network is any group of computers that have a physical communication link between them. Networks allow computers to share information and other resources quickly and securely.

DOS 3.2 introduced the XCOPY command, enabling the user to identify more than one file at a time to be copied, and it made important modifications to other DOS commands. It was also the first version to support IBM's Token Ring network topology and the first to allow for 720KB 3.5" floppies. Version 3.3, introduced in 1987, offered additional enhancements to numerous existing commands and introduced support for 1.44MB floppy disks. Logical partition sizes could be up to 32 MB, and a single machine could support both a primary and a secondary partition on each disk.

NOTE   Partitions and other disk concepts will be covered in more depth in Chapter 4.

Around the same time that DOS 3.3 was introduced, Microsoft and IBM announced the creation of a second PC operating system, OS/2. I'll discuss OS/2 later in this chapter.

MS-DOS 4

By 1988 it was apparent that the wave of the future was the graphical interface, and DOS 4 provided users with the DOS Shell, a utility much like the Windows File Manager. Actually, DOS Shell was simply a scaled-down version of Windows (which we will look at in a minute) that allowed users to manage files, run programs, and do routine maintenance all from a single screen. The DOS Shell even supported a mouse. (That's right, there was no ability to use a mouse within DOS before this version.) For all versions of DOS after version 4, most of the improvements were relatively small and involved tinkering with and refining existing utilities and commands.

NOTE   A *shell* is a program that runs "on top of" the operating system and allows the user to issue commands through a set of menus or some other graphical interface. Shells make using an operating system easier to use by changing the user interface. The two shells we will be looking at most closely are Microsoft's DOS Shell (a menuing system) and Windows (a fully graphical user interface).

MS-DOS 5

There were several important features introduced in the 1991 release of DOS 5.0. First of all, the ability to load drivers into reserved (upper) memory was a relief to those people who were constantly running out of conventional memory. This feature allowed more complex DOS programs (that took up more conventional memory) to be developed.

In addition to this feature, several software utilities made their debut. The most commonly used utility introduced at this time was EDIT.COM. This ASCII text editor has since become one of the most popular text editors for simple text files (and a welcome relief from the single-line view of EDLIN.COM—previously the only choice for a text editor). In DOS 5 (and 6), MS-DOS included the program QBASIC.EXE, which EDIT required in order to run. QBASIC also allowed BASIC programs to be written and run.

Another DOS 5 utility that has become a favorite among technicians is DOSKEY.COM. When loaded, this utility allowed DOS *macros* to be programmed and executed. Additionally, this utility stores, in memory, the last few commands typed at the DOS prompt. The user can press the up arrow key to cycle through the last few commands instead of retyping them. This feature makes issuing repetitive commands much simpler.

Finally, with DOS 5 came the release of the "uns," UNFORMAT .EXE and UNDELETE.EXE. The UNFORMAT utility can recover from an accidental disk format, as long as the format had been performed with the /U (unconditional) switch. The UNDELETE utility can recover accidentally deleted files.

TIP   When performing file or disk maintenance on a machine set up for DOS 5, never interrupt a format or deletion. If you let it finish, you improve the chance that you can then use the UNDELETE or UNFORMAT commands to undo it.

MS-DOS 6

Released in 1993 to excellent sales (and a lawsuit for patent infringement), DOS 6.0 offered a number of new commands and configurable options. It included new antivirus and backup software, a defragmentation utility, drive compression, and the ability to pool EMS and XMS memory using EMM386.EXE.

DOS 6.0 has subsequently been revised a number of times, including once (DOS 6.2 to 6.21) because of a court order. Microsoft was found to have violated Stac Electronics' patent rights in the creation of the DoubleSpace utility for 6.0 and 6.1, and the only real difference between 6.2 and 6.21 is that DoubleSpace is removed. Never to be denied, Microsoft soon released DOS 6.22 with a disk compression program called DriveSpace.

As of this writing, DOS 6.22 is the most current version available as an operating system. (Although Microsoft has made modifications to certain DOS commands for use within Windows 95, Microsoft does not consider DOS a separate operating system under Windows 95, and so does not sell it separately as a new version, or even identify it as such.)

Microsoft Windows

Any real understanding of the success of DOS after 1987 requires a knowledge of Windows. In the early years of its existence Microsoft's DOS gained great acceptance and became a standard as a PC operating system. Even so, as computers became more powerful and programs more complex, the limitations of the DOS command-line interface were becoming apparent (as well as the aforementioned conventional memory limitation).

The solution to the problem was to make the operating system easier to navigate, more uniform, and generally more "friendly" to the user. IBM had understood that the average user did not want to receive their computer in pieces but preferred to have it ready-to-go out of the box. Oddly, they did not understand that the same user who wanted their *hardware* to be ready-to-go did not want to edit batch files or hunt through directories using CD or DIR commands either. Because of this, when Microsoft came to IBM with a graphical user interface (GUI) based on groundbreaking work done by Xerox labs, IBM was not interested, preferring to go onward with the development of OS/2, a project it had already started with Microsoft.

NOTE   The Xerox corporation maintained a think-tank of computer designers in Palo Alto, California called the Palo Alto Research Center (PARC). One of the results of their work was the Alto workstation, which is generally thought to be the forerunner of all modern graphical operating systems. The Alto had a mouse and a GUI interface and communicated with other stations via ethernet. Oh, and it was finished in 1974! Both Microsoft and Apple viewed the Alto and incorporated its technology in their own systems.

Regardless of IBM's interest, Microsoft continued on its own with its development of the GUI—which it named *Windows* after its rectangular work areas—and released the first version to the market in 1985. Apple filed a lawsuit soon after, claiming that the Microsoft GUI had been built using Apple technology, but the suit was dismissed. Apple's Macintosh and Microsoft's DOS-with-Windows combo have both continued to evolve, but until a recent deal between Apple and Microsoft, tensions have always been high. Mac and PC *users*, of course, still remain adamantly chauvinist about their respective platforms.

The Windows interface to MS-DOS is really just a shell program that allows users to issue DOS commands through a graphical interface. The introduction of a mouse—a legacy of the Xerox Alto computer on which both the Macintosh and Windows GUIs are based—further freed users from DOS by allowing them to issue commands without using the keyboard. Word processors, spreadsheets, and especially games were revolutionized as software manufacturers happily took advantage of the ease of use and flexibility that Windows added to DOS.

After the development of Windows, many of the enhancements made to subsequent versions of DOS were designed to help free up and reallocate resources to better run Windows and Windows-based applications. Similarly, PC hardware continued to evolve far past the limits of DOS's ability to effectively use the power available to it, and later versions of Windows would be designed to hide and overcome the limitations of the operating system.

Windows 1

Version 1 of Windows featured the tiling windows, mouse support, and menu systems that still drive next-generation operating systems such as Windows 95, Windows 98, and Windows NT. It also offered "cooperative multitasking"—meaning that more than one Windows application could run concurrently. This was something that MS-DOS up to this point could not do.

However there were several things Windows 1 could *not* do. For one thing, it didn't use icons. Windows 1 was basically a fuller-featured graphical version of the DOS SHELL.EXE program.

Windows 2

Version 2, released in 1987, added icons and allowed application windows to overlap each other as well as tile. Support was also added for PIFs (program information files), which allowed the user to configure Windows to run their DOS applications more efficiently.

Later in 1987 Microsoft also released another version of Windows, designed for the Intel 386 processor, which came to be known as Windows/386. (Because of this, version 2 is often referred to as Windows/286.) Windows/386 allowed for multiple DOS sessions in extended memory, but in most other ways was the same as Windows 2. Although these versions were improvements over version 1, it would not be until the 1990 release of Windows 3.0 that the Windows interface would be widely used.

Windows 3

Windows 3.0 featured a far more flexible memory model, allowing it to access more memory than the 640KB limit normally imposed by DOS. It also featured the addition of the File Manager and Program Manager, allowed for network support, and could operate in "386 Enhanced mode." 386 Enhanced mode used parts of the hard drive as "virtual memory" and was therefore able to use disk memory to supplement the RAM in the machine. Windows today in fact is still quite similar to the Windows of version 3.0.

In 1992, a revision of Windows 3, known as Windows 3.1, provided for better graphical display capability and multimedia support. It also improved the Windows error-protection system and let applications work together more easily through the use of object linking and embedding (OLE).

Windows after the introduction of version 3.1 took a marked turn for the better, in that Microsoft started making a serious effort to make the change to a full 32-bit application environment. With version 3.11, also known as Windows for Workgroups, Windows could offer support for both 16-bit and 32-bit applications. (Windows 3.1 could only support 16-bit applications.) Significant progress on the

32-bit front was not to be made, however, until very late in 1995, when Microsoft introduced Windows 95.

> **NOTE** With the introduction of Windows for Workgroups (Windows 3.11), people who knew that there were two "flavors" of Windows 3.1 started referring both to version 3.1 and to version 3.11 as *Windows 3.x*.

Windows 95

Although it dominated the market with its DOS operating system and its add-on Windows interface, Microsoft found that the constraints of DOS were rapidly making it difficult to take full advantage of rapidly improving hardware and software developments. The future of computing was clearly a 32-bit, preemptively multitasked system such as IBM's OS/2, but many current users had DOS-based software or older hardware—generally referred to as "legacy" devices—that were specifically designed for DOS and would not operate outside of its Windows 3.1, cooperatively multitasked environment.

> **NOTE** Legacy devices are generally defined as devices (sound cards, modems, etc.) that do not support the Plug-n-Play standard used by Windows 95 or are simply too old to properly interface with more modern computers. Legacy devices are either not able to dynamically interact with the Windows 95 system or not able to function at all. They therefore require manual configuration (which is not generally necessary on newer devices) or must be replaced by newer devices.

Because of this problem, in the fall of 1995 Microsoft released a major upgrade to the DOS/Windows environment. Called Windows 95, the new product integrated the operating system and the shell. Where previous versions of Windows simply provide a graphic interface to the existing DOS OS, the Windows 95 graphical interface *is* the OS. Moreover, Windows 95 was designed to be a hybrid of the features of previous DOS versions and newer 32-bit systems. To this end, it is a preemptively multitasked system that is able to emulate and support cooperative multitasking for programs that require it. It also supports both 32-bit and 16-bit drivers as well as DOS drivers, although the 32-bit drivers are strongly recommended over the DOS ones, as they are far more stable and faster.

Windows 98

As this book is written, Microsoft is putting the finishing touches on their next revision of Windows 95, called Windows 98. It has several major changes in its architecture to make it more stable (meaning that fewer crashes will occur). Microsoft has also integrated their Web browser into the operating system using their Internet Explorer 4.0 technologies so that the distance between the operating system and the Internet is shortened. Microsoft expects to have this product shipping in summer of 1998.

TIP   Currently the A+ test does not test your knowledge of the Windows 98 operating system. An unfortunate fact of the computer industry is that about the time you master a product, it is obsolete. The only defense against this pitfall is constant re-education and studying.

Windows NT

The DOS/Windows 3.*x* combo and Windows 95 are currently the most important PC operating systems on the market. Still, for users who need more power, other options are available. One of these is the Windows NT operating system. NT (which unofficially stands for New Technology) is an OS that was designed to be far more powerful than any previous Windows version. It uses an architecture based entirely on 32-bit code and is capable of accessing up to 4 gigabytes (4,000 megabytes) of RAM.

Windows NT can support huge drive sizes and more than one processor and has numerous other advantages over Windows 95 and DOS. NT is often used as a workstation for users who use large files or complex programs. CAD (computer-aided design) programs are a good example of the sort of applications that run better under NT than under other versions of Windows.

Windows NT also allows for better security than previous versions of Windows and is more stable. Naturally, each version of NT that has come out has been more expensive than the current version of Windows 3.*x* or 95 and needed a significantly more powerful machine to run well. NT 3.1 was released as both a workstation and a server product in 1993 and has subsequently been upgraded to 3.5, 3.51, and 4.0. Versions 3.1 through 3.51 look much like Windows 3.1, while 4.0 uses the Windows 95 GUI.

TIP   Microsoft is also developing a new version of their Windows NT software, version 5.0. There are two major new features in NT 5.0: integrated Web browsing and Active Directory. The integrated Internet Explorer software will allow you to extend your desktop with HTML and ActiveX controls so that your desktop computer can be part of the Internet. The Active Directory is a central repository of user configuration information that can be distributed and replicated throughout a network. Active Directory is being developed in response to Novell Netware's directory called NDS (Novell Directory Services). Some say that Active Directory will be greater than sliced bread. Most others think it's too little too late. That, and it won't be ready until late 1999 or early 2000.

OS/2

Even as Windows 3.1 was in development, Microsoft was participating in a joint effort with IBM to create a next-generation operating system for use with 286 and higher processors. This operating system was the second generation OS, or OS/2. The creation of the initial version caused a number of disagreements, though, and the partnership soon broke up. IBM continued the development of OS/2, while Microsoft took part of the technology and began to develop LAN Manager, which would eventually lead to the development of Windows NT.

With OS/2 version 2, IBM made OS/2 a 32-bit system that required at least a 386 processor to run. Although this made it vastly more stable and powerful than Windows 3.1, both it and Microsoft's NT product had a problem finding a market. The main reason for this was probably that most users simply did not have powerful enough computers (or couldn't afford them) to properly use the system.

With version 3 (OS/2 Warp), IBM created a multitasking, 32-bit OS that required a 386 but preferred a 486. Warp also required a staggering 4 MB of RAM just to load. With a graphical interface and the ability to do a great deal of self-configuration, the Warp OS was a peculiar cross between DOS and a Macintosh. Warp featured true preemptive multitasking, did not suffer from the memory limitations of DOS, and had a desktop similar to the Macintosh.

For all of its tremendous features, OS/2 Warp had a funny name and was badly marketed. It never really established a wide user base. Nonetheless, until Windows NT 3.51 was released in 1995, OS/2 was the operating system of choice for high-end workstations, and the OS retains a small but faithful following.

Multitasking—or How to Do More Than One Thing at a Time!

Preemptive and cooperative multitasking are two ways that computers are able to manage the way that the processor is controlled. Cooperative multitasking depends on the application itself to be responsible for using and then freeing access to the processor. This is the way that Windows 3.1 manages multiple applications. Because of this, if any application locks up while using the processor, the application will be unable to properly free the processor to do other tasks, and the entire system will lock, usually forcing a reboot.

Pre-emptive multitasking is different, in that the operating system allots each application a certain amount of processor time and then forcibly takes back control and gives another application or task access to the processor. This means that if an application crashes, the operating system takes control of the processor away from the locked application and passes it on to the next app, which should be unaffected. Although unstable programs still lock, only the locked application will stall, not the entire system.

High-End Operating Systems

High-end operating systems are those that are used by *power users* (users who do several high-end tasks concurrently—for example, people involved in the process of software development must perform several types of tasks simultaneously as they write, compile, debug, and test their programs). Generally speaking, these operating systems have higher hardware requirements than the personal computer systems used by typical business workers. Some of these operating systems may require the use of more than one processor.

UNIX

One option for high-end users is UNIX, which is an operating system that has been in use for more than two decades in some form. UNIX is compatible with DOS or Windows applications through the use of additional software, and there are versions of UNIX that run on Intel-based PC hardware (like Linux, FreeBSD, Solaris X86, and SCO for Intel). UNIX is an extremely powerful and extremely complex system. It features many of the advantages of Windows NT, and UNIX machines can be made to perform many different tasks. The most popular use of UNIX today is as the foundation of the Internet. All of the protocols and programs used on the Internet have their basis in UNIX in some form or another. For example, World Wide Web server software was only available on the UNIX OS before the Internet really took off.

The most important disadvantage of UNIX is that it is not totally compatible with PC software. Additionally (although I have some friends who would disagree), UNIX is not what most people would describe as a "user-friendly" operating system .

NeXTSTEP

In addition to these operating systems, other companies have been developing their own "next generation" operating systems. One company that had its own operating system was NeXT Computer. Founded by ousted Apple Computer executive Steve Jobs, NeXT Computer started by developing hardware (basically a souped-up Macintosh) that ran their special operating system called NeXTSTEP. Their operating system was unique in that it represented every entity in the operating system with logical "objects." Hence the term *object-oriented OS.*

Eventually Jobs realized that the OS was where the money was to be made, and NeXT abandoned its hardware ventures. The

NeXTSTEP OS was primarily used by programmers and system administrators.

Rhapsody

Recently, Apple acquired NeXT and the rights to use its operating system technologies and incorporate them into Apple's next operating system release, called Rhapsody. Rhapsody has been in development for some time now. The main benefit to this operating system is supposed to be that it will be hardware independent. It is intended to run on both Intel and Motorola-based computers.

It is important that we know where we have been and how we have gotten to where we are. Although the information in this chapter is not literally included on the A+ exam, knowing this background is an essential part of being an informed and effective computer support person or service technician and certainly accords with the overall goals of certification. Customers and clients will be more confident of your abilities when you can show that you have a solid understanding of your industry.

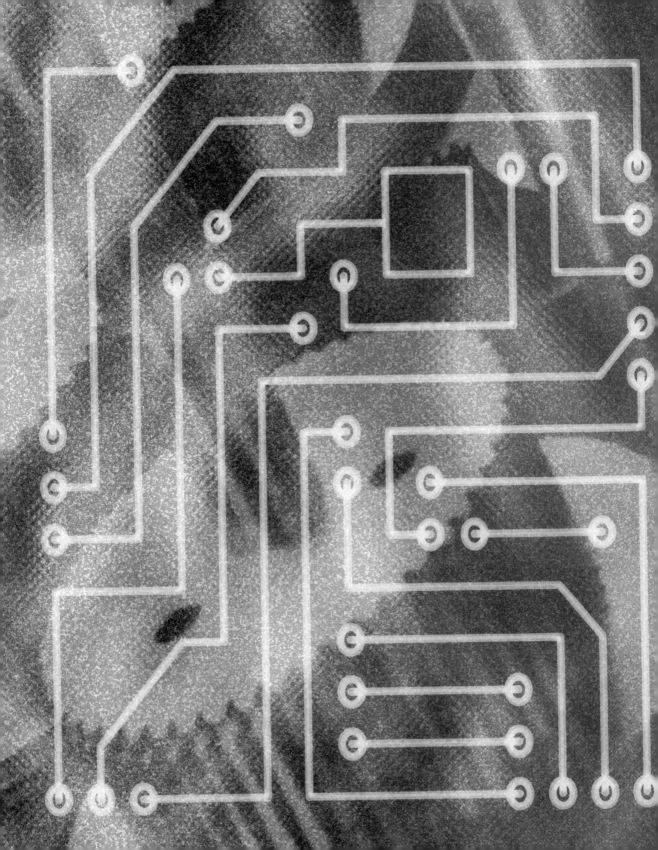

CHAPTER
TWO

Using Microsoft Operating Systems

■ Identify ways to navigate the operating system and how to get to needed technical information.

■ Identify basic concepts and procedures for creating, viewing, and managing files and directories, including procedures for changing file attributes and the ramifications of changes (for example, security issues).

The A+ Windows/DOS Exam covers three main operating systems in use today (all, coincidentally, made by Microsoft). It covers MS-DOS, Windows 3.*x* (including 3.1 and 3.11), and Windows 95. This chapter details the way each of them handles common tasks like running programs, organizing files, and answering your questions.

Using MS-DOS

The Microsoft Disk Operating System, or MS-DOS, was never meant to be extremely friendly. It has its roots in an operating system known as CP/M, which, in turn, has its roots in UNIX. Both of these older operating systems (OSes) are command line-based. In other words, they use long strings of words typed in at the computer keyboard to perform operations. This type of interaction with the computer is preferred by some people. Most often, people with technical backgrounds (including yours truly) like the command-line interface.

Executing Programs

The primary reason for having a computer is to use it for particular tasks. Whether in word processors, spreadsheets, or games, all tasks that need to be completed on a computer must be implemented in the form of some sort of *program*.

NOTE   Even the command-line DOS utilities we will be looking at later are technically just programs provided with DOS. But in general, when a person is talking about a program, they're referring to a piece of software that is purchased separately from DOS. Examples of this are WordPerfect 5.1, Paradox 4 for DOS, and even—of course—Windows 3.1!

Programs consist of at least one file that is accessed by DOS, which then issues instructions. These instructions are interpreted by DOS and then passed on to the processor, which executes the code. This will then produce a result, which the operating system will pass on to the monitor, the printer, or another device.

Installing and Running a Program

In early versions of DOS, most PCs had little or no hard drive storage space, and programs were normally written with the idea that they would be run directly off a single diskette and that the user would have to insert another diskette if work needed to be saved for later use. This worked but was incredibly tedious, and keeping track of disks and finding files was a user management headache.

As PC hardware evolved, and greater amounts of storage became available, programs began to get larger and more feature-laden. This made running programs from the floppy drive difficult if not impossible, and software needed to be transferred to the hard drive—that is, *installed*—before it could be used. This process works well, and most vendors supply an installation program with their software products to make the process as painless as possible. This program, usually named either INSTALL.EXE or SETUP.EXE, has a dual purpose: to transfer the program files for the desired program to the hard drive and to configure DOS to use that product. Some DOS programs do not need any particular configuration and will run as long as the files they need are available to them. Others need additional changes to be made to DOS. These changes, and how they can be made, will be discussed in Chapter 6.

NOTE The setup process for two different software packages—MS-DOS and Windows 3.1—are described in depth later in this book. Chapter 5 deals with installing DOS, while Chapter 9 is dedicated to the Windows 3.1 setup. Remember that Windows 3.1 is actually just a program that runs on top of DOS (like WordPerfect 5.1 or other software), and it needs DOS to already be installed before it can be put on the system.

You will find that the newer a piece of software is, the more resources it is likely to consume. These programs also are more likely to make system modifications, and it is partly because of this that you can't just copy files from the installation disk to the hard drive—you have to run the installation program.

You must be certain before you spend your money on a new program that the software you want to use does not require a different operating system than the one you have. If you do not have Windows, make certain that the program is not designed to run under Windows. Even DOS programs often require more overhead than your old machine might be able to offer. For example, a new DOS program may require any or all of the following:

- Greater amounts of free drive space to install the software
- A newer version of DOS in order to run properly
- More memory (RAM)
- A faster system (updated CPU, etc.)
- A CD-ROM drive as the preferred installation drive

Windows applications, such as Microsoft's Word for Windows, simply do not function without Windows installed and running.

Once a DOS program has been installed, the process of running that program is relatively straightforward. Each program will have either an executable file or a batch file that must be run to begin the execution of the program. Until this file has been executed, the computer acts as though the program does not exist and will not contain in its memory any information on how to complete that program's tasks. As a matter of terminology, the program is only active while the executable file is *open*. Exiting the program usually unloads its code from memory and stops execution of any tasks that are underway. In this way, DOS allows another program to be started and to make use of the resources previously used by another program.

TIP

The executable file or batch file for a program is usually specified in the setup instructions for the program, but these files are also recognizable by their filename *extensions*. Extensions are the characters that appear after the dot in a DOS filename (the extension is one, two, or three characters long; most files use all three). The extension defines the file's type and function. Executables, for instance, have a .EXE extension, and batch files, which have a different function, have a .BAT extension.

NOTE

See Chapter 7 for a more detailed discussion of programs and their installations.

Managing Files

Another important task of the operating system is file management. File management is accomplished through the use of a number of "external" commands. The basic idea is that for a program to run it must be able to read information off of the disk and write information back. In order to be able to organize and access information—especially in larger new systems that may have thousands of files—it is necessary to have a structure and an ordering process.

DOS provides this process by allowing you to create directories in which to organize files, and it also regulates the way that files are named and what the properties of the file are. Each file created in DOS has to follow certain rules, and any program that accesses files through DOS must comply with these rules. Files created on a DOS system will have the following:

- A filename of one to eight characters, with no spaces or punctuation
- An optional extension of one to three characters

The TREE command allows you to examine your file structure by letting you see the relationships of the directories and subdirectories you have created. The DOS file system is arranged like a filing cabinet. In a filing cabinet, paper is placed into folders, which are inside dividers, which are in a drawer of the filing cabinet. In the DOS file system, individual files are placed in subdirectories that are inside directories, which are stored on different disks. See Figure 2.1 for a simple DOS file system tree.

DOS also protects against duplicate filenames, as no two files on the system can have exactly the same name and *path*. A path indicates the location of the file on the disk; it is composed of the logical drive letter the file is on, and if the file is located in a directory or subdirectory, the names of the directories. For instance, an important DOS file named COMMAND.COM is located in the "root" of the C: drive—that means it is not within a directory, and so the path to the file is simply C:\COMMAND.COM. Another important DOS file, the file FDISK, is located in the DOS directory off of the root of C:, so the path to FDISK is therefore C:\DOS\FDISK.EXE.

FIGURE 2.1:

A DOS tree

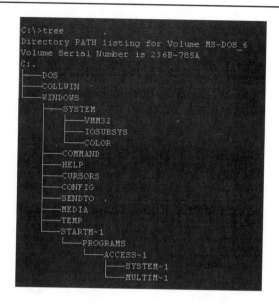

```
C:\>tree
Directory PATH listing for Volume MS-DOS_6
Volume Serial Number is 236B-785A
C:.
├───DOS
├───COLLWIN
└───WINDOWS
    ├───SYSTEM
    │   ├───VMM32
    │   ├───IOSUBSYS
    │   └───COLOR
    ├───COMMAND
    ├───HELP
    ├───CURSORS
    ├───CONFIG
    ├───SENDTO
    ├───MEDIA
    ├───TEMP
    └───STARTM~1
        └───PROGRAMS
            └───ACCESS~1
                ├───SYSTEM~1
                └───MULTIM~1
```

WARNING Saving a new file named WORK.TXT into a directory that already has a file of that name will overwrite the old file and replace it with the new one. To avoid this, either name the new file something different—for instance, WORK2.TXT—or put the file into a different directory. Both C:\WORK.TXT and C:\FILES\WORK.TXT can exist on the same system because although the files have the same name, they have different paths. Also, DOS is not case sensitive. To the DOS OS, WORK.TXT and work.txt are the same file.

Additionally, DOS provides four attributes that can be set for files to modify their interaction with the system. These attributes are:

Read-only   Prevents a file from being modified, deleted, or overwritten

Archive   Used by backup programs to determine whether the file has changed since the last backup and needs to be backed up

System   Used to tell the OS that this file is needed by the system and should not be deleted

Hidden   Used to keep files from being seen in a normal directory search. This is useful to prevent system files and other important files from being accidentally moved or deleted

Attributes are set for files using an external DOS command called ATTRIB.EXE using the following syntax:

ATTRIB <filename> [+ or -][attribute]

To set the read-only attribute on the file TESTFILE.DOC, you would use the following series of commands:

```
ATTRIB TESTFILE.DOC +ro
```

WARNING If you don't know the options for a DOS command, you can usually find them out using the online help for that command. Simply type the command followed by a forward slash (/) and a question mark (?). This will display all the options for that command and how to use them properly. It may not always be clear, but you can usually use "/?" to figure out the general use of the command.

Managing Disks

Besides governing the way in which files are named and organized, DOS also has utilities that allow it to manage physical disks—both hard drive and floppy disks—so that they are usable. DOS provides a number of disk-related services, including:

- Creating and deleting partitions on hard drives
- Formatting partitions and floppy drives

- Copying and backing up disks
- Compressing files to increase the number of files stored on a drive

System Management

Not all functions of DOS are directly related to running applications, but they are still important to the health of your system. One example of this is the ability of DOS to adjust a PC's internal clock. The hour, minute, and second can be set with the TIME command, and the date can be changed with the DATE command, as shown below. This can be crucial to some programs, as different applications may access the computer's internal clock to time-stamp or date-stamp a document.

```
C:\>date
Current date is Sat 12-13-1997
Enter new date (mm-dd-yy):

C:\>time
Current time is  7:18:19.53p
Enter new time:
```

DOS gives you utilities to gather statistics and information about the computer it's running on as well. DOS has utilities built into it that allow you to examine the system's configuration and resource usage. Two such programs are MEM, which allows you to examine the total memory and used memory on the system and MSD, which stands for Microsoft Diagnostics. MSD is a program that gives you the ability to examine many different aspects of a system's hardware and software setup. A screen shot of the main MSD menu, showing the various category "buttons" you can activate to show more information, is shown in Figure 2.2.

FIGURE 2.2:

The main Microsoft Diagnostics (MSD) menu

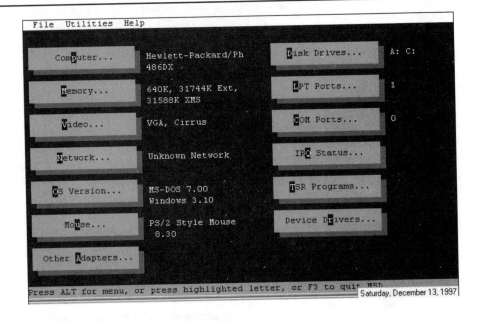

```
 File   Utilities   Help

   Computer...        Hewlett-Packard/Ph    Disk Drives...    A:  C:
                      486DX

   Memory...          640K, 31744K Ext,     LPT Ports...      1
                      31588K XMS

   Video...           VGA, Cirrus           COM Ports...      0

   Network...         Unknown Network       IRQ Status...

   OS Version...      MS-DOS 7.00           TSR Programs...
                      Windows 3.10

   Mouse...           PS/2 Style Mouse      Device Drivers...
                      8.30

   Other Adapters...
```

Press ALT for menu, or press highlighted letter, or F3 to quit MSD
Saturday, December 13, 1997

Using Microsoft Windows 3.x

As I discussed in our exploration of the Microsoft DOS operating system, the Windows interface to DOS has become an integral addition to most modern desktop PCs. In this section, I will look a little more deeply at this interface and how Windows helped to add functionality and ease-of-use that would have been difficult or even impossible under DOS alone.

The chapter will look at how the major program elements of Windows work and give you a basic introduction to how to use the interface. It will then examine how to configure and customize systems based on the particular needs and tastes of each user.

Interface Components

The key to the success of the Windows product has been the way in which its GUI (graphic user interface) has allowed programmers to hide the inner workings of the DOS operating system and its command-line input process from users. In order to do this, Windows provided simplified access to three major functions that users needed to use on a regular basis. These are:

- Running applications
- Managing Files
- Printing

The programs that make this possible, as well as the Windows Desktop itself, will therefore be the topic of this section. Note that these features are exactly the same in both Windows for Workgroups and Windows.

TIP   As you read the following information, you should follow along on a computer that has Windows 3.1 or 3.11 installed on it. If such a computer is not available to you, you should come back later to step through these exercises. Windows installation is covered in Chapter 4.

The Desktop

The Windows Desktop is best understood if you think of it as an actual, physical desktop. When you put papers on a desk, no matter how you organize those documents, they are still all sitting on the workspace. The Windows Desktop is a similar entity, in that it is the back wall of the Windows environment. As you learn to open, close, and move individual program windows around on the screen, all of these windows will have to fight for space on the Desktop, which is only as large as your screen.

The Desktop does not have any configurable options, and it does not perform any tasks. Rather, it simply contains the visible elements of Windows and defines the limits of the graphic environment. To see the Desktop on your own Windows system, start your computer, start Windows, and click the Minimize button on the Program Manager. Assuming you have nothing else running and the system has not been modified, you will now see a flat wall on your screen with an icon that says Program Manager in the lower left (the Program Manager is shown below). If the system has been modified, you may see a pattern or a picture on the screen.

The Program Manager

When you initially start Windows, the program that starts on Windows load is called the Shell program. By default, this shell is PROGMAN.EXE, a program that is located in the Windows directory. PROGMAN.EXE is the file that runs the Program Manager, or the interface that allows you to organize and execute numerous commands from a single graphical window. The Program Manager shell is designed to allow users to easily access needed applications and also allows access to various utilities used to customize their Windows environment.

Program manager works through the use of two major types of objects: program windows and icons. Windows, as the name of the product would suggest, are crucial to the design and use of the Windows environment. They provide the space in which a particular program or utility can function. Icons are the doors through which programs are started, and they are therefore used to spawn windows. A third object, the group, is a special type of window only found in Program Manager.

NOTE The difference between *Windows* and *windows* is confusing but important. The proper noun refers to the product, while the lowercase "window" is used when describing a particular window within the interface, or program windows in general.

Program Windows

A program window is a rectangular area created on the screen when an application is opened within Windows. This window can have a number of different forms, but most windows include at least a few basic elements. Figure 2.3 shows the Control Box, Title Bar, Minimize Button, Restore Button, and Resizable Border.

FIGURE 2.3:

The basic elements of a window

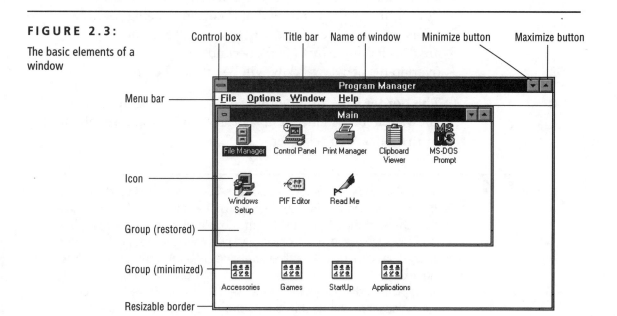

The Control Box is used to examine the state of the application, and can be used to maximize, minimize, and close the application. Clicking it once brings into view a selection menu. Double-clicking it closes the window and shuts down the application.

The Minimize and Restore buttons are used to change the state of the window on the Desktop, and they will be discussed in the section on the three states of a Windows window coming up later in this section.

The Title Bar simply states the name of the program and in some cases gives information as to the particular document being accessed by that program. As we learn about multitasking, the color of the Title Bar will indicate whether or not a particular window is the active window. The active window is simply the window that is currently being used, and it has two attributes: First, any keystrokes that are entered are directed there by default. Second any other windows that overlap the active window will be pushed behind it.

The border is a thin line that surrounds the window and allows it to be widened and shortened. This will be explained further later in the chapter.

NOTE   Double-clicking is an important mouse skill. The mouse is used far more in Windows than it is in DOS. The mouse has four main functions: the click, the right-click, the drag, and the double-click. To click, simply place the mouse pointer over an object and press and release the left button once. Right-clicking (also called *alternate clicking*) is the same as clicking, except that you use the right mouse button instead of the left. To drag, press and hold down the mouse button and move the object to a new location. The double-click is the final function, and the toughest to get used to. Double clicking involves rapidly clicking an object twice without moving the mouse in the process. The double-click and the drag can be challenging skills to learn, and if you are not mouse-proficient, you should plan to give yourself and your users some learning time.

These elements are not all found on every window, as programmers can choose to eliminate or modify them. Still, in most cases these will be constant, with the rest of the window filled in with menus, toolbars, a workspace or other application-specific elements. For instance, Microsoft Word, the program with which this book was written, adds an additional control box and minimize and maximize buttons for each document. It also has a menu bar, a number of optional toolbars, scroll bars at the right and bottom, and a status bar at the very bottom. Application windows can become very cluttered.

Notepad, on the other hand, is a very simple Windows program. It has only a single menu bar and the basic elements seen previously in Figure 2.3. Both of these programs are used to create and edit documents, but Word is far more configurable, far more powerful, and therefore has many more optional components available within its window.

More than the physical parts of a window itself, though, is involved in understanding what the Windows interface allows a user to do. Windows also are movable, stackable, and resizable; and they can be hidden behind other windows (often unintentionally!).

When an application window has been launched, it will exist in one of three states:

- Maximized

- Restored

- Minimized

Maximized Windows

A Maximized window is one that takes up all available space on the screen. When it is in front of the other programs, it is the only thing visible. Even the Desktop is hidden. For an example of a maximized application, see Figure 2.4. Note that in the upper-right corner the restore button displays a down-pointing triangle, and the sides of the window no longer have borders. The window is flush with the edges of the screen. Maximizing a window provides the maximum workspace possible for that window's application, and the window can be accessed actively by the user. Still, in the process every other window is covered, making multitasking more difficult. In general, maximized mode is the preferred window size for most word processing, graphics creation, and other user applications.

FIGURE 2.4:

A Solitaire window that has been maximized

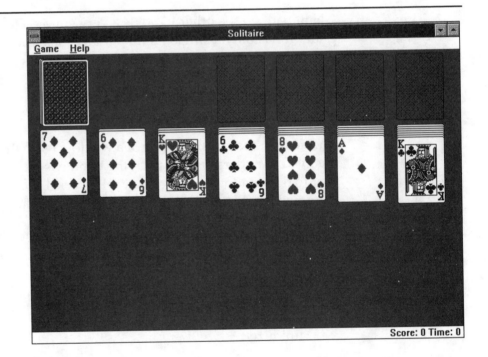

Restored Windows

A restored window is one that can be used interactively and is identical in function to a maximized window, with the simple difference that it does not necessarily take up the entire screen.

Restored windows can be very small, or they can take up almost as much space as maximized windows. Generally, how large the restored window becomes is the user's choice. Restored windows have a restore box with an up pointing triangle (used to maximize the window) and they have a border going around their edge. Figure 2.5 shows an example of a restored window.

FIGURE 2.5:

A Solitaire window that has been restored

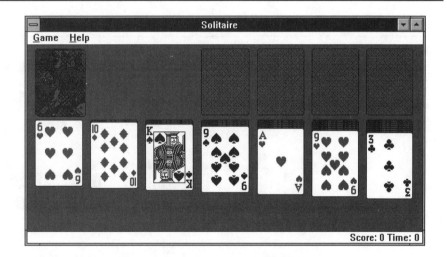

Minimized Windows

The last window state is minimized. Minimized program windows are represented by nothing but an icon on the Desktop (we'll get to icons soon!) and they are not usable until they have been either maximized or restored. The only difference between a minimized program and a closed program is that a minimized program is out of the way but is still in the same place when you return to it as when you minimized it. Let's take the Solitaire program we have been looking at in the graphics. The program is opened, and a game of Solitaire is started. If you need to open another program (or maybe need to stop playing because your boss has entered the room), you have two choices. You can close the program and re-open it later. If you do this, though, your current game will be lost, and you will have to start over. Minimizing the Solitaire window, on the other hand, will leave the program open but will remove the open window from the screen and put nothing more than an icon in the lower-left corner of the Desktop, as shown in Figure 2.6. Cover the icon with a different active window and later you can restore the window to its previous size and finish the game in progress.

FIGURE 2.6:

A Solitaire window that has been minimized

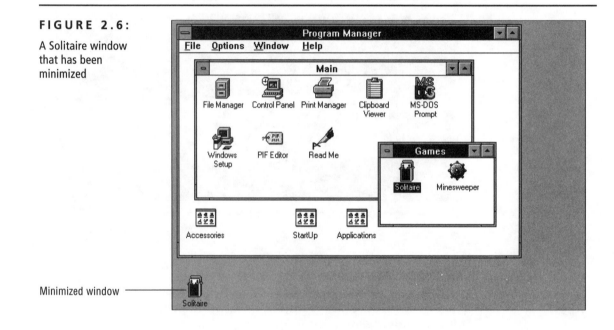

Minimized window

Icons

Icons are not nearly as complex as windows can be, but they are very important nonetheless. Icons are shortcuts that allow a user to open a program or a utility without knowing where that program is or how it needs to be configured. Icons consist of four elements:

- Icon Label

- Icon Graphic

- Program Location

- Working Directory Location

The label and graphic simply tell the user the name of the program and give a visual hint as to what that program does. Solitaire, for instance, is labeled "Solitaire," and its icon graphic is a deck of cards. By clicking on an icon once, you make that icon the active icon (programmers call this "setting the focus on an object"). Once an icon is active, the commands in the Program Manager menu bar now will affect it only. By clicking on the word File on the menu, a drop-down menu appears. One of the selections is *Properties*. Clicking properties will bring up the attributes of an icon (Figure 2.7) and is the only way to see exactly which program an icon is configured to start.

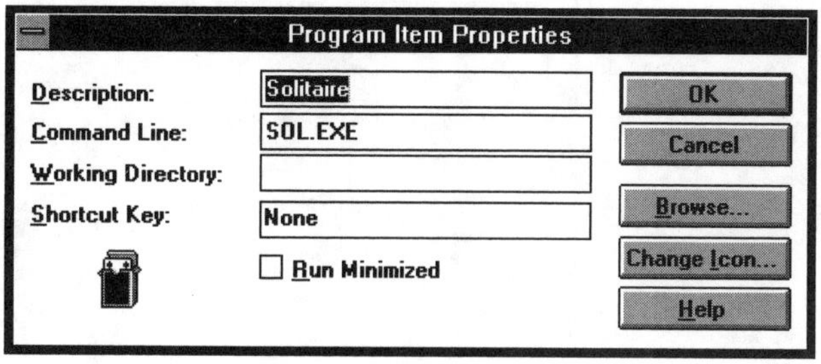

FIGURE 2.7:

The properties window of Solitaire with the active icon to the left

The working directory simply tells Windows where to save documents created through this icon. This is default and can be over-ridden.

Remember that program icons are very specialized objects and that they occur only in the Program Manager or on the Desktop to identify a minimized window. Other types of icons do occur, and we will look at the Control Panels icons later, as well as at Group icons immediately.

Groups

Within Program Manager, there is actually a second type of icon besides the program icons. These are the group icons. Groups are created to allow icons with like purposes to be stored together. No program icon can be stored directly on the workspace of the Program Manager. All program icons must belong to a group, which then has an icon on the workspace. To use a particular icon, a user must double-click the group the program's icon is in. This then brings up a window containing program icons. The user can then double-click the program icon itself to launch the program window. In Figure 2.8, the Main and Games groups are open, and the Applications, Accessories and StartUp groups are closed. Which is the active window? How about the active icon?

FIGURE 2.8:

Group windows and icons

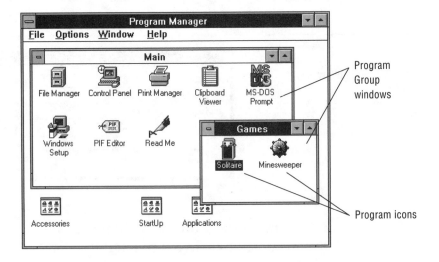

The File Manager

As we have now seen, the Program Manager is responsible for allowing a user access to applications. To manage files, though, requires the use of a different program. The Windows File Manager is a utility that allows the user to accomplish a number of important file-related tasks from a single interface. Moreover, the ability to use drag-and-drop techniques and other graphical tools to manage the file system makes the process far simpler.

The commands whose jobs are done in full or part by file manager include:

- DIR
- MD
- CD
- MOVE
- COPY
- XCOPY
- DEL
- DELTREE
- REN
- DISKCOPY
- ATTRIB
- UNDELETE
- BACKUP
- FORMAT

You can also use File Manager to print documents, check for viruses, and run programs.

To open the File Manager, find its icon in the Main group (it looks like a yellow file cabinet) and double-click. The window will open (see Figure 2.9) and will have three major areas, plus a menu bar and a status bar.

FIGURE 2.9:

Windows File Manager

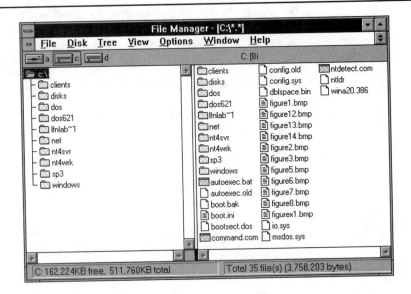

Along the top of the workspace, just under the menu, is a drive bar where the logical drives accessible to the machine are listed. Each drive has a small icon, with a letter to the right of it. Below this are two spaces. The one to the left shows the directory structure of the current drive while the one to the right displays the contents of the currently selected directory. The machine in Figure 2.9 has two local logical drives (C: and D:) as well as a floppy drive (A:). In the root of the C: drive are 10 directories—displayed in yellow—and 26 files which have icons resembling pieces of paper. Note that the directories are listed in both panes, but the files are only on the right.

In DOS, displaying the contents of the directory C:\APLUS\ DOCS would require the following steps:

1. Type **a:\> c:** and press Enter. The C:> prompt will appear.

2. Type **CD aplus** and press Enter to change to a directory named APLUS. The prompt will change to include the path (i.e. C:\APLUS).

3. Type **CD DOCS** and press Enter to change to the DOCS subdirectory.

4. To view the directory listing, type **DIR** and press Enter.

With the File Manager, all of these commands can be executed simply by using the mouse:

1. Click on the icon for the C: drive in the drive bar. This will change the contents of the directory window below to that of the C: drive and will display the contents of the root of C: in the right window pane.

2. Double-click the APLUS directory in the left pane. This will show the contents of the APLUS directory on the right and will display any subdirectories of APLUS.

3. Double-click on the docs subdirectory in the left pane. This will display the contents of the directory in the right pane.

WARNING We are now going to look for a minute at how easy deleting and moving files is within Windows. This makes it even more likely than under DOS that you or one of the people you support will delete or misplace a file or a number of files that are still needed. In some cases, the UNDELETE utility can be used to recover these files, but using this utility is risky and often does not work. Educate your users on the dangers of playing in the File Manager and take care yourself when cleaning out files.

Most of the common file commands that you have learned to execute in DOS can be accomplished through the Windows File Manager. You are really using Windows as an interface to the DOS system, and your mouse clicks are actually causing the Windows interface to issue the same commands to DOS that you could have typed in yourself previously does this. Copying, moving, and deleting directories is now accomplished simply by selecting the files you wish to work with. To move or copy, simply click and drag to the new location. To delete, click the Delete key after selecting the files to be purged.

TIP Selecting objects in the File Manager usually just involves clicking the drive, directory, or file you wish to use. At times, though, multiple files or directories may need to be selected. This can only be accomplished in the right window where subdirectories and files are displayed and involves the use of the Ctrl or the Shift key. Holding down the Ctrl key allows you to click multiple files, and instead of changing the focus to a new file as you click it, the focus is shared between files already selected and the new file. Clicking a file and then holding down Shift and selecting another file selects both files—and all files between them. If the File Manager is new to you, try these to see how they work.

Some other utilities in the File Manager are also very useful. The Search option in the File menu is used to scan the files and directories on a drive looking for a particular name, phrase, or pattern. (The text of the files is not searched.) Standard DOS wildcards can also be used, allowing, for instance, a search for all files with text (.TXT) extensions. To perform such a search, you'd use an asterisk (*) as a stand-in for the filename. Asterisks are used to take the place of any number of characters in a search, while question marks (?) are used to take the place of a single number or letter.

To try this:

1. Click on File, and then on Search. The Search window will open (Figure 2.10) and you will be prompted for the Search information.

2. Type ***.TXT** in the Search For text box.

3. In the Start From box enter **C:**.

4. Make sure the check box allowing you to search subdirectories is marked and click OK.

FIGURE 2.10:

The Search window

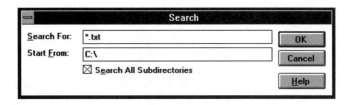

Windows will now search the C: drive and will eventually display a Search Results window with all of the files it has found.

Besides simplifying most file management commands, the File Manager also allows you to more easily complete a number of disk management tasks. Floppy disks can be formatted and labeled, as well as having the DOS system files installed. They can also be copied through the Copy Disk option (which uses the DOS DISKCOPY utility). These commands are all located in the Disk menu.

NOTE   Most formatting and management of your fixed drives will still be done with the FDISK and FORMAT utilities found in the DOS directory. The File Manager cannot modify partitions or format hard drives.

Network Options

One of the areas in which the basic Windows product and its Windows for Workgroups cousin differ is the way in which they access information on the network. While Windows depends on a third-party DOS client (such as the DOS Client for Microsoft Networks or the NetWare client software) Windows for Workgroups has networking software built into it, and the Workgroups File Manager has the additional functionality of being able to attach the user to network resources. The regular Windows File Manager cannot do this but will display and allow access to any drive mappings that already have been mapped using a DOS client. Figure 2.11 shows such a drive (I:) being accessed within Windows 3.1's File Manager.

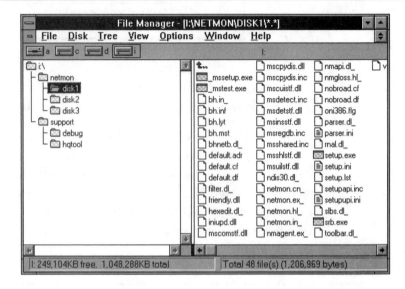

It is a good idea to remember that the Workgroups networking capability does add functionality unavailable in Windows. Don't be caught unaware if you run into it.

> **NOTE** Networking is covered in more detail in Chapter 10.

Print Manager

Like file management, the creation and use of printers has been integrated into the Windows interface. This allows you to capture printer ports, install Windows printer drivers, and even examine the print queue Windows creates for your documents. Moreover, Windows is able to help make the print process more efficient and can save a great deal of time for your users.

The Print Manager is the program that manages all of this, and its icon (a picture of a printer with paper coming out) is in the Main group. If you have not yet installed a printer, the Print Manager window (Figure 2.12) will be relatively blank when you first open it. The Pause, Resume, and Delete buttons will be unavailable (their icons will appear in gray) until a printer is installed. This graying of unavailable options is a characteristic of all well-written Windows programs. The first step in using this utility is installing a printer, and to do this you need to click on the Options menu, and then select Printer Setup....

FIGURE 2.12:

The Printers window

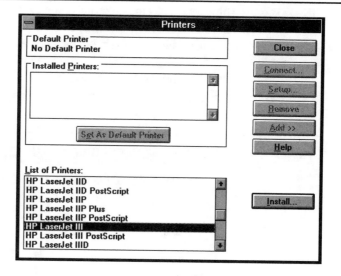

If you have a printer that is listed in the box labeled List of Printers, you should select the printer and click install. You will then be asked to insert at least one of the Windows installation disks (probably Disk 6). If your printer is not listed, you have to acquire the Windows driver for your particular printer and then select Install Unlisted or Updated Printer. You will then be asked for the location of the updated driver.

Once the printer is installed, it will appear in the Installed printers list. You can then select the printer and click on the Setup... button to the right. Doing so will allow you to see additional configuration information for that particular printer. In Figure 2.13 you can see that these options can include the installed fonts, the paper source, and other settings. Generally, these do not need to be configured, as the defaults work well in most situations, but if the printer is not providing you with adequate results using the defaults, check its documentation to see if any of its settings may be modified to remedy the situation.

TIP

As some printers are far more complex than others, they also have more options. For instance, a color printer will have color settings options that are not listed on printers where color is not available. Check each new printer types you install to see what options are available for that model.

FIGURE 2.13:

The Setup window for an HP LaserJet III

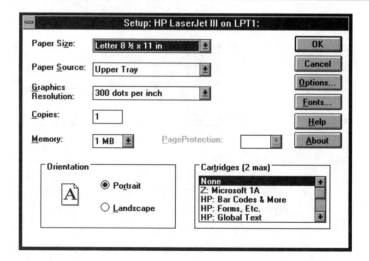

NOTE The top of the screen also tells you which local port the printer is being redirected to. As with DOS, Windows needs to be able to send the job to a specific place. In Figure 2.13 this is LPT1:, but it could have potentially been any of a number of different ports listed in the Connect... window. Remember that any printer, even one on the network, must be routed through a logical port in DOS and Windows.

Once one printer is installed, other printers may be added, or by clicking close you can return to the main Print Manager window. The Pause and Resume buttons will now be active, and the printer will be listed below them, as shown in Figure 2.14. Notice that you do not have to have the printer physically installed on the port to add the print driver. Nonetheless, you will get errors if you try to print and the device is not present. Also, as drivers are specific to each printer, if you change the printer you must install the new printer's driver for best performance.

FIGURE 2.14:

The Print Manager window

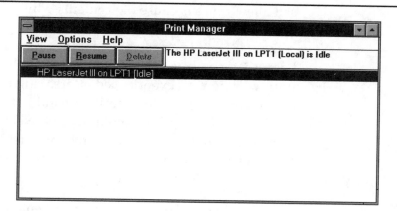

Customizing the Windows Interface with the Control Panel

Although for the most part the Windows system is functional from the time it is first installed, Microsoft realized that if someone were going to be using computers regularly, the person would probably want to be able to customize their environment so that it would be better suited to their needs, or at least more fun to use. Because of this, the Windows environment has a large number of utilities that are intended to give the user control over the look and feel of the Desktop.

This was, of course, an excellent idea. It was also a bit more freedom than some less-than-cautious users seem to be capable of handling, and you will undoubtedly serve a number of customers who call you in to restore their configuration after botched attempts at changing one setting or another.

More than likely, you will also have to re-install Windows yourself a few times because of accidents while studying or testing the system's limits. This is actually a good thing since no competent computer technician can say that they have never had to reinstall because of an error. You can't really know how to fix Windows until you are very experienced at breaking it. Because of this, it is extremely important to experiment and to find out what can be changed in the Windows environment, what results from that change, and how to undo any unwanted results! To this purpose, we will be examining the most common configuration utility in Windows: the Control Panel.

Located in the Main group and represented by a computer with a clock, the Control Panels are the graphical entryway to the heart of Windows' configurable settings. One of the few applications in Windows that contains icons of its own; the Control Panel utility houses a number of other options. The standard Control Panel icons are shown in Figure 2.15, but various applications and add-on products can add others. We will be taking only a brief look at the uses of these panels, but many of them are worth exploring closely on your own.

FIGURE 2.15:

The Control Panel

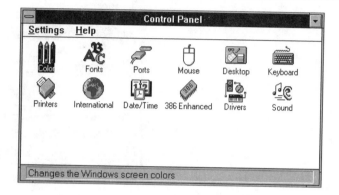

The Color Panel

The Color panel (Figure 2.16), represented by three crayons, is one of the most commonly used control panels. Its purpose is to allow a user to select a color scheme for their Windows Desktop that is easier to see or more appealing aesthetically than the default gray, white, and blue that loads when Windows is first installed.

The top part of the Color panel has a drop-down menu with a list of different color combinations that can be used on the system. Each of these color combinations—called *schemes*—specifies the color to be used by every element of the Windows environment, from the Desktop color to the color of the menus to the color of the buttons and their text.

FIGURE 2.16:

The Color Panel

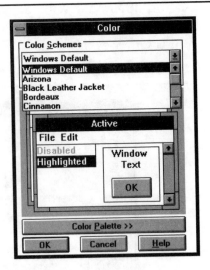

NOTE Drop-down menus are a common method of allowing a user to enter input graphically. The drop-down menu is easily recognized as a selection box with a button on its right side that has a down arrow. You can make a selection using the mouse to drop down a list box or clicking the up and down arrows on the keyboard.

Experiment a bit with the different schemes available, and look to see what your options are. I highly recommend trying Hot Dog Stand, just so you can see the hideous results that color scheme modifications can produce. Notice that as you select a color scheme, the small window below the menu changes to show the way that the different screen elements will be colored. To test a scheme on the system as a whole, click OK. (Watch the screen on this one. The OK in the display window doesn't do anything. The real OK is in the lower left!)

To change the scheme back, or to try a different one, double-click Colors again. To modify the color patterns even further, click the Color Palette >> button near the bottom of the control panel.

Pressing this button increases the color of the control panel, and gives you a color palette from which you can assign particular colors to individual elements, as shown in Figure 2.17.

FIGURE 2.17:

The Color control panel customization window

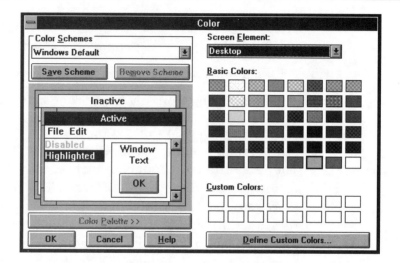

Moreover, the Define Custom Colors... button in the lower right of this new, larger window allows you to further customize by actually creating colors from the spectrum brought up on the left.

NOTE   If all this hoopla over color schemes seems a bit ridiculous to you, you are almost certainly in the majority. Still, it is Microsoft's success at giving people options and making an interface that is almost ludicrously changeable that has made Windows successful.

One of the only real dangers with the color panel is that an unwary user can accidentally set their foreground and background colors to the same value. This effectively makes some parts of the interface invisible and makes the system extremely annoying to use. Fortunately, you should be able to simply select a different color scheme (probably the trusty Windows Default) and return the components to usable colors.

The Desktop Panel

Much like the Color control panel, the Desktop panel is used to configure the system so that it is more easily usable and more attractive to look at. The Desktop panel allows the following:

- Setting a Pattern or a Wallpaper for the Desktop
- Turning Alt+Tab switching on and off
- Enabling and configuring a screen saver
- Configuring Icon spacing, border sizing, and cursor blink rate

The Pattern and Wallpaper options both apply only to the Windows Desktop, and both affect the way that the Desktop looks. They are different, though, in that the Pattern option applies a texturing or pattern to the surface, while the Wallpaper option places a bitmap file of top of it. Bitmaps are uncompressed image files, and bitmap files can be relatively large. For this reason, loading a Wallpaper consumes more system resources than the comparably small Pattern files do. For highest performance, of course, it is best to use neither and accept the flat Desktop background.

NOTE   Bitmaps are the default image type for Windows. Windows bitmaps have a .BMP extension and are usually created and modified using the Paintbrush application in the Accessories group.

Before going further in this chapter, go into the Desktop panel and try some of the patterns and wallpapers. Make sure your Program Manager is restored so that you can see the Desktop behind it. Figure 2.18 and 2.19 show the Desktop with two different backgrounds. Figure 2.18 shows a Desktop with the Weave pattern, and the one in Figure 2.19 shows a Desktop with the EGYPT.BMP wallpaper.

FIGURE 2.18:

The Desktop with a pattern (Weave)

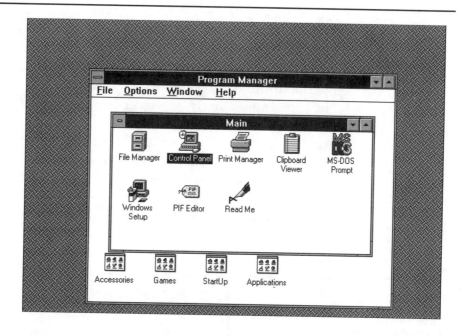

FIGURE 2.19:

The Desktop with wallpaper (EGYPT.BMP)

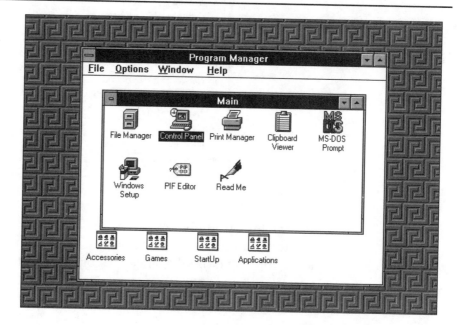

Another option is the Screen Saver. Screen savers were initially designed to prevent burn-in on older monitors, which could develop permanent "shadows" of screen images left on for too long. Screen savers were designed to assure that after a certain period of time the screen would be active, and the monitor would be safe. Interestingly, as newer monitors came out that do not generally get damaged by being left on with a static image, the screen saver has taken on an entertainment function instead, and Windows comes with a number of interesting—and sometimes hypnotizing—screen saver options. Click the down arrow in the Name box under the Screen Saver area, and select Starfield Simulation. Figure 2.20 shows the Desktop control panel with this option selected.

FIGURE 2.20:

The Desktop panel with Starfield Simulation selected

The Delay option below the Name box allows you to set the number of minutes the machine must be idle (no keyboard or mouse input) before the screen saver is loaded. In Figure 2.21, the Delay has been set to 10 minutes. Next, click the Setup button to the right. Here, we can set the particular properties of this screen saver. We can also set a password so that once the screen saver has loaded it won't deactivate until the correct password has been entered. Note that the other screen savers all have the password option but differ in their other options.

TIP

If a user forgets their password, go to the CONTROL.INI file (located in C:\WINDOWS, typically) and locate a section entitled [ScreenSaver], Delete this section, and you can now reset the screen saver with a new password.

FIGURE 2.21:

The Starfield Simula-
tion Setup window

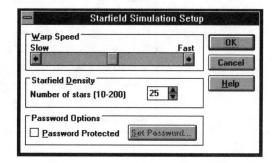

The other features of the Desktop panel are less often changed and usually should be left alone unless they specifically need to be changed. For an explanation of what Sizing Grid granularity and other options do, click the Help button in the Desktop panel and then click on Sizing Grid.

TIP

Help can be a very useful aid in finding out simple facts about the interface. Remember, though, that help files are specific to a particular application. Help on the Desktop panel will provide no assistance on how to change a color scheme, but Help in the Color panel will.

The 386 Enhanced Panel

Unlike the previous two panels we have looked at, the options in the 386 Enhanced Control Panel (shown in Figure 2.22) are not intended to make the system more aesthetically pleasing or more fun to work with. Rather, the 386 Enhanced panel has a number of options that can distinctly affect the performance of your system. Inexperienced users should stay out of this panel altogether.

FIGURE 2.22:

The 386 Enhanced panel

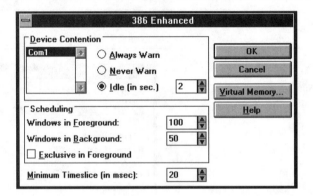

The three options configured in the 386 Enhanced panel are:

- Device contention

- Scheduling

- Virtual Memory

The device contention configuration allows you to specify how the system should deal with conflicts over resources. If, for instance, two devices are sharing an interrupt, how does the system monitor arbitrate that relationship? The default here is to use an Idle time of two seconds to see if the conflict disappears. Other options are available, but the default is usually right here.

The Scheduling option is an interesting one and determines how much of the system's resources are dedicated to foreground applications. (The *foreground application* is the application that currently is in front of all the other apps. In other words, it is the application whose window is on top of all other open windows.) The higher the number of the Scheduling option, the greater the number of timeslices that will be dedicated to the foreground application. To increase the number of timeslices devoted to the background app, increase the value in the second spinner box. The Exclusive in Foreground check box takes scheduling to the extreme and gives 100 percent of the processor time to the foreground app. If this is checked, the foreground application will run faster, but other applications will not run at all until they are given the focus again (thus bringing them to the foreground).

NOTE A *spin box* and a *check box* are two types of graphical input tools. A spin box allows the user to select a number from one value range to another simply by clicking the up or down arrow. The value can also be typed in. In the case of the Scheduling spin boxes, the values can range from 1 to 10000. A check box is a Boolean field, which has only two values: on (checked) and off (unchecked). Click once to check a box; click again to uncheck it.

Probably one of the most important buttons in the Control Panel, and also one that should generally be left alone, is the Virtual Memory button in the 386 Enhanced panel. This button opens a window (Figure 2.23) where you can define the way that your machine will use space on the hard drive to supplement your physical RAM. Because the use of this drive space as virtual memory is crucial to Windows' performance, you should be careful not to set this value too low or too high.

FIGURE 2.23:

The Virtual Memory
window

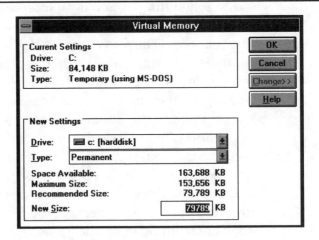

A virtual memory setting that is too low will reduce the *swap file*—the file on the hard drive that acts as virtual RAM—to the point that Windows will not be able to run as many applications concurrently or may begin to have memory errors. Similarly, a setting that is too high will make it unnecessarily difficult to search for needed information in the swap file and will result in a slower system. Because of these pitfalls the Recommended Size: value in the Virtual Memory window is almost always the correct value to go with.

A swap file stores information Windows isn't currently using to a special file on disk. When the particular information is needed by Windows, the information is swapped back to main memory for use by Windows. There are two types of swap files: permanent and temporary. Each swap file has its own unique characteristics:

Permanent swap files are created by Windows the first time it is started. When Windows creates a permanent swap file, it actually creates two files: SPART.PAR and 386SPART.PAR. The first file (SPART.PAR) points to the location of the actual swap file (386SPART.PAR). In order to use a permanent swap file with Windows, you must be running Windows in

386Enhanced mode. Permanent swap files reserve a chunk of the available disk space for their use. That space is not available for use for other files, even if Windows isn't running! Permanent swap files give the best performance but exact a large price in disk space.

TIP

If you ever see 386SPART.PAR, don't delete it! Even though it takes up a lot of disk space, Windows won't function properly if you delete it. If you need to reclaim some of the space used by this file, run Windows and use the Virtual Memory option in the 386 Enhanced control panel to adjust the size of the permanent swap file.

Temporary swap files are created every time you start Windows and are deleted when you exit Windows. The temporary swap file is named WIN386.SWP. Temporary swap files are more flexible because their size is dynamic, based on how much disk space is available during Windows startup. Beware, however—they slow Windows down, primarily because they are not as efficient and it takes time during windows startup to recreate. The swap file can be deleted, just like any other file, but only if Windows is not running—i.e., it must be deleted through a DOS utility. It will, however, be recreated the next time Windows starts. Do not delete or reduce the size of the swap file to save room on a full drive! Instead, either delete other little-used files or buy an additional or larger hard disk.

If you do want to move or resize the swap file, watch carefully to see how the system performs after the change, and then make changes as necessary until the performance of the system is adequate.

Additional Control Panels

The three Control Panel selections we have examined are by no means the only ones you should take the time to examine. Most of the other options are rather like the 386 Enhanced, in that they will not need to be changed under normal conditions. Nonetheless, the Printers, Drivers, Sound, and other panels do have valuable options, and you should definitely examine them closely.

TIP Because Windows is a graphical system, the key to success is to click on every option and examine every window. By exploring the system to find out what it can do, you will be better prepared to later decipher what a user has done! Moreover, remember that when you are first learning Windows the solution to a support issue is most often found through your eyes, not your memory. If you have a problem to troubleshoot, begin by looking in all of the windows you can find that may have settings relating to the problem. Often, the answer actually is staring you in the face! If you get really stuck, try pressing F1 or looking for a Help button or Help menu item.

Using Microsoft Windows 95

At the time this book is being written, the most current version of Windows is Windows 95. There are quite a few similarities (and more than a few differences) between Windows 3.*x* and Windows 95. In this chapter we'll take a look some of the most significant ones.

The major topics we'll cover in this section are as follows:

- Windows 95 System Requirements
- The Windows 95 Interface

NOTE For more detailed information on Windows 95, check out *Mastering Windows 95*, by Robert Cowart, or browse Microsoft's Web site at http://www.microsoft.com/.

As with any software requirements, as the version number increases, the hardware requirements increase as well. Because Windows 95 is a newer generation of software than Windows 3.*x*, a more powerful computer is required to run it. For information about system requirements, refer to Chapter 4.

The Windows 95 Interface

The most obvious difference between Windows 95 and Windows 3.*x* is the new interface. Figure 2.24 shows an example of the Windows 95 interface. Each major component is labeled in the figure.

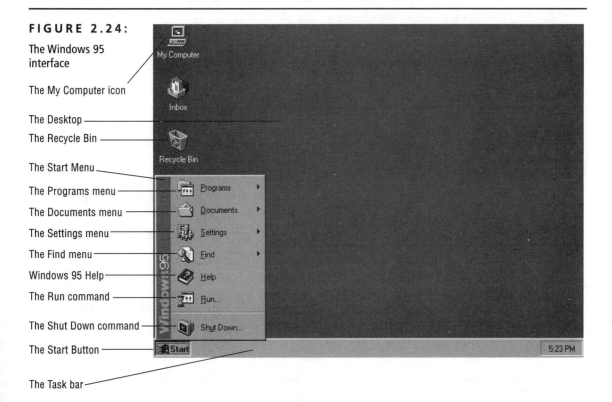

FIGURE 2.24:

The Windows 95 interface

The My Computer icon

The Desktop

The Recycle Bin

The Start Menu

The Programs menu

The Documents menu

The Settings menu

The Find menu

Windows 95 Help

The Run command

The Shut Down command

The Start Button

The Task bar

Let's take a look at some of the more common elements of the Windows 95 interface.

The Desktop

You can change the Desktop's background patterns, screen saver, color scheme, and Desktop size easily by right clicking on any area of the Desktop that doesn't contain an icon. When you right click, you'll get a menu that pops up in front of the Desktop. This menu allows you to do several things, like creating new icons (now called *shortcuts*), new directories (now called *folders*), a command for arranging icons, and a special command called *Properties*. This command is available through several other right-click options throughout Windows 95.

When you right-click the Desktop and choose Properties, you will see the Display Properties screen shown in Figure 2.25. From this screen you can click the various tabs at the top to move to the different screens of information about the way Windows 95 looks. For example, if you want to change the screen saver, click the Screen Saver tab, then choose a different screen saver from the drop-down list. Make any other changes you want (like changing the Desktop pattern wallpaper or screen resolution) and click OK to save them.

TIP   The Display Properties screen performs the same function as the Desktop control panel under Windows 3.*x*.

FIGURE 2.25:

The Display Properties screen

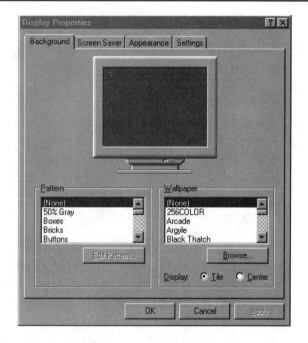

TIP   You can also access the Display Properties settings by using the Display control panel under Start ➤ Settings ➤ Control Panel.

The Taskbar

The Taskbar (Figure 2.26) is another new feature of the Windows 95 interface. It contains two major items: the Start Menu and the System Tray. The Start menu is discussed in the next subsection. The System Tray is located on the right side of the Taskbar and contains a clock (by default). Other Windows 95 utilities (for example, screen savers, virus-protection utilities) may put their icons here when running to indicate that they are running and to provide the user with a quick way to get access to their features.

FIGURE 2.26:

The Taskbar

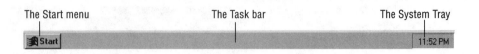

The Start menu   The Task bar   The System Tray

Whenever you open a new window or program, it gets a button on the Taskbar with an icon that represents the window or program. To bring that window or program to the front (or maximize it if it was minimized), you can click on the representative button on the Taskbar. As the Taskbar fills up with buttons, the buttons become smaller in order to fit.

You can increase the size of the Taskbar by moving the mouse pointer to the top of the Taskbar and pausing until the pointer turns into a double-headed arrow. Once this happens, you can click the mouse and move it up to make the Taskbar bigger. Or, you can move it down to make the Taskbar smaller. You can also move the Taskbar to the top or sides of the screen by simply clicking on the Taskbar and dragging it to the new location.

NOTE   You can make the Taskbar automatically "hide" itself when not being used (thus freeing up that space for use by the Desktop or other Windows). To do this, right-click the Taskbar and choose Properties. (You can also do this by selecting Start ➤ Settings ➤ Taskbar.) This will bring up the Taskbar Properties screen. From this screen you can customize the appearance of the Taskbar (for example, removing the clock from the System Tray, making the Start menu's icons smaller so they take up less room, and choosing which programs appear on the Start menu). If you check the Auto Hide option and then click OK, the Taskbar will minimize itself when the pointer is not over it. When you move the mouse pointer back to the area of the screen where the Taskbar is hidden, the Taskbar will pop up and can be used as normal.

The Start Menu

When Microsoft officially introduced Windows 95 to the world, it bought the rights to use the Rolling Stones song "Start Me Up" in its advertisements and at the introduction party. The reason they chose that particular song is because it's the Start menu that is the central point of focus in the new Windows 95 interface. It functions a lot like the File menu does in the Windows 3.x Program Manager, except that it has a lot more functions.

To display the Start menu, click on the word "Start" in the Taskbar. From the Start menu, you can select any of the various options the menu presents. An arrow pointing to the right means that there is a submenu. To select a submenu, move the mouse pointer over the submenu title and pause. The submenu will then appear; you don't even have to click. (You have to click to choose an option *on* the submenu, though.) Let's discuss each of the default Start menu's submenu options and how to use them.

Programs Submenu

The Programs submenu holds the program groups and program icons that you can use (a lot like the Program Manager does under Windows 3.x). When you select this submenu, you will be shown yet another submenu, with a submenu for each program group (Figure 2.27). You can navigate through this menu and its submenus and click on the program you wish to start.

FIGURE 2.27:

Using the Programs submenu to launch Solitaire

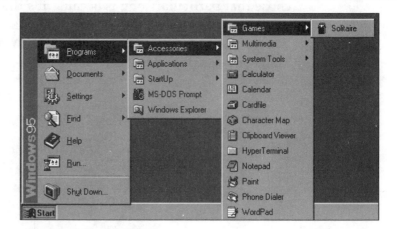

You can add programs to this submenu in many ways. The three most popular ways are as follows: via the application's installation program, via the Taskbar Properties screen, or via the Windows 95 Explorer program. The first (and simplest) way is to use the application's installation program. The installation program will not only copy the files for the program but will automatically make a program group and shortcuts for the programs under the Programs submenu.

> **TIP**
>
> You can add shortcuts to the top of the Start menu (above the Programs submenu) by clicking on a program or shortcut and dragging it to the Start menu. A shortcut for that item will appear in the Start menu above a divider between Programs and the new shortcut.

Another way to make shortcuts under the Programs submenu is to use the Taskbar Properties screen to add them. To get to this screen, right click the Taskbar and choose Properties. When the Taskbar Properties screen appears, click the Start Menu Programs tab to bring it to the front. You will then see the screen shown in Figure 2.28. From here you can click Add to add a new program or Remove to remove one. A *wizard* (a special sequence of screens designed to walk you through the necessary steps to accomplish certain tasks) will help you create or delete the shortcut(s).

FIGURE 2.28:

Using the Taskbar Properties screen to add and remove programs from the Programs submenu

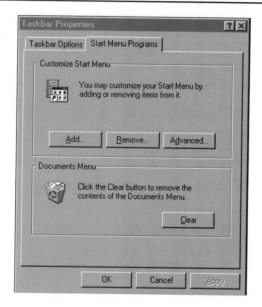

Finally, you can add program shortcuts to the Programs submenu by using another new component introduced in Windows 95: the Windows 95 Explorer (EXPLORER.EXE). Explorer performs a lot of the same functions of the File Manager under Windows 3.*x* but adds quite a few more features. Start the Explorer by navigating to Start ➤ Programs ➤ Windows Explorer. You will see a window similar to the one in Figure 2.29. From here you can see all of the crucial elements in Windows 95. Navigate on the C: drive to C:\WINDOWS\START MENU by either double-clicking parent folders or clicking the + signs next to the parent folders. This will display any subfolders. Once you click the plus sign next to START MENU you should see the PROGRAMS subfolder. You can either navigate further to a particular program group, or create the shortcut at the root of the Programs submenu. To create a shortcut in Explorer, right-click *in the right pane* and follow the steps in the wizard to create the new shortcut.

FIGURE 2.29:

The Windows 95 Explorer

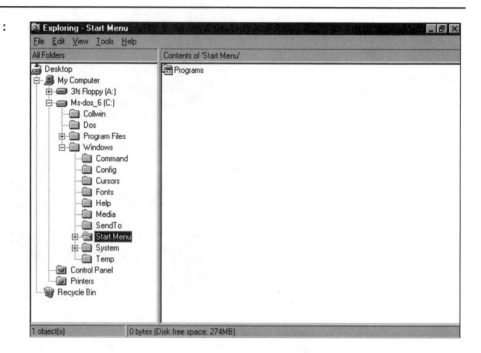

Documents Submenu

The Documents submenu has one and only one function: to keep track of the last 15 data files you open. Whenever you open a file, a shortcut is automatically made in this menu. This menu makes it easier to open the same document again if you need to. Just click on the document in the Documents menu to open the document in its associated application.

TIP
If you want to clear the list of documents shown in the Documents submenu, go to the Taskbar Properties screen. Then, click the Clear button within the Documents Menu section.

Settings Submenu

The Settings submenu is provided so you have easy access to the configuration of Windows 95. There are three submenus to the Settings submenu: Control Panel, Printers, and Taskbar. These submenus give you access to the Control Panel, printer driver, and Taskbar configuration areas, respectively. You can also access the first two areas from the My Computer icon, but they are placed here together to provide a common area to access Windows 95 settings.

Find Submenu

The Find submenu is used to find things. The Find command can be used to find either files (stored on a local computer or a network drive) or to find a computer that is hooked to the same network.

NOTE   If your Windows 95 computer is networked, there will probably be an extra option (Computer) under the Find submenu. The computer I installed Windows 95 on was not hooked to a network, so the graphic in this book does not show a Find ➤ Computer option.

When you select the Find submenu then select Files or Folders, you will be presented with a figure similar to the one in Figure 2.30. Next to the Named: field in this dialog box, simply type in the name of the file or directory you are looking for and click Find Now. Windows 95 will search whatever is specified in the Look In: parameter for the file or directory. Matches will be listed in a window underneath the Find window. You can use wildcards (* and ?) to look for multiple files and directories. You can also click the Advanced tab to further refine your search.

FIGURE 2.30:

The Find Files screen

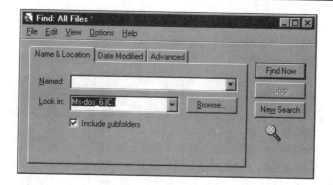

Help Command

Windows 95 includes a *very* good help system. Not only is it arranged by topic, but it is fully indexed and searchable. Because of its usefulness and power, it was placed into the Start menu for easy access. When you select this command, it will bring up the Windows 95 Help screen (Figure 2.31). From this screen you can double click on a manual to show a list of subtopics then click on a subtopic to view the text of that topic.

FIGURE 2.31:

Windows 95 Help
Contents tab

Or, you can click the Index tab to show an alphabetic listing of topics (Figure 2.32). To select a topic, type the first few letters of the topic (for example, type **prin** to move to the section that talks about printing) then click Display to display the text on the topic.

You can also click the Find tab to find any text you want in the help files (Figure 2.33). Simply type the text. As you type, Help will display a list of topics that contain the characters you are typing. You will see the list of topics get shorter as you type, because the more you type the more you are narrowing down your search. When the topic you want appears in the list, click on the one(s) you want to read about, then click Display.

FIGURE 2.32:

Windows 95 Help
Index tab

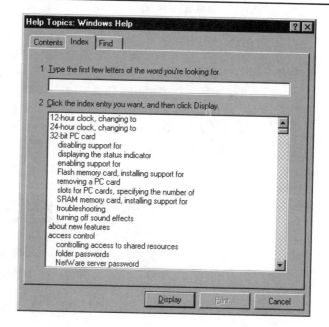

FIGURE 2.33:

Windows 95 Help
Find tab

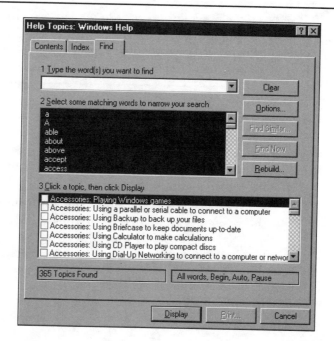

Run Command

The Run command can be used to start programs if they don't have a shortcut on the Desktop or in the Programs submenu. When you choose Run from the Start menu, the screen in Figure 2.34 appears. To execute a particular program, just type its name and path into the Open: field. If you don't know the exact path, you can browse to find the file by clicking the Browse button. Once you have typed in the executable name and path, click OK to run the program.

FIGURE 2.34:

The Start menu's Run command

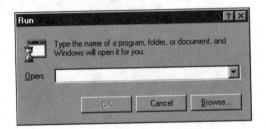

TIP   If the program you want to run has been run recently, you can find it listed on the drop-down list next to the Run box's Open: field. Click the down arrow to display the list, then select the program you want by clicking its name and then clicking OK.

Shut Down Command

Windows 95 is a very complex operating system. At any one time, there are several files open in memory. If you accidentally hit the power switch and turn the computer off while these files are open, there is a good chance these files will be corrupted. For this reason, Microsoft has added the Shut Down command under the Start menu. When you select this option, Windows 95 presents you with three choices, as shown in Figure 2.35.

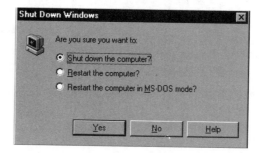

The three Shut Down choices are:

Shut Down the Computer. This option will write any
unsaved data to disk, close any open applications, and get
the computer ready to be powered off. When you see a black
screen with the message "It's now safe to turn off your computer" in orange text, it is, in fact, safe to power off the computer. You can also hit Ctrl+Alt+Del to reboot the computer at
this point.

Restart the Computer. This option works the same as the
first option but instead will automatically reboot the computer with a warm reboot.

Restart the Computer in MS-DOS Mode. This option is
special. It does the same as the previous option, except upon
reboot, Windows 95 will execute the command prompt only
and will not start the graphic portion of Windows 95. You
can then run DOS programs as though the machine were a
DOS machine. When you are finished running these programs, type **exit** to reboot the machine back into the "full"
Windows 95 with the GUI.

The My Computer Icon

Another new addition to the Windows 95 Desktop is the My Computer icon. If you double-click this icon, it will display all the disk drives installed in your computer as well as the Control Panel and Printers folders, which can be used to configure the system. If you double-click a disk drive, you will see the contents of that disk drive.

You can delve deeper into each disk drive and open window for each subdirectory by double-clicking them. You can copy and move files between drives and between directories using these windows.

If you were to right-click the My Computer icon and choose Properties, you would see a screen similar to the one in Figure 2.36. This screen is called the System Properties screen and can give you information about the current configuration of your computer—for example, what type of processor your computer uses and how much RAM is installed. It also will tell you what version of Windows 95 is being used.

FIGURE 2.36:

System Properties
screen

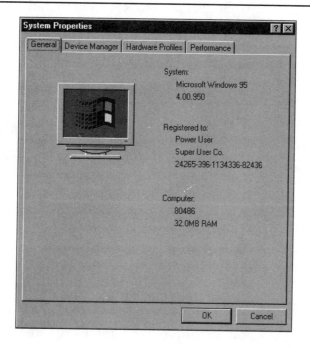

The Recycle Bin

Under Windows 3.*x*, when you delete a file from Windows, it warns you, then allows you to permanently delete the file. In Windows 95, when you delete a file, it still asks you, but instead of deleting it permanently from the disk, it places it in the Recycle Bin.

You can retrieve a file that you have deleted by simply opening the Recycle Bin icon, then dragging the file from the Recycle Bin back to the disk it came from. To permanently erase the file, you need to "empty" the Recycle Bin. You accomplish this by right-clicking the Recycle Bin and choosing *Empty Recycle Bin*. Figure 2.37 shows the difference between a full Recycle Bin (one that contains deleted files) and an empty Recycle Bin (one without any deleted files).

FIGURE 2.37:

The full (left) and empty (right) Recycle Bins

Windows

The final interface component that has changed is the set of buttons in the upper-right corner of any window. Figure 2.38 shows these buttons. Under Windows 3.*x*, there are only two buttons, but in Windows 95, there are three. The leftmost button is the *Minimize* button. When clicked, it causes the window to be minimized into an icon on the Taskbar. The middle button is the *Minimize/Maximize* button. Depending on the size of the screen when you click this button, the window is either maximized so that it takes up the whole screen or reduced if the window is already at its largest size. The rightmost button is the *Window Close* button. This button, when clicked, will close the window.

FIGURE 2.38:

Window control buttons

Other Differences between Win 95 and Win 3.x

Another difference between Windows 95 and Windows 3.x is that Windows 95 is an operating system that manages its own resources, whereas Windows 3.x is a Graphical User Interface (GUI) for DOS. As such, any hardware that Windows 95 needs to talk to must have its own drivers installed for Windows 95.

Additionally, Windows 95 can run 32-bit (Windows 95) applications simultaneously with older, 16-bit (Windows 3.x) applications. This provides for backwards compatibility with 16-bit applications. However, if a 16-bit application misbehaves it can adversely affect all other 16-bit apps and perhaps take down the whole system. This drawback is one of the reasons you should upgrade all of your older, 16-bit applications to their newer, 32-bit counterparts.

Review Questions

1. Which of the following is not a standard feature of DOS?

    A. Network support

    B. Running programs

    C. Managing files

    D. Managing disks

2. Which of the following is a program?

    A. Windows 3.1

    B. WordPerfect 5.1

    C. FORMAT.EXE

    D. All of the above

3. Which of the following filenames is invalid in DOS?

    A. myfile.txt

    B. my file.txt

    C. myfile

    D. MYFILE.TXT

4. Which is a disk-related service provided by DOS?

    A. Creating and deleting partitions on hard drives

    B. Compressing files to increase the number of files stored on a drive

    C. Copying and backing up disks

    D. All of the above

5. Which utility allows you to view memory usage?

    A. MEM

    B. MEMORY

    C. TIME

    D. FORMAT

6. Which utility allows you to view the system's processor type?

    A. MEM

    B. MSD

    C. FDISK

    D. PROC

7. Which of the following actually talks to a computer's hardware?

    A. The ROM BIOS

    B. The DOS System Files

    C. COMMAND.COM

    D. The processor

8. What is the Basic Input/Output System also known as?

    A. RAM

    B. ROM

    C. COMMAND.COM

    D. BIOS

9. Which is not a function of COMMAND.COM?

    A. Providing a consistant user interface to all DOS system files

    B. Presenting the results of a command to the user

    C. Receiving input from the user

    D. Formatting requests so they can be sent directly to the processor

10. Which DOS attribute is used by backup programs?

    A. Read-only

    B. Archive

    C. Hidden

    D. System

11. Which DOS command allows you to see the syntax of the DATE command?

    A. DATE /?

    B. DATE ?

    C. HELP /DATE

    D. HELP /DATE /SYNTAX

12. To run a Windows-based program in DOS without the Windows interface you have to:

    A. Use the DOS Shell to run the program.

    B. Configure DOS to support a mouse.

    C. Run the Windows program as the only program on the machine.

    D. Windows programs do not run under DOS alone.

13. Which of the following is not an important function of Windows?

    A. Running applications

    B. Preparing hard disks for use

    C. Managing files and directories

    D. Managing printing

14. Which of the following is not included within the Program Manager?

    A. Icon

    B. Group

    C. Desktop

    D. Menu

15. Which of these best describes an Icon?

    A. Any Windows-based program file

    B. The graphical configuration file needed to run all Windows apps

    C. The graphical shortcut to a file

    D. A graphical application

16. Which of these is used to close a window?

    A. Restore button

    B. Title bar

    C. Minimize button

    D. Control box

17. Which of the following is not a mouse function?

    A. Double-click

    B. Skip

    C. Drag

    D. Click

18. Which is not configurable through an Icon's properties window?

    A. Its Label

    B. Its Working directory

    C. Its Group

    D. Its Icon graphic

19. Where can you *not* find Icons?

    A. On the Desktop

    B. On the Program Manager workspace

    C. In a Group

    D. In the Control Panel

20. Which DOS wildcard is used in File Manager to represent any number of characters in a string?

    A. *

    B. %

    C. @

    D. ?

21. In which area do Windows and Windows for Workgroups differ the most?

    A. File management

    B. Network support

    C. Local printing

    D. Virtual Memory settings

22. The Control Panel is used to configure:

    A. System settings

    B. DOS settings

    C. Applications

    D. I/O drivers

23. A set of colors that define the appearance of Windows elements is a:

    A. Scheme

    B. Group

    C. Palette

    D. Rainbow

24. Which of the following is not an option under Windows Setup in Windows 3.1?

    A. Display

    B. Keyboard

    C. Mouse

    D. Network

25. Selecting the Exclusive in Foreground option in the 386 Enhanced Control Panel affects the foreground application by:

    A. Slowing it down

    B. Speeding it up

    C. Assigning it specific memory

    D. Assigning it specific hard disk space

26. Which of the following input devices is used to represent a Boolean (on or off) option?

    A. A check box

    B. A spinner box

    C. A drop-down menu

    D. An icon

27. Which of the following Control Panels is used to password protect a Windows 3.x workstation?

    A. Colors

    B. Keyboard

    C. Enhanced

    D. Desktop

28. You can install Windows 95 on a 386DX.

    A. True

    B. False

29. Which Windows 95 interface component contains the Settings submenu?

    A. Desktop control panel

    B. Right-click menu

    C. Start menu

    D. Network control panel

30. You can change the size of the Taskbar.

    A. True

    B. False

31. To turn off a Windows 95 machine you should:

    A. Exit Windows, then turn off the machine

    B. Run SHUTDOWN.EXE

    C. Just turn it off

    D. Choose Shut Down from the start menu and shut the computer off when Windows 95 says it's okay.

32. Which command is used to find files on a Windows 95 machine?

    A. Program Manager

    B. Find under the Start menu

    C. FINDFILE.EXE

    D. You can't find files on a Windows 95 machine.

33. How do you access the Control Panel in Windows 95?

    A. Select Start menu ➤ Settings ➤ Control Panel.

    B. Select Start menu ➤ Control Panel.

    C. Select Start menu ➤ Programs ➤ Control Panel.

    D. Right-click My Computer and select Control Panel.

34. You can't search the help system in Windows 95.

    A. True

    B. False

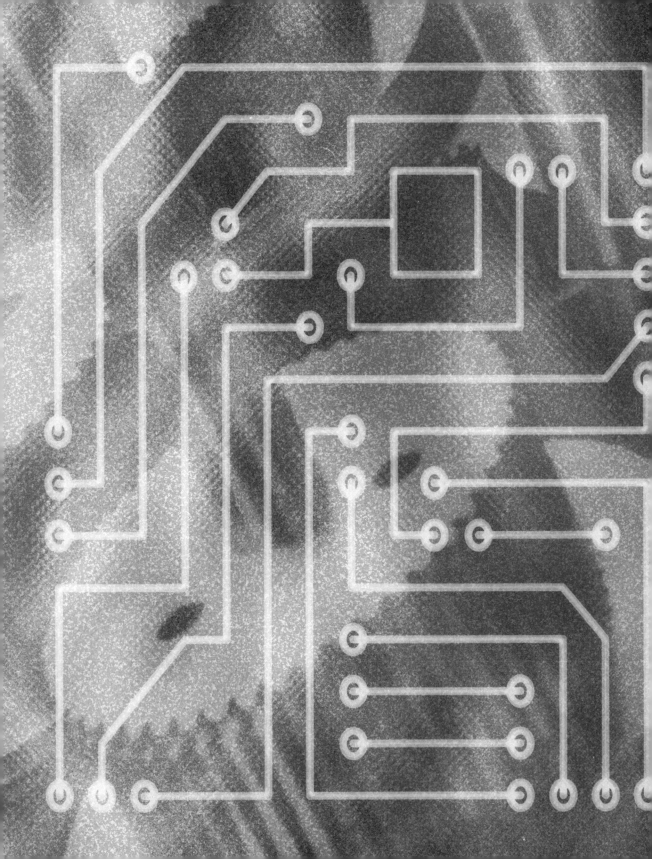

CHAPTER

THREE

3

Operating System Architecture

- Identify the operating system's functions, structure, and major system files.

- Identify the basic system boot sequences and alternative ways to boot the system software, including the steps to create an emergency boot disk with utilities installed.

This chapter is a general overview of Operating System (OS or O/S) architectures, specifically DOS (Disk Operating System), Windows 3.*x*, and Windows 95. As you learned in Chapter 1, an operating system is a computer program (or more often, a set of computer programs) that is designed to allow the convenient operation of a computer. While this may seem simple enough, there are two key ideas in this definition that may have gone unnoticed:

The operating system is convenient. Parts of today's operating systems may have been separate utility programs from third party software companies last year or some years before. One example of this phenomenon is the DriveSpace program that is now part of DOS. So what is included in an operating system depends partly on what the current idea of "convenient" happens to be.

The OS *allows* **the operation of the computer.** Computers simply will not operate without some kind of instruction. These instructions may be embedded in a chip or integrated circuit, in which case they are called firmware, or they may be kept on some other medium, such as a floppy disk or a hard drive, in which case they are called software. Either way, the program "allowing" the operation of the computer is the operating system.

The term "architecture" refers to the structure that is given to the various parts of an operating system.

In this chapter, we will examine the major parts of the common operating systems used on IBM compatible personal computers, we will see how the parts fit together, and we will examine the flow of information or the processing that occurs, particularly in the boot up process.

NOTE Sometimes pieces, even external commands, can become part of an operating system. In our example above, DriveSpace started out as a program called Stacker from Stac Electronics. Anyone could buy it, and it was not required as part of the operating system. In the DOS 6.22, DriveSpace is still a separate program, but it is sold as *part of the operating system* because it is a very convenient way to make room on hard drives. This type of program that is distinctly standalone, yet part of the OS is called an external command. Other commands, known as internal commands, are so necessary that they are built into the core of the operating system.

DOS Architecture

DOS interacts with computer hardware, so while the hardware is not a true part of DOS, DOS would not be functional without the hardware. The hardware basically consists of a variety of parts, such as motherboard circuits, drives, peripheral interfaces, etc. The activity of DOS takes place primarily in the motherboard circuitry, comprised of a CPU, memory chips, memory controller circuits, ROM BIOS, and so on (see Figure 3.1).

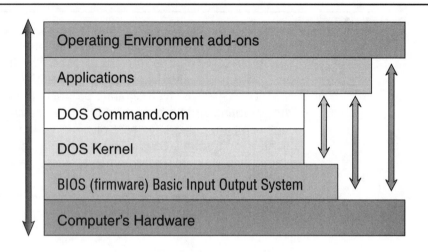

The DOS Kernel and Command Shell

The *kernel* is the core executable code that makes up the operating
system and allows the other pieces of the operating system to talk
to each other. The DOS kernel is composed of two files loaded into
memory when DOS is booted. The names of the two files will vary,
depending on the variation of DOS; they are generally named IO
.SYS and MSDOS.SYS. (But for example, in IBM's older versions of
PC-DOS, these files are named IBMBIO.COM and IBMDOS.COM.
The names are of little consequence until we begin our examination
of Windows 95.) A third file, named COMMAND.COM is loaded at
boot up but may be displaced from and replaced into memory. This
file is called a *command shell* or a *command interpreter*.

How Applications Use the Command Interpreter and the Kernel

Well behaved applications will generally "talk" to the hardware by way of the DOS command interpreter and the DOS kernel. Some DOS applications can talk directly to the system BIOS or even directly to the hardware itself.

The intent of this second approach is usually to speed up system performance. Unfortunately, it can backfire on certain systems, when certain pieces of hardware are present, or when certain combinations of software are running.

IO.SYS

IO.SYS is a piece of programming code that allows the rest of DOS and the programs to interact directly with the system hardware and the system BIOS. A part of this code is hardware drivers for common hardware devices.

> **NOTE**   Briefly, a *driver* is a small program or piece of program code that runs in the background and translates the information going to and from an application and a piece of hardware. For example, a program such as WordPerfect doesn't keep track of all the different types of printers that are available; instead, it uses a printer driver. (DOS applications use their own specific printer drivers.) WordPerfect is loaded into memory along with a printer driver that is specific to the user's printer. If a different printer is attached to that system, then a different printer driver may be required.

IO.SYS has built in drivers for such things as printer ports, serial or communication ports, floppy drives, hard drives, auxiliary ports, console I/O (input and output), etc. Because these drivers come preloaded when the system boots up, users need not concern themselves with installing common drivers. Other not-so-common drivers are generally loaded in a customized manner through a file called CONFIG.SYS.

MSDOS.SYS

MSDOS.SYS is the second kernel file found in DOS. Its function is primarily to handle disk I/O, hence the name *disk operating system*. Just like IO.SYS, MSDOS.SYS is loaded into memory at boot up and remains in memory at all times.

COMMAND.COM

COMMAND.COM is called the *DOS shell* or the *command interpreter*. It provides the command line interface that the DOS user sees. This is usually, but not always, the C:\> prompt. This prompt may be customized in a file called the AUTOEXEC.BAT.

COMMAND.COM also serves the purpose of providing some built-in commands that are commonly used and interpreting some other commands that are less commonly used. A glance at the DOS subdirectory on a DOS based computer will show a list of commands, including SHARE.EXE, XCOPY.COM, and others. These commands are called *transient commands* and usually assume the function of a utility. COMMAND.COM processes the transient commands as they occur.

Commonly used commands, such as COPY, TYPE, and DIR, are not listed in the DOS subdirectory. These commands are resident commands. The resident commands need no processing.

COMMAND.COM is a program that violates a rule of DOS program, namely the restriction in DOS that a program must occupy a contiguous memory space. All other programs follow this rule, which leads to memory management problems (see Chapter 6). COMMAND.COM is split into two pieces:

- The first piece is a small core that loads into the lowest part of the memory space just after IO.SYS and MSDOS.SYS.

- The second part is loaded into the highest part of conventional memory space, leaving the rest of conventional memory space free for applications to run in.

When an application is larger than the free space, it may elect to erase the upper portion of COMMAND.COM in order to free up space for itself. After the program is executed and finished, DOS reloads COMMAND.COM into conventional memory. Failure to reload COMMAND.COM is a common problem that the technician should be aware of. It often occurs when a special pointer (called an *environmental variable*) to the location of COMMAND .COM has been changed. If COMMAND.COM fails to load, then the system halts with an error message.

And Now for the Real World...

COMMAND.COM is the command shell that comes with DOS, but it is not a requirement. There is a shareware program called 4DOS that may be used to replace COMMAND.COM. This "enhanced" command interpreter has a variety of useful resident commands built into it.

Some of the 4DOS command line features are:

- Command line history with editing capabilities

- Copying and rename groups of files and directories

- Finding files on your system

- Viewing files

- File descriptions up to 511 characters long

continued on next page

Some of the 4DOS batch file features are:

- Batch language subroutines and IF/THEN/ELSE logic

- Batch file debugger executes line by line

Check out JP Software's Web site at www.jpsoft.com for more information or to download a copy of 4DOS.

Drivers

We saw that the IO.SYS kernel file loads certain built-in device drivers. There is also a group known as *installable device drivers*. A mouse driver is an example. Originally, PCs had no mice, and DOS had no mouse drivers. When mice became popular, they were originally sold with their own installable drivers. Later, most mice became compatible with the Microsoft standard and could use the Microsoft DOS installable mouse driver.

A very important device driver that is loaded with IO.SYS is the *console device driver* (CON). The PC is worthless without a mechanism for inputting and outputting information. Some early experimental PCs used lights and switches, but that system was pretty cumbersome. The console driver allow the use of a keyboard for input and a monitor for output.

In the original DOS, the console driver left something to be desired, especially with regard to monitor output. The original adapter was, after all, called a *Monochrome Display Adapter*, with no mention of the word, "graphics." A new device driver called *ANSI.SYS* was created that could allow for primitive screen graphics to be displayed. This driver is an installable driver, and it completely replaces the console driver. Most DOS programs with graphics features required that the ANSI.SYS driver be loaded in the CONFIG.SYS. You'll learn more about this topic in Chapter 5.

The Memory Map

In order to introduce two other special DOS commands, EMM386 .EXE and the HIMEM.SYS, we will need to review the concept of a memory map (see Figure 3.2). Because the memory maps use the hexadecimal numbering system, resulting in strange looking numbers with the letters A through F embedded in them. I've provided a brief explanation of hexidecimal numbering here. For more information, refer to the *A+: Core Module Study Guide*.

A Crash Course in the Hexadecimal Numbering System

Computer scientists and programmers use three alternate number systems to describe the events that occur in programming and in the CPU. These are the *binary* system and the *octal* and *hexadecimal* systems. The binary system is an accurate representation of what occurs inside the computer. The binary system uses zeros and ones as its only digits, which is where the term *bit* comes from: a *bit* is a <u>bi</u>nary dig<u>it</u>.

To represent the number nine in the decimal system, we just write down the numeral 9. To represent the number ten, we put a numeral 1 in the tens column, and a numeral 0 in the ones column.

In binary, we don't have a tens column, but we do have a ones column, and a twos column and a fours column, and so forth. Zero is used as a placeholder, just as it is in decimal.

For the number one in binary, we just write down a 1. For the number two in binary, we put a 1 in the twos column and a zero as a placeholder in the ones column, so it appears as 10_2 (where the subscript 2 is used to indicate that this is not the normal, decimal system 10 but is a binary number). The number nine in binary looks like 1001_2: a 1 in the eights column, placeholders in the fours and twos columns, and a 1 in the ones column.

continued on next page

Hexadecimal uses more digits than decimal does to represent number, as opposed to binary which uses fewer. Where binary uses two digits and decimal uses ten digits, hexadecimal uses sixteen digits. The extra digits are A, B, C, D, E, and F. F is a digit that is used to represent the decimal number 15. The number after F is 10h. (The h indicates that the hexadecimal number system is being used.) The 1 is in the sixteens column, and the 0 is a placeholder in the ones column.

Hexadecimal is used for memory maps because it conveniently corresponds to natural groupings of binary numbers. All the binary numbers from 0000_2 to 1111_2 can be represented by the hexadecimal numbers 0h to Fh. Every hexadecimal digit in a hexadecimal number can easily be converted to a group of four binary digits.

When examining the memory map, like the one shown in Figure 3.2, we see sixteen natural breaks. These are segments that end in an address xFFFFh, where any number from 0 to F can be substituted for x. Although 64 is not a convenient number for us to think about that is exactly what these segments are: 64KB (kilobytes). The first ten segments add up to 640KB (kilobytes), which is generally considered the largest memory space that DOS can work with. (You may have heard people refer to the "640KB limit.")

Notice that the top six segments, which add up to 384KB, appear to be reserved or set aside as "open" for an adapter. Remember that earlier we said that DOS programs must have contiguous memory space, which means that the available memory cannot be broken up into chunks that don't touch each other. So, while memory addresses may be free and available in the upper six segments, they are generally not available to DOS or DOS programs without help.

FIGURE 3.2:

A DOS memory map

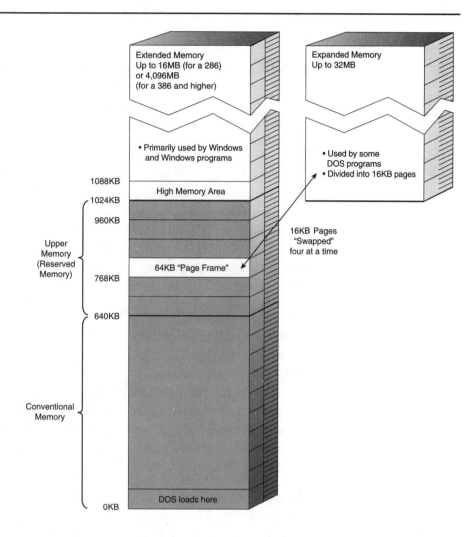

EMM386.EXE

To understand the EMM386.EXE and the HIMEM.SYS commands, which were added to DOS as DOS evolved, we actually need to step back into history a bit. The name, "EMM386.EXE" sounds like something that would apply to 386 computers, and that's true. But it is based on earlier concepts and memory management techniques.

Originally, programmers wrote programs that used less than 64KB. But, as a rule, programs will be written to fill available memory, even today. Programs grew quite large, by yesterday's standards and pretty soon left little room for the data that the programs were designed to manipulate.

A very common program in the early 1980s was Lotus 1-2-3, a popular spreadsheet used for accounting. Lotus wanted a way to fit more data into the memory of the computer while using a program that kept getting bigger as more features were added. Lotus teamed up with Intel and Microsoft to create a concept called expanded memory (not to be confused with extended memory). Their teamwork brought to market the LIM (Lotus Intel Microsoft) Spec Expanded Memory.

Remember that the DOS program must use contiguous memory. However, there is no such constraint on where the data itself must reside. Often, in the memory map perspective, there are free unallocated gaps in the memory address space reserved for hardware. What if some real memory could reside at that address? Could data be stored there? The answer is yes. Not only could data be stored there, but it could also be stored there temporarily and switched with some other data.

Building on these ideas, Lotus spreadsheets were soon able to be as large as 32MB. The user added memory on a card placed into an expansion slot. DOS loaded a LIM Spec Expanded Memory Manager, a small program that controlled the card and its memory chips. The memory manager would assign, as needed, a free unallocated memory address in the hardware range (640KB to 1MB) to a chunk of memory on the card.

These chunks of memory could be removed from or added to the memory map in 16KB blocks called *pages*. Up to four pages could be placed into memory space normally reserved for hardware. This space was called a *page frame*. When the program needed other data, the memory manager would swap the page out of the page frame in trade for another page of data. LIM Spec allowed for up to 32MB of expanded memory to be swapped into the page frame, one to four pages at a time.

Moving forward in time, the 80286 and the 80386 CPUs were developed. With many more address lines and advanced CPU core functions, these chips could see a great deal more memory, called extended memory. Designers created motherboards with room for more memory. Other operating systems, such as UNIX and Xenix, could use extended memory, but DOS could not. It became desirable and convenient to be able to use extended memory as if it were expanded memory.

NOTE   Remember, expanded memory has no direct memory address. It resides on an add-in card and is swapped in and out of memory space based on the control of the expanded memory manager. Extended memory actually has addresses associated with it, because the new CPUs have more address lines (actual wires that can be turned on and off to switch on and off access to a particular address).

EMM386.EXE provides the operating system with a mechanism to see extended memory, on a 386 computer system, as if it were expanded memory. It does this with the cooperation of the 386 CPU by taking control of the unallocated memory addresses between 640KB and 1MB. There are other programs with similar capabilities for the 286 computers. The memory space that EMM386.EXE controls has come to be known as *upper memory*, and the spaces occupied by programs in that region are known as *upper memory blocks* (UMBs).

There are two net effects of this process: First, the obvious effect that expanded memory is now available for use by DOS programs.

Second, clever programmers quickly found a way to use space in this address range for other purposes.

DOS programs need a contiguous memory space, but it does not have to be in conventional memory. If the program is small enough, it can run in the space normally reserved for hardware. A classic example of a small program is a driver such as a mouse driver or network interface card driver. Place the small drivers into this upper memory space, and more room is available in the larger conventional memory space for larger programs to run.

HIMEM.SYS

Next we examine the HIMEM.SYS command. Going back into history even further, remember that DOS was in some ways based on the older operating system, CP/M. CP/M was designed to run on 8080 and Z80 CPUs, which had only 16 address lines.

Feel free to work the math yourself, but trust me, this works out to a 64KB address space. That number should sound familiar, as it is exactly the size of the segments we looked at in the memory map. That's right: CP/M and all of its programs were restricted to the space of one segment of our DOS memory map.

Programmers of the CP/M era were used to a memory map based on a 64KB address space. Programs used memory addresses represented by four hexadecimal digits, not five as we see in our DOS memory map. Programmers continued to work in four digits addresses, as they were used to creating very small programs. If a program got big enough to pass the bounds of a memory address segment, the programmer used an address style called segmented addressing. Later, we will contrast segmented memory with flat memory.

A segmented address uses four digit hexadecimal for most of the memory addresses and adds a segment address when the program crosses segment bounds. So a program in the first segment would use address of 0000h to FFFFh. If it passed into the second segment, it would add the segment address 1, so 1:0000h to 1:FFFFh could be address in the second segment. A more common way to see this would be with two groups of four digits, where the first group represents the four most significant digits of the segment address and the second group represents the last four least significant digits. An example would be 1000:789Ah.

With an 8088 processor, the largest segment address that may be used is F:FFFFh, or more conventionally F000:FFFFh. Each F represents four binary digits or address wires that can be activated, and the 8088 had a total of 20 address lines, names A0 to A19. However, DOS was created, in theory, to accept segmented addresses up to FFFF:FFFF. The extra address space allowed by segmented addressing simply isn't available with the 8088's twenty address lines.

With the advent of the 80286 processor came four more address lines. These address lines mean that the 286 can literally see up to 16MB of memory address space, even though DOS cannot. And they mean that, by using one extra address line, the A20 line, an address of 1FFFFFh can be achieved. The full hexadecimal number represented by the segmented address of FFFF:FFFFh is 10FFEFh, well within the range allowed by the physical address lines A0 to A20. With the proper coaxing, DOS could now see address up to FFFF:FFFFh. This was almost a full 64KB segment of extra memory.

This 64KB (minus 16 bytes) is now known as the *High Memory Area* (HMA). It is created and managed by a device driver called HIMEM.SYS. The most common use of the HMA is to relocate parts of the DOS kernel, thus freeing space in the conventional memory area for larger DOS programs.

TIP The use of the A20 line (address line 20) is actually controlled by the keyboard controller chip, the i8042, which is on the motherboard. The i8042 interacts with the keyboard. If you have problems with the use of the HMA (or other memory problems) try switching the keyboard.

Booting

Several events occur during the startup of a computer system. This startup process is often called the boot up or booting.

The first events that occur in the boot process are governed by the system BIOS chip. It has instructions embedded in it called *firmware* that give some basic structure to the boot up. First, the chip runs the power on self test (POST), which tests a variety of devices. Then the chip adds adapter card ROM BIOS extensions to the BIOS (basic input output system). The firmware then instructs the system to look for a hard drive or floppy drive that might have an operating system on it. If that OS is DOS, then the chip runs the boot loader program, which is part of the Master Boot Record. The boot loader program looks for the IO.SYS and the MSDOS.SYS parts of the kernel, loads these into memory, and relinquishes main control of the system to the kernel.

The kernel then loads the command processor, which is usually COMMAND.COM, and executes two configuration files:

- The first is the CONFIG.SYS file, which stands for system configuration. This file sets certain OS parameters and loads most of the various installable device drivers. This is where HIMEM.SYS gets loaded.

- The second configuration file is AUTOEXEC.BAT. A batch file, named with a BAT extension, is simply a set of commands that DOS can execute or run. These commands may be simple utilities, like a virus checker, or they may be full-blown applications, like WordPerfect or Windows 3.1. The AUTOEXEC.BAT is a batch file that is automatically executed when the system starts up.

The process of configuring or setting up these files will be covered in Chapter 5. Once these files have been executed, DOS has booted up. What happens next is up to the computer user; often the user runs Windows 3.1 or Windows 3.11.

The Architecture of Windows 3.*x*

Windows was developed to run on IBM compatible computers, primarily the 286 and the 386 compatibles. As it was developed, it needed to be able to run on various configurations, which in turn required that it run using different processors' *modes*.

An Intel compatible processor has three modes of operation: real, protected, and enhanced. (Enhanced mode allows another feature called *virtual*—more on that later.).

Real mode The real mode places the processor in an emulation of an 8088 CPU, assuming of course that it is a high level processor. An 8088 can only run in real mode. An *x*86 CPU (80286, 80386, 486, or Pentium) running in real mode has the same limitations that an 8088 has. It uses only the first 20 address lines and is limited to 1MB of address space, etc. Because Windows 3.*x* allows real mode operation, it can actually be run on an XT type computer. I once ran it on a 12 MHz XT just to prove this point. Of course, it ran very slowly.

Protected mode The protected mode of CPU operation was introduced with the 80286 to utilize its 24 address lines. The protected mode allows the use of up to 16MB of RAM. DOS won't run in protected mode, but Windows will and some other OSes will as well.

Virtual mode The virtual mode allows the processor to pretend that it is multiple 8086 or 8088 processors. Each version of the multiple processors is called a virtual processor and has the same restrictions of a real 8088 processors, but each virtual processor can run separate copies of programs.

Windows was designed to switch back and forth between the processor modes for desirable performance. Multiple DOS programs could be run in virtual mode, large Windows programs could be run in protected mode, and so forth.

Windows 286 was an early version that allowed for real mode of operation. It came in versions 2.1, 2.1a, 2.1b, 2.1c, and 2.1d. It was improved with version 2.2, and it really arrived with version 3.0 released in 1990. With Windows 3.0 came three modes of operation—real, standard and enhanced—and the now familiar look and feel of the Windows interface.

Windows 3.1 was released in 1992. It made some modifications to the user interface but appeared substantially the same. One major addition was the inclusion of TrueType technology, which allowed screen fonts to more closely resemble actual printed fonts. Gone was the old UAE message that came with almost every Windows 3.0 session: UAE stands for unexplained application error, which was generally but not always a protected memory error. Windows 3.1 called these memory errors General Protection Faults (GPF), which is more descriptive, and other errors were given more appropriate names. And GPFs occurred with much less frequency than UAEs did.

Another significant addition in version 3.1 was networking capability, which was further developed into an integral part of the Windows program in Windows 3.11, also known as Windows for Workgroups.

In this section, we will focus on Windows 3.*x* (including 3.0, 3.1, and 3.11). The main parts of Windows 3.*x* are:

- The Graphical User Interface (GUI)
- Object Linking and Embedding (OLE)
- WIN.COM
- The kernel files: KRNL286.EXE and KRNL386.EXE
- GDI.EXE
- USER.EXE
- The INI files: WIN.INI and SYSTEM. INI

The Graphical User Interface (GUI)

The Graphical User Interface (GUI—pronounced goo-ey) is perhaps the most noticeable feature of Windows to end users. The GUI provides users with a whole new way of accessing programs. A mouse is used to point at objects on the screen, most commonly icons that are pictorial representations of programs and program groups but also other objects as defined in various programs.

A graphical user interface is an alternative way for the user to interact with a computer. While DOS requires that the user have some understanding of the underlying process (e.g. the file tree structure, the disk naming conventions, etc.) and that the user type a variety of commands into the keyboard, the graphical user interface relieves the user of many of these tasks. The user can accomplish many commands with simply a double-click of the mouse or a drag-and-drop operation.

GUIs such as Windows 3.*x* are termed *Operating Environment add-ons* because, while relying on the underlying DOS as an operating system, they give a whole new perspective on the user interaction with the computer. Windows 3.*x* is not an operating system in and of itself but is an evolutionary step toward a complete graphically oriented operating system, such as Windows 95.

The Players in the GUI Market: Xerox, Apple, GEOS, and Microsoft

There are primarily two graphical user interfaces available today, although others exist. The two that come to mind are those provided by Microsoft and by Apple. The Microsoft GUI was developed after the Apple Macintosh was created, so many people think that Microsoft copied from Apple. That may be the case; but Apple, in turn, copied from Xerox.

continued on next page

Some Apple people, back in the days of the Apple IIc, visited the Xerox Palo Alto Research Center (PARC) and saw a device (which we now know as a mouse) being used to control a graphical user interface (which we now know as a GUI). The Apple folks went back to their labs and invented the Apple Lisa, which later evolved into the Apple Macintosh. I have personally owned a Lisa and several Macintoshes, and I have seen a Xerox GUI computer. The similarities are remarkable.

Microsoft's first efforts at the Windows environment were shaky at best. Few programs were available, and the operating environment was not stable. It frequently locked up and crashed. The first Windows environment was announced in 1983 but was not actually seen until 1985. The late 1980s saw the evolution of Windows 2.*x* and Windows 386. This roughly parallels the evolution of the Lisa and Macintosh from Apple.

At the same time, the UNIX world developed X-Windows, and in reaction to the hardware and software "bloat" seen in the MS Windows world, GEOS (created by Geoworks) was developed as a GUI that would run well on PCs, XTs, and 286 computers.

Object Linking and Embedding (OLE)

OLE stands for *object linking and embedding*. In this case, the notion of object is not a screen representation, rather it is a document or file. An example might be one spreadsheet linked to another. Instead of having two copies of the same data, one copy can be referred to by another spreadsheet. The referred or linked copy will appear to the user as if it were in the referring spreadsheet. Further, any changes made in the original data will be reflected immediately in the linked image of that data.

In a similar fashion, a spreadsheet can be linked into a word processor. Changes made to the spreadsheet will appear automatically in the word document, which has a point embedded in it that locates the original data.

Program, Configuration, and Initialization Files

In this section, we will discuss the most important Windows system files: WIN.COM, the kernel files, the main system drivers (GDI.EXE and USER.EXE), and the initialization or INI files.

WIN.COM

The WIN.COM file is created during Windows setup and combines the WIN.CNF file with startup screen logo files. WIN.COM is used to load the startup logo screen and load the kernel files and other core components. WIN.CNF is actually a piece of executable code. If it were to be renamed to WIN.COM, it would start up Windows without loading the logo screens.

If you are starting Windows in standard mode, then WIN.COM runs DOSX.EXE in order to provide extended memory support. DOSX.EXE in turn loads the standard-mode kernel, KRNL286.EXE.

The Kernel Files: KRNL286.EXE and KRNL386.EXE

The kernel files, KRNL286.EXE and KRNL386.EXE, are responsible for loading and running applications and management of resources. Specifically, the kernel files control memory management and scheduling resources. Scheduling resources control the flow of tasks in a multitasking environment.

KRNL286.EXE is the executable loaded for the standard mode of operation, which allows the processor to be placed into real and protected modes. KRNL386.EXE is the kernel for the virtual or 386 enhanced Windows mode. This kernel allows the processor to be placed into all three modes of operation: real, protected, and virtual 86.

The Graphical Device Interface (GDI.EXE)

The GDI.EXE (Graphical Device Interface) file controls and creates the GUI. It is a set of text and graphics display routines that Windows programs can call when needed for graphical screen output. This set of routines is technically called a library. Programs do not need to do special graphics programs because the display routines are already available.

USER.EXE

The USER.EXE file is the Windows input and output manager. The types of input managed include keyboard, mouse, and communications, such as ports. The output managed includes sound and communications hardware. Various Windows components, such as the GDI, receive interpreted input from the USER.EXE; and the components perform actions, such as opening or closing a window.

INI Files: WIN.INI and SYSTEM.INI

INI's initialization files (pronounced eye-en-eye or in-knee) are made up of sections that start with a section head. The section head is contained by square left and right brackets. Within each section are lines containing keyword and value strings, and comments. A keyword and value string has a keyword, then an equal sign, then a value. This value may be a numerical value, or it may be a Boolean value. (Boolean values have two choices, such as True/False, Yes/No, On/Off, or 1/0.) Comments and remarks are preceded with a semi-colon. Any keyword line may be turned off simply by inserting the semi-colon at the beginning of that line.

The WIN.INI file was the primary configuration file for Windows in earlier versions, however with the release of version 3.0, configuration was split into two files. The WIN.INI file contained the settings that let users personalize their Windows installations. Frequently, various programs would also use the WIN.INI to contain their settings. Some hardware settings might also be found here, for example the serial and printer port setting.

The SYSTEM.INI file is now the primary configuration file for hardware setting. SYSTEM.INI would include the console input and output devices (usually a keyboard and monitor), the mouse, various network interface settings, and so forth.

Starting Up Windows 3.x

If you start Windows in standard mode, then WIN.COM runs DOSX.EXE in order to provide extended memory support. DOSX .EXE in turn loads the standard-mode kernel, KRNL286.EXE. As startup continues, the KRNL286.EXE loads the following files: Windows drivers (identified by the DRV extension in the SYSTEM.INI), the GDI.EXE, the USER.EXE, and various supporting files (for example fonts and network access files). Finally the KRNL286.EXE starts the shell specified in the SYSTEM.INI, usually Program Manager.

If you start Windows in the enhanced mode, WIN.COM starts the Windows 386 enhanced mode system loader, WIN386.EXE. WIN386.EXE in turn loads the following: Virtual Machine Manager or VMM and the virtual device drivers, designated by the "386" extension as specified in SYSTEM.INI. Network support may also be loaded at this time. The WIN386.EXE goes on to start KRNL386.EXE. The KRNL386.EXE starts or loads the Windows drivers, GDI.EXE, USER.EXE, and supporting files such as fonts and network drivers. The KRNL386.EXE also starts the Windows shell, usually Program Manager.

The Architecture of Windows 95

While DOS is a versatile operating system, it has its failings in the modern world of computing. It has an imposed memory limitation of 640KB (with some minor exceptions) and a programming structure that is based on segmented memory addressing. While tricks to gain more memory for application programs have extended the useful life of DOS, most people are no longer interested in dealing with its limitations.

Windows 3.*x* (including 3.0, 3.1, and 3.11) improved that situation somewhat. It allowed access to larger and larger memory spaces. But Windows 3.*x* retained some of the old DOS problems. In particular, the memory mode for Windows is still the segmented memory architecture. The segmented memory space leads to problematic programming techniques, and this in turn leads to UAEs (unexplained application errors) and GPFs (general protection faults). In essence, most of the time Windows 3.*x* runs in extended memory using the protected mode of the CPU. A GPF occurs when a program attempts to access part of the memory space that is reserved by another program. If that other program happens to be the Windows operating environment, then the system may hang, programs will quit, and data will get lost. Not a pretty picture.

Another characteristic of Windows 3.*x* is cooperative multitasking. Under this scheme, certain activities will take control away from the keyboard and therefore away from user intervention. One such activity is simply formatting a floppy disk. At other times, the activity could be an application that has gone awry. Often, if something goes wrong, the only recourse is to reboot the computer.

In an effort to solve these problems, Microsoft developed Windows 95, a new OS that still works with old applications (more or less). In many ways, Windows 95 appears to be built on DOS and

Windows 3.*x*, but this appearance exists only for purposes of backwards compatibility with older programs. We will see, for example, that the Windows 95 boot process is similar to the DOS boot process but with a very important difference. The look of Windows 95 borrows a great deal from Windows 3.*x*, but it has some features that go far beyond those of Windows 3.*x*.

This section will provide a general overview Windows 95, examine the details of functions of several important Windows 95 system files, and review the Windows 95 boot sequences.

In general, Windows 95 is designed to do the same job as Windows 3.*x*, only better. It provides a GUI but an enhanced one. It supports multitasking but does it preemptively rather than cooperatively. Windows 95 keeps the networking features introduced with Windows 3.11 but makes them better, easier to work with, and more stable. The file system is very similar to DOS but allows the use of long file names. A new version of Windows 95 offers very large drive partition sizes.

NOTE
The newer versions of Windows 95 have been slipstreamed, meaning that they are brought to market under the same name. These are usually referred to as OSR 1, OSR 2, and OSR 2.5, where OSR stands for "operating system release."

The GUI

The Windows 95 GUI uses overlapping windows, as does Windows 3.*x*. These windows are now arranged a bit differently in a space called the Desktop. The windows that appear on the Desktop are generally either an open application, such as Word 97, or a graphic representation of an organizational object called a Folder. Folders are somewhat equivalent to the group icon window in

Windows 3.*x*. However, Folders have certain significant added features:

- First, a Folder can contain another Folder.
- Second, a Folder may contain a shortcut.
- Third, the Folders can be manipulated in the traditional ways but also in some new ways.

Also appearing on the Desktop are program and program shortcut icons. In the old Windows, only group icons appeared in the Program Manager window.

Multitasking

Multitasking is a big issue with users, especially with so-called "power users." The ability to have a wide variety of programs open at one time (see Figure 3.3) enables the user to be more productive.

In the cooperative multitasking model that we saw with Windows 3.*x*, these programs that are simultaneously opened can interfere with one another causing UAEs or GPFs or grabbing the full attention of the processor. Windows 95 uses a variety of multitasking termed *preemptive*.

In preemptive multitasking, the control of the processor remains in with the operating system, not with the programs. This means that Windows 95 has control. If a program needs attention, (for example, if a communications program has incoming data), then Windows 95 will give that task the processor power it needs, even while running another program. A user can, therefore, download a file from the Internet and also work on a Word 97 document, without fear that the file download will be incomplete.

FIGURE 3.3:

Several programs open
at one time

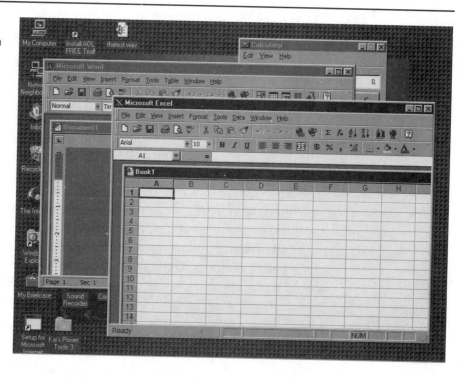

FIGURE 3.3:

Several programs open at one time

Networking

Networking is tightly integrated into Windows 95. No longer is modem access to other computers considered an added-in program. Now, when a computer accesses others, for example by connecting to the Internet, the user's computer becomes an extension of a computer network. This integration also covers the more traditional local area network (LAN), where a network interface card is used to attach the user's computer to others.

File Structure

The new file system allows for long file names, much like its Macintosh counterpart. The old file system used an 8.3 (eight-dot-three) naming convention, where the first part of the name was 1 to 8 characters long and the second part of the name, the file extension, was 0 to 3 characters in length. In the new system, there is a 255 character limit to a name, and it may have embedded spaces and certain special characters. The result is that a Windows 95 file name is very readable.

Further, the new file structure is backward compatible with older applications and even DOS. It accomplishes this feat by using a file name alias that is constructed according to special rules. For example, a long Windows 95 file name, such as LONGFILENAME.TXT, would translate into a short 8.3 filename, such as LONGFI~1.TXT.

Partitioning

When hard drives are installed, at least one partition must be created. DOS 6.22 supports a partition size of up to 2GB. This is based on a FAT, or file allocation table. Older versions of DOS would support smaller partitions. For example, DOS 3.3 would only see a drive partition of 32MB or less. With the introduction of Windows 95 Service Release B, we can now have drive spaces of up to 2,048GB or 2 terabytes, through the use of something called FAT32.

NOTE   FAT32 will support large drive partitions, however it is not compatible with earlier versions of Windows 95 or with Windows NT. This does not, however, mean that Windows 95 with FAT32 installed can not be used on a network. It can see a network or be seen by a network just fine.

Memory

In order to use extended memory efficiently, Windows 95 is constructed using a flat memory model, instead of a segmented memory model. Remember, in the segmented memory space, memory is addressed using a segment address and an offset address. This system is one of the primary reasons that ill-behaved programs can cause a general protection fault. In a flat memory model, all memory address have a complete address in one part, instead of a two part segmented address. This leads to more secure addressing, and very large programs are easier to write.

Sometimes, it's necessary to get a program based on segmented memory to run in a flat memory space. Windows 95 uses a process called *thunking* to translate from a 16-bit application to a 32-bit flat memory model and back again to 16-bit. This process is the reason that certain programs, notably older Windows 3.1 programs, might run slower under Windows 95.

Drivers

Device drivers are those little bits of program code that serve to translate between the main operating system and a piece of hardware. As computers get more and more complicated in design, the requirement for more drivers and larger drivers becomes apparent. Windows 3.*x* used 16-bit drivers, with the exception of Windows for Workgroups, which commonly used 32-bit drivers for networking and some other tasks.

A primary disadvantage to 16-bit drivers is that they must reside in DOS memory space (i.e., the first megabyte of memory). Placing the drivers there takes away from space for applications and data. Further, the CPU runs in real mode while accessing DOS memory space, so 16-bit drivers are slower. The 32-bit drivers used by Windows 95 reside in the flat memory space and do not require the processor switch modes.

TIP Sixteen-bit Windows drivers can be used in Windows 95, but they are not efficient. Sixteen-bit Windows virtual drivers cannot be used in Windows NT.

Configuration Files

By now, you should be familiar with the program files IO.SYS, MSDOS.SYS, and COMMAND.COM. These files also exist in Windows 95, although the MSDOS.SYS file is a dummy file with a few configuration settings in it.

NOTE MSDOS.SYS is not needed by Windows 95, but is included for those DOS programs that expect an actual MSDOS.SYS file to exist.

IO.SYS (and MSDOS.SYS)

The functions that were previously found in both IO.SYS and MSDOS.SYS have been combined into one IO.SYS file, along with several others, including HIMEM.SYS (memory manager), IFSHLP.SYS (installable file system), SETVER.COM, and WIN .COM. IO.SYS truly starts the Windows operating system.

Because some older programs won't function if they cannot find MSDOS.SYS, a dummy MSDOS.SYS file exists. Much of this file is taken up by wasted space so it will be large enough to fool the programs looking for it. MSDOS.SYS also contains a configuration line that tells the system whether to boot into the GUI or into a DOS command shell at startup time.

COMMAND.COM

COMMAND.COM is still the DOS shell or command interpreter. External DOS commands are examined by COMMAND.COM before they are executed. If you select Start ➤ Run and type in **COMMAND.COM** or simply **command**, a DOS window will appear.

The INI Files: WIN.INI, SYSTEM.INI, and PROGMAN.INI

Recall that Windows 3.x used INI files for program configuration information, in particular WIN.INI, SYSTEM.INI, and PROGMAN .INI. These files are retained by Windows 95 for compatibility with older Windows programs. For example, many of the early Windows 3.x applications wrote their configuration information to the SYSTEM.INI file. Later applications commonly wrote similar information to their own INI files and thus are less dependent on the SYSTEM.INI file.

The Registry: SYSTEM.DAT and USER.DAT

Windows 95 exploits the registry file in a way that early versions of Windows could not. The registry file is a central repository of configuration information. A complete examination of the Registry is beyond the scope of this book, as it is an advanced topic. However, it is important to know that the Registry may be edited with the REGEDIT command. And it is important to know that the careless technician can create a royal mess by editing the Registry.

The Registry is comprised of two files: SYSTEM.DAT and USER .DAT. *DAT* is short for data file. The SYSTEM.DAT is a complex file containing a wide variety of system setting and application program settings. The USER.DAT file contains primarily configuration settings for individual users, such as user rights and personal desktop settings.

Boot Up Sequence

The Windows 95 boot up sequence is similar to the DOS boot up sequence: The processor, usually a Pentium or 486 CPU, starts out in real mode. Very quickly in the boot up sequence, the operating system loads extended memory or protected mode program code and sheds the real mode program code altogether.

The boot up sequence is also referred to by Microsoft as the *startup process*. It starts with a real mode startup process under BIOS control. This part is the same for any computer, regardless of operating system. The real mode startup process initiates the system startup files, including IO.SYS and various MS-DOS drivers and TSRs, which are loaded for compatibility with older programs. Drivers and TSRs are found in the CONFIG.SYS and AUTOEXEC.BAT files.

IO.SYS loads and initializes real mode Windows drivers, such as HIMEM.SYS, IFSHLP.SYS, SETVER.EXE, and DRVSPACE.BIN. The file MSDOS.SYS is then examined for special startup configuration values. These include the path to the Windows directory, whether to load the GUI, and several other values.

The real mode startup process then examines the SYSTEM.INI and WIN.INI files. Most of what was stored in these files is now located in the registry files, but some settings are retained in these INI files for backaward compatibility. At this time the system switches to the protected mode configuration manager, which examines the system for currently attached hardware and whether the hardware is functioning. Next, Windows 95 loads the KRNL386 .EXE, the GDI, and USER.EXE.

Windows 95 accesses the Registry for other resources. These resources, such as fonts used by Windows 95, are installed. The Desktop setup, including its appearance, is loaded and the user is allowed access to the system

Accessing DOS from Windows 95

Compatibility with older programs is important because people have a significant investment in the money spent on their programs and in their time learning how to use them. Microsoft built a number of features into Windows 95 that allow previous users of Windows 3.x to capitalize on their investment and that allow technicians access to DOS-based troubleshooting.

There are three different ways a Windows 95 machine can access DOS:

- The user can boot the computer straight into DOS.
- The user can exit from Windows 95 into DOS mode.
- The user can initiate a DOS shell from inside of Windows 95.

In the first two scenarios, the computer runs a true DOS in real processor mode. In the third scenario, the computer creates something called a Virtual DOS Machine (VDM). A virtual machine is a program that pretends to be hardware. With a VDM, the Windows 95 programs creates a sub-program that pretends to be DOS.

Running DOS from inside Windows 95 involves creating a VDM. You can use the Start ➤ Run menu and type **command** to create a DOS shell window, or you can click the DOS Prompt icon located on the Desktop.

To boot into DOS at start up, press the F8 key and select one of two DOS choices from the menu that appears:

- The first choice will load any 16-bit drivers found in the CONFIG.SYS and AUTOEXEC.BAT files. These drivers might include CD-ROM or network drivers.

- The other choice is DOS safe mode, which will start DOS without loading any drivers. (Another way to enter DOS safe mode is to press the F5 key).

Another trick is to use the F4 key to enter the old operating system (either DOS or DOS and Windows 3.*x*)—press the F4 key during the Starting Windows 95 message. The F4 method requires that an old operating system actually be present. All the other methods I've discussed don't take the user to an old operating system; they take the user into DOS 7, the DOS that is underlying Windows 95.

Finally, the choice to enter into DOS mode is presented when the user exits from Windows. This method will load drivers and will leave loaded 16-bit drivers in memory, and so this method is not as desirable for troubleshooting purposes where a clean and safe boot is often needed.

Review Questions

1. Which of the following files is not needed under Windows 95?

    A. USER.DAT

    B. IO.SYS

    C. MSDOS.SYS

    D. AUTOEXEC.BAT

2. Which of the following components starts a Windows 3.*x* session?

    A. WIN.CNF

    B. WIN.COM

    C. KRNL286.EXE

    D. KRNL386.EXE

3. Which technology allows Windows 95 to use up to 2 terabytes of drive space?

    A. FAT32

    B. IDE

    C. Enhanced IDE (EIDE)

    D. SmartDisk

4. Which Windows 3.*x* component is responsible for drawing windows and scroll bars?

    A. USER.EXE

    B. GDI.EXE

    C. KRNL286.EXE

    D. WINDOW.EXE

5. Which of the following files is the command interpreter for MS-DOS?

    A. COMMAND.COM

    B. COMMAND.EXE

    C. MSDOS.SYS

    D. KRNL386.EXE

6. Generally speaking, you can run Windows 3.*x* programs under Windows 95.

    A. True

    B. False

7. Which key could you press at the "Starting Windows 95 . . ." screen to boot directly to an old operating system instead of starting Windows 95?

    A. F1

    B. F2

    C. F4

    D. F5

8. One of the disadvantages of the FAT32 file system is:

    A. It isn't compatible with Windows NT or earlier versions of Windows 95 (before service release B).

    B. It is slower than other types of file systems.

    C. It is expensive.

    D. It can't be used on computers with a National Semiconductor 80753 pre-processor integrator.

9. Which Windows 3.*x* core component controls display of windows, icons, and menus?

    A. KRNL286.EXE

    B. KRNL386.EXE

    C. GDI.EXE

    D. None of the above

10. If you save a file called MYLONGFILENAME.DOC under Windows 95, what does it look like in a directory listing in a DOS window?

    A. MYLONGFILENAME.DOC

    B. MYLONG~1.DOC

    C. MYLONG~1.FIL

    D. MYLONGFI.DOC

11. Place the following MS-DOS files in order by placing a number next to them to indicate their loading order (i.e., 1=first, 2=second, and so on)

    _3_ MSDOS.SYS

    _2_ CONFIG.SYS

    _1_ IO.SYS

    _5_ AUTOEXEC.BAT

    _4_ COMMAND.COM

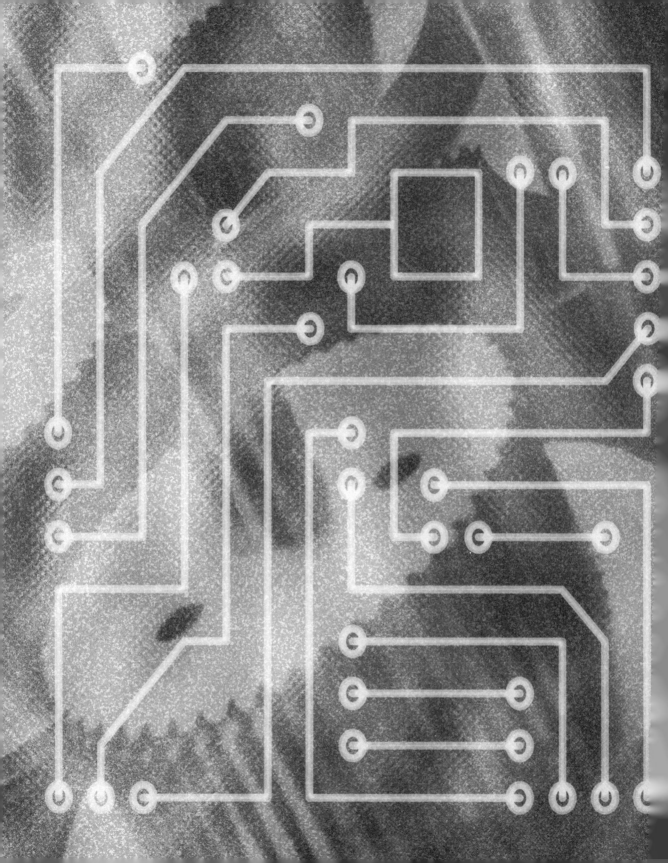

CHAPTER

FOUR

4

Installing Microsoft Operating Systems

■ Identify the procedures for installing DOS, Windows 3.*x*, and Windows 95 and for bringing the software to a basic operational level.

■ Identify steps to perform an operating system upgrade.

Installing an operating system on a computer is a task every technician will be asked to perform. Because it is such an important part of a technician's routine, it is included on the A+ Exam. This chapter deals with the steps necessary to install any of the three major operating environments.

Installing DOS

Installing DOS is a relatively simple task. There are menus at every step to guide you through the process. For these sections we will make a few assumptions. First, we'll assume that you are installing MS-DOS version 6.22, the most current version available for installing on a PC. IBM's PC-DOS installation is very similar. Second, we'll assume that the disk has already been partitioned and formatted (with the /S switch to make it a bootable hard disk), as detailed in Chapter 6. Finally, we'll assume that you are installing DOS to a hard disk. We will make special notations for installing to a floppy disk, where appropriate.

Starting SETUP.EXE

There are three disks used to install MS-DOS. They are labeled Disk 1, Disk 2, and Disk 3, surprisingly enough. Disk 1 is the disk that is bootable and contains the SETUP.EXE program that is used to install DOS. In order to install DOS, you need to insert Disk 1 in the A: drive and turn the computer on.

If you have more than one floppy drive, you can boot to a floppy in drive A: and place Disk 1 in drive B:. In order to get SETUP.EXE to execute in this case, you will need to manually type the following at a command prompt:

```
A:\> B:
B:\> SETUP
```

The setup program will then start and you can begin the installation process.

Because this disk is bootable, the computer will boot and automatically start the SETUP.EXE program. You will know that this process has completed successfully when you see a blue screen with the following message:

```
Please Wait.
Setup is determining your system configuration.
```

At this point, you know that SETUP.EXE is functioning normally. After a small delay (a few seconds), a welcome screen will appear that indicates that you are ready to install DOS. If you press F1 at this point, you will see a help screen detailing information about the installation process. You can press F3 twice to escape to the DOS command prompt at this point (or at any time during the installation). Also, you can press F5 at any time to change the screen colors that Setup uses to display information. This may be useful to you if you are color blind and can't see certain contrasting colors. Additionally, if you are installing to a floppy disk, you need to press F7 and Enter to choose this option.

When you are ready to continue with the installation, press Enter.

Entering MS-DOS Machine Settings

At this point, Setup has determined what type of machine you are installing DOS on and will present you with the system settings information it has found. Figure 4.1 shows a screen similar to what you might find.

FIGURE 4.1:

The MS-DOS system settings information setup screen

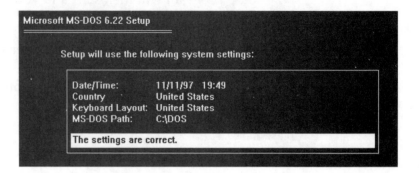

In this menu, Setup will display both the configuration it detected for your system and the default installation parameters to use for this installation. The settings it normally shows are those for Date/Time, Country, and Keyboard Layout. Notice that the default for the selection bar is These Settings Are Correct. MS-DOS Setup is rather arrogant in its assumption that it did everything right the first time and that you want to put everything where it tells you to. However, it can afford to be arrogant because it's usually right.

On the off chance that Setup made an error, you do have the ability to change the settings. To change a setting:

1. Use the arrow keys on your keyboard to move the selection bar so that the value you want to change is highlighted.

2. Press Enter.

3. You will be prompted to either enter a new value (Date/Time) or be presented with a list of possible settings (Country and Keyboard Layout). Enter the new value for the setting and press Enter to accept the new value.

4. Repeat steps 1 through 3 for any other settings that need to be changed.

When you've finished changing the installation parameters, highlight These Settings Are Correct and press Enter. This indicates to Setup that all configuration information is correct and installation can proceed normally.

Setting the DOS Installation Directory

The next screen that is presented asks where you would like to install the DOS files (Figure 4.2). The default directory, C:\DOS, is normally the directory in which you'll want to place these files. To change the path where Setup puts the DOS files, simply hit Backspace to delete the nameof the current installation directory and enter your own. If the directory doesn't exist, Setup will create it for you. When you have entered the correct directory (or if you want to use the default directory), press Enter and the Setup program will continue.

FIGURE 4.2:

Selecting the location for the MS-DOS files

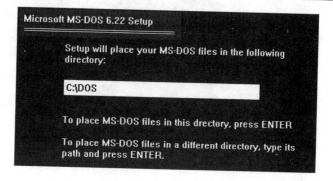

NOTE   As soon as you press Enter, Setup will begin copying files and making changes to your system. If you press F3 to exit, no changes will have been made to your system (except any FDISKing or FORMATing you may have done).

Copying MS-DOS Files

At this point, Setup starts copying files. An installation progress bar at the bottom of the screen will indicate to you how far Setup is into the installation with a yellow barometer that increases in size as the installation progresses. Setup also indicates progress with a % Complete figure above the progress bar. This setup screen will also tell you that now is a good time to fill out your registration card (Figure 4.3). That is, in fact, a good idea because it lets Microsoft know who you are and that you have legally purchased their software.

FIGURE 4.3:

MS-DOS Setup shows the progress by means of a % Complete barometer.

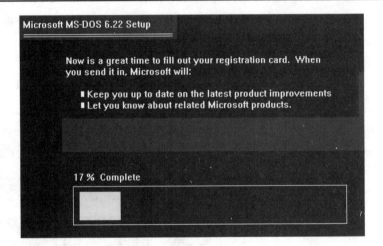

```
Microsoft MS-DOS 6.22 Setup


        Now is a great time to fill out your registration card.  When
        you send it in, Microsoft will:

            ▪ Keep you up to date on the latest product improvements
            ▪ Let you know about related Microsoft products.




        17 % Complete
```

TIP Watch the lower-right corner of the Setup screen during installation. Setup will display what files it is reading from the setup disk, then what files it is writing to the hard disk (or floppy disk). If you encounter a problem reading or writing a file, you will know which file is causing the problem by paying attention to this corner of the screen.

When the Setup progress bar reaches around 25 percent complete, a screen will appear that tells you to insert the next MS-DOS setup disk into your A: drive (Figure 4.4). Eject the first disk by pushing the eject button on your floppy drive. Insert the MS-DOS setup disk that is labeled Disk 2 (remember, there are three MS-DOS setup disks). Press Enter to continue.

FIGURE 4.4:

Setup asking you to insert Disk 2

At this point, Setup goes into what I like to call "the long copy," during which it will copy several files to your hard disk. During this time, Setup will flash several screens of information about some of the new features of MS-DOS 6.22, including MemMaker, Disk Compression, and MS-DOS Anti-Virus.

When the progress indicator reaches around 58 percent, Setup will present another screen that asks for MS-DOS Setup Disk 3 (Figure 4.5). Remove Disk 2 and insert Disk 3. Press Enter to continue and start the final file copy.

FIGURE 4.5:

Setup asking you to insert Disk 3

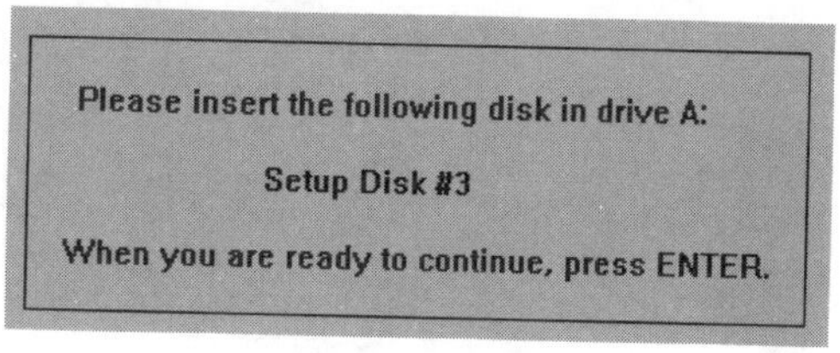

Please insert the following disk in drive A:

Setup Disk #3

When you are ready to continue, press ENTER.

The final file copy will take slightly less time than the second. When the indicator reaches 100 percent complete, the disk activity stops and the screen in Figure 4.6 appears, telling you to remove the MS-DOS setup disk from the floppy drive in preparation for a restart. At this point, all files have been copied and the computer has DOS installed. Remove all disks from all floppy drives and press Enter.

FIGURE 4.6:

At the end of the install process, Setup asks you to remove the floppy disks.

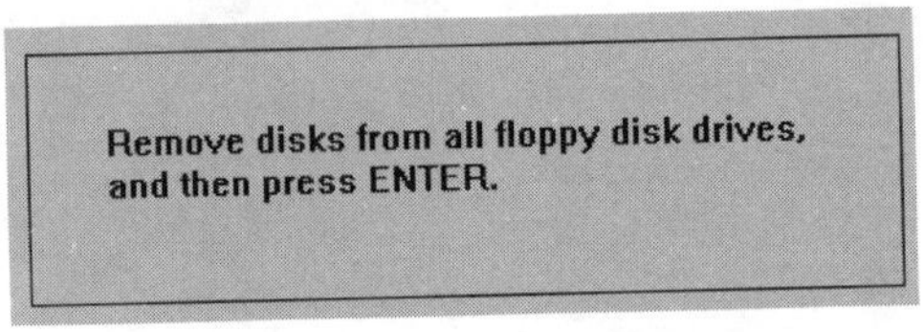

> Remove disks from all floppy disk drives, and then press ENTER.

Finalizing Setup

When you press Enter at the previous screen, the screen shown in Figure 4.7 is displayed. This screen instructs you what to do next. If you want to reboot the computer and start MS-DOS 6.22, go ahead and press Enter.

FIGURE 4.7:

The MS-DOS final setup screen

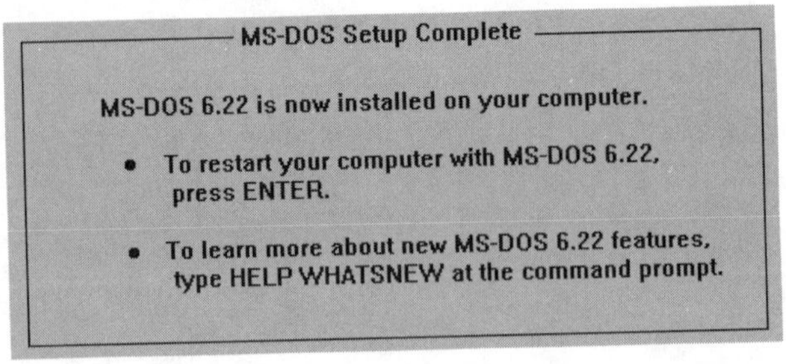

> ── MS-DOS Setup Complete ──
>
> MS-DOS 6.22 is now installed on your computer.
>
> • To restart your computer with MS-DOS 6.22, press ENTER.
>
> • To learn more about new MS-DOS 6.22 features, type HELP WHATSNEW at the command prompt.

Note that if you want to learn about the new features, you still have to press Enter to reboot first. However, after you've rebooted, you can type the following to get information about the new commands:

```
HELP WHATSNEW
```

This will bring up a DOS help file that explains what's new in MS-DOS since the previous version.

After you've pressed Enter, the machine will reboot and the default AUTOEXEC.BAT and CONFIG.SYS will be executed. You can make changes to them if you wish. You can also install new hardware and install the drivers for them at this point, now that the AUTOEXEC.BAT and CONFIG.SYS have been created.

Pat yourself on the back. You have just successfully installed MS-DOS.

Installing Windows 3.*x*

Installing Windows is a relatively simple act that every technician will have to perform several times throughout their career. The A+ exam covers several Windows installation topics, so I will pay particular attention to the major installation steps. I will actually go into more detail than the exam does. However, you may install Windows so often, you might not think about the exact steps. This chapter may also detail some installation options you may not have used before.

For this section we need to make two assumptions:

- First, that the version of Windows you are installing is version 3.1. Installation for Windows 3.11 (Windows for Workgroups) is mostly the same as for Windows 3.1. (Also, the A+ exams cover the Windows 3.1 version only.)

- Second, we assume that you are installing from 3½" floppy diskettes. This is the default medium, but it is also possible to get Windows on 5¼" disks by writing to Microsoft.

Prerequisites for Windows 3.1 Installation

Just as with the installation of DOS, Windows has its own set of prerequisites. Because Windows is a graphical interface, instead of keyboard-command based interface, it has a longer list of prerequisites (as well as more stringent ones).

Computer System Windows 3.1 requires a 286 or better processor. A 286 is required for running Windows in Standard mode, and a 386 or better is required for running Windows in 386-Enhanced mode. (See the sidebar *What Is a Windows Operating Mode?* for an explanation of Standard and 386-Enhanced modes.)

Operating System Windows is only a shell for an existing operating system and therefore requires that one is installed before you can install Windows. Windows can be installed over MS-DOS version 5.0 or later or PC-DOS version 3.1 or later.

Disk Space Windows requires more disk space than DOS alone, so you must take into account your current disk space situation. A new installation of Windows 3.1 requires at least 2MB (possibly up to 11MB) available. An upgrade from an earlier version of Windows will require anywhere from 5MB up to 5.5MB (in addition to what the current version already uses).

Memory Windows 3.1 requires at least 640KB of conventional memory and 1024KB (1MB) of extended memory for 386-Enhanced mode (approximately 2,048KB). In Standard mode, those requirements are reduced, somewhat, to 640KB of conventional and

256KB of extended. Also, in order to access extended memory, you must make sure that there is an extended memory manager (like HIMEM.SYS) loaded. If there isn't one currently loaded, the Windows Setup program will make the changes to your CONFIG.SYS to load it.

Mouse Windows is a graphical interface. As such, it uses a pointer and icons to represent files, programs, and disks. To move this pointer, you need to use a mouse. It is possible to run Windows without a mouse, but it is very difficult. Also, some commands in some Windows programs don't have keyboard shortcuts.

Video DOS uses video circuitry differently than Windows does. DOS uses a video card's character mode (also called text mode). Character mode is faster than graphics mode, but graphics mode has a higher resolution and can take advantage of most of any particular video card's features. For this reason, a video card that has a *Windows driver* is also required, as well as a monitor that is compatible with that type of video card.

TIP

Remember that these *prerequisites* are just that. They are *bare minimums*! You can get Windows to run without these settings, but don't expect to get any work done. Windows 3.1 *should* be run on nothing less than a 386 with 4MB of RAM and 30MB of disk space free for adequate performance. Increasing any of these resources will improve Windows' performance. I have actually installed Windows on a 286 machine with 1.5MB of RAM, and it *does* run, but I couldn't do much with it. The NOTEPAD program took a full minute to launch. And, when typing in windows, I had to wait a second or two between pressing a key and seeing the character appear on the screen!

What Is a Windows Operating Mode?

When Windows 1.0 came out, it was pretty basic. It was designed to run on any PC. At that time, the fastest PC was one based on a 286 processor. When Windows 3.0 was going to come out, Microsoft had a problem. The fastest processor then was the 386 processor, which had several new features (multitasking, access to more memory, etc.). They wanted to use the new features of the 386 processor but still provide compatibility for people running Windows on older hardware. To deal with this, they introduced the *operating mode* feature. When Windows is first started, it detects what kind of hardware it's running on. If the hardware can support it, Windows runs in *386-Enhanced mode* to take advantage of all of the features that the 386 processor has to offer. If the hardware can't support it, Windows drops into what is called *Standard mode*. This mode makes Windows run as if it is running on a 286 processor, even though it may actually be running on a 486.

Installing Windows 3.1 Using the Express Setup: The DOS Portion

Assuming the machine you are going to install Windows on has met the prerequisites, you now have two choices: Install Windows using Express Setup or install it using Custom Setup. When you run SETUP.EXE from the A: drive, you will be presented with a somewhat familiar blue installation screen. This screen will, eventually, ask if you want install via Express or Custom.

Express Setup makes a few assumptions about the way you would like Windows installed. For example, it automatically picks which Windows applications and utilities will be installed (i.e., Notepad, Solitaire, and Windows Write). We will detail a little later which specific settings can be chosen.

Windows' installation has been divided into two parts: the DOS portion and the Windows portion.

The first part of Windows installation is the DOS Setup portion. In this portion, the files for Windows Setup portion are copied to the hard disk and decompressed—which brings up an important point: Installing Windows (and most programs these days) doesn't mean simply copying the files from the installation disk to the hard disk. It usually also involves *decompression*. The files were compressed to fit more files on the floppy disks in the first place. Therefore, when you run an installation program (like SETUP.EXE), it decompresses the files as it copies them to the hard disk.

Let's run through a typical Windows Express installation.

Starting Setup

The installation program that you use to install Windows to your hard disk (Windows *cannot* be installed to a floppy disk—there isn't nearly enough space) is called SETUP.EXE and is located on the first Windows installation disk. This disk is labeled "Disk 1." Normally, to install Windows, you type **Setup** at the A: prompt. However, sometimes there are special situations to consider. For this reason, the Setup program has a few command-line options that can be used to customize how Setup runs. Table 4.1 details these options.

TABLE 4.1:   Windows Setup Command-Line Options

Option	Example	Description
/A	Setup /A	Administrative Setup. Decompresses the Windows files, places them in a server directory you specify, and marks them Read-Only. Use this option if you are planning to run Windows from the network. (Used with the /N option)

TABLE 4.1 (CONTINUED):   Windows Setup Command-Line Options

Option	Example	Description
/N	Setup /N	Sets up a workstation from a network (shared) copy of Windows (set up with the /A option above). Run Setup from the network with this option
/I	Setup /I	Ignores Setup's hardware detection. With this option, Setup ignores any hardware types it detects, and the person installing Windows must manually verify all hardware type information during Setup. Use this option if Setup is locking up before getting to the first screen
/S:path	Setup /S:C:\WINSETUP	Specifies the path to the Windows compressed files
/O:file	Setup /O:C:\WINSETUP\SETUP.INF	Specifies the path and filename of the SETUP.INF file
/B	Setup /B	Runs Setup with monochrome video options. If you have a black-and-white monitor, run Setup with this option
/H:file	Setup /H:C:\ACME.INF	Runs Setup in batch mode, where file specifies the name of the systems settings file. (See Microsoft's Windows 3.1 Web site for information on creating this file)
/T	Setup /T	Searches the target installation drive for possible conflicting memory-resident (TSR) programs. Check with the manufacturer of a particular TSR to see whether or not it's compatible
/C	Setup /C	Disables the search for TSR programs. If you need to install Windows and Setup doesn't recognize one of the memory-resident programs, run Setup with this switch

To start your Windows installation, place the Windows installation disk labeled Disk 1 into your A: drive and type the following:

```
A:SETUP
```

Setup will present you with a message that says, "Please wait…" while it checks the hardware configuration of your computer. After a few seconds, the blue installation welcome screen (Figure 4.8) will appear and welcome you to Windows Setup.

FIGURE 4.8:

Windows Setup's welcome screen

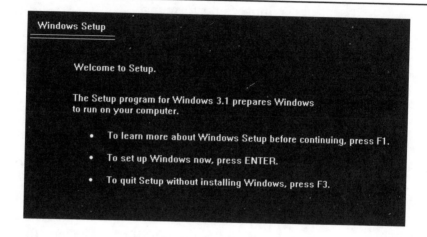

Just like the MS-DOS Setup covered earlier, the Setup program for Windows has a few keys that perform certain functions during the Setup process. F1 is for help, F3 is for exiting Setup, Enter accepts, and the arrow keys navigate through menu choices. If you wonder what keys you can press, look at the gray bar at the bottom of the screen. It displays which keys are active.

If you want to read the HELP information, go ahead and press F1. Otherwise, press Enter to continue.

Choosing Express Setup

At this point, you will see the screen shown in Figure 4.9. This screen allows you to choose which type of Setup to use: Express or Custom. Choosing Express Setup allows Setup to make the following decisions for the user:

- Setup automatically configures mouse, keyboard, language, and network (if there is any). It will also automatically configure AUTOEXEC.BAT and CONFIG.SYS files for optimum Windows performance.

- Setup will suggest that you install Windows to C:\WINDOWS. If there is a version of Windows already installed, it will ask you if you want to upgrade.

- Setup searches for available disk space on other local disk drives if there is not enough space available on the C: drive.

- Setup will recommend a partial Setup if there is not enough disk space for the standard installation of Windows.

- If you are upgrading from Windows 3.*x*, Setup will set up any currently installed printers.

- Setup will automatically make icons for any existing Windows (and certain DOS) applications that are on your hard disk. Setup scans your hard disk, looks for Windows applications (and some DOS applications, like EDIT.COM), and makes icons for them.

- When Setup is finished, it will offer some basic instruction on how to use the mouse and some basic Windows concepts.

If you would like to make any of these decisions yourself, you will have to choose the Custom Setup option by pressing the C key. We will discuss the Custom Setup option later in this chapter.

To continue setting up Windows, press Enter to choose Express Setup and begin copying files to your hard disk.

FIGURE 4.9:

Choosing Express or
Custom Setup

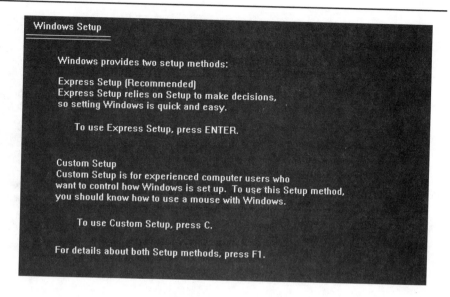

Windows Setup

Windows provides two setup methods:

Express Setup (Recommended)
Express Setup relies on Setup to make decisions,
so setting Windows is quick and easy.

    To use Express Setup, press ENTER.

Custom Setup
Custom Setup is for experienced computer users who
want to control how Windows is set up. To use this Setup method,
you should know how to use a mouse with Windows.

    To use Custom Setup, press C.

For details about both Setup methods, press F1.

NOTE   As soon as you press Enter, Setup will begin copying files to your hard
disk. You can press F3 at any point during the installation to cancel it.
If you press F3 now, no changes will have been made to your disk.

DOS Setup File Copy

At this point, Setup will detect your current hardware configuration and begin copying files to your hard disk and decompressing
them (Figure 4.10). You can watch this process in the lower-right
corner of the screen. This corner will indicate what file is being
copied. There is also a status bar at the bottom of the screen that
indicates the percentage of files copied.

FIGURE 4.10:

The DOS portion Setup's file-copy screen

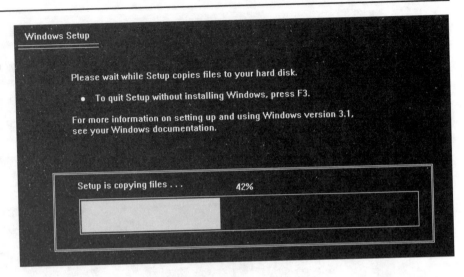

When the status bar reaches about halfway across the screen, Setup will stop and ask you to insert the second disk (Figure 4.11). Remove the first disk from the floppy drive and insert Disk 2. Once this is done, press Enter to continue copying files.

FIGURE 4.11:

The DOS portion of Setup, asking for Disk 2

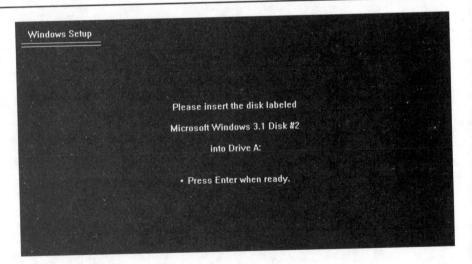

When the file copy has completed, Setup will notify you to wait while it starts Windows. Windows will execute, and the Windows portion of Setup will start.

TIP   If Windows doesn't start, it is most likely due to one of two errors: either the video card is misconfigured or your network card isn't set up correctly. Double-checking the configuration of these two items during the DOS portion can save you a lot of headaches later in the Windows portion.

Installing Windows 3.1 Using the Express Setup: The Windows Portion

At this point in the installation, you are now running Windows. It is really a scaled-down version of Windows since it isn't loading all the drivers and the Program Manager. Once Windows has executed, it will run the Windows Setup utility. This utility performs the same function as its DOS counterpart. The Windows portion of the installation finalizes the installation and modifies both the Windows configuration files and the DOS configuration files.

This portion of the installation is easier with a mouse attached because you can click the mouse buttons to answer the various questions that Setup asks you. If a mouse has been detected by Windows, then when Windows starts you will see a white mouse pointer (See Figure 4.12). If the mouse pointer does not appear, you can still install Windows; just use the Tab key to switch between active buttons and the Enter key to select them. (An active button has an extra dark line around it.)

FIGURE 4.12:

The Windows mouse pointer

Entering User Information

The next step in the installation of Windows is to enter the name and company of the person who is going to use Windows. This information is stored for future use by other installation programs (Microsoft products pull some of their registration information from these two fields). Figure 4.13 shows an example of the name and company screen.

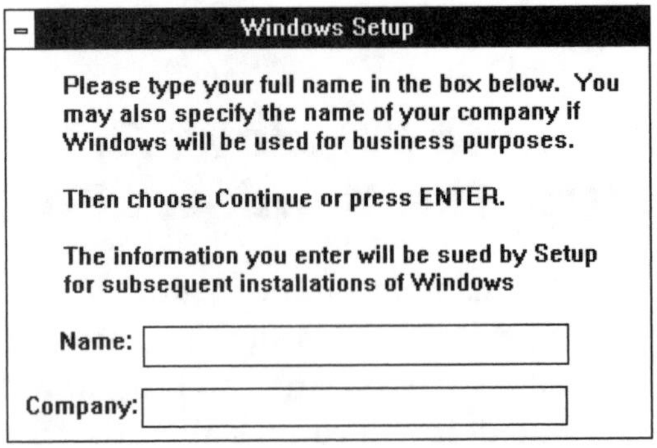

FIGURE 4.13

Entering user and
company information

```
┌─────────────────────────────────────────────────┐
│ ▬            Windows Setup                        │
├─────────────────────────────────────────────────┤
│   Please type your full name in the box below.  You │
│   may also specify the name of your company if      │
│   Windows will be used for business purposes.       │
│                                                     │
│   Then choose Continue or press ENTER.              │
│                                                     │
│   The information you enter will be sued by Setup   │
│   for subsequent installations of Windows           │
│                                                     │
│   Name:  [                                      ]   │
│                                                     │
│   Company: [                                    ]   │
└─────────────────────────────────────────────────┘
```

Once you have entered the name and company information, click Continue. A window will appear asking you to verify that you typed your information correctly. If you have entered your information correctly, click Continue again. If not, click Change and you will be taken back to the screen in Figure 4.13 and asked to enter that information again.

Windows Portion Setup File Copy

Now that Windows knows who you are, it can proceed to copy files. During the copying of files, you will see a screen similar to the one in Figure 4.14.

FIGURE 4.14:

Windows portion
Setup's file-copy screen

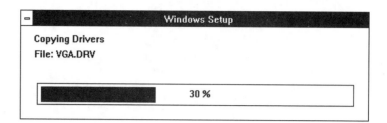

This screen has several similarities to the DOS Copy Files screen shown back in Figure 4.10: Both screens have a copy status bar (in the Windows copy screen, the status bar is blue instead of yellow). Both screens have an area that displays which file is being copied. (In the Windows file-copy screen, this area is in the upper left, instead of the lower right. This difference is vitally important, because if you're propping your head on your hands at this point and you're staring generally downward, you may miss the message that can change your life.)

When the file copy gets to approximately 30 percent, Setup will ask for Disk 3 by displaying a screen similar to the one in Figure 4.15. Insert the disk in the floppy drive and click Continue or hit Enter to allow the file copy to continue.

FIGURE 4.15:

Windows portion Setup
asking for Disk 3

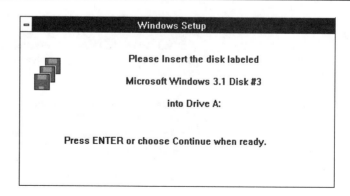

When the file copy gets to approximately 80 percent, Setup will ask for Disk 4 and display another Insert Disk… screen like the one in Figure 4.15. Remove Disk 3 and insert Disk 4. Click Continue or hit Enter to allow the file copying to continue.

When the file copy reaches 100 percent, the file copy is finished and Setup will start setting up any DOS and Windows applications.

Setting Up Applications

Once the file copy has finished, Setup will create the main program groups (Main, Accessories, Games, Startup, and Applications). Then it will search the hard disk for Windows applications and DOS applications (that it knows about through entries in its APPS.INF file). When it finds one, it will create an icon for it in the Applications program group. If there are many, it will create a second program group, called Applications 2.

For some reason, Microsoft can never recognize one of its own programs: the MS-DOS Editor (EDIT.COM). Setup always asks what this program is. It does this by presenting you with a dialog box that gives you a choice between MS-DOS Editor and None of the Above (see Figure 4.16). Click on MS-DOS Editor and click OK.

FIGURE 4.16:

Application setup for EDIT.COM

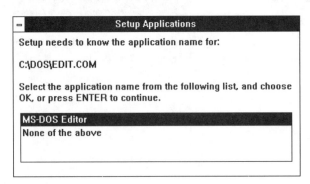

Windows Tutorial

After making the icons for the Windows and DOS applications, Setup is pretty much finished. The last thing it does is ask you if you want to run the tutorial (Figure 4.17). Personally, I don't run the tutorial because I have used Windows several times. If you are in the same situation, click Skip Tutorial. (Skip Tutorial is not the default, so you will have to hit Tab or the down arrow key once before you hit Enter.)

FIGURE 4.17:

You can run the Windows tutorial at this point if you wish.

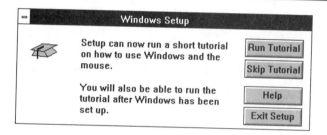

Finishing Up

Windows is now installed. A screen appears telling you just that (Figure 4.18). From this point, you have two choices: restart Windows or Return to MS-DOS. Restarting Windows loads Windows with the Program Manager and all drivers. Returning to DOS exits Windows and returns you to the DOS command prompt.

NOTE   It is best to choose Return to MS-DOS at the Finished screen. Once you've done so, you can reboot the computer so that any changes that may have been made to the CONFIG.SYS or AUTOEXEC.BAT can take effect. If you don't do this, Windows may not function properly.

FIGURE 4.18:

Setup finished!

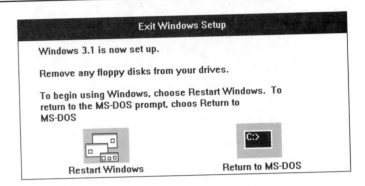

Installing Windows 3.1 Using the Custom Setup: The DOS Portion

The other option for setting up Windows is to use the Custom Setup option. You will choose this option if you want to be able to choose the Windows settings that the Express Setup chooses for you automatically. (See the list earlier in this chapter for a list of the possible settings and assumptions that Express Setup makes for you). Just like Express Setup, the installation of Windows under Custom Setup is divided into two portions, the DOS Setup Portion and the Windows Setup Portion.

> **NOTE** Several items in the Custom Setup are the same as in Express Setup. I will indicate which are the same and which are different as we discuss the Custom Setup.

The DOS portion of the Custom Setup is responsible for copying files and preparing for the Windows portion, exactly like the DOS portion of the Express Setup. The major difference between the two is that the DOS portion of the Custom Setup allows you to make more choices.

Starting Setup

This Setup program is started the same way as Express Setup. Simply insert Disk 1 into the A: drive and type the following at your C: prompt.

```
A:SETUP
```

This will start the Setup program. At this point, Setup will show the Please Wait... then the Welcome to Setup Screen (as shown previously in Figure 4.8). The same options exist at this screen as in the Express Setup (get help, quit, or set up Windows now). To begin the Setup of Windows, press Enter.

Choosing Custom Setup

At this point, you will see the Choose Your Setup Method screen (as shown previously in Figure 4.8) This is the step where the first difference between Express and Custom Setups appears. Instead of pressing Enter to continue with an Express Setup, you need to press the letter C to perform a Custom Setup. This choice will give you more options during the installation.

Specifying a Windows Directory

Another difference between the Custom and Express Setup is that Custom Setup lets you specify which directory to install Windows in (Figure 4.19). If C:\WINDOWS is the directory you want to install Windows in, go ahead and press Enter to continue. However, if you want to install Windows to another directory, hit Backspace several times to delete C:\WINDOWS from the entry field and type in a new path (for example, C:\WIN31). Once you have accepted the default path or entered a new one, press Enter to continue the installation.

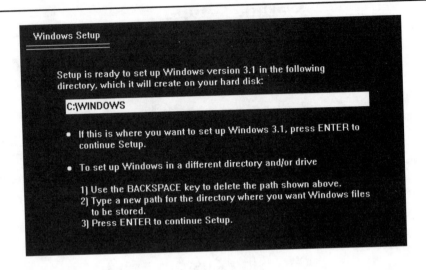

Specifying Windows Settings

The next screen, which appears only in the Custom Setup process, is the Windows settings screen (Figure 4.20). This screen displays the hardware and software Setup detected on your machine when it was first started. Check this list over carefully. If there are any discrepancies between the settings Setup chooses and what hardware and software is installed on your computer, you can change them. To do this, use the up and down arrow keys on your keyboard to move the selection bar to the setting you want to change. Then press Enter. This will bring up another screen with a list of possible choices for the setting. Use the up and down arrows to select the new choice and press Enter. This will accept the change and return you to the screen shown in Figure 4.20. Table 4.2 describes the Windows settings that can be changed from this screen.

FIGURE 4.20:

Changing Windows
settings

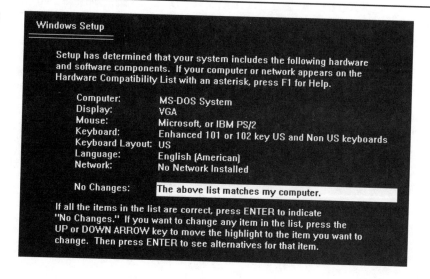

TIP

Remember that these settings are detected by Setup and should be considered accurate, unless your documentation says otherwise.

TABLE 4.2: Possible Windows Settings

Setting	Description
Computer	Most often this setting is set to MS-DOS System (for generic MS-DOS–based computers). If the computer has special concessions (like a low-power processor that needs to go to sleep every once in awhile) that need to be made, you will need to choose the driver that most closely matches your system. If one isn't listed, check your documentation
Display	This is a very important setting. This setting is the Windows video driver. If this setting is set to the wrong driver, the Windows portion of Setup won't function correctly (You won't be able to see the Setup screens). Your video card documentation will contain information about which driver to use. It may also include a disk with that driver on it. To use that driver, select the option "Other (Requires disk provided by a hardware manufacturer)" in the drop-down list. Setup will ask you for the location of the driver, which you can type in and press Enter. (This option is available in all of these configuration lists)

TABLE 4.2 (CONTINUED):   Possible Windows Settings

Setting	Description
Mouse	This setting allows you to select the mouse driver that Windows uses. This is also an important setting because Windows can't use the computer's mouse unless the driver is correct. It's not as important as the video driver, however, because you can still finish the installation with only a keyboard if you have to (it's mostly pressing Enter)
Keyboard	This setting controls which type of keyboard Windows will be using. Like the Computer setting, most keyboards use one setting (Enhanced 101 or 102 Key US and Non US Keyboards). You would only need to choose a different one if there is a special situation. See your computer's or keyboard's documentation for details if you suspect you're in one of those situations
Keyboard Layout	This setting controls which keys, when struck, make which extended characters (characters such as @#$!%^;:"'> and < among others). Also, foreign keyboard layouts may contain extra characters (like accented letters) that will need to be mapped to a keyboard
Language	This setting controls the language of the Windows dialog boxes and help files
Network	This setting indicates which network Windows will support. With Windows 3.1, it relies on DOS for most network software, but Windows components must be installed to allow Windows to take advantage of the network. If you are not installing Windows on a computer that is hooked to a network, this setting should be No Network Installed

When you are finished changing settings or you agree with the settings Setup has chosen for you, highlight The Above List Matches My Computer and hit Enter to begin copying files.

DOS Setup File Copy

The DOS Portion file copy is exactly the same as in the Express Setup. Both file copy operations copy the Windows portion files and expand them (decompress them) to the hard disk. The copy screens both have status bars that indicate the installation's progress. There is only one difference between the DOS file copy for Custom Setup and the DOS file copy for Express Setup, and it's really a trivial one: The screen that asks for Disk 2 looks different. Compare Figure 4.11 earlier in the chapter (Express Setup) with Figure 4.21 here (Custom Setup). Notice in Figure 4.21, Setup is actually asking you where the Setup disk is, instead of assuming that it's in Drive A:. To continue, type in the path to the Windows files from Disk 2 (or the drive where Disk 2 is located) and press Enter.

FIGURE 4.21:

The DOS portion file copy asking for Disk 2

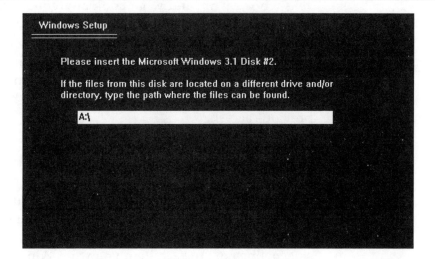

The file copy will continue until the DOS file-copy status bar reaches 100 percent. At this point, the DOS portion of Setup starts Windows and executes the Windows Setup program.

Installing Windows 3.1 Using the Custom Setup: The Windows Portion

The Windows portion of the Custom Setup has the exact same responsibilities as the Windows portion of the Express Setup: copying files and configuring the Windows user interface. When the DOS portion of the Custom Setup is finished, it will start

Windows. Because this is the first time Windows has been executed, it will start the Windows Setup program. The installation can then continue.

Entering User Information

Once the Windows portion of the Custom Setup has begun, it asks who you are and what company you work for. (This step was shown previously in Figure 4.13.) Enter your name, press Tab to move to the next field, enter your company name (if applicable), then press Enter or click Continue. Setup will ask you to verify that you have entered the correct information. If it is correct, click Continue. If it is not correct, click Change to be taken back to the previous screen.

Windows Setup Choices

This step is unique to the Custom Setup. Figure 4.22 shows the next screen to appear. This screen allows you to choose how the Custom Setup proceeds. There are three check boxes in this screen, one next to each item you want Windows to install. All three items in the list are checked by default.

If you want Windows to make a default installation of all programs, you need to click in the check box next to the first item in the list (Set Up Only Windows Components You Select) so that the X is removed from the box. If you leave this check box checked, you will be asked which programs and utilities you want Setup to install.

If you want to select a printer driver as part of the installation, make sure the second box is checked (the default). If not, uncheck this box.

Finally, if you want Setup to search for Windows applications on the hard disk and make icons for them in the Program Manager, leave the last box checked. If not, uncheck this box.

For the purposes of our installation, leave all three check boxes checked and click Continue.

FIGURE 4.22:

You can make your choice of Windows components.

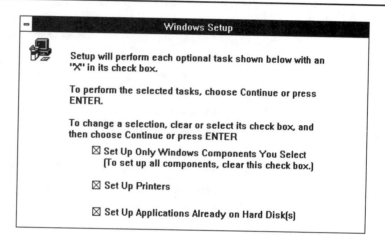

NOTE   If one of these check boxes is unchecked, you won't see the corresponding screen for the sections we discuss next. For example, if you uncheck Set Up Printers you won't be given the option to add a printer.

Choosing Windows Components

The next screen allows you to choose which Windows applications and utilities to install (Figure 4.23). They are grouped into several categories that Setup calls *components*. Just as in the previous step, if you don't want to install a component, uncheck the box in front of it.

FIGURE 4.23:

Choosing Windows applications and utilities

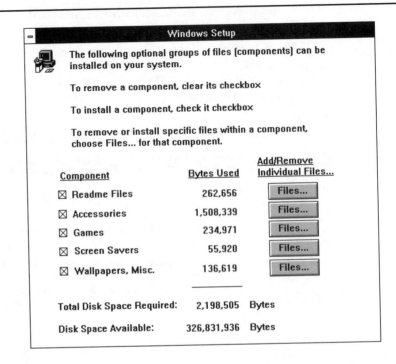

Let's say, for example, you want to install Solitaire but not Minesweeper. Make sure Games is checked so that the Games group gets installed. Then click the Files button to display the files within that group. This will bring up the screen in Figure 4.24. To prevent Minesweeper from being installed (as I have done in Figure 4.24), click Minesweeper and Minesweeper Help and then click the Remove button. Once you have clicked both files, click OK to accept these changes. You can do a similar operation for each group of Components. When you've finished selecting and deselecting the files you want installed, click Continue.

FIGURE 4.24:

Preventing
Minesweeper from
being installed

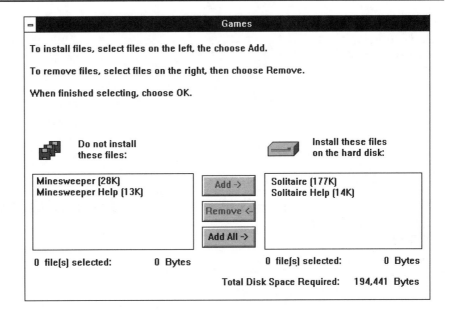

To install files, select files on the left, the choose Add.

To remove files, select files on the right, then choose Remove.

When finished selecting, choose OK.

Do not install
these files:

Install these files
on the hard disk:

Minesweeper (28K)
Minesweeper Help (13K)

Add →

Remove ←

Add All →

Solitaire (177K)
Solitaire Help (14K)

0 file(s) selected: 0 Bytes

0 file(s) selected: 0 Bytes

Total Disk Space Required: 194,441 Bytes

Changing Virtual Memory (Swap File) Settings

At this point during the Custom Setup, you have the option to
select the size and type of your swap file. If you have enough contiguous disk space available, Setup will choose a permanent swap
file for you automatically (as it did in our case in Figure 4.25) and
choose the best size possible. If you want to change the type or
style, however, you can do so, by clicking the CHANGE>> button.
This will expand the window so it looks like the one in Figure 4.26.

FIGURE 4.25:

Setup displaying the virtual memory setting it chose

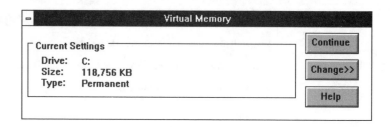

FIGURE 4.26:

Changing the virtual memory setting

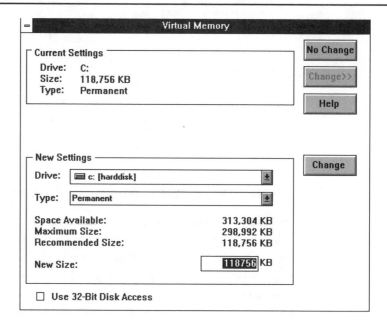

If you want to change the setting, select the new type and type the new size for the swap file in the box next to New Size. Click Change to accept the setting and continue the installation. If you don't want to change the swap file size settings that Setup detected, click No Change to continue the installation.

The 32-Bit Disk Option (Fast Disk)

Notice I didn't discuss the 32-bit disk option (also called FastDisk) shown in Figure 4.26. There's one reason for this: This option can be *dangerous*! If you aren't using a Western Digital WD1003 or compatible hard disk, or you don't have a 32-bit disk access driver for your hard disk, you can seriously mess up the data on your hard disk by using this option.

This option enables Windows to write directly to your hard disk, bypassing the BIOS. If there is any sector translation (or any other strange disk stuff) going on, data can be corrupted almost instantly. If you are, in fact, using a WD1003-compatible hard disk (or have a 32-bit compatible Windows driver for your disk), and want to speed up Windows, you *can* check this option.

Windows File Copy

After these settings have been made, Setup will start copying files. After a few files have been copied (at around the 30 percent mark), Setup will ask for Disk 3. Just as you would in Express Setup (Figure 4.15), Insert Disk 3. Click OK to continue copying files. At approximately 80 percent, Setup will ask for Disk 4. Insert Disk 4 and click OK to finish the file copy.

Setting Up a Printer

When the Windows portion file copy has finished, Setup continues the installation process by asking which printer you want to install (Figure 4.27). If you don't have a printer attached to this computer (either directly or through a network) that you need to install a driver for, you can just click Continue.

FIGURE 4.27:

Printer installation

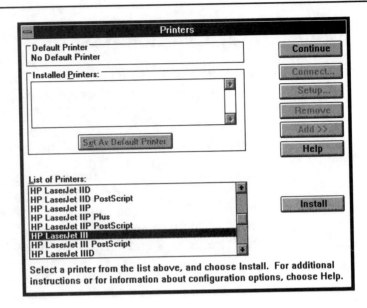

If you do, in fact, have a printer attached to your computer you will need to install a driver for that printer and configure it. Use the scroll bar at the side to scroll down the list of available printer drivers until you can see your printer listed. Click the name of your printer and click Install... to install the driver for your printer. (You will have to insert Windows Setup Disk 5 to install any printer driver listed here.) If the printer you have is not in the list, scroll back to the top of the list and choose Install Unlisted or Updated Printer and click Install. This will bring up a screen asking you to insert the disk from the manufacturer. This disk should have come in the box along with the printer and should be labeled something like Windows Printer Driver or Disk 1: Setup. Insert this disk and click OK to install the printer driver.

When the printer driver has been installed, the new printer will show up in the Installed Printers list. By default, the printer is set to use LPT1. If you happen to have more than one parallel port in the computer and your printer is hooked to a port other than LPT1 (including a network), you can use the Connect... button to choose a different port. Select the port from the list of available ports and click OK to accept the port configuration.

Repeat this whole process for any other printers that need to be configured for your machine. When you're finished, click Continue to continue the installation; and it will proceed to the next step in sequential fashion as before, one screen at a time, with subsequent screens following their predecessors, in a logical, orderly, and almost predictable way until it stops or is otherwise deterred from its progress.

Setting Up Applications

And so it goes. The next step is yet another step that's similar to the Express Setup. At this point, Setup continues by creating the five program groups—Main, Accessories, Games, Startup, and Applications—and populating them with icons for the Windows programs and applications you selected earlier under Choosing Windows Components.

After creating the program groups and icons, Setup asks you where you want Setup to look for Windows applications (Figure 4.28). You have three choices: The DOS PATH variable, the entirety of each hard disk, or both. To choose one, click it and then click Search Now. To choose all disks plus the PATH variable, click the first item in the list (Path), then hold down the Shift key while clicking the last item in the list (in this case, the C: drive). Both items will now be selected. You can then click Search Now to start the search.

FIGURE 4.28:

Telling Setup where to
search for applications

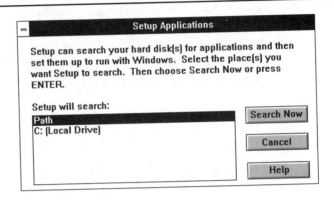

As with the DOS portion, Setup will find EDIT.COM and get
confused, so it will ask you what it is (remember Figure 4.16?).
Respond by clicking MS-DOS Editor and then clicking OK.

The new wrinkle in this procedure is shown in Figure 4.29. Once
Setup has found all the Windows applications, it will present you
with a list of the applications it found. You can pick which applications you want Setup to make icons for by clicking on each one
and then clicking Add to move it to the list under Set Up for Use
with Windows. Or you can click Add All if you want all the applications that Setup found installed. When you finish picking which
icons you want made, click OK to continue.

FIGURE 4.29:

Choosing which icons
to create

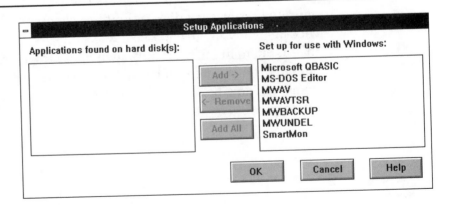

Running the Tutorial

The final step in the Custom Setup is to vote on running the tutorial, just as in Express Setup (see Figure 4.17 earlier in this chapter). As in Express Setup, it's up to you, though if you're reading this book you probably don't need the tutorial, especially at this point. Click Skip Tutorial if you don't want to run the tutorial.

Finishing Up

Setup has now finished installing Windows. It presents you with the same screen it did in Express Setup (Figure 4.18). You have a choice to either restart Windows or return to MS-DOS. You may want to reboot the computer first so that any changes made to the AUTOEXEC.BAT or CONFIG.SYS files can take effect. To that end, click Return to MS-DOS to quit Windows and return to DOS. Then, press Ctrl+Alt+Del to reboot your computer. When your system comes back up again, type **WIN** to start Windows.

The overall steps in Express and Custom Setup are detailed in Table 4.3. This is a good table to study in depth as part of your preparation for the A+ exam.

T A B L E   4 . 3 :   Steps Involved in Express Setup and Custom Setup

Express Setup	Custom Setup
Run SETUP.EXE	Run SETUP.EXE
Welcome screen	Welcome screen
Choose Express Setup	Choose Custom Setup
DOS file copy	Specify Windows directory
Enter user information	Specify Windows settings
Windows file copy	DOS file copy
Set up all applications	Enter user information

TABLE 4.3 (CONTINUED): Steps Involved in Express Setup and Custom Setup

Express Setup	Custom Setup
Windows tutorial screen	Windows file group choices
Restart or exit to DOS	Choose Windows components
	Change swap file settings
	Windows file copy
	Printer setup
	Setup asks where to search for apps
	Setup asks which icons to make
	Windows tutorial screen
	Modify Startup Files
	Restart or exit to DOS screen

Installing Windows 95

Windows 95 has become the operating system of choice for thousands of users. Most people that have computers today have upgraded to Windows 95 so that they can take advantage of its many features. This section details the steps needed to install Windows 95 on a computer.

Windows 95 can be installed from either floppy disks or CD-ROM. If you buy the package that includes the installation CD-ROM, you get a few extra things like a neat game called Hover, a quick tutorial, and the Windows 95 Administration tools for setting up Windows 95 in special situations (like networks). Most people choose the CD-ROM because it's faster.

Before we discuss the actual installation steps, let's take a minute to review the prerequisites a computer must have in order to run Windows 95.

Installation Prerequisites

Let there be no doubt about it, Windows 95 is a resource hog. It requires more RAM, hard disk space, and processor speed than any of its predecessors. Table 4.4 lists the hardware requirements for installing Windows 95 on a computer.

TABLE 4.4: Windows 95 hardware prerequisites

Hardware	95 Requirement
Processor	386DX or386DX or higher processor (486 recommended)
Memory	4MB (8MB Recommended)
Free hard disk space	50–55MB for typical install (40MB if upgrading from a previous version of Windows). Could go as high as 85MB for a custom install with all options
Floppy Disk	One 3.5" Disk drive (if doing installation from floppy disks)
CD-ROM	Required if installing from CD (preferred method)
Video	VGA or better
Mouse	Required
Keyboard	Required

In addition to the hardware requirements, the disk must be partitioned using FDISK (just as with a DOS installation). And, if you are performing the installation via CD, you must set up an AUTOEXEC.BAT and CONFIG.SYS that will load a CD-ROM driver so you can access the CD. This step is required because you cannot boot to the installation CD. A sample CONFIG.SYS and AUTOEXEC.BAT follow:

```
CONFIG.SYS:
    Files=25
    Buffers=9,256
    DEVICE=C:\PANCD.SYS /B:25 /N:PANCD001


AUTOEXEC.BAT
    PATH=C:\;C:\DOS
    MSCDEX.EXE /D:PANCD001 /L:D /M:100
```

Notice that they aren't very big. These files only have to get the CD-ROM functional under DOS; once Windows 95 is loaded, they won't be needed.

Starting the Installation

The program that performs the installation is called SETUP.EXE and is located in the root directory of either Disk 1 of the set of installation floppies or on the installation CD-ROM. It examines your hard disk and makes sure there is enough room to install Windows 95, then copies a few temporary files to your hard disk. These temporary files are the components of the Installation wizard which will guide you through the installation of Windows 95.

There are a few options that you can use with the Setup program. To use them, you place them after the SETUP at the command line, separated by a single space. Table 4.5 details these Setup startup switches.

TABLE 4.5: Windows 95 SETUP command line options

Option	Function
/d	This switch ignores the setup of your existing copy of Windows. It only applies during an upgrade

TABLE 4.5 (CONTINUED): Windows 95 SETUP command line options

Option	Function
\<filename\>	Used without the "\<" and "\>," it specifies the pre-configured setup file that Setup should use. (e.g. SETUP MYFILE.INI causes Setup to run with the settings contained in MYFILE.INI)
/id	Skips the Disk Space check
/im	Skips the available memory check
/in	Runs Setup without setting up network components
/ip	Skips the check for any Plug-n-Play devices
/iq	Skips the test for cross-linked files
/is	Skips the routine System check
/it	Skips the check terminate–and–stay-resident programs (TSRs) that are known to cause problems with Windows 95 Setup
/l	Use this switch if you have a Logitech mouse and want it enabled during Setup
/n	This switch causes Setup to run without a mouse
/T:C:\tmp	Specifies which directory ("C:\tmp" in this case) Setup will copy its temporary files to. If this directory doesn't exist, Setup will create it

To start the installation, you simply change to the drive letter where the installation files are and type **SETUP** (with the appropriate startup switches), like so:

```
C:>D:
D:>SETUP
```

Setup will tell you that it's going to check your system and that you must press Enter to continue. If you want to cancel the installation without continuing, you can hit Esc. When you press Enter, Setup copies a very basic Windows system to your computer from the CD and starts it. Setup then executes in a Windows environment and welcomes you to the installation (Figure 4.30).

FIGURE 4.30:

Windows 95 Setup
Welcome Screen

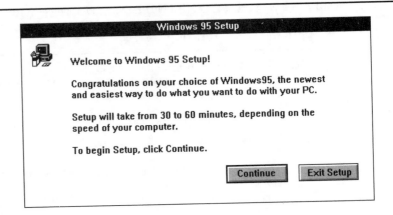

To begin the installation, click Continue. Setup will then copy some more files your computer while it builds the Setup wizard. The Windows 95 Setup wizard guides you through the installation step by step. At each step you will be asked questions about how you would like Windows 95 configured. Then, you simply click a button called Next or Continue.

The Setup wizard will ask you questions about three main categories:

- Gathering Information
- Copying files to your computer
- Finishing the installation

These three general steps will be presented to you when you begin the installation and at various times during the installation.

After the welcome screen, Setup will present you with the text of the license agreement. The Windows 95 License agreement (Figure 4.31) basically says that you are being sold a copy of this software for use on one computer and that you won't give it away or sell it to anyone else for a profit. There's a bunch more to it, so you should read the entire agreement. When you are done, click

Yes to accept the agreement and move on. If you click No, you are telling Setup (and Microsoft) that you don't agree to the terms of the contract. This will cancel the installation.

FIGURE 4.31:

The Windows 95 license agreement

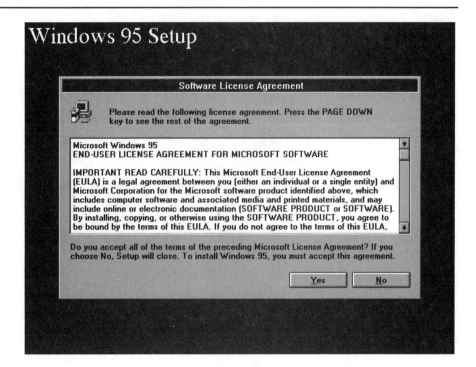

Step 1: Collecting Information About Your Computer

After accepting the Windows 95 License Agreement, you will be presented with the screen in Figure 4.32. This screen gives you the basic outline of the Windows 95 Installation process. In the first step, Setup asks you questions about how your computer is currently configured and which options you would like to install.

NOTE

From now on, the Setup screens will have a Back button and a Cancel button. The Back button will show you the previous screen, whereas the Cancel button will allow you to completely exit the installation. If you exit the installation before it's completely finished, Setup will restore your system to its former state.

FIGURE 4.32:

Windows Setup start screen

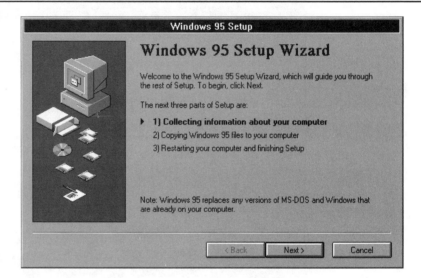

To begin the gathering of information, click the Next button (or press Enter).

Choosing the Windows Installation Directory

Just like it does in a Windows 3.*x* installation, Setup will allow you to choose where you would like to Install Windows 95. The screen in Figure 4.33 shows that Setup picks C:\WINDOWS by default. However, if you want to have both Windows 3.*x* and Windows 95 on the same system, you should install Windows 95 to a directory other than C:\WINDOWS. To do this, click the radio button next to Other directory and click Next. Setup will then ask you which directory you want to put Windows 95 in.

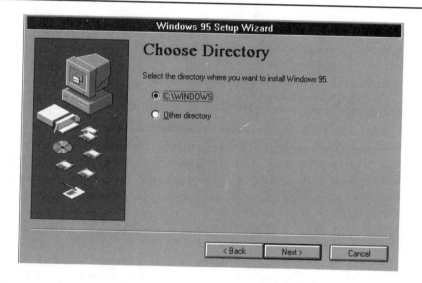

For most installations, you will want to install Windows 95 to the C:\WINDOWS directory. If this is the case, leave C:\WINDOWS checked and click the Next button to continue. Setup will check to see if you have enough disk space and memory to install Windows 95. If either of these two requirements are below the recommendations, Setup will issue an error and quit. If they pass, Setup will continue to the next step, choosing the type of Setup you want to perform.

Choosing the Setup Options

The screen shown in Figure 4.34 allows you to select which type of installation you want. There are four options:

Typical   This option allows Setup to choose the most popular options

Portable	This option sets up the most common applications and utilities for portable computers. This option will install PCMCIA support and Advanced Power Management (APM)
Compact	This option, when selected, will install the bare minimum components Windows 95 needs to function
Custom	This option will allow you to choose which components to install. If you select this option, Setup will present you with a list of utilities and programs to install. This option allows you to make the most choices about how Windows 95 gets installed. This is the method most commonly used by technicians to install Windows 95

Because it's the most popular option for technicians, select Custom by clicking in the circle next to Custom. Then click Next to continue the installation.

FIGURE 4.34:

Selecting the type of setup you want to perform

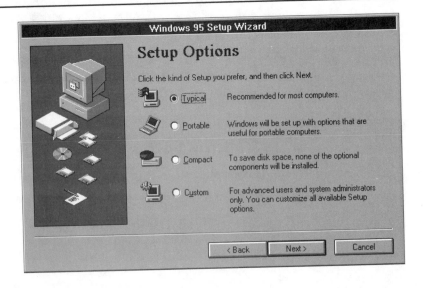

Entering User Information

The next screen (Figure 4.35) allows you to enter information about yourself and your company (if applicable). This information will be used when you install most other Microsoft applications. To enter this information, simply start typing your name. The text will appear next to Name: in the white area. Then, hit Tab to move to the next field, Company. Type in your company name (or the name of the company whose computer this is) and click Next to continue.

FIGURE 4.35:

User information
screen

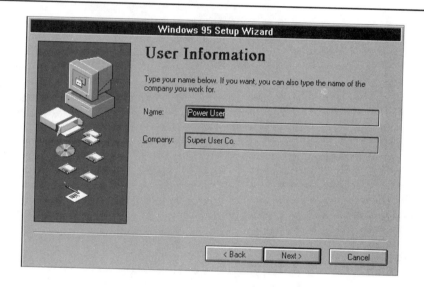

Entering the Product Identification Number

The product identification number helps to ensure that you aren't illegally installing Windows 95 from a pirated copy. There is a number you must enter that is usually found on the back cover of the CD case (look for a yellow sticker with the words CD KEY). It might also be found on the warranty registration card. You should send this card in so that you can receive technical support if you ever need it. From this screen (Figure 4.36), simply type in the number *exactly* as it appears on the back of the CD case.

FIGURE 4.36:

Entering the Product Identification Number

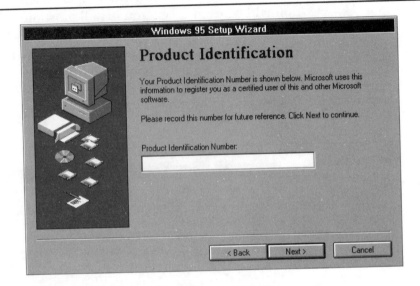

After you finished typing the number, you can click Next. If you type the wrong number, Setup will tell you and ask you to enter it again.

Analyzing Your Computer and Setting up Hardware

Setup is now ready to start looking for the hardware devices it needs to install drivers for. It will present you with the screen shown in Figure 4.37. To let Setup search for the devices, select the Yes (Recommended) option. To specify all the hardware that your computer has manually, select the No, I Want to Modify the Hardware List option. Windows 95 does a pretty good job of detecting hardware in the computer and installing device drivers for those devices. For most computers, you'll want to select the Yes option and click Next as shown in Figure 4.37.

FIGURE 4.37:

Allowing Setup to search for hardware devices

After you click Next, Setup will present you with a screen like the one shown in Figure 4.38. If you have a network adapter, sound card, or CD-ROM drive, mark the appropriate check box(es). A check box will appear to tell Setup to install drivers and software for those items. When you have finished selecting hardware drivers from this screen, click Next to continue the installation and begin the hardware detection process.

The hardware detection process may take several minutes. During this time, you will see a screen like the one in Figure 4.39 and you will hear the hard drive searching for files (or at least you'll see the hard drive light flash madly). When Setup finds a piece of hardware, it will make a note of which driver to install; if it finds something it doesn't have a driver for, it will ask you if you want to provide one or not install the device at all.

FIGURE 4.38:

Choosing special Setup options

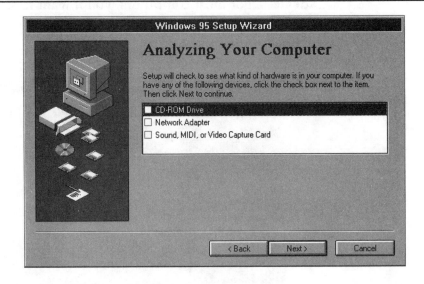

FIGURE 4.39:

Analyzing the computer's hardware to determine which drivers to install

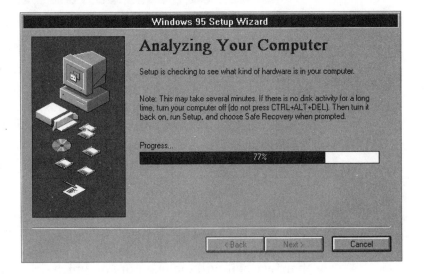

TIP
　　If the progress bar stops moving for more than ten minutes, and there is no hard disk activity, more than likely the machine is locked up. Reboot the computer and rerun setup. Setup will detect that a previous installation wasn't completed and it will try to resume where it left off. Neat, huh?

After the hardware detection is finished, Setup will automatically move on to the next step.

Choosing E-Mail and Fax Software to Install

Windows 95 comes with several pieces of software to get you connected to the rest of the world. From the screen in Figure 4.40, you can choose to installed Microsoft's own version of America Online called The Microsoft Network (MSN). In addition, Windows 95 comes with the software to send and receive faxes (although you must have a fax modem installed in your computer to use it). This software is called Microsoft Fax and is integrated into Windows 95's Universal Mailbox called the Exchange Client (meaning you must have the Exchange Client installed to use MS Fax). The Exchange Client is actually called Microsoft Mail in the Setup window. This name, although confusing, stems from the fact that this mail client has its roots in the old MS Mail software. It looks surprisingly similar to the old Windows Mail client.

If you want to install any of these components, check the appropriate box. When you're done selecting items, click "Next" to continue.

WARNING
　　These checkboxes just tell Setup whether you want the e-mail and fax software installed. Setup doesn't let you configure these components until after Windows 95 is installed.

FIGURE 4.40:

Choosing which online tools to install

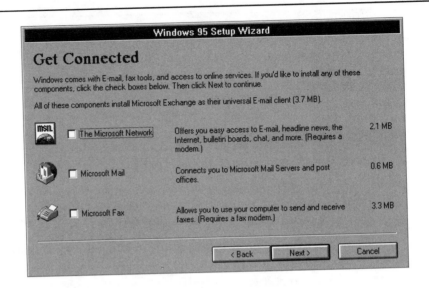

Choosing Which Windows 95 Components You Want Installed

If you choose a Standard installation type (under Choosing the Setup Options, above), Setup will ask you if you want it to choose all the components automatically (Figure 4.41) or give you the screen in Figure 4.42 and let you choose. If you choose a Custom installation type, Setup will automatically present you with a screen to select which components you want to install (Figure 4.42).

If a check box is gray with a check mark in it, that means that not all the components of that category are going to be installed. If you highlight the category that has the gray check box and click the Details button, a screen will appear that will allow you to select or deselect additional components. Figure 4.43 shows the screen that appears when you highlight Accessories and click Details. Notice that Games is not checked by default. If you want Solitaire installed (and most people do), click the check box next to Games and click OK.

FIGURE 4.41:

Standard Setup component selection

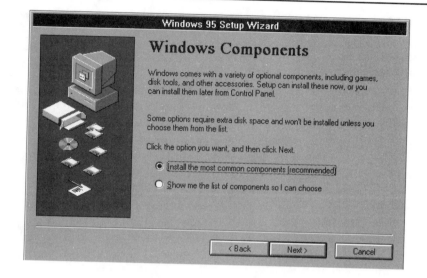

FIGURE 4.42

Custom Setup component selection

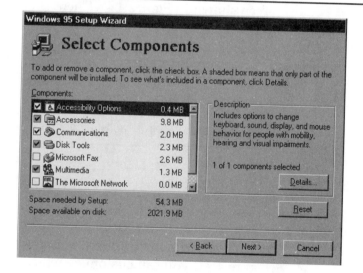

FIGURE 4.43:

Adding or removing
components from an
installation group

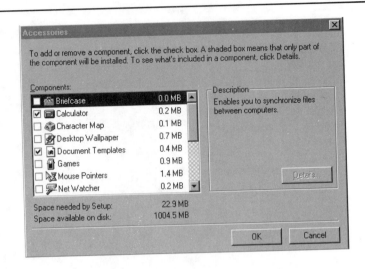

Once you have selected all the components you want installed,
accept all selections by clicking OK until you get back to the
screen shown in Figure 4.42. Then, click the Next button to continue the installation.

TIP   If you make a mistake selecting items, you can click the Reset button
to reset the selections to the Setup defaults. However, be aware that
the selections made in the e-mail/fax section of the installation will
also be reset to their defaults, all of which are not installed.

Network Configuration

The next step in the installation of Windows 95 shows up only if
there is a network card installed in the machine. From this screen
(Figure 4.44) you can customize which networking components

are installed and how they are configured. Click Next to continue this installation.

NOTE   Because Windows 95 Networking configuration is covered in Chapter 9, we won't cover it again here. Refer to Chapter 9 for information about the details of configuring the Network Properties screen.

FIGURE 4.44:

The Setup Network Configuration screen

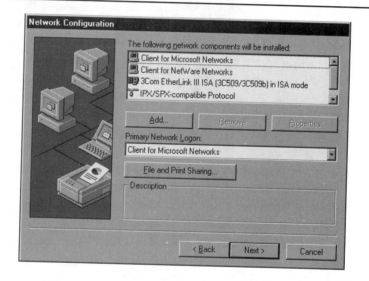

If you have networking installed, the next screen you will see will be the computer identification screen shown in Figure 4.45. This only applies if you have the Client for Microsoft Networks installed because, on Microsoft networks, each computer has to have a name and should belong to a workgroup (these concepts will also be discussed in Chapter 9). After entering the information for these parameters, click Next to continue to the next step in the installation.

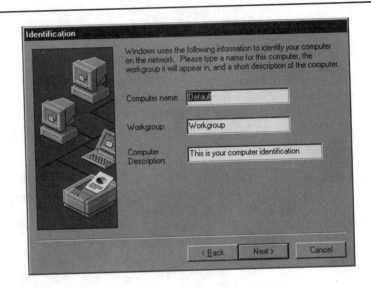

Verifying Computer Settings

Now that Setup has detected all the hardware in your machine in a Custom setup, the Setup Wizard will present you with a list of the hardware (Figure 4.46) that it found and allow you to modify which driver Windows 95 will use. If any of the drivers in the list are incorrect or have Unknown next to them, click on the driver description, then click the Change button. Setup will present you with a list of alternatives. If none of the alternatives fit, leave the driver unchanged and install a new one after the installation.

Once you have verified that all hardware drivers are correct, click Next to continue.

NOTE Installing new drivers and updating existing drivers is covered in Chapter 5.

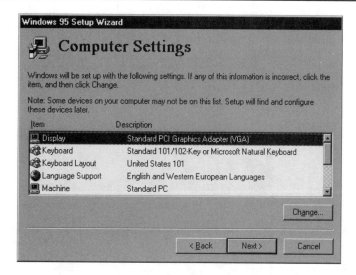

FIGURE 4.46:

Verifying computer settings

Creating a Startup Disk

The next step in the Windows 95 installation is to decide whether you want a startup disk (see Figure 4.47). A startup disk can be used to boot the machine in case of a problem. You can copy diagnostic utilities to it so that they are available when you have the machine up and running. You can choose to make one at this time (the Yes option) or to make one at a later time (the No option). Most technicians make their own Windows 95 startup disk, copy all their diagnostic utilities to it, and never use this option again. So, choose No and click Next to continue the installation.

FIGURE 4.47:

Choosing not to create
a startup disk

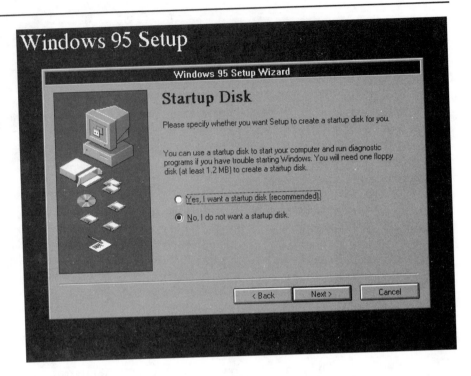

Step 2: Copying Files to Your Computer

At this point, you have given the Setup wizard all the information it needs to begin installing Windows 95. It will present you
with a screen (Figure 4.48) telling you this and giving you one last
chance to cancel before copying files to your computer. If you
think you made any mistakes, you can click the Back button. You
can also click Cancel to abort the entire installation. If you believe
you have entered all information correctly, click Next to start the
file copy.

FIGURE 4.48:

Starting the file copy

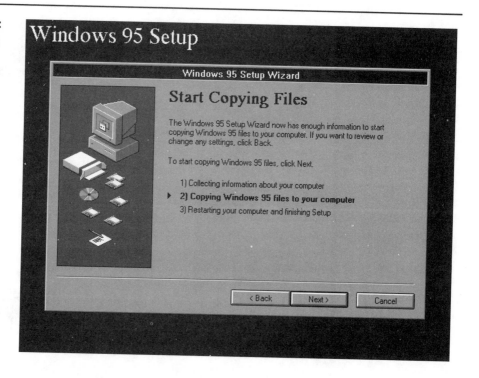

The bottom of the next screen displays a progress bar (see Figure 4.49) to indicate how far along the file copy process is. You can cancel the file copy at any time by clicking the Exit button in the lower-right corner of the screen or by pressing the F3 key on your keyboard. The file copy may take several minutes, depending on the speed of your computer. The nice part is, you don't have to watch a boring, blue bar go across the screen. Instead, you get to read several screens that give you information about the features of Windows 95.

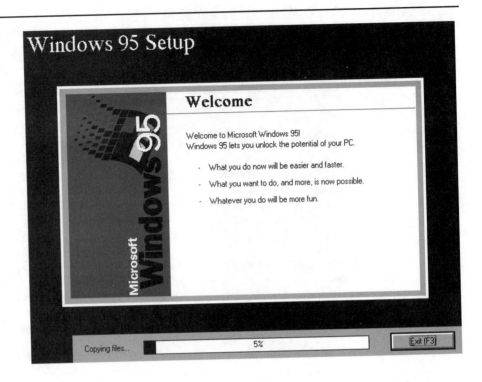

FIGURE 4.49:

The file copy screen (with progress bar)

NOTE At this point, you may also get a screen asking you if you want to create a startup disk. You can do this at a later time from the Add/Remove Programs control panel (see *Creating a Startup Disk* later in this chapter). So for now, click No and continue the installation.

Step 3: Restarting the Computer and Finishing Setup

When the file copy is finished, you will see a screen like the one in Figure 4.50. This screen is telling you that the majority of the installation is finished. You just need to reboot the computer and customize the way Windows 95 operates. To restart the computer and run Windows 95, remove any disks from their respective disk drives and click Finish. This will cause the computer to reboot.

FIGURE 4.50:

Finishing the installation

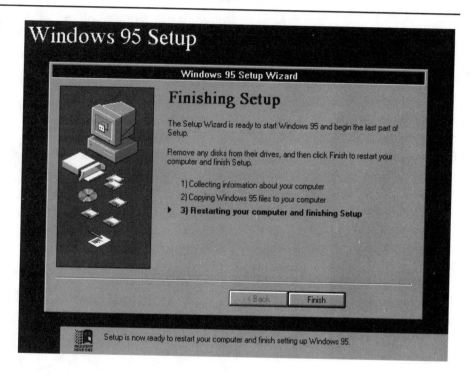

Upon rebooting, you'll see a blue screen with the words, "Getting ready to run Windows 95 for the first time..." in red at the bottom of the screen.

NOTE   If you have a network client installed, you may see a network login screen. The first time you run Windows 95, you won't be able to use your network connection anyway, so click Cancel for any screens you see that deal with network logins.

Setting Up Hardware and Software After Installation

The next screen you will see will tell you that Windows 95 is setting up hardware and any Plug-n-Play devices you might have (Figure 4.51). If there are any devices for which Windows 95 can't determine the settings (or find drivers), it will pop up a screen asking you to specify them. It will then pop up another screen telling you what settings it is configuring (Figure 4.52). It will automatically continue to the next screen.

FIGURE 4.51:

Setting up hardware

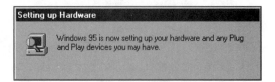

FIGURE 4.52:

Setting up Windows settings

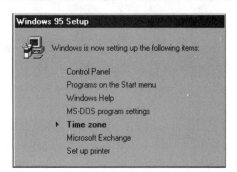

Setting the Date/Time Properties

After you set the hardware and software parameters, Windows 95 will present you with a screen that will allow you to set the date, time, and time zone (Figure 4.53) of the computer. There are two tabs at the top of the window:

- The Time Zone tab will allow you to click on a map to set your time zone (click your current location on the map and it will set the time zone to the correct zone automatically, or if you know it, you can select your time zone from a drop-down list). You can click the check box next to Automatically Adjust Clock for Daylight Saving Changes, and Windows 95 will set the clock automatically forward or backwards on the appropriate day.

- The other tab (which can be brought forward by clicking Date & Time) is the Date & Time tab (Figure 4.54). From here you can set the current date and time by clicking the appropriate date in the calendar. You move to different months by selecting them from the drop-down list. If you need to move forward or backward a year, click the up or down arrows, respectively, that are to the right of the year. To change the time, click the area that indicates the time and use the arrows to the right to move the hours, minutes, seconds and AM/PM forward or backwards.

FIGURE 4.53:

The Time Zone tab of the Date/Time property box

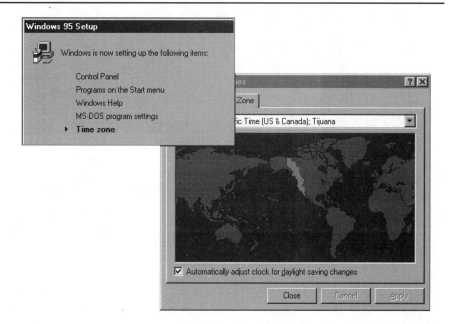

FIGURE 4.54:

Setting the date and
time during Windows
95 setup

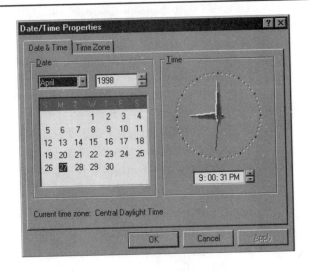

When you've finished setting the date, time, and time zone, you
can click OK to continue the installation.

Windows 95 and the Year 2000

If you are wondering whether Windows 95 is Year 2000 compliant, the
answer is: Sort of. The DIR and DATE commands in the command prompt
window only display dates in two digits. There is a patch, however, and
you can download it from the Microsoft support Web site at `http://`
`support.microsoft.com/download/support/mslfiles/win95y2k.exe`.

Setting Up Your Universal Inbox

If you chose to install either Microsoft Mail or Microsoft FAX, Windows 95 will ask you to install Microsoft Exchange using the Inbox

Setup wizard. This wizard will guide you through the setup of the e-mail and fax services. If you have a modem installed in your computer, the wizard will help you to configure it to work with these services. Because this material isn't covered on the exam, I will refer you to the Windows 95 help file that comes on the installation CD to help guide you through the installation of this feature.

Setting Up a Printer

The final step to configuring Windows 95 is setting up a printer. To do this, Windows 95 starts up the Add Printer wizard (Figure 4.55). This wizard is designed to guide you through the installation of a printer. We will cover this in more detail in Chapter 5, so we won't devote a great deal of time to discussing it here. If you don't want to install a printer now (or don't have one connected to your computer), click Cancel.

FIGURE 4.55:

Configuring a printer

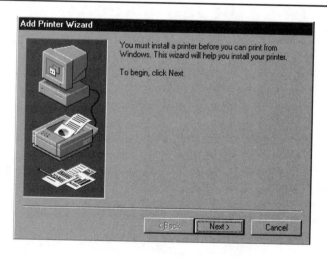

Final Installation Steps

After configuring a printer, Windows 95 is finally fully configured and will present you with a screen instructing you that it will reboot one final time (Figure 4.56). To reboot your computer and bring up Windows 95, click OK. Voilà! Windows 95 is installed!

FIGURE 4.56:

The final Windows 95 setup screen

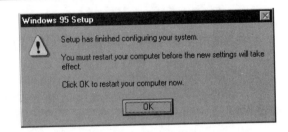

After the Installation

Once Windows 95 comes up for the first time (without any wizards), you can log in to the network and start using Windows 95. You can further customize the interface using the techniques discussed in the previous chapter.

Upgrading to Windows 95 from MS-DOS or Windows 3.x

If you are currently running Windows 3.x and want to upgrade to Windows 95, you're not alone. By the time of the millennium, most Intel-based computers will be running Windows 95. That's due, in part, to the benefits and ease of use that Windows 95 offers. It can also be attributed to the fact that the upgrade process is very easy (almost painless, in fact). Let's run through a typical upgrade.

Starting the Upgrade

There are three major steps that you need to follow when upgrading from an earlier version of Windows. They are the same steps used to install Windows 95. The steps are, in order:

1. Gather information about your computer.

2. Copy files to your computer.

3. Finish Setup.

These steps are performed by the Windows 95 installation program, SETUP.EXE. In order to start the upgrade, you need to start the SETUP.EXE program. If you are upgrading to Windows 95 using the floppy disk installation method, insert the first disk (the one labeled Disk 1-SETUP) into your A: drive. Then, from Windows, select the Run command under the File menu in Program Manager and type the following in the box that appears:

A:\SETUP.EXE

To run the program, click OK.

To run SETUP.EXE from a CD-ROM drive, follow the exact same procedure, but replace the A: with the letter of your CD-ROM drive. To upgrade from DOS, type A:\SETUP.EXE at the C: prompt. Aside from this difference, upgrading from DOS or Windows is exactly the same.

After you start the Setup program, the screen in Figure 4.57 will appear, after a short examination of your hard disk to make sure it doesn't have any serious flaws. This screen asks you to read the license agreement and either accept it or decline it. If you decline,

Setup will exit and the installation will not continue. To continue the installation, click Yes.

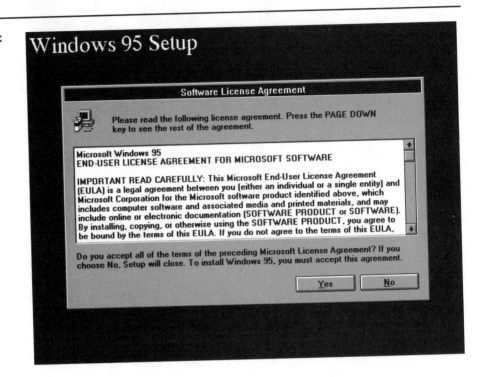

Step 1: Gathering Information

The next screen that Setup shows you is the one that details what the generic steps in the installation are (Figure 4.58). As we have already discussed, there are three general steps to the upgrade: Gathering Information, Copying Files, and Finishing Setup. To continue, click the Next button.

FIGURE 4.58:

Gathering Information screen

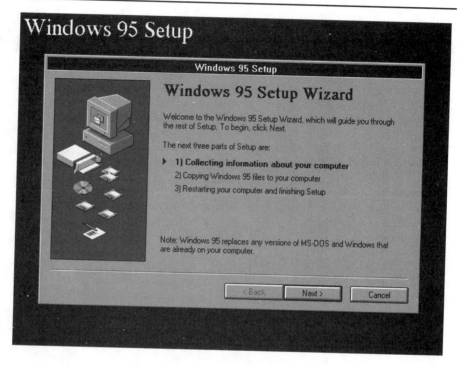

Specifying Windows Directory

There are several pieces of information that Setup needs to gather before it can complete the setup. The first of these is the directory you want to install Windows in. By default, Setup wants to install Windows 95 in the C:\WINDOWS directory (Figure 4.59), which is the same directory it was installed in for Windows 3.1. You can change it if you want by clicking the box next to Other Directory: and typing in a new path for the Windows installation. If C:\ WINDOWS is acceptable, click Next to continue the installation.

FIGURE 4.59:

Selecting Windows directory

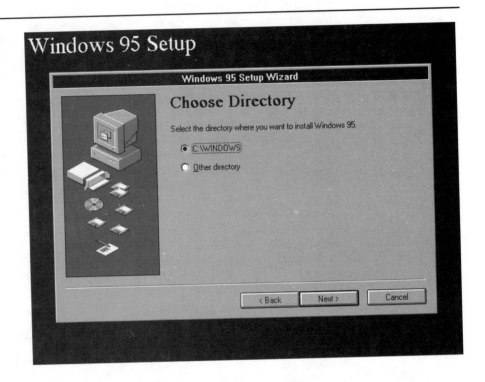

TIP   If you want to be able to use your DOS/Windows 3.x combination after the upgrade, you still can. You may need to revert to DOS or Windows 3.x for an application that is incompatible with Windows 95. (Any DOS program that accesses hardware directly will fall into this category.) To make sure the Windows files don't get overwritten and are available, you must install Windows 95 in a directory other than C:\WINDOWS (for example, C:\WIN95). Then, after the installation is complete, you can press F8 during boot-up and select *Previous version of MS-DOS*. Your computer will boot up as it was immediately before the upgrade.

Once you have specified the installation directory, Setup will scan the hard disk and make sure the C:\WINDOWS directory exists. If it doesn't, Setup will make it. It will also scan the disk and check to see that there is enough disk space to upgrade Windows (Figure 4.60). You can click Cancel at any time to cancel the scan.

FIGURE 4.60:

Windows checking
the disk

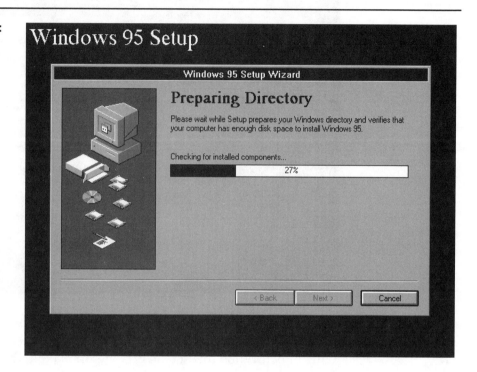

Saving Existing System Files

At this point, Setup asks you if you want to save your old system files (Figure 4.61). This should be done, in case the installation doesn't work properly and you want to uninstall Windows 95. If you answer Yes to this question, Setup will make a duplicate of the existing DOS and Windows files (this will take about 6MB of extra disk space) that can be used to uninstall Windows 95.

FIGURE 4.61:

Do you want to save
your system files?

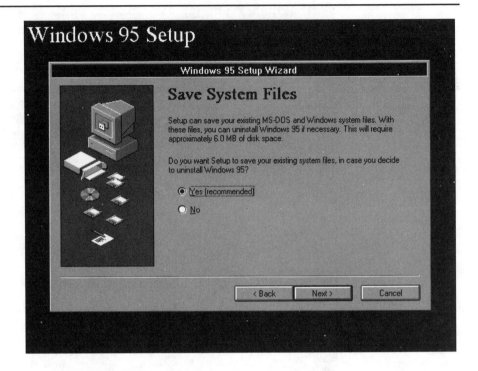

Click Next to continue the installation. The screen in Figure 4.62 will appear. While this screen is being displayed, the system files are being compressed and tucked away until they are needed. If not needed, they can be deleted using the Add/Remove Programs control panel. When you open this control panel, there will be a listing of all the programs that were installed since the time Windows 95 was installed. In this list will be two categories: Old Windows 3.*x* and MS-DOS System Files, and Windows 95. If you want to uninstall Windows 95, click the Windows 95 entry and click the Add/Remove button. It will then start the uninstall and ask you to reboot. After you reboot, your system will be as it was before the upgrade.

FIGURE 4.62:

Saving your existing
system files

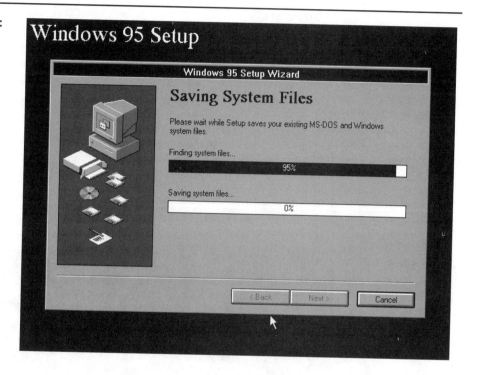

Choosing a Typical Installation

When Setup is done saving the system files, it will present you
with the screen shown in Figure 4.63. This screen allows you to
choose from the following options to customize the way Setup
runs:

Typical   This option allows Setup to choose the most
popular options

Portable   This option sets up the most common appli-
cations and utilities for portable computers.
This option will install PCMCIA support and
Advanced Power Management (APM)

Compact	This option, when selected, will install the bare minimum components Windows 95
Custom	This option will allow you to choose which components to install. If you select this option, Setup will present you with a list of utilities and programs to install. This option allows you to make the most choices about how Windows 95 gets installed

For this discussion, choose Typical and click Next.

FIGURE 4.63:

Choosing a typical installation

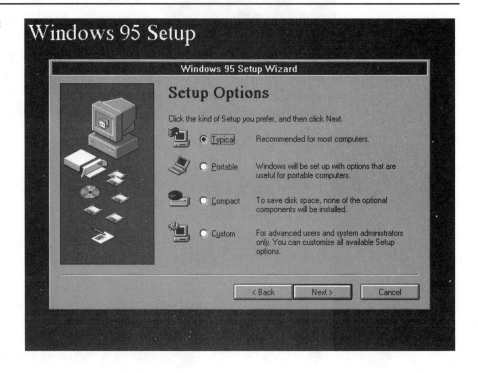

Verifying Name and Company Information

The next step in the upgrade is to verify the registration information you typed in when you installed Windows 3.*x*. This is a very simple process. The user and company are automatically entered (Figure 4.64). All you need to do is click Next.

FIGURE 4.64:

Verify company information.

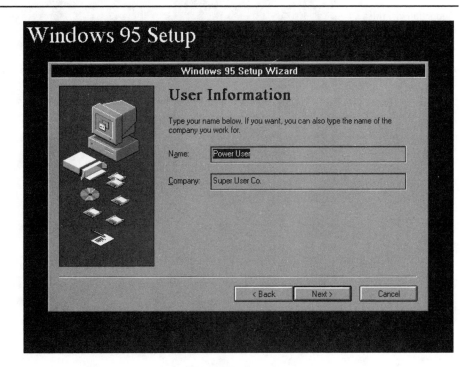

Product Identification Number

Another screen that requires your acknowledgement is the Product Identification Number screen. This number is used by Microsoft to register the product in your name, for things like Technical

Support. This screen displays the Product Registration ID number for your installation of Windows 95 (Figure 4.65). Before you send in your warranty card for Windows 95, you should write this number on it in the space provided.

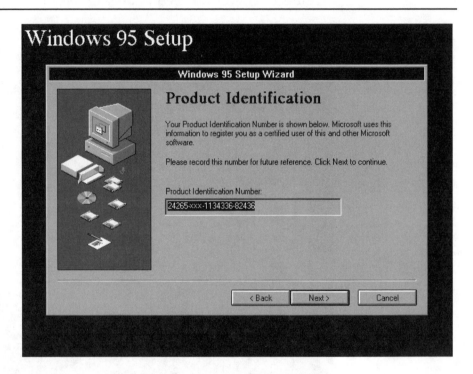

When you have written the number down and are ready to continue, click Next to continue the installation.

Analyzing Your Computer

The next thing that Setup does is check to see what hardware is installed in your computer. It does that so that you don't have to manually choose every driver that Windows needs. To start this process, it presents you with a list of the multimedia and network components you might have installed in your computer (Figure 4.66). If you have any of those devices installed in your computer, click the appropriate check box(es). Click the Next button to continue the hardware device detection.

FIGURE 4.66:

Selecting multimedia and network components to install

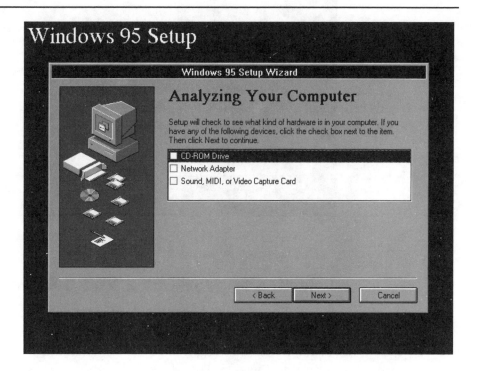

Setup will now scan the system and look for hardware devices (Figure 4.67). For each device it finds, Setup will install the drivers and utilities for each type of device you have installed in your computer. This screen will disappear automatically when the progress bar reaches 100 percent.

FIGURE 4.67:

Hardware detection process

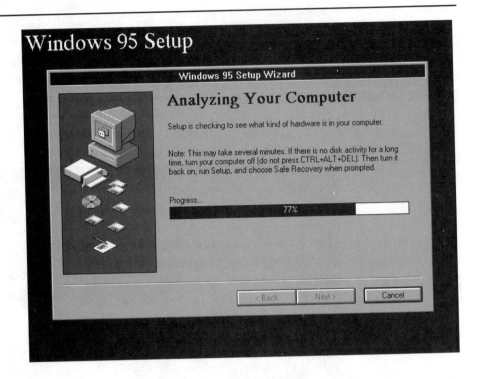

Selecting Windows 95 E-Mail Options

When the hardware detection is complete, Setup presents you with the screen in Figure 4.68. This screen allows you to select which e-mail services you want to install and configure for use with Windows 95. The Microsoft Network (MSN) is Microsoft's own, private online service (similar to America Online). If you choose not to install it now, you can install after Windows 95 is installed. Microsoft leaves it right there on the Desktop and all you have to do is double-click.

NOTE The Set Up the Microsoft Network icon on the Desktop can't be dragged to the trash, but you can delete it by right clicking it and then selecting Delete from the popup menu.

FIGURE 4.68:

Windows 95 e-mail
options

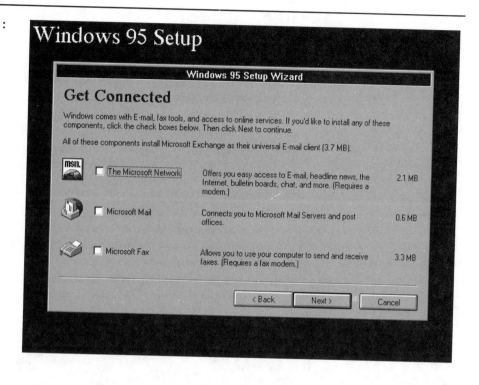

The second mail option is Microsoft Mail. This option will install the MS Exchange Universal Inbox client that can connect to Internet (POP3) mail servers and MS Mail or Exchange post offices. If you want to use this mail client, mark the check box next to it, otherwise leave it blank. The final mail option isn't really an e-mail option; it's a fax option. Microsoft Fax allows you to send faxes from within almost any Windows 95 application (assuming you have a fax-capable modem installed in your computer). When installed, a Microsoft Fax printer will be created. When you select this printer from within an application, instead of printing the document, a window will pop up and allow you to fax the page to someone using your fax/modem.

Select which option(s) you want to install, then click Next to continue the installation.

Selecting Windows 95 Components

After choosing which e-mail options you want, you can customize the Windows 95 installation and decide which components you want to install. At this point in the installation, Setup will present you with the screen shown in Figure 4.69. If you want to let the Setup program install the most common components, choose the Install the Most Common Components (Recommended) option by checking the button next to that item. This is the most common option to choose during installation if you want the installation to be as simple as possible. If you choose the other option—Show Me a List of Components So I Can Choose—and click Next, Setup will present you a list of the possible components and you can select the ones you want to install.

For your upgrade, allow Setup to choose your components and click Next to continue.

FIGURE 4.69:

Telling Setup to automatically choose which components are installed

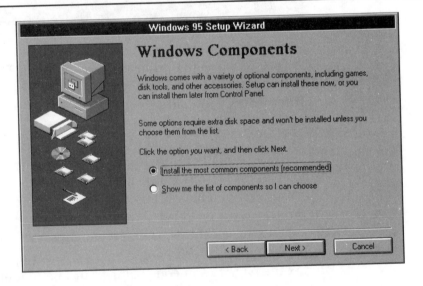

Creating a Startup Disk

It should already be apparent that Windows 95 and DOS are different. We have discussed several differences between Windows 95 and the DOS/Windows combination. There is another difference that we haven't discussed. There is a different way to create a startup disk. During the upgrade, Setup will ask you if you want to create a startup disk (Figure 4.70). If you select Yes, you will need to insert a blank floppy disk (either a 1.2MB 5¼" floppy disk or 1.44MB diskette) so that Setup can copy the startup files to the diskette.

FIGURE 4.70:

Creating a Windows 95 startup disk

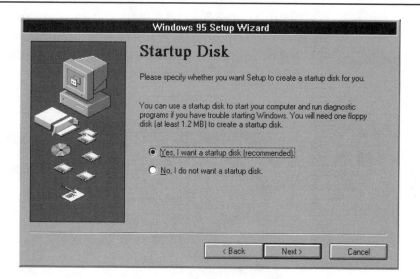

TIP   You can create a startup disk after installation (if you select No to the Create Startup Disk question during the upgrade installation process, for example). Go to the Start ➤ Settings ➤ Control Panel and double click on the Add/Remove Programs control panel. Within this control panel is a tab called Startup Disk. Click this tab to bring it to the front. On this page will be a button that says Create Startup Disk. When you click it, it will start the startup disk creation process.

Step 2: Copying Files to Your Computer

Once the information is entered, the next step is to copy all the Windows 95 component files to your computer. During this step, Setup will copy the files from their compressed archive files on the disk or CD (called *CAB files* because they have the extension *.CAB) to the hard disk. This step is the simplest of the three steps because there are only two parts: initiating the file copy and the file copy itself.

Start Copying Files

To initiate the file copy, Setup returns you to a screen similar to the one presented back in Figure 4.58. Figure 4.71 shows the screen that Setup presents to allow you to initiate the file copy. To start the file copy, click the Next button.

FIGURE 4.71:

Starting the file copy

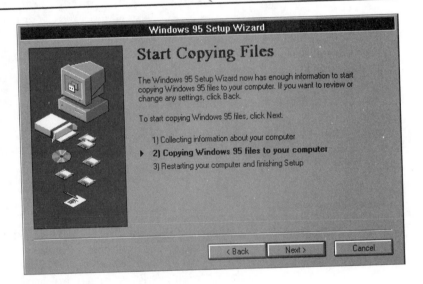

Copying Windows 95 Files

During the file copy, a status bar will appear and indicate how far along the file copy is (Figure 4.72). You will also see various screens that indicate the various features of Windows 95. During this process, you can cancel the file copy by pressing the F3 key at any time (or by clicking the Exit button).

FIGURE 4.72:

Windows 95 installation file copy

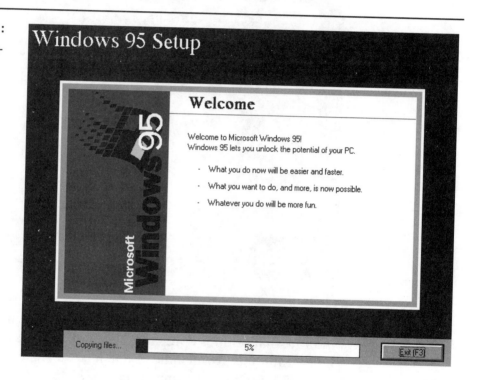

Step 3: Finishing Setup

After the file copy, the installation is basically complete. To complete the installation, you need to do only two things: reboot the computer and enter final Windows settings. As soon as the file copy is complete, Setup will present you with the screen shown in

Figure 4.73. To finish the installation, click Finish and the computer will reboot.

FIGURE 4.73:

Finishing Setup

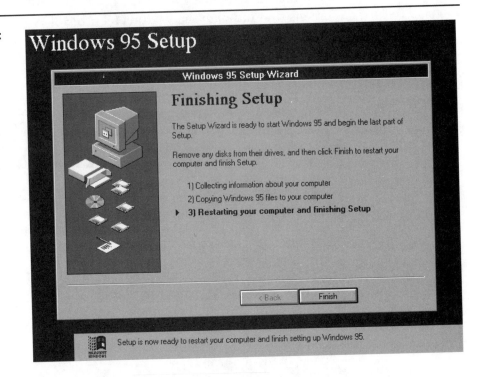

FIGURE 4.73:

Finishing Setup

After the machine has rebooted, Windows 95 will start up and indicate that setup is "preparing to run Windows 95 for the first time." After this, it will indicate that it is "finalizing settings for Windows 95" and present a small list of the settings it is making permanent. Setup will make icons for the control panel and upgrade your Windows 3.x Program Manager program groups and program icons into groups and icons for the Start menu. After that, Setup will index the Windows Help file so it can be searched. Then, Setup will modify the generic MS-DOS program properties so that DOS programs can be run under Windows 95.

The final step is to set up the time zone that this computer resides in (Figure 4.74). This gives Windows 95 information it can use to automatically adjust the time when sending e-mail across time zones, for example. Windows 95 can also automatically adjust the built-in BIOS clock during daylight savings time.

FIGURE 4.74:

Setting Windows 95 time information

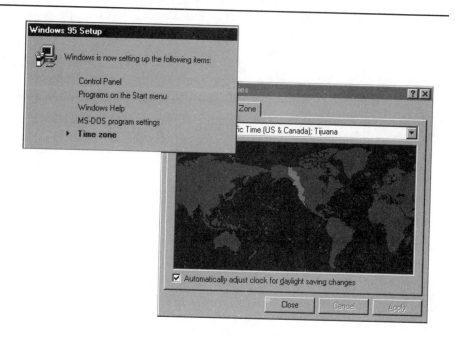

To select the proper time zone, choose the time zone from the drop-down list. I live in Fargo, ND, which is in the Central Time Zone, six hours behind GMT (Greenwich Mean Time). To finish the installation, click Apply to make the settings permanent, then click Close.

After you set the time zone, Setup will restart the computer for a final time. After this restart, the computer will be a fully functional Windows 95 computer.

TIP If the computer doesn't function properly, try rebooting in *Safe Mode*. This mode of operation loads Windows 95 with a minimal set of drivers and can help you determine if the problem is hardware or software related. To boot the computer in safe mode, turn the computer on and press the F8 key when you see Starting Windows 95. Doing so will present you with a list of boot-up choices, the third of which is Boot Computer in Safe Mode. Select this option (number 3) and press Enter. When Windows 95 comes up, it will be running in safe mode, indicated by the words Safe Mode in all four corners of the screen. To exit safe mode, restart the computer. Upon reboot, the computer will be operating normally.

Review Questions

1. Which program is used to install DOS?

   A. INSTALL.EXE

   B. INSTALL.BAT

   C. SETUP.EXE

   D. STEPUP.EXE

2. Which utility (or utilities) can be used to determine the amount of disk space on a machine that already has a version of DOS installed? (Choose all that apply.)

   A. DIR

   B. CHKDSK

   C. SPACE /DISK

   D. DISK /SPACE

3. When upgrading DOS, Setup renames the AUTOEXEC.BAT to what?

   A. AUTOEXEC.BAK

   B. AUTOEXEC.001

   C. AUTOEXEC.OLD

   D. AUTOEXEC.DAT

4. DOS can be installed on IBM-compatible computers. True or false?

   A. True

   B. False

5. How many disks are required to do a regular DOS installation?

    A. 1

    B. 2

    C. 3

    D. 4

6. If you are upgrading from MS-DOS 6.20 to 6.22, how many disks (not counting uninstall disks) will you use to do the upgrade?

    A. 1

    B. 2

    C. 3

    D. 4

7. It is necessary to back up the entire hard disk before doing a DOS upgrade. True or false?

    A. True

    B. False

8. Prior to installing DOS onto a hard disk for the first time, you must do which of the following?

    A. FDISK and FORMAT the disk.

    B. Delete any unnecessary files.

    C. Back up the entire disk.

    D. Turn off the computer, then turn it back on.

9. When you are installing DOS 6, you have to install to one of your floppy drives.

    A. True

    B. False

10. Which function key, when pressed, will halt Setup and leave you at a DOS command prompt?

    A. F1

    B. F3

    C. F5

    D. F7

11. Which function key will display help in the Setup program?

    A. F1

    B. F3

    C. F5

    D. F7

12. A computer with an AMD K5 processor (an Intel-compatible CPU) can run MS-DOS.

    A. True

    B. False

13. To install Windows 3.*x* to a computer, you can copy the files to your hard disk from the A: drive and then start Windows by typing WIN at the C:> prompt. True or false?

    A. True

    B. False

14. Which of the following Windows 3.*x* Custom Setup steps is *not* included in the Express Setup?

    A. DOS File Copy

    B. Windows File Copy

    C. Printer Setup

    D. Specify Windows Directory

15. If you don't want to install Notepad, which Windows 3.*x* installation method do you use? (Choose all that apply.)

    A. Easy Setup

    B. Difficult Setup

    C. Custom Setup

    D. Express Setup

16. What is the name of the Windows 3.*x* installation program?

    A. SETUP.EXE

    B. INSTALL.EXE

    C. INSTALL.BAT

    D. Setup.BAT

17. If you want the simplest possible installation, in which Windows 3.*x* Setup makes all the choices for you, which Setup method do you use? (Choose all that apply.)

   A. Easy Setup

   B. Difficult Setup

   C. Custom Setup

   D. Express Setup

18. Which Windows 3.*x* Setup switch is used to decompress the Windows compressed files onto a network drive?

   A. /A

   B. /B

   C. /C

   D. /N

19. Which Intel processor must your computer have (at minimum) in order to install Windows 3.*x*?

   A. 8086

   B. 8088

   C. 80286

   D. 80386

20. Which Windows 3.*x* Setup switch is used to ignore the hardware detection?

   A. /A

   B. /B

   C. /C

   D. /I

21. How much memory (minimum) does Windows 3.*x* require to run in 386 Enhanced mode?

    A. 512KB

    B. 640KB

    C. 1024KB

    D. 2048KB

22. Which key, when pressed, will stop Setup in either Windows 3.*x* or Windows 95 and exit you to DOS?

    A. F1

    B. F3

    C. F5

    D. F7

23. Which Windows 3.*x* Setup mode allows you to verify which type of computer you are installing Windows 3.*x* on?

    A. Easy Setup

    B. Difficult Setup

    C. Custom Setup

    D. Express Setup

24. Which Windows 3.*x* Setup mode allows Setup to automatically configure the swap file type and size? (Choose all that apply.)

    A. Easy Setup

    B. Difficult Setup

    C. Custom Setup

    D. Express Setup

25. During an Windows 3.x Express Setup, if you have just completed inserting Disk 2 in the DOS portion of the Setup, the next step you have to do is:

    A. Enter user information.

    B. Run the Windows Tutorial.

    C. Select Express Setup.

    D. Select Windows components to install.

26. When choosing a printer in a Windows 3.x Custom Setup, you notice that your printer type isn't listed. What option do you choose to install your printer?

    A. Generic/Text Only

    B. Install Unlisted or Updated Printer

    C. HP LaserJet III

    D. Install New Printer

27. Which Windows 3.x operating mode is used for older hardware and slower performance machines?

    A. 386 Enhanced Mode

    B. Real Mode

    C. Standard Mode

    D. Slow Mode

28. The Windows 95 Setup type that is most like the Windows 3.x Express setup is:

    A. Typical

    B. Laptop

    C. Minimum

    D. Custom

29. Which of the following Windows 95 Installation steps is *not* done during the course of a normal Custom installation:

    A. Copy system files

    B. Save old system files

    C. Select the Windows installation directory

    D. Install the Exchange client

30. How much RAM does Windows 95 require?

    A. 2MB

    B. 4MB

    C. 6MB

    D. 8MB

31. Which processor is required in your computer in order to install Windows 95?

    A. 286

    B. 386SX

    C. 386DX

    D. 486DX

    E. Pentium

32. Which software component(s) must be installed in order to use Microsoft Fax to send and receive faxes with a fax modem? (Choose all that apply.)

    A. Microsoft Fax

    B. WinFax Pro

    C. Exchange Client

    D. Fax-o-la

33. You must install at least a basic installation of DOS before installing Windows 95.

    A. True

    B. False

34. True or false: the Windows 95 installation has a DOS portion.

    A. True

    B. False

35. Which Windows 95 component is an online service, similar to AOL or CompuServe?

    A. The Microsoft Channel

    B. The Microsoft BBS

    C. The Microsoft News Network

    D. The Microsoft Network

36. How many times do you have to reboot to install Windows 95?

    A. 1

    B. 2

    C. 3

    D. 4

37. You have just finished entering your name and company information. What is the next step in installing Windows 95?

    A. Copy system files.

    B. Set up Microsoft Exchange.

    C. Select Components to Copy.

    D. Enter the product identification number.

38. What is the name of the Windows 95 installation executable?

    A. INSTALL.BAT

    B. SETUP.BAT

    C. SETUP.EXE

    D. INSTALL.EXE

39. After upgrading Windows 3.*x* to Windows 95 (and installing 95 to a directory called C:\WIN95) you can no longer run Windows 3.*x* on that computer.

    A. True

    B. False

40. Which of the following is *not* a Windows 95 installation type?

    A. Express

    B. Custom

    C. Laptop

    D. Minimum

41. The Custom installation allows you to choose which Windows 95 components you want to install.

    A. True

    B. False

42. You can configure networking software during an installation of Windows 95.

    A. True

    B. False

43. If you don't agree with the Microsoft License Agreement, Setup will let you install Windows 95 anyway.

   A. True

   B. False

44. In a Typical installation of Windows 95, you have the option of picking which Windows 95 components you want to install.

   A. True

   B. False

45. The last step in installing Windows 95 is:

   A. Configuring Microsoft Exchange

   B. Copying system files

   C. Setting the time, date, and time zone

   D. Entering the Product Identification Number

46. Which of the following Setup switches will cause Setup to forgo the initial disk scan?

   A. /id

   B. /is

   C. /i

   D. /noscan

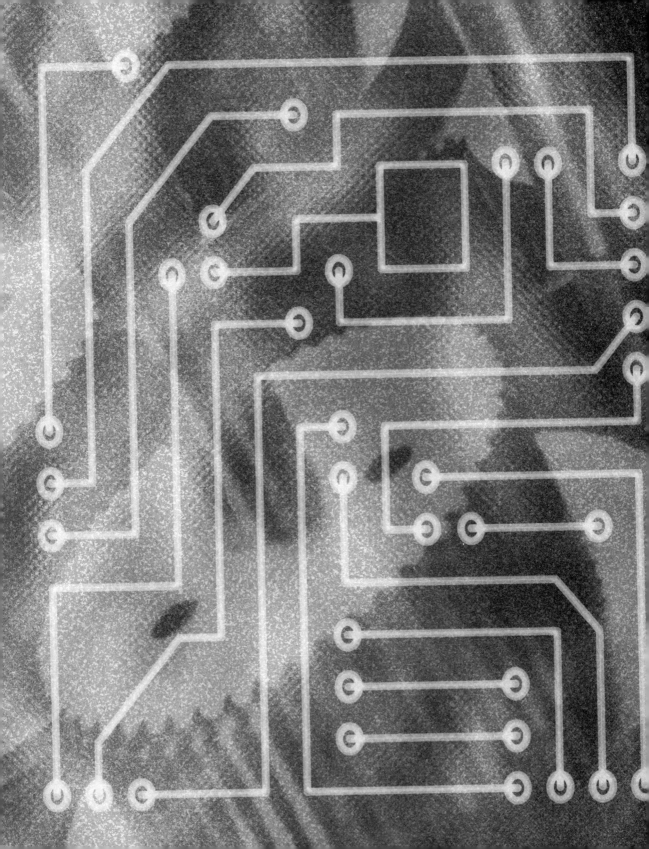

CHAPTER
FIVE

Operating System Configuration

■ Identify the operating system's functions, structure, and major system files.

■ Identify procedures for loading/adding device drivers and the necessary software for certain devices.

■ Identify the procedures for changing options, configuring, and using the Windows print subsystem.

Everyone needs to add functionality to their computer, whether hardware or software. This chapter deals with the configuration of the major operating system environments. It also deals with configuring the operating system to recognize new hardware like modems, sound cards, and printers.

Configuring MS-DOS and the Startup Files

Startup of a computer is generally referred to as *booting* or *bootstrapping*. This term is derived from an expression that was more meaningful in an older age of lesser technology—to pull oneself up by the bootstraps.

This section of the chapter describes what happens when you flip the power switch on a DOS-based computer and devotes special attention to the software involved in that process. An understanding of what *should* be taking place during bootup will aid you greatly in any effort to diagnose a malfunctioning system.

Configuring CONFIG.SYS

We have already looked at the elements of DOS that are unalterably programmed into your computer (Chapter 3). Unless you're a DOS programmer, undertaking to change these elements would be tantamount to wreaking havoc on the operating system.

Unlike the files discussed in Chapter 3, however, CONFIG.SYS is a system file that is *made* to be changed, much like a new car is made to be individually adjusted according to the taste of its owner. When buying a new car, a prospective buyer selects from a list of possible options and pays to have those options included in the vehicle. The CONFIG.SYS file can be compared to the dashboard of your car. A standard-model automobile's dashboard contains, in addition to the standard dials and buttons, various unused "plugs" that are waiting to be utilized should the buyer decide to purchase additional special features. The dashboard's dials and plugs correspond to the commands located within the CONFIG.SYS file—they are device drivers and commands that are placed in the CONFIG.SYS file. The unused plugs in this hypothetical dashboard correspond to the full range of available commands that may be used in the CONFIG.SYS file, many of which are described in detail later in this chapter.

This file can be used for vital tasks such as memory management, which has to do with arranging the memory addresses used by DOS programs. Many users include the DOUBLESPACE program in their CONFIG.SYS, allowing the doubling of disk space through disk compression. There are also multi-configuration options available, which allow you to change your configuration at bootup depending on your occasional needs. Other options include things like the VSAFE command, which allows for automatic virus-protection for your system.

In the bootup process, CONFIG.SYS loads into memory prior to COMMAND.COM. To view its contents, you must be in the root directory of your hard drive, indicated by the C:\> prompt. At the prompt, type the following:

```
EDIT CONFIG.SYS
```

In all likelihood you will see a CONFIG.SYS file that contains something like this:

```
DEVICE=C:\WINDOWS\HIMEM.SYS
DEVICE=C:\WINDOWS\EMM386.EXE NOEMS
BUFFERS=23,0
FILES=30
DOS=UMB
LASTDRIVE=E
FCBS=4,0
```

(Or you may see something longer and somewhat more intimidating.)

NOTE   The rest of this chapter will explain much of what you're likely to see in the CONFIG.SYS file.

Make a Copy of CONFIG.SYS Before You Make Any Modifications

Before editing the CONFIG.SYS file it is a good idea to make a copy of it so you can restore its previous settings. This may be necessary because it is possible to render your system nonfunctional through incorrect changes to the file. To make a copy, type the following command:

```
COPY CONFIG.SYS CONFIG.BAK
```

If you later need to restore the previous settings, use the following commands, in the following order:

```
RENAME CONFIG.SYS CONFIG.OLD
RENAME CONFIG.BAK CONFIG.SYS
```

These commands will replace the existing CONFIG.SYS with original one.

Main Parameters of CONFIG.SYS

The following sections describe the most commonly used parameters for CONFIG.SYS and how they are used. The commands must follow a certain format, as shown in the command's syntax.

FILES The FILES command describes how many *file handles* DOS can keep track of simultaneously. A file handle is simply another name for an open file. If DOS discovers that a program exceeds this limit as it tries to open a file, DOS responds by saying that there are too many files open. In light of that, it seems logical to make FILES the highest number the system will allow (which is 255), except that the memory available to the system is reduced slightly whenever this number is increased. Setting the FILES to 30 would be typical. Documentation that comes with programs will often specify the minimum FILES setting for their program.

Syntax	Example
FILES=n	FILES=30

BUFFERS Like the FILES command, the BUFFERS command determines the number of buffers DOS creates so that it can store disk information in RAM rather than on disk. This will lessen the need for constantly accessing the hard drive, reducing the number of reads and writes, and speeding up overall operation of the computer. The higher this number is set, the more memory it will use. Setting BUFFERS to 50 would be typical on a hard drive of 120MB or more. The BUFFERS command should be reduced on systems running a disk caching program such as SMARTDRV. In this case, BUFFERS should be set to a lower number, such as 15. Windows automatically installs SMARTDRV in the AUTOEXEC.BAT file, so a Windows computer should have the BUFFERS command set low.

Syntax	Example
BUFFERS=n	BUFFERS=50

DEVICE Every device that is connected to a computer, such as a hard drive, CD-ROM, or printer, relies on a piece of software called a *device driver* in order to communicate with the operating system. These drivers are sometimes included with DOS. Drivers for those devices that are not included with DOS (a CD-ROM is a typical example) must have a pointer in the CONFIG.SYS file that directs DOS to the correct address for the driver. This pointer is the DEVICE command. Typically, the driver for a piece of hardware will come on a disk included with the hardware. In the hardware's documentation there will be instructions explaining how to load the driver on your hard drive and how to modify your CONFIG .SYS file so that DOS can find the driver when it boots up. When the DEVICE command is executed at bootup, DOS will find the driver and load it into memory.

Syntax

DEVICE=[*d:path*]*filename*

Example

DEVICE=C:\SB16\SB16.SYS

> **NOTE** Many kinds of *software* also require the use of a device driver. DOS includes many examples of such software, such as its own memory management software. The memory management drivers are HIMEM.SYS and EMM386.EXE. Other drivers include DOUBLESPACE.SYS, which is the device driver for DOS's DoubleSpace disk compression program. We will look at the memory management programs in detail later in this chapter.

Memory Management Parameters of CONFIG.SYS

Memory management involves loading portions of DOS or complete DOS programs into areas of memory that are not normally accessible. This is an essential aspect of optimizing DOS for high performance, as it makes more memory available to other programs, including Windows. Some DOS programs require contiguous blocks of memory to run, and using memory management may allow them to fit into memory, even in cases where they may have been squeezed out and rendered nonfunctional before.

DOS is capable of working with 1,024KB of memory addresses under most circumstances. The reason for this is that DOS was originally designed to work with the Intel 8088 CPU that IBM picked out for the original PC back around 1980. The 8088 could address 1,024KB of memory, which at the time was a colossal amount.

These early programmers also had to decide how those 1,024KB of memory addresses would be used. They decided that the first 640KB would be used for programs, data, and the operating system itself. This first 640KB is referred to as *conventional memory*. Most programs written for DOS are designed to work within this first 640KB, which is sometimes referred to as the *640K barrier*. The area from 640KB to 768KB is reserved for video memory. The upper area from 768KB to 1,024KB is referred to as the *reserved memory area* (this area is also sometimes called the *upper memory area*). This reserved memory area contains the BIOS ROM and is reserved for ROMs on circuit boards such as LAN cards or hard disk controller cards. Figure 5.1 illustrates these memory areas.

Originally, the programmers for DOS envisioned that this 640KB would be enough memory space to run any software built for DOS. Programs grew quickly, however, and it became necessary to utilize the upper areas of memory for more and more purposes. The device drivers and commands described in this section provide ways to do that.

Memory above 1,024KB is called extended memory and is used by Windows and Windows-based programs. Extended memory cannot be accessed unless the HIMEM.SYS memory manager is used. The lowest 64KB of extended memory, from 1,024KB to 1,088KB, is called the High Memory Area (HMA). Portions of DOS can be loaded into this area using a memory manager.

NOTE   For more detailed information about the DOS memory map and other PC memory topics, refer to the first book in the A+ Study Guide series, the *A+: Core Module Study Guide*.

FIGURE 5.1:

DOS's main memory areas

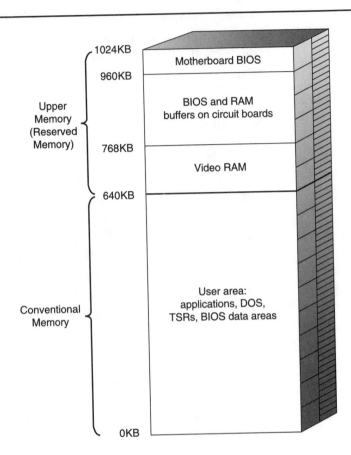

HIMEM.SYS is the DOS memory manager that enables extended memory above 1,024KB on your system, including the High Memory Area from 1,024KB to 1,088KB. Windows cannot load at all without HIMEM.SYS, and for this reason it automatically invokes it whether it is present in the CONFIG.SYS file or not.

The syntax for HIMEM.SYS is as follows:

```
DEVICE=[d:\path]HIMEM.SYS [switches]
```

Here is an example of HIMEM.SYS being used:

```
DEVICE=c:\dos\HIMEM.SYS /int15=1024
```

Table 5.1 describes the switches that can be used with HIMEM.SYS.

TABLE 5.1:   Switches used with the HIMEM.SYS command

Switch	Purpose
/a20control:onloff	Determines status of the HMA A20 line
/cpuclock:onloff	Determines whether HIMEM.SYS will modify system clock speed. The default is off
/eisa	Allocates maximum amount of extended memory. Required for EISA systems with 16MB of memory or more
/hmamin=*nnn*	Specifies minimum memory space a program must request in order for DOS to load it into the HMA. The number nnn will be in kilobytes. Only one program can load into HMA. The default size is 0KB
int15=*nnn*	Reserves nnn kilobytes for handling of Int 15, which is used by certain older programs. The default size is 0KB
/machine:*name*	Defines the specific computer type using a predefined code. (Required by some systems that HIMEM.SYS cannot detect)
/numhandles=*nn*	Maximum memory block handles for extended memory. The default is 32
/shadowram:onloff	Sets the status of shadow RAM
/verbose	Calls for status messages by HIMEM.SYS when it starts up

The DOS=HIGH command is used to load part of DOS into the High Memory Area between 1,024KB and 1,088KB. The DOS=UMB command enables DOS to manage *upper memory blocks* (*UMBs*). Upper memory blocks are the blocks of free memory in the upper memory area between 640KB and 1,024KB. Using DOS=UMB will mean that DOS is empowered to load programs and device drivers into UMBs.

DOS=HIGH and DOS=UMB can be left as separate commands or combined into one statement as shown here:

```
DOS=HIGH,UMB
```

The syntax for this command is as follows:

```
DOS=HIGH|LOW[,UMB|,NOUMB]
```

TIP The "|" symbol that appears twice in the preceding syntax line above indicates that you can use one or the other, but not both, of the items that are separated by the symbol.

The DOS=HIGH command will not work unless the HIMEM .SYS device driver is installed. The DOS=UMB command requires that the EMM386.EXE driver be loaded.

The EMM386.EXE reserved memory manager provides DOS with the ability to utilize upper memory blocks (UMBs) to store programs and device drivers. UMBs reside in the 640KB to 1,024KB region of memory. The EMM386.EXE is also used to simulate expanded memory for DOS applications that utilize 386 Enhanced mode.

The syntax for the command is:

```
DEVICE=[d:\path]EMM386.EXE [switches]
```

An example of the EMM386.EXE invocation is:

```
DEVICE=C:\DOS\EMM386.EXE NOEMS I=B000-B7FF
```

EMM386.EXE comes with numerous optional switches, which are summarized in Table 5.2.

TABLE 5.2:   Switches used with EMM386.EXE

Switch	Purpose
N*nnn*	Quantity of extended memory allocated for expanded memory emulation, represented in kilobytes
on I off I auto	Set or change operational status of EMM386.EXE
/p*nnnn*	Specifies page frame address
/p*n*=address	Specifies address for segment *n*
a=*altregs*	Assigns alternate register sets used for multitasking. The default is 7
Altboot	Enables an alternate process for warm boots initiated by Ctrl+Alt+Del; for use when warm boots malfunction
b=*address*	Specifies the starting address for EMS memory swapping; the default is hex address 4000h
d=*nnn*	Retains DMA buffering equal to *nnn* KB
Frame=*address*	Specifies the 64KB page frame's starting address
h=*handles*	Number of file handles that EMM386.EXE can utilize
i=*range*	Include this memory range as available memory addresses
l=*nnnn*	Directs EMM386.EXE to leave available a specified quantity of extended memory after loading itself
min=*nnnn*	Describes minimum amount of expanded memory provided by EMM386.EXE. The default EMS memory is 256KB
M*n*	Specifies a page-frame address; will be a number from 1 to 14, representing a pre-defined base address
Noems	Prevents LIM3.2 expanded memory
Novcpi	Disallows VCPI
Nohi	Directs EMM386.EXE to load itself into memory below 640KB
Highscan	Restricts upper memory scanning
Quiet	Suppresses display of EMM386.EXE loading messages
ram=*range*	Specifies segment addresses for UMBs; also enables UMBs and expanded memory

TABLE 5.2 (CONTINUED):   Switches used with EMM386.EXE

Switch	Purpose
Rom=*range*	Allocates memory addresses for shadow RAM
Verbose	Calls for status messages by EMM386.EXE when it starts up
win=*range*	Specifies an address range to be used by Windows rather than EMM386.EXE
x=*range*	Excludes this memory range from available memory addresses

NOTE   All the *range* addresses specified in Table 5.2 are in hexadecimal.

NOEMS is a commonly used option for disabling expanded memory. The *i=range* and *x=range* switches are commonly used both by the MemMaker program and by anyone performing manual memory mapping of the system.

The EMM386.EXE driver is often used in conjunction with the DEVICEHIGH and LOADHIGH commands. The LOADHIGH command is covered in detail later in this chapter, in the section pertaining to the AUTOEXEC.BAT file. LOADHIGH or LH is used to load an application program into an upper memory block.

The DEVICEHIGH command functions precisely as the device command, but with the following exception: It will load the device drivers into upper memory blocks, thereby freeing up space in conventional memory. If there is insufficient space in the UMBs, DOS will load the device driver into conventional memory. This command requires the EMM386.EXE invocation to be in place in CONFIG.SYS. It is possible that you may encounter some older drivers that will not execute properly if they are loaded into UMBs. If you know you're using some older drivers, you may want to load one driver at a time into upper memory. After rebooting you should verify that the system is working correctly.

The syntax for the command is:

```
DEVICEHIGH=[d:path]filename
```

An example of the DEVICEHIGH command is:

```
DEVICEHIGH=C:\lsrjt\lsr.sys
```

Once the preceding commands are in place, you can view the results of memory management by rebooting to initiate the changes and then typing **MEM** at the command prompt. The MEM command displays statistics as shown in Figure 5.2.

FIGURE 5.2:

Output from the MEM command in DOS 6.22

```
C:\WINDOWS>mem

Memory Type         Total        Used        Free
----------------    --------    --------    --------
Conventional          640K         44K        596K
Upper                   0K          0K          0K
Reserved              384K        384K          0K
Extended (XMS)     15,360K      2,240K     13,120K
----------------    --------    --------    --------
Total memory       16,384K      2,668K     13,716K

Total under 1 MB      640K         44K        596K

Total Expanded (EMS)              20M (20,463,616 bytes)
Free Expanded (EMS)               13M (13,434,880 bytes)

Largest executable program size   596K (609,968 bytes)
Largest free upper memory block     0K       (0 bytes)
MS-DOS is resident in the high memory area.
```

The row displaying Upper Memory is most significant for memory optimization. In Figure 5.2 notice that the Upper Memory row shows that there is no upper memory available (and none being used).

Typing **MEM /C** at the command prompt displays a very useful and important table. This table describes where each specific program loads, whether into conventional or upper memory. After setting up memory optimization on your system and rebooting, use the MEM /C command. Read the name of those drivers or programs that you attempted to load into UMBs, then check the

Upper Memory column to see which of them *did* in fact load into the upper memory area. If a program loaded into conventional memory instead, there may not be sufficient contiguous memory space available for it in a UMB.

NOTE Contiguous memory is memory that occurs in a single continuous block. Programs usually won't function when loaded into different areas of memory; for this reason DOS requires that there be a single memory block available that is large enough to contain an entire program before it will load the given program.

The task of working out which programs can fit into upper memory becomes time-consuming, and for that reason it is often simpler to run the MemMaker program included with DOS to optimize memory.

Using Multiconfig to Customize PC Startup

One of the most powerful and attractive features that came along with version 6.2 of DOS is *Multiconfig*. Before Multiconfig, it was necessary to maintain different CONFIG.SYS files if you wanted to utilize different system configurations at different times. The real problem with this approach was that you either had to rename or move your CONFIG.SYS files after booting up and then boot the system again in order to use the altered configuration. Users who required programs that used a lot of memory, or users who liked to run scads of memory-gripping TSRs were often forced into this tedious repetition.

DOS 6.2 included special commands that allowed different configurations to be maintained within a single CONFIG.SYS file. These different configurations are made available to choose from at bootup, when a menu appears offering a choice of bootup configurations. The menu can also be set to default to a certain configuration for occasions when no user is present to make a menu selection. This is helpful for those who hate to sit idly by while their computer boots; they can still go off and grab a coffee during the moments it takes for the computer to boot.

The following analysis will provide step-by-step explanations for a multiple configuration. Suppose you had two simple CONFIG .SYS files that you wanted to merge into one Multiconfig. The first file describes a very basic setup:

```
FILES=30
BUFFERS=30
DEVICE=C:\DOS\ANSI.SYS
DEVICE=C:\WINDOWS\SETVER.EXE
```

The second CONFIG.SYS file is set up to use upper memory in order to effectively run a hypothetical memory-hogging DOS game called BigRAMhog.

```
DEVICE=C:\DOS\HIMEM.SYS
DEVICE=C:\DOS\EMM386.EXE NOEMS
DOS=HIGH,UMB
FILES=30
BUFFERS=30
DEVICEHIGH=C:\DOS\ANSI.SYS
DEVICE=C:\BIG\BIGRA.SYS
```

Once you combine the two files into one CONFIG.SYS file, you need to add titles in square brackets. A bracketed title must precede each section that was formerly a complete CONFIG.SYS file. These sections are called *blocks*. The result of joining the two files would be this:

```
[basicsetup]
FILES=30
BUFFERS=30
DEVICE=C:\DOS\ANSI.SYS
DEVICE=C:\WINDOWS\SETVER.EXE
[bigramsetup]
DEVICE=C:\DOS\HIMEM.SYS
DEVICE=C:\DOS\EMM386.EXE NOEMS
```

```
DOS=HIGH,UMB
FILES=30
BUFFERS=30
DEVICEHIGH=C:\DOS\ANSI.SYS
DEVICE=C:\BIG\BIGRA.SYS
```

Now, a *menu block* must be factored into the picture. This block of commands goes at the top of the Multiconfig file. Again, this is also created with a bracketed title, and this block will contain specific *menuitem* commands. Additionally, each menuitem must have a corresponding BlockName in the CONFIG.SYS. The syntax of the menuitem command is this:

```
MENUITEM BlockName,[menutext]
```

Blockname refers to the bracketed name preceding the two configurations. *Menutext* is what will actually appear on the menu that is seen during bootup. After adding in these commands under the [menu] block title, here is what the CONFIG.SYS file looks like:

```
[menu]
menuitem basicsetup,Basic setup
menuitem bigramsetup,Bigramhog setup
[basicsetup]
FILES=30
BUFFERS=30
DEVICE=C:\DOS\ANSI.SYS
DEVICE=C:\WINDOWS\SETVER.EXE
[bigramsetup]
DEVICE=C:\DOS\HIMEM.SYS
DEVICE=C:\DOS\EMM386.EXE NOEMS
DOS=HIGH,UMB
FILES=30
BUFFERS=30
DEVICEHIGH=C:\DOS\ANSI.SYS
DEVICE=C:\BIG\BIGRA.SYS
```

NOTE   It is also important to create a common block at the end of the Multi-config file (by adding the word "common" in brackets at the end of the CONFIG.SYS file, like this: [common]). The [common] block loads drivers that are common to all configurations. This is important because installation programs will sometimes update your CONFIG.SYS file automatically, by tacking a command at the end of the file. Commands in the common block are automatically executed by all configurations. If the common block is missing, automatic updates to CONFIG.SYS will land at the end of last configuration block, and thus will take effect only if the last configuration block is selected. This is generally undesirable. Some software will edit existing lines in CONFIG.SYS when installed, and will do this with no awareness of Multiconfig. After automatic installations, it is wise to check to see if this has occurred. If it has, the changes will need to be manually made to any blocks that were not updated.

The next step is to assign a default configuration and a timeout specifying how long the system will wait until it boots into the default configuration. This can be accomplished with the *menu-default* command:

```
menudefault BlockName,[timeoutvalue]
```

The *timeoutvalue* specifies in seconds how long Multiconfig will wait for you to select one of the configurations. The menudefault command should be placed into the menu block in CONFIG.SYS. Suppose your primary interest in the computer is to play video games. To this end, you would want the default configuration to be bigramsetup. Type this in the menu block:

```
menudefault bigramsetup,5
```

CONFIG.SYS now appears like this:

```
[menu]
menuitem basicsetup,Basic setup
menuitem bigramsetup,Bigramhog setup
menudefault bigramsetup,5
```

```
[basicsetup]
FILES=30
BUFFERS=30
DEVICE=C:\DOS\ANSI.SYS
DEVICE=C:\WINDOWS\SETVER.EXE
[bigramsetup]
DEVICE=C:\DOS\HIMEM.SYS
DEVICE=C:\DOS\EMM386.EXE NOEMS
DOS=HIGH,UMB
FILES=30
BUFFERS=30
DEVICEHIGH=C:\DOS\ANSI.SYS
DEVICE=C:\BIG\BIGRA.SYS
[common]
```

Reboot the computer at this point and DOS will display the following:

```
MS-DOS 6 Startup Menu
=====================
1. Basic setup
2. Bigramhog setup
Enter a choice: 2       Time remaining: 5
```

The Enter a Choice line contains a 2 because the menudefault command in CONFIG.SYS specifies that bigramsetup will be the default configuration. Pressing Enter at this point will automatically select the default configuration, and the processing of the Bigramsetup block in CONFIG.SYS will begin immediately. Hitting 1 and then Enter will select the Basic setup.

Meanwhile, the time remaining will count down to zero, and if nothing is pressed prior to this, the computer will begin processing the Bigramsetup block. If any number is pressed, DOS stops its countdown while waiting for the Enter key.

Another valuable command in Multiconfig is *Include*. Here's the syntax for it:

```
Include [blockname]
```

Include is especially useful in CONFIG.SYS files that contain numerous commands that are common to more than one configuration block. To use it, the common commands must be placed in a separate block, and the block must be given a name. The Include command is then invoked from within the other blocks.

In the example configuration, the following lines are common to both blocks:

```
FILES=30
BUFFERS=30
```

Revising the configuration with the Include command would produce the following results:

```
[menu]
menuitem basicsetup,Basic setup
menuitem bigramsetup,Bigramhog setup
menudefault bigramsetup,5
[all]
FILES=30
BUFFERS=30
DEVICEHIGH=C:\DOS\ANSI.SYS
[basicsetup]
INCLUDE all
DEVICE=C:\WINDOWS\SETVER.EXE
[bigramsetup]
INCLUDE all
DEVICE=C:\DOS\HIMEM.SYS
DEVICE=C:\DOS\EMM386.EXE NOEMS
DOS=HIGH,UMB
DEVICE=C:\BIG\BIGRA.SYS
[common]
```

Note here that the DEVICEHIGH command will load ANSI.SYS into conventional memory (below 640KB) rather than upper memory if the basic setup is selected. This is because the basic setup does not contain the HIMEM.SYS and the EMM386.EXE drivers that it needs in order to utilize upper memory.

Bypassing CONFIG.SYS

Certain occasions of troubleshooting hardware or software mal-functions may necessitate using the *clean boot* feature of DOS. The way to perform a clean boot is to press the F5 key while your machine is booting up. Please note that the keystroke must occur *after* the message comes up that says:

```
Starting MS-DOS...
```

When you press F5 during the appropriate interval, a message informs you that DOS is booting without the CONFIG.SYS and AUTOEXEC.BAT files. The system will then use built-in default values in its revised minimal configuration. Memory manage-ment, for example, will not take place, and any customized PROMPT or PATH settings will be eliminated. You can obtain a similar result by pressing and holding down the Shift key instead of F5; if you use the Shift key, you must hold it down until the bootup process is completed.

TIP   DoubleSpace, DOS's disk compression program, will load regardless of whether you bypass the configuration files by means of the F5 key. If you want to bypass DoubleSpace, use Ctrl+F5 instead.

The typical scenario for problems that necessitate your using a clean boot is that some new hardware or software has just been installed and your computer fails to boot (or otherwise malfunc-tions) in the aftermath. The device driver for the new equipment may prove incompatible with your system or with another installed program or driver. If the computer successfully boots with the F5 option, then the problem lies with a particular line in CONFIG.SYS or AUTOEXEC.BAT.

Another option during bootup is the F8 key. Press it as DOS is starting up if you want to engage the DOS interactive boot fea-ture. The F8 option is useful when you have already determined that a problem lies in CONFIG.SYS or AUTOEXEC.BAT but you must narrow it down to a particular line of text. In the earlier years of DOS, a troubleshooting technique used in this situation consisted of putting the REM command at the beginning of suspect lines in CONFIG.SYS or AUTOEXEC.BAT. The REM would classify that line as a "remark," thus rendering it non-executable. This method was time-consuming, however, as every reboot required further editing of CONFIG.SYS or AUTOEXEC.BAT. The interactive boot offered by the F8 option is far more efficient. When F8 is pressed during the interval between the "Starting MS-DOS" message and what would have been the next message, each command in the CONFIG.SYS file will be displayed one at a time during bootup, followed by a [Y, N]? query, as in the following example:

```
DEVICE=C:\HIMEM.SYS [Y,N]?
```

Here, DOS is requesting that you tell it whether you want this particular command to be processed or ignored. After you respond, it will bring up the next command in your CONFIG.SYS file. When you have answered Y or N to each query, another question will appear:

```
Process Autoexec.bat [Y,N]?
```

If you answer Y to this question, then DOS will step you through the AUTOEXEC.BAT file in a similar manner. If you answer N, AUTOEXEC.BAT will not run at all.

Customizing DOS with the AUTOEXEC.BAT

A *batch file* is a file with a .BAT extension that contains other DOS commands. The power of a batch file is that by simply typing the name of the batch file and pressing Enter, DOS will process all of the batch file commands without need for any additional user input. Once created, a good batch file will save you time every time you use it. The batch file will also save you from lost time due to typos and looking up commands for which you can't remember the correct syntax or the optional switches. Batch files are the subject of Chapter 7. In this section we will describe one batch file, the AUTOEXEC.BAT file, because of its special role in the startup and configuration of DOS-based system.

The power of the AUTOEXEC.BAT file is simply this; it runs every time you boot your computer. It is the last stage of the bootup process and is automatically executed by COMMAND .COM before your C:> prompt appears.

There are certain programs and commands that are pertinent to your system configuration, and these are often most effective when placed in the AUTOEXEC.BAT file. A few of these programs and commands will be examined in the next several sections.

An example of an AUTOEXEC.BAT file follows:

```
@ECHO OFF
PATH C:\DOS\;C\WINDOWS;C:\UTILITY
PROMPT $P$g
cls
C:\DOS\SMARTDRV
MOUSE
```

The first line, @ECHO OFF, issues a command reversing a DOS default setting. By default, DOS will display, or "echo" on screen, every command that it processes. Normally, this happens when you type in the command. However, DOS will also display the commands as they run from a batch file, just as if you'd typed them in, which may amount to unwanted screen output. Turning off this echo with the ECHO OFF command will prevent DOS from doing this. The @ symbol acts as an ECHO OFF command but affects only its own command line. Without the @ symbol, AUTOEXEC.BAT will actually display the words "ECHO OFF" before executing the command.

The CLS command in the fourth line is a directive to clear the screen of all text except the command prompt. The MOUSE command invokes the mouse driver. The other elements require a more detailed explanation and will be discussed below.

Customizing the DOS Prompt Using the PROMPT Command

The PROMPT command is used to modify the appearance of the command line prompt, which usually appears as the C:\> for the hard drive or A:\> prompt for the floppy disk drive. In this case, the C: or A: refers to the current drive; the backslash refers the current directory, and both are followed by the > symbol. The command used to produce this prompt is PROMPT pg. In this command, the "p" directs DOS to include the current drive and path in the DOS prompt, and the "g" directs DOS to include the greater-than sign.

The syntax for the command is:

```
PROMPT $symbolcode$symbolcode
```

The symbol codes that can be used with the PROMPT command are given in Table 5.3. They can be used to display features like date and time within the DOS prompt, or to invoke more complex video alterations (like making the prompt flash on and off or appear in a different color) by calling on the ANSI.SYS driver. The $ sign followed by a character is used to delineate a special code, summarized in Table 5.3.

NOTE   With the introduction of DOS 6, the command PROMPT PG no longer needs to appear in the AUTOEXEC.BAT. This setting is set in the DOS environment by default.

TABLE 5.3:   Symbols for use after $ in the PROMPT command

Symbol	Output in the Prompt
a	The & symbol
c	The (symbol
f	The) symbol
e	The Esc key, used to invoke ANSI.SYS
s	Blank space
p	Designates the current drive and path
g	The > symbol
n	Designates the current drive
d	Date
t	Time
v	The DOS version in use
l	The < symbol
b	The I symbol
q	The = sign
h	Backspace (deletes character left of cursor)
_	Underscore (moves cursor to next line)

Additionally, the PROMPT command can be used to place text onscreen instead of (or in addition to) using one PROMPT's special symbols. Type this line at the DOS prompt:

PROMPT Yeah?

Enter it, and your command line will henceforth display a little more personality:

Yeah?_

Understanding the PATH Command

As mentioned earlier in the chapter, COMMAND.COM is the lucky agent who gets to do the dirty work when DOS is looking for a program. If COMMAND.COM does not locate the program in the current directory as a .COM, .EXE, or .BAT file, it will search along the current *path*. The current path on your system refers to the order in which COMMAND.COM searches specified subdirectories for programs typed in and entered at the command prompt. The current path can be ascertained by typing PATH without any parameters at the command line:

```
PATH
```

The current path, which is the output from the preceding command, may appear like this:

```
PATH C:\DOS;D:\
```

The path statement indicates to DOS that if COMMAND.COM is unable to find a requested program in the current directory, it will search the C:\DOS subdirectory and then the D:\ root directory in search of it. When failing to find a particular program along the path, it will display the message

```
Bad command or file name
```

The PATH command is used to view or modify the current path. The syntax for the command is as follows:

```
PATH d1:\path1;d2:\path2...
```

If your path statement is poorly configured, if you have added programs that reside in their own separate subdirectories or disk partitions, or if you'd like to rename directories or move critical files to different locations, your path statement becomes very important. Understanding how it functions is dependent upon an understanding of how the DOS directory system works.

As an example, suppose your job entails frequent travel and you need to download compressed files from your headquarters on a regular basis. To access the files, you need to run your DOS decompression program, PKZIPW, which your company purchased for you and loaded into a PKWARE subdirectory. When you boot up each morning, the computer displays the familiar C:\ prompt. One morning, a little sleepy, you forget to change to the PKWARE directory before you type PKZIPW. You are abruptly informed:

`Bad command or file name`

This occurs, of course, because DOS cannot process this command until you have switched to the PKWARE subdirectory:

`CD\pkware`

Instead of issuing this CD command before each downloading session, you could add the PKWARE subdirectory to your path statement, as follows:

`PATH C:\dos;C:\pkware`

From that point on, you can type PKZIPW and run the program without having to switch directories. Typically, the external commands for DOS will be found in the DOS subdirectory. It is logical, therefore, to make sure that the DOS subdirectory is included on the path. The path can be eliminated completely by typing the following:

`PATH ;`

In this case, DOS will produce the following message when the current path is next requested:

`No Path`

While you can use the PATH command to rewrite the entire current path, the APPEND command is the best way to simply modify the path. The syntax for APPEND is:

`APPEND d1:\path1;d2:\path2... /x`

The subdirectories included with the APPEND command will also be examined when DOS is looking for a program. The /x switch must be used for this command to work.

Using SMARTDRV.EXE to Cache Disk Reads and Writes

SMARTDRV.EXE is a disk-caching program that will almost always improve performance on a DOS-based system. A disk-caching program's job is to intercept data that is being read from disk. The program will store this data in RAM, in a place referred to as the *cache*. Often, the operating system or an application will make multiple calls for the same piece of data. Frequently, this data can be retrieved from the cache, suspending the need to access the hard drive, and thus taking advantage of the vastly superior speed of RAM memory.

Writes to disk can also be cached by most disk-caching programs. This works the same way, but in reverse. When a program calls for data to be written to disk, it is intercepted and stored in the cache for a specific interval of time, at the conclusion of which it will be written to disk.

The syntax for invoking the SMARTDRV command is:

`[d:path]SMARTDRV.EXE [switches]`

Software cache programs must be configured when the system is started. For this reason Smartdrive should be placed in the AUTOEXEC.BAT file. Alternatively, it can be placed in CONFIG .SYS with the following command:

`DEVICE=[d:path]SMARTDRV.EXE [switches]`

Options for SMARTDRV.EXE consist of the switches shown in Table 5.4.

TABLE 5.4: Switches for use with SMARTDRV

Switch	Purpose
Device [+I-]	Enables or disables read/write caching
InitCacheSize WinCacheSize	Defines cache size
/C	Forces data in the write cache to be written to disk
/F	Empties cache before returning to command prompt
/L	Forces SMARTDRV to load itself in memory below 640KB
/N	Displays a command prompt without forcing cached data to disk
/Q	Tells SMARTDRV to forego the display of status messages when loading
/R	Restarts SMARTDRV after clearing cache
/S	Displays status information on SMARTDRV's efficiency
/U	Prevents CD-ROM caching portion of SMARTDRV from loading
/V	Tells SMARTDRV to display status messages when loading
/X	This default setting disables write-caching for all drives and is countered by the d:+ parameter
/E:elementsize	Minimum number of bytes SMARTDRV will process at once
/B:buffersize	Number of bytes in read-ahead buffer

The Device [+ I -] option overrides the SMARTDRV default setting, which is to cache read and write requests for hard disks, to cache read requests from floppy disks, and to overlook network drives completely. Multiple drives can be indicated here if they are separated by spaces. The plus sign tacked onto a drive will enable both read and write requests for that drive, while the minus sign will negate them. Adding the drive letter without the plus or minus sign will result in the caching of reads but will disable write caching.

The *Initial Cache* Size (set by the *InitCacheSize* option as it's listed in the Table 5.5) is the amount of cache memory SMARTDRV reserves at the outset when running DOS. It is also the maximum size of the cache. *Windows Cache Size* (or *WinCacheSize*) describes the smallest cache that Windows must preserve for SMARTDRV if it chooses to allocate additional memory to its operations. This additional memory can actually be taken temporarily out of the cache reserved under InitCacheSize. This tends to make the cache fluctuate during operations. Upon exit from Windows, the cache is restored to its InitCacheSize value.

The default cache sizes, which are usually adequate, are shown in Table 5.5.

TABLE 5.5: DOS 6.22 default cache sizes

Extended Memory	InitCacheSize	WinCacheSize
Up to 1MB	All extended	Zero (no caching)
Up to 2MB	1MB	256KB
Up to 4MB	1MB	512KB
Up to 6MB	2MB	1MB
6MB or greater	2MB	2MB

The size of the cache can be changed easily in the AUTOEXEC.BAT file. An example of this that will create a 1MB InitCacheSize and a 1MB WinCacheSize would be the one created by the following command:

```
C:\DOS\SMARTDRV 1024 1024
```

The /E:*elementsize* option determines the minimum number of bytes SMARTDRV will process at once. Although 8KB is the default, smaller values may be entered.

/B:*buffersize* refers to the SMARTDRV buffer. The buffersize value, a multiple of the elementsize, is the number of bytes that will be placed into memory cache during disk reads. The default is 16KB.

The /L option is irrelevant unless upper memory is enabled with EMM386.EXE. SMARTDRIVE loads into upper memory by default unless forced into low memory with the /L option.

The /S option is a useful tool that can be used to analyze the performance of SMARTDRV. Output from invoking SMARTDRV /S will look like Figure 5.3. This screen informs us that the cache size is 256KB and remains 256KB while running Windows. This information indicates Windows is not requiring the use of cache for running applications. A *cache miss* indicates that the system did not find required data in the cache, which necessitated a disk read. A *cache hit* indicates a successful read from the cache. Figure 5.3 shows about a 75 percent rate of cache hits. This percentage could be increased by increasing the WinCacheSize, which at 256KB is set below its default and may be too low for optimum performance on this system.

FIGURE 5.3:

Output from the SMARTDRV /S command in DOS 6.22

```
Room for    32 elements of   8,192 bytes each
There have been    1,643 cache hits
      and    498 cache misses

Cache size:    262,144 bytes
Cache size while running Windows:    262,144 bytes

            Disk Caching Status
drive    read cache    write cache    buffering
---------------------------------------------------
  A:        yes            no           no
  B:        yes            no           no
  C:        yes            yes          no
  D:        yes            yes          no
Write behind data will be committed before command prompt returns.
```

> **TIP**
>
> If the drives displayed by SMARTDRV /S all read No under the Buffering column, be sure your CONFIG.SYS file does not contain the /DOUBLE-BUFFER option following a SMARTDRV invocation. The double buffering may be necessary on some older equipment, but if so, the SMARTDRV /S option will reveal that by displaying a least one yes in the buffering column.

Configuring Windows 3.*x*

The Windows interface, as previously discussed, is a graphical interface for DOS. And, as such, it will use the same configuration files (AUTOEXEC.BAT and CONFIG.SYS) that DOS uses. It also has a few of its own. Let's discuss the configuration files that Windows 3.*x* uses and their various options.

Program Configuration Files

Windows stores program configuration information in three main areas: INI files, the Windows Registry, and group files. Each area has its own benefits and configuration issues. Let's look at each of these areas separately.

Initialization (INI) Files

Almost every Windows program has an initialization (INI) file. INI files are simply text files used to store program settings. These files are easily identified by their .INI extension. When an application executes, it reads the INI file, loads the settings into memory, and configures the program according to the settings contained in the file.

INI files are made up of sections and entries. A *section* breaks up an INI file into logical groupings of settings and is denoted within an INI file by a set of square brackets around the name of the section ([*section name*]). Here is an example of a section from an application INI:

`[PREFERENCES]`

On the other hand, an *entry* is one of the application's possible settings and a value for that setting. Entries that control similar settings are grouped together under a section. Here is an example of an entry that you may find under the section example given above:

`USEDEFAULT=ON`

INI files are changed every time you change the application's settings within the program. (You usually change a setting under Options or Preferences.) This change is written to the INI file. The next time you start the application, it reads the INI file and keeps the new setting in the application.

Sometimes, you may not want a particular item to load (when troubleshooting, for example). To prevent a line in an INI file from loading, place a semicolon (;) in front of that entry. This will effectively "REM out" the line, and Windows will ignore the line when the INI file is read. It's also a great way to provide commentary and documentation within an INI file.

In addition to the INI files for applications, Windows has its own set of INI files. Each file contains special settings that control how Windows operates. Windows components use four main INI files:

- WIN.INI
- SYSTEM.INI
- PROGMAN.INI
- CONTROL.INI

WIN.INI contains Windows' environmental settings, which control the general function and appearance of Windows. Any changes you make through the Control Panel application normally get stored here. Wallpaper settings, extension mappings (double-clicking a file with a particular extension opens a particular Windows application), language settings, sound mappings, and general device information are found in WIN.INI.

Listing 5.1 shows a typical WIN.INI file. Table 5.6 details some of the most common sections and entries found in a WIN.INI file and their functions. When an entry immediately follows a section, you can assume that the entry is found in that section in the INI file.

Listing 5.1:   A typical WIN.INI file

```
[windows]
spooler=yes
load=
run=
Beep=yes
NullPort=None
BorderWidth=3
CursorBlinkRate=530
DoubleClickSpeed=452
Programs=com exe bat pif
Documents=
DeviceNotSelectedTimeout=15
TransmissionRetryTimeout=45
KeyboardDelay=2
KeyboardSpeed=31
ScreenSaveActive=0
ScreenSaveTimeOut=120
DosPrint=no
device=Generic / Text Only,TTY,LPT1:
[Desktop]
Pattern=(None)
Wallpaper=(None)
```

```
GridGranularity=0
[Extensions]
cal=calendar.exe ^.cal
crd=cardfile.exe ^.crd
trm=terminal.exe ^.trm
txt=notepad.exe ^.txt
ini=notepad.exe ^.ini
pcx=pbrush.exe ^.pcx
bmp=pbrush.exe ^.bmp
wri=write.exe ^.wri
rec=recorder.exe ^.rec
hlp=winhelp.exe ^.hlp
[intl]
sLanguage=enu
sCountry=United States
iCountry=1
iDate=0
iTime=0
iTLZero=0
iCurrency=0
iCurrDigits=2
iNegCurr=0
iLzero=1
iDigits=2
iMeasure=1
s1159=AM
s2359=PM
sCurrency=$
sThousand=,
sDecimal=.
sDate=/
sTime=:
sList=,
sShortDate=M/d/yy
sLongDate=dddd, MMMM dd, yyyy
[ports]
; A line with [filename].PRN followed by an equal sign causes
; [filename] to appear in the Control Panel's Printer Configuration
; dialog
```

```
; box. A printer connected to [filename] directs its output into this
; file.
LPT1:=
LPT2:=
LPT3:=
COM1:=9600,n,8,1,x
COM2:=9600,n,8,1,x
COM3:=9600,n,8,1,x
COM4:=9600,n,8,1,x
EPT:=
FILE:=
LPT1.DOS=
LPT2.DOS=
[FontSubstitutes]
Helv=MS Sans Serif
Tms Rmn=MS Serif
Times=Times New Roman
Helvetica=Arial
[TrueType]
[Sounds]
SystemDefault=ding.wav, Default Beep
SystemExclamation=chord.wav, Exclamation
SystemStart=chimes.wav, Windows Start
SystemExit=chimes.wav, Windows Exit
SystemHand=chord.wav, Critical Stop
SystemQuestion=chord.wav, Question
SystemAsterisk=chord.wav, Asterisk
[mci extensions]
wav=waveaudio
mid=sequencer
rmi=sequencer
[Compatibility]
NOTSHELL=0x0001
WPWINFIL=0x0006
CCMAIL=0x0008
AMIPRO=0x0010
REM=0x8022
PIXIE=0x0040
CP=0x0040
JW=0x42080
```

```
TME=0x0100
VB=0x0200
WIN2WRS=0x1210
PACKRAT=0x0800
VISION=0x0040
MCOURIER=0x0800
_BNOTES=0x24000
MILESV3=0x1000
PM4=0x2000
DESIGNER=0x2000
PLANNER=0x2000
DRAW=0x2000
WINSIM=0x2000
CHARISMA=0x2000
PR2=0x2000
PLUS=0x1000
ED=0x00010000
APORIA=0x0100
EXCEL=0x1000
GUIDE=0x1000
NETSET2=0x0100
W4GL=0x4000
W4GLR=0x4000
TURBOTAX=0x00080000
[fonts]
Arial (TrueType)=ARIAL.FOT
Arial Bold (TrueType)=ARIALBD.FOT
Arial Bold Italic (TrueType)=ARIALBI.FOT
Arial Italic (TrueType)=ARIALI.FOT
Courier New (TrueType)=COUR.FOT
Courier New Bold (TrueType)=COURBD.FOT
Courier New Bold Italic (TrueType)=COURBI.FOT
Courier New Italic (TrueType)=COURI.FOT
Times New Roman (TrueType)=TIMES.FOT
Times New Roman Bold (TrueType)=TIMESBD.FOT
Times New Roman Bold Italic (TrueType)=TIMESBI.FOT
Times New Roman Italic (TrueType)=TIMESI.FOT
WingDings (TrueType)=WINGDING.FOT
MS Sans Serif 8,10,12,14,18,24 (VGA res)=SSERIFE.FON
Courier 10,12,15 (VGA res)=COURE.FON
```

```
MS Serif 8,10,12,14,18,24 (VGA res)=SERIFE.FON
Symbol 8,10,12,14,18,24 (VGA res)=SYMBOLE.FON
Roman (Plotter)=ROMAN.FON
Script (Plotter)=SCRIPT.FON
Modern (Plotter)=MODERN.FON
Small Fonts (VGA res)=SMALLE.FON
Symbol (TrueType)=SYMBOL.FOT
[embedding]
SoundRec=Sound,Sound,SoundRec.exe,picture
Package=Package,Package,packager.exe,picture
PBrush=Paintbrush Picture,Paintbrush Picture,pbrush.exe,picture
[PrinterPorts]
Generic / Text Only=TTY,LPT1:,15,45
[devices]
Generic / Text Only=TTY,LPT1:


[Windows Help]
H_WindowPosition=[213,160,213,160,0]
M_WindowPosition=[188,-14,425,476,0]
```

TABLE 5.6: Common WIN.INI sections and entries

Section or Entry	Function
[Windows]	Contains general Windows environmental parameters for items such as the mouse, keyboard, printers, and monitors
load=filename	Automatically runs the program specified in filename when Windows starts up. This program will run as if Minimize on Use has been set for that program. You can include multiple programs on this line
run=filename	This entry is similar to load=, but instead of running the programs minimized, it runs them normally. Items placed in the Startup group get an entry on this line. You can include multiple programs on this line as well
[Desktop]	Contains settings that relate to Windows' desktop appearance, including items such as wallpaper, icon spacing, desktop patterns, and icon appearance. You can also make entries in this section using the Desktop control panel

TABLE 5.6 (CONTINUED): Common WIN.INI sections and entries

Section or Entry	Function
[Extensions]	Tells Windows which extensions on a file should use which applications. The general format for these commands is *extension= application ^.extension*. For example, to associate text files with the Notepad application, make an entry such as TXT=NOTEPAD .EXE ^.TXT
[intl]	Contains entries for Windows' international settings, including items such as default language, country, time zone, currency character, type of measuring system (standard or metric), and keyboard layouts for the different language characters. You can also make entries in this section using the International control panel
[ports]	Defines the logical ports that Windows can use. You can define up to ten ports. If Windows doesn't have a port defined here, it can't use a device on that port, even if the device is hooked up correctly
[FontSubstitutes]	Substitutes known Windows fonts for known non-Windows fonts that are similar. For example, one entry specifies that the Macintosh font Times is the same as the Windows font Times New Roman (the Times=Times New Roman entry). If you open a Macintosh file that has been formatted with Times, Windows substitutes Times New Roman in its place
[TrueType]	Sets TrueType options for TrueType fonts. For example, it specifies whether Windows applications will list TrueType fonts in their Font selection dialog boxes
[Sounds]	Specifies which sounds will be used for which events. If you have a sound card installed in your PC and Windows is set up to use it, you can assign sounds to various system events. You can also modify this section using the Sounds control panel
[mci extensions]	This section is very similar to the [Extensions] section, except that this section associates certain extensions with their multimedia applications. For example, the entry wav=waveaudio associates any .WAV files with the waveaudio application that is set up to play this type of file.
[Compatibility]	Contains a list of programs that are somewhat compatible with Windows 3.1 and the operational changes Windows has to make when running these programs. You should never need to change this section. Installation programs may possibly make changes here
[fonts]	Contains a list of the font names that Windows loads when it starts up and their associated filenames. You can also modify this section using the Fonts control panel

TABLE 5.6 (CONTINUED): Common WIN.INI sections and entries

Section or Entry	Function
[embedding]	Contains Object Linking and Embedding (OLE) information, which is used when some programs need to communicate with each other—for example, when one program needs to update a picture in another program
[PrinterPorts]	Contains a list of the available printers. This is the list that pops up in an application when you select Print. The information contained here specifies the name of the printer driver, the printer port it's attached to, and the timeout information. You can also modify this section using the Printers control panel
[devices]	This section is almost a duplicate of the [PrinterPorts] section, except that the information is slightly different: it contains only the driver name, driver file, and port. It exists to provide compatibility with older, Windows 2.*x* applications
[Windows Help]	Specifies the location of the various Help windows on-screen. You can also modify this section by bringing up the Help windows and dragging them to a different position on-screen
[network]	Contains information about the network resources Windows uses and how to reconnect network drives and printers at startup time (and if it is necessary to do so). You can also modify this section using the Network control panel
[colors]	Defines the color scheme for Windows components (if different from the default). Lists each component and the color values for each component as a code of Red, Green, and Blue. You can also modify this section using the Colors control panel

NOTE

The list in Table 5.6 is by no means comprehensive. These sections and entries are the most important ones (the ones that may be on the test).

The second Windows INI file, SYSTEM.INI, contains Windows configuration settings. Settings for most of the hardware that Windows uses can be found here. This file is probably the most important INI file because it contains the majority of the information on Windows configuration and most of the drivers that

Windows uses. If a new hardware device is installed, an entry for its driver is made in SYSTEM.INI so that Windows can communicate with it.

Listing 5.2 shows a typical SYSTEM.INI file. Table 5.7 details some of the most common sections and entries in SYSTEM.INI.

Listing 5.2:   **A typical SYSTEM.INI file**

```
[boot]
shell=progman.exe
mouse.drv=MOUSE.DRV
network.drv=
language.dll=
sound.drv=mmsound.drv
comm.drv=comm.drv
keyboard.drv=keyboard.drv
system.drv=system.drv
386grabber=vga.3gr
oemfonts.fon=vgaoem.fon
286grabber=vgacolor.2gr
fixedfon.fon=vgafix.fon
fonts.fon=vgasys.fon
display.drv=vga.drv
drivers=mmsystem.dll
[keyboard]
subtype=
type=4
keyboard.dll=
oemansi.bin=
[boot.description]
keyboard.typ=Enhanced 101 or 102 key US and Non US keyboards
mouse.drv=Microsoft, or IBM PS/2
network.drv=No Network Installed
language.dll=English (American)
system.drv=MS-DOS System
codepage=437
woafont.fon=English (437)
aspect=100,96,96
```

```
display.drv=VGA
[386Enh]
mouse=*VMD
network=*dosnet,*vnetbios
ebios=*ebios
woafont=dosapp.fon
display=*vddvga
EGA80WOA.FON=EGA80WOA.FON
EGA40WOA.FON=EGA40WOA.FON
CGA80WOA.FON=CGA80WOA.FON
CGA40WOA.FON=CGA40WOA.FON
32BitDiskAccess=OFF
device=*int13
device=*wdctrl
keyboard=*vkd
device=vtdapi.386
device=*vpicd
device=vtda.386
device=*reboot
device=*vdmad
device=*vsd
device=*v86mmgr
device=*pageswap
device=*dosmgr
device=*vmpoll
device=*wshell
device=*BLOCKDEV
device=*PAGEFILE
device=*vfd
device=*parity
device=*biosxlat
device=*vcd
device=*vmcpd
device=*combuff
device=*cdpscsi
local=CON
FileSysChange=off
PermSwapDOSDrive=C
PermSwapSizeK=118756
[standard]
```

```
[NonWindowsApp]
localtsrs=dosedit,ced
[mci]
WaveAudio=mciwave.drv
Sequencer=mciseq.drv
CDAudio=mcicda.drv
[drivers]
timer=timer.drv
midimapper=midimap.drv
```

TABLE 5.7: Common SYSTEM.INI sections and entries

Section or Entry	Use	Function
[boot]	[boot]	Details the parameters needed for system startup, including drivers, system fonts, and the Windows shell. You can also make entries to this section using the Windows SETUP program
shell=filename	shell=PROGMAN.EXE	Details which Windows program the user will use to run programs and interact with Windows. You can change this entry if you don't want to use the Program Manager (PROGMAN.EXE), but the program you include in the entry must be able to do the things you would normally do with the Program Manager. If you include CLOCK.EXE, for example, you won't be able to do anything except look at the clock. When you close the Clock program, Windows exits
[keyboard]	[keyboard]	Specifies which keyboard settings are used if the keyboard isn't a U.S. English keyboard. Other types of keyboards (for example, a Spanish keyboard) have a special DLL file that needs to be loaded so that the keyboard can work (an entry will be included in this section). You can also modify the entries in this section by changing the Keyboard entry in the Windows SETUP program
[boot.description]	[boot.description]	Maps English descriptions to the drivers for the various devices in Windows. These descriptions can be seen in SETUP

TABLE 5.7 (CONTINUED):   Common SYSTEM.INI sections and entries

Section or Entry	Use	Function
[386Enh]	[386Enh]	These settings apply only in 386Enhanced mode. Drivers in this section control how Windows uses virtual memory, hard disk access, and other items. Any items that contain an asterisk (*) are virtual device drivers. These drivers are built into the WIN386.EXE file and provide access to basic Windows services
32bitDiskAccess=	32bitDiskAccess=Off	Controls whether Windows can use 32-bit disk access. If this entry is set to ON, Windows will try to access the disk directly, bypassing the computer's BIOS. This increases Windows performance. Most computers can use this option (any computers that are compatible with the WD1003 disk controller). If you activate this option and Windows hangs during startup, your disk controller is not 100 percent compatible with WD1003. You can also modify this setting in the 386Enhanced control panel in the Virtual Memory dialog box
device=*int13 device=*wdctrl	device=*int13 device=*wdctrl	These two virtual device driver entries are added to SYSTEM.INI when SETUP detects that a WD1003-compatible disk controller capable of 32-bit disk access is installed. These entries work with the 32bitDiskAccess =ON entry in the same section to provide Windows with 32-bit disk access
EMMExclude= address range	EMMEXCLUDE= CD000-CDFFF	Corresponds to any exclusions made on the command line of EMM386 in CONFIG.SYS. If you make an exclusion with EMM386 .EXE (for example, DEVICE=EMM386.EXE X =CD000-CDFFF), you have to put the same entry in the [386Enh] section in SYSTEM.INI if you want Windows to behave correctly
NoEMMDriver=On/Off	NoEMMDriver=On	Set this entry to ON when you don't have EMS memory installed (or aren't using an EMS driver such as EMM386.EXE). Windows will not use any expanded memory

TABLE 5.7 (CONTINUED):   Common SYSTEM.INI sections and entries

Section or Entry	Use	Function
[Standard]	[Standard]	Contains settings that Windows uses only when it runs in Standard mode
[NonWindowsApp]	[NonWindowsApp]	Controls parameters for DOS sessions. Some of these settings are taken care of if you use a PIF file
MouseInDosBox=0/1	MouseInDosBox=1	Affects whether a mouse can be used within a DOS application running in Windows. When you set this entry to 1, a mouse can be used in the application while it's running in Windows. When you set this entry to 0, mouse support in the DOS box is disabled
[drivers]	[drivers]	Contains entries for Windows drivers for various hardware devices. It usually contains an entry for the system timer (TIMER.DRV)

As already discussed, the Program Manager contains all the icons for all the programs you may want to run. PROGMAN.INI contains two major sections: [Settings] and [Groups]. [Settings] contains specific settings for the Program Manager (such as which driver it uses and where the Program Manager window is located on the screen). [Groups] contains a list of the Program Manager group files that the Program Manager uses to display icons. Any new groups created in the Program Manager automatically get entries in PROGMAN.INI.

Listing 5.3 shows a typical PROGMAN.INI file. Table 5.8 details the most common settings placed into it.

Listing 5.3:   **A typical PROGMAN.INI file**

```
[Settings]
Window=68 48 580 384 1
display.drv=vga.drv
Order=1 6 2 4 5 3 7
[Groups]
Group1=C:\WINDOWS\MAIN.GRP
Group2=C:\WINDOWS\ACCESSOR.GRP
Group3=C:\WINDOWS\GAMES.GRP
Group4=C:\WINDOWS\STARTUP.GRP
Group5=C:\WINDOWS\APPLICAT.GRP
```

TABLE 5.8:   Common PROGMAN.INI sections and entries

Section or Entry	Use	Function
[Settings]	[Settings]	Details the overall settings for the Program Manager. Settings such as the Program Manager window's position and the driver used can be found and changed here. This section is updated when you make changes to the Program Manager
[Groups]	[Groups]	Detail which program groups will show up in the Program Manager. Every program group that appears in the Program Manager has an entry in this section, including the name of its group file. (See "Program Manager Group Files" later in this chapter.) This section is updated when a new program group is created

The Control Panel application is used to change several settings—the settings that are changed most often are the ones that affect Windows' appearance. The Color and Desktop control panels are the most popular ones. The settings for these two control panels are contained in CONTROL.INI.

CONTROL.INI contains the different colors, patterns, and color schemes that Windows can use. When a user changes any of these items, CONTROL.INI is updated with the changes. Listing 5.4

shows a typical CONTROL.INI file. Table 5.9 details the most
common sections and entries in CONTROL.INI.

Listing 5.4:   **A typical CONTROL.INI file**

```
[current]
color schemes=Windows Default
[color schemes]
Arizona=804000,FFFFFF,FFFFFF,0,FFFFFF,0,808040,C0C0C0,FFFFFF,4080FF,
➥C0C0C0,0,C0C0C0,C0C0C0,808080,0,808080,808000,FFFFFF,0,FFFFFF
Black Leather Jacket=0,C0C0C0,FFFFFF,0,C0C0C0,0,800040,808080,FFFFFF,
➥808080,808080,0,10E0E0E0,C0C0C0,808080,0,808080,0,FFFFFF,0,FFFFFF
Bordeaux=400080,C0C0C0,FFFFFF,0,FFFFFF,0,800080,C0C0C0,FFFFFF,FF0080,
➥C0C0C0,0,C0C0C0,C0C0C0,808080,0,808080,800080,FFFFFF,0,FFFFFF
Cinnamon=404080,C0C0C0,FFFFFF,0,FFFFFF,0,80,C0C0C0,FFFFFF,80,C0C0C0,
➥0,C0C0C0,C0C0C0,808080,0,808080,80,FFFFFF,0,FFFFFF
Designer=7C7C3F,C0C0C0,FFFFFF,0,FFFFFF,0,808000,C0C0C0,FFFFFF,C0C0C0,
➥C0C0C0,0,C0C0C0,C0C0C0,808080,0,C0C0C0,808000,0,0,FFFFFF
Emerald City=404000,C0C0C0,FFFFFF,0,C0C0C0,0,408000,808040,FFFFFF,
➥408000,808040,0,C0C0C0,C0C0C0,808080,0,808080,8000,FFFFFF,0,FFFFFF
Fluorescent=0,FFFFFF,FFFFFF,0,FF00,0,FF00FF,C0C0C0,0,FF80,C0C0C0,0,
➥C0C0C0,C0C0C0,808080,0,808080,0,FFFFFF,0,FFFFFF
Hotdog Stand=FFFF,FFFF,FF,FFFFFF,FFFFFF,0,0,FF,FFFFFF,FF,FF,0,
➥C0C0C0,C0C0C0,808080,0,808080,0,FFFFFF,FFFFFF,FFFFFF
LCD Default Screen Settings=808080,C0C0C0,C0C0C0,0,C0C0C0,0,800000,
➥C0C0C0,FFFFFF,800000,C0C0C0,0,C0C0C0,C0C0C0,7F8080,0,808080,800000,
➥FFFFFF,0,FFFFFF
LCD Reversed - Dark=0,80,80,FFFFFF,8080,0,8080,800000,0,8080,800000,
➥0,8080,C0C0C0,7F8080,0,C0C0C0,800000,FFFFFF,828282,FFFFFF
LCD Reversed - Light=800000,FFFFFF,FFFFFF,0,FFFFFF,0,808040,FFFFFF,
➥0,C0C0C0,C0C0C0,800000,C0C0C0,C0C0C0,7F8080,0,808040,800000,FFFFFF,
➥0,FFFFFF
Mahogany=404040,C0C0C0,FFFFFF,0,FFFFFF,0,40,C0C0C0,FFFFFF,C0C0C0,C0C0
➥C0,0,C0C0C0,C0C0C0,808080,0,C0C0C0,80,FFFFFF,0,FFFFFF
Monochrome=C0C0C0,FFFFFF,FFFFFF,0,FFFFFF,0,0,C0C0C0,FFFFFF,C0C0C0,C0C
➥0C0,0,808080,C0C0C0,808080,0,808080,0,FFFFFF,0,FFFFFF
Ocean=808000,408000,FFFFFF,0,FFFFFF,0,804000,C0C0C0,FFFFFF,C0C0C0,C0C
➥0C0,0,C0C0C0,C0C0C0,808080,0,0,808000,0,0,FFFFFF
```

```
Pastel=C0FF82,80FFFF,FFFFFF,0,FFFFFF,0,FFFF80,FFFFFF,0,C080FF,FFFFFF,
➥808080,C0C0C0,C0C0C0,808080,0,C0C0C0,FFFF00,0,0,FFFFFF
Patchwork=9544BB,C1FBFA,FFFFFF,0,FFFFFF,0,FFFF80,FFFFFF,0,64B14E,
➥FFFFFF,0,C0C0C0,C0C0C0,808080,0,808080,FFFF00,0,0,FFFFFF
Plasma Power Saver=0,FF0000,0,FFFFFF,FF00FF,0,800000,C0C0C0,0,80,
➥FFFFFF,C0C0C0,FF0000,C0C0C0,808080,0,C0C0C0,FFFFFF,0,0,FFFFFF
Rugby=C0C0C0,80FFFF,FFFFFF,0,FFFFFF,0,800000,FFFFFF,FFFFFF,80,FFFFFF,
➥0,C0C0C0,C0C0C0,808080,0,808080,800000,FFFFFF,0,FFFFFF
The Blues=804000,C0C0C0,FFFFFF,0,FFFFFF,0,800000,C0C0C0,FFFFFF,C0C0C0,
➥C0C0C0,0,C0C0C0,C0C0C0,808080,0,C0C0C0,800000,FFFFFF,0,FFFFFF
Tweed=6A619E,C0C0C0,FFFFFF,0,FFFFFF,0,408080,C0C0C0,FFFFFF,404080,
➥C0C0C0,0,10E0E0E0,C0C0C0,808080,0,C0C0C0,8080,0,0,FFFFFF
Valentine=C080FF,FFFFFF,FFFFFF,0,FFFFFF,0,8000FF,400080,FFFFFF,C080F,
➥C080FF,0,C0C0C0,C0C0C0,808080,0,808080,FF00FF,0,FFFFFF,FFFFFF
Wingtips=408080,C0C0C0,FFFFFF,0,FFFFFF,0,808080,FFFFFF,FFFFFF,4080,
➥FFFFFF,0,808080,C0C0C0,808080,0,C0C0C0,808080,FFFFFF,0,FFFFFF
[Custom Colors]
ColorA=FFFFFF
ColorB=FFFFFF
ColorC=FFFFFF
ColorD=FFFFFF
ColorE=FFFFFF
ColorF=FFFFFF
ColorG=FFFFFF
ColorH=FFFFFF
ColorI=FFFFFF
ColorJ=FFFFFF
ColorK=FFFFFF
ColorL=FFFFFF
ColorM=FFFFFF
ColorN=FFFFFF
ColorO=FFFFFF
ColorP=FFFFFF
[Patterns]
(None)=(None)
Boxes=127 65 65 65 65 65 127 0
Paisley=2 7 7 2 32 80 80 32
Weave=136 84 34 69 136 21 34 81
Waffle=0 0 0 0 128 128 128 240
Tulip=0 0 84 124 124 56 146 124
```

```
Spinner=20 12 200 121 158 19 48 40
Scottie=64 192 200 120 120 72 0 0
Critters=0 80 114 32 0 5 39 2
50% Gray=170 85 170 85 170 85 170 85
Quilt=130 68 40 17 40 68 130 1
Diamonds=32 80 136 80 32 0 0 0
Thatches=248 116 34 71 143 23 34 113
Pattern=224 128 142 136 234 10 14 0
[installed]
3.1=yes
TTY.DRV=yes
TTY.HLP=yes
[MMCPL]
NumApps=12
X=44
Y=44
W=430
H=240
```

TABLE 5.9: Common CONTROL.INI section and entries

Section or Entry	Use	Function
[current]	[current]	Specifies which color scheme is currently used
[color schemes]	[color schemes]	Specifies the color schemes that Windows can use and the colors for the various items in Windows. The hexadecimal numbers after the style names are separated by commas. Each hexadecimal number represents a particular color for a particular item in Windows. You can make additional entries to this section using the Color control panel
[patterns]	[patterns]	Defines the various patterns that can be used for the desktop. You can also modify this section using the Desktop control panel
[installed]	[installed]	Contains the Windows version number and lists installed printer drivers and DLL files
3.1=?	3.1=Yes	If set to Yes, indicates that Windows 3.1 is installed
[MMPCL]	[MMPCL]	Defines settings for multimedia devices

> **TIP**
> INI files can be edited with any ASCII text editor (including the DOS EDIT command and NOTEPAD.EXE in Windows). Some INI files can be edited with the SYSEDIT utility, which will be discussed in "Windows Configuration Utilities" later in this chapter.

The Registry

Configuration information is also stored in a special configuration database known as *the Registry*. This centralized database contains environmental settings for various Windows programs. It also contains what is known as *registration* information, which details which types of file extensions are associated with which applications. So, when you double-click a file in File Manager, the associated application runs and opens the file you double-clicked.

The Registry is unique in a couple of ways. First, it is a database. Most of the configuration files that have been discussed so far have been ASCII text files, which can be edited with almost any text editor. However, the Registry database is contained in a special binary file named REG.DAT, which can be edited only with the special Registry Editor provided with Windows. The Registry Editor program is called REGEDIT.EXE, and its icon is not typically created during Windows installation—you must create the icon manually. You can also run the program manually by choosing File➤ Run from the Program Manager, typing **REGEDIT**, and clicking OK.

Once you have successfully run REGEDIT.EXE, you will see a screen similar to the one shown in Figure 5.4. This screen lists the types of files that have been registered with Windows. This registration is another difference between INI files and the Registry. When a program is installed, the installation program registers the file types with the Registry database so that Windows is familiar with the file types that the application uses. INI files just store the configuration information. If you want the information to be centralized, you have to edit the WIN.INI or SYSTEM.INI file.

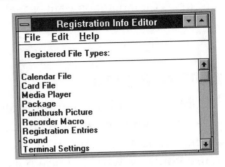

FIGURE 5.4:

REGEDIT.EXE window

> **NOTE** Windows 95 extensively uses the Registry to store all kinds of information. In Windows 95, it replaces the functionality of SYSTEM.INI and WIN.INI and holds most, if not all, of the configuration information for Windows 95. It is a major task to modify the Registry in Windows 95—you should try it only under the direction of a Technical Support Engineer.

Program Manager Group Files

Program Manager group files are the files in the Windows directory (for example, C:\WINDOWS) that store information about which application icons are contained in which Program Manager groups. Group filenames always have a .GRP extension and names similar to their actual program group names. The names may be truncated to fit within the DOS naming convention of eight letters, a period, and a three-letter extension. For example, the Accessories group has a group file named ACCESSOR.GRP, and the Main group has a group file named MAIN.GRP.

You cannot edit group files with a text editor. You must make an icon in the associated program group in Program Manager. When you add an icon to a program group, the group file is updated with information such as the path to the application, the name of the icon, the icon's picture, and the icon's position within the group.

When you delete a program group in Program Manager, the group file gets deleted as well.

TIP

If a program group gets deleted from the Program Manager accidentally and you have a backup of the group file, you can restore the program group without needing to create new icons. First, copy the group file back into the Windows directory. Then, select File ➤ New in Program Manager. When asked whether you want to create a group or an icon, select Group. Finally, instead of typing a new name for the group, type the name of the group file (for example, TEST.GRP) and click OK. The group will be created with its old name, and all the icons will be exactly where they were (as of the last backup).

Font Files

Font files are one of the Windows components that receive very little attention (and people know very little about them). Fonts (also called *typefaces*) are different ways of presenting letters. A font usually has a name and a size. The size is measured in points (a point is 1/72 of an inch). Several fonts come with Windows, and you can add several more using the Fonts control panel. Figure 5.5 shows some examples of the fonts that came with Windows 3.1. Font files are stored in C:\WINDOWS\SYSTEM (unless Windows was installed in a different directory).

FIGURE 5.5:

Font examples

```
Arial
Courier
Courier New
Modern
MS Sans Serif
Σψμβολ  ("Symbol")
System
Times New Roman
♦✗■ℽ⟡♦✗■ℽ⟡♦ ("WingDings")
```

Windows uses three main types of font files: raster fonts, vector fonts, and printer fonts. Each type has a specific use.

Raster Fonts

Raster fonts (also called *bitmap* or *screen* fonts) are designed pixel by pixel, and each size family is stored as a separate file (for example, 12-point fonts are stored in one file, 10-point fonts in another). These fonts display quickly and are great for viewing text on-screen. You cannot scale a raster font without losing image quality (the letters will look as if they were drawn with blocks instead of smooth, continuous lines), and you cannot rotate them. Typically, these files have a .FON extension.

The main disadvantage of raster fonts is that you must have the font file installed for the type and size you need to display (for example, if you need to display 12-point Arial, you must have the .FON file for that type and size installed on your system). This problem was addressed with the introduction of vector fonts.

Vector Fonts

Vector fonts (also called *scalable* or *TrueType* fonts) are stored as mathematical formulas. When a vector font is displayed, Windows reads the instructions in the formula—for example, *draw a line from X to Y, then from Y to Z, then from A to B.* (See Figure 5.6 for an illustration of this process.) To enlarge the font size, Windows just moves A, B, X, Y, and Z farther apart (also shown in Figure 5.6). These fonts scale and rotate well. However, they are more complex and take more time for Windows to process so that they can be displayed. TrueType fonts have the extensions .TTF and .FOT. One file of each type must be installed on the system for each TrueType font Windows uses.

FIGURE 5.6:

Drawing a vector font

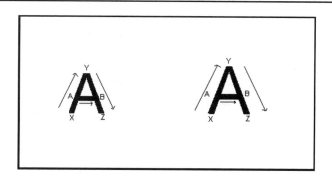

Printer Fonts

Printer font files contain the instructions that the printer needs to print a particular font. There are three types of printer fonts

- Device fonts

- Printable screen fonts

- Soft fonts

Device Fonts *Device* fonts (also called *hardware* fonts) print the quickest because the routines needed to draw these fonts are stored inside the printer. These fonts are either hardwired in the printer's control circuitry or added through a removable cartridge.

Printable Screen Fonts It is difficult to find a device font for some of the TrueType and bitmap fonts. In these cases, the screen font is translated into a printer font by Windows and downloaded to the printer. This type of printer font is called a *printable screen font*. These fonts are the regular fonts used to display text on-screen (either raster or vector fonts) but are translated and downloaded to the printer so that they can be printed. Printable screen fonts are probably the most popular type of font for the average user. Their main advantage is that they allow any screen font to be printed. Their main disadvantage is that this process takes resources away from Windows. If you print a several-page document with only printable screen fonts, it may take longer than it would with only screen and printer fonts.

Soft Fonts *Soft* fonts come on a disk and are downloaded via a special utility to the printer's memory or hard disk. (Some printers have hard disks on which they store fonts and print jobs.) Soft fonts usually include a screen font.

Most publishers use a combination of screen fonts and either device or soft printer fonts. To use a font in a design program, you must make sure that both the screen and printer fonts for that typeface are available. If they aren't, the screen font will be translated and downloaded to the printer, and the printing process will take several minutes longer.

Windows Configuration Utilities

Windows configuration utilities are a class of Windows components that don't get much attention. These utilities are provided by Microsoft to make managing Windows parameters easier. There are two main utilities used for this purpose: SYSEDIT.EXE and the Windows PIF Editor.

SYSEDIT.EXE

Often, you have to modify DOS and Windows configuration files simultaneously. For this reason, Microsoft included the SYSEDIT .EXE program (see Figure 5.7). This utility typically doesn't have an icon created for it during installation. However, you *can* create an icon for it. It's located in the C:\WINDOWS\SYSTEM directory. You can also run the utility by choosing File ≻ Run in the Program Manager.

FIGURE 5.7:

SYSEDIT.EXE's main screen

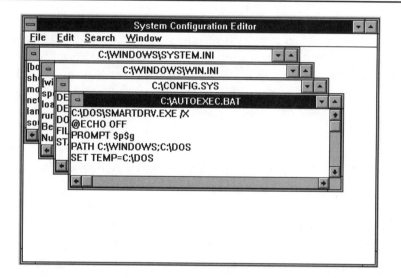

In Figure 5.7, notice that the only files SYSEDIT.EXE can edit are SYSTEM.INI, WIN.INI, and DOS's CONFIG.SYS and AUTOEXEC .BAT. All other configuration files must be edited by some other means (using either DOS's EDIT.COM or the Windows Notepad).

To edit any of the files listed above, just click the window that represents the file you wish to edit. Then, make the change (delete an entry, add an entry, or modify an entry). To make the change permanent, choose File ≻ Save. Or, exit the program and select Yes when SYSEDIT.EXE asks you whether you want to save the changes you made.

TIP   The SYSEDIT.EXE program can also give you information about available system resources. Choose File ➢ About. At the bottom of the dialog box that appears, you will see the amount of system resources available (as a percentage).

PIF Editor

A common practice these days is to run DOS applications in Windows, as shown in Figure 5.8. There are no special requirements to run a DOS application in Windows. (Although, if you want a DOS application to show within a window instead of full-screen, you must run Windows in 386Enhanced mode.) However, some older DOS applications try to access hardware directly instead of going through the operating system and BIOS. If this type of application tries to run in Windows, Windows may not know how to handle it.

FIGURE 5.8:

Running a DOS application (EDIT.COM) in Windows

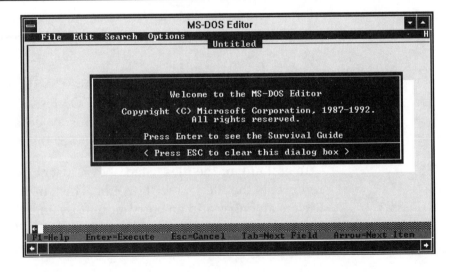

For this reason, Windows includes a utility for making *program information files* (PIFs), which tell Windows how to handle DOS applications that try to run in the Windows environment. PIF files are associated with a DOS application and have .PIF extensions. The PIF Editor (found in the Main program group) is the utility used to create these files.

NOTE   If a DOS application doesn't have its own PIF file, Windows will use the settings from a PIF file called _DEFAULT.PIF (located in the C:\ WINDOWS directory).

When you first open the PIF Editor, you will see a screen similar to the one shown in Figure 5.9. Notice that there are several options for making a DOS application run in Windows. Some settings (such as any settings that relate to memory) are crucial, while others don't affect the way the application runs—they are simply cosmetic (such as the Windows Title setting).

FIGURE 5.9:

The PIF Editor's main screen

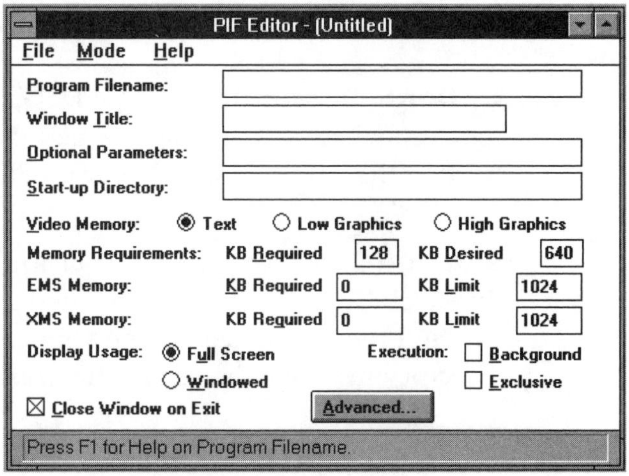

NOTE   You will see the screen shown in Figure 5.9 only if you run Windows in 386Enhanced mode and are making a PIF file to run in 386Enhanced mode. You can change the PIF file type by selecting an operating mode from the Mode menu.

Let's discuss each setting and what it does. If you need more details, press F1 while in the PIF Editor—the Windows PIF Editor Help program will give you a description of the parameter and how to use it.

Program Filename   This field should include the name and path of the DOS executable. When you double-click the icon for this executable in Windows, Windows looks for the application specified in this field.

Window Title   This field specifies the text that appears at the top of the window when running the application in Windows. In Figure 5.8 (shown earlier in the chapter), this field has been filled in (in the PIF Editor for EDIT.COM) with MS-DOS Editor.

Optional Parameters   Some DOS applications require parameters (or switches) after their name to run properly. Instead of putting the parameters in Program Filename, put them here.

Start-up Directory   Some DOS applications require a working directory. This directory is specified so that the DOS application can find the files it needs. The application usually uses the same directory in which the application resides.

Video Memory   This setting specifies the video mode the DOS application uses in Windows. It also specifies how much memory the video portion takes. Text mode uses the least amount of memory;

High Graphics mode uses the most. If you are unsure of which mode to use, check the documentation for the application. This setting is important—if you don't give the application enough memory, it may hang or scramble the video display when switching between the DOS application and Windows. Or, it may not run at all.

Memory Requirements   This setting specifies how much conventional memory the application requires. There are two values here: KB Required and KB Desired. The amount *required* is how much available conventional memory the manufacturer recommends. The amount *desired* is usually set to 640 so that the application uses as much conventional memory as is available.

EMS Memory   This setting is similar to Memory Requirements, except that these fields specify the minimum amount of expanded memory the application needs and the maximum amount it can use.

XMS Memory   This setting is also similar to Memory Requirements, except that it is used for extended memory.

Display Usage   This radio button specifies how the application runs, either using the whole display (Full Screen) or running in a window (Windowed). This setting is important—the Windowed mode requires more resources from Windows and isn't as efficient (but it's easier to switch between Windows and DOS applications). No matter which setting you've specified, you can usually switch between Windowed and Full Screen mode by holding down the Alt key and pressing Enter.

Execution   This setting specifies how Windows treats this application with regard to the multitasking abilities of Windows. When the Background option is checked, this application continues to run in the background, even if it is not the active application. For example, this option allows you to switch to another program in Windows while this application calculates a long list of numbers. When the Exclusive option is checked, no other application can run in the background while this application is active (even DOS applications with PIF files that have the Background option checked). You can check one or both of these options.

Close Window on Exit   This option controls what happens to the window when you exit the DOS application from its own menus (for example, by pressing Esc or Ctrl + Q). If this option is checked, Windows closes the window automatically. If this option is unchecked, Windows leaves the window open and puts the word "Inactive" in front of the application name at the top of the window. To close the window, you must double-click the box in the upper-left corner or click it once and choose Close.

Advanced   The Advanced button opens the window shown in Figure 5.10, which details the 386Enhanced options for the PIF Editor. If you are in Standard mode, this button won't be available. Click it to bring up the next set of PIF options

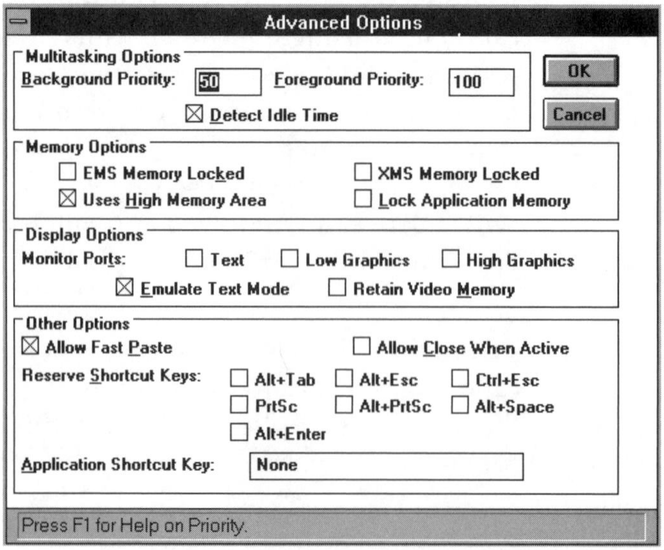

FIGURE 5.10:

The PIF Editor's Advanced Options screen

Multitasking Options These options control how the application receives processor time. The numbers in Background Priority and Foreground Priority specify the priority of receiving processor time (the range of these numbers is 0 to 10,000). If you want the application to receive most of the processor time in one of these situations, set the corresponding value to 10,000.

Background Priority This number specifies the priority of the application when it runs in the background. The larger the number, the more processor time the application receives when running in the background.

Foreground Priority This number specifies the priority of the application when it runs in the foreground. The larger the number, the more processor time the application receives when running in the foreground as the active application.

Detect Idle Time If this option is checked, another application can steal CPU cycles from this application while waiting for keyboard input. You should keep this option checked most of the time so that other applications can benefit from a user's indecision. If an application hangs while waiting for keyboard input, uncheck this option.

Memory Options These options specify the memory settings unique to running this application in 386Enhanced mode:

EMS Memory Locked When an application is pushed to the background, the information it had in memory is sometimes swapped to the disk. When this option is checked, the information the application had in expanded memory will not be swapped to the disk—it will remain in memory. Most applications don't have a problem with swapping memory. However, if you have an application that does, check this box so that the information stays put.

XMS Memory Locked This option is similar to EMS Memory Locked, except that it prevents the application's extended memory from being swapped to the disk. If this box is unchecked, the application can use Windows' virtual memory. However, some DOS applications don't like memory swapping and may crash if this option is unchecked, especially if the application tries to directly access memory instead of going through DOS.

Lock Application Memory When this option is checked, it performs the same functions as EMS Memory Locked and XMS Memory Locked, except that it functions for conventional memory. It prevents the application's conventional memory from being swapped to the disk when the application goes to the background.

Uses High Memory Area This option allows the application to use the High Memory Area (HMA). Most recent DOS applications have access to the DOS HMA, but only if there is nothing loaded there. If the HMA is available when Windows starts, the DOS application can allocate its own HMA. If the HMA is unavailable when Windows starts, uncheck this box so that the application won't try to use HMA.

Display Options These options specify how an application uses video in Windows in 386Enhanced mode:

Monitor Ports This setting specifies whether Windows can verify the settings that the application uses for video while it runs in a particular mode. For example, if Text is checked, Windows will monitor all video transactions that the application makes while in Text mode. If there is a problem, Windows tries to correct the display. If you have problems switching between graphics modes, check the option that corresponds to the mode that has the problem. If none of these options are checked, the application can access the full-screen display quicker.

Emulate Text Mode Some DOS applications run in Text mode and display information using standard ROM BIOS services for output. If your application does this, check this box to increase the speed of the video display. If you get garbage on your screen when you display information in the application, uncheck this option.

Retain Video Memory When this option is unchecked, it allows Windows to allocate the memory given to the DOS application for displaying information to other applications when the DOS application is in the background. If this option is checked, the memory is allocated to the DOS application for video memory and is not given back to the system until the application is closed.

Other Options This is the miscellaneous section of the PIF Editor. It contains the options that don't fit into any of the other areas:

Allow Fast Paste This option allows Windows to use a faster method of pasting information from the Windows Clipboard to the DOS application. Some applications can handle this faster method, others cannot. Test it by trying to paste information from the Clipboard to the application. If it works, you can use this option.

Allow Close When Active This option allows you to make Windows automatically force the application to shut down when you close Windows. This is dangerous because an application that is forcibly shut down can corrupt data. Never use this option for applications that consistently use the hard disk (such as word processors or graphics-intensive applications).

Reserve Shortcut Keys These checkboxes deactivate the selected key combinations in Windows so that when the key combinations are pressed, they perform a function in the DOS application rather than in Windows. If you use a DOS word processor, you may have to reserve several of these key combinations. Check the box next to the key combination that you want the DOS application to be able to use.

Application Shortcut Key This option allows you to start a DOS application from within Windows by typing a key combination. To set the key combination, click within this field and press the keys that you want to use to start the application (the key combination that you press can't already be used by another application). As you press the keys, their names are displayed in this field.

When you are finished entering settings for the application, save the PIF file with a name similar to the name of the application (for example, if the DOS application is called FURBLE.EXE, you should name the PIF file something like FURBLE.PIF). To finish, make an icon for the PIF file in the Program Manager. When you double-click the PIF file, Windows runs the DOS application with the settings contained in the PIF file.

NOTE   Before you create your own PIF file for a DOS application, check the installation directory for an existing PIF file. If there isn't one, check the technical support Web site of the company that made the application for an updated PIF file.

Adding New Hardware and Software to DOS and Windows

When you add new hardware or software to Windows, remember one thing: it will change your configuration. Before you change a machine running Windows, back up your INI files, GRP files, AUTOEXEC.BAT, and CONFIG.SYS, either to a floppy disk or to another directory. If the installation is unsuccessful, you can return the machine to its former state by copying those files back to the correct directories in place of the current, nonworking ones.

Adding New Hardware

When adding new hardware to Windows, there are very few new elements in addition to the ones you encountered when adding new hardware to DOS. The key items that Windows requires so that it can use the new hardware are drivers. If you install a new sound card in the computer and install drivers for DOS, it doesn't necessarily mean that Windows can take advantage of the new hardware. Windows needs its own drivers.

Typically, when you install a new piece of hardware, you will install software immediately after installing the device in the computer. Most installation programs install two portions of software for the new device: the DOS portion and the Windows portion. The DOS portion usually consists of drivers for CONFIG.SYS or AUTOEXEC.BAT and, possibly, one or two DOS utilities. The Windows portion consists of Windows applications needed to use the new device. Usually, there are *no* Windows drivers. Access to the device is provided to the application through its DLL files via their communication to DOS and the device drivers.

Adding New Software

When you add new software to Windows, the process is usually the same as adding new software to DOS. Insert the installation disk into the disk drive. Then, choose File ➤ Run in the Program Manager. When the Run dialog box appears (see Figure 5.11), type **A:\SETUP.EXE** or **A:\INSTALL.EXE**, depending on the application—check your documentation to find out the name of the installation program—to run the installation program. Follow the prompts that appear.

FIGURE 5.11:

The Run dialog box

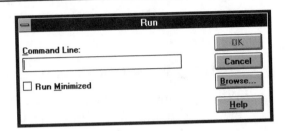

Remember that a new application adds additional INI files and takes up disk space. Some of the Office Suites take up more than 150MB (and that's the Typical installation).

Configuring Windows 95

Because Windows 95 is almost an entirely new operating system, it only shares a few configuration similarities with its ancestors (Windows 3.*x* and DOS) for compatibility's sake. The AUTOEXEC .BAT and CONFIG.SYS are used to a limited extent, but only for older hardware compatibility. Additionally, INI files are still used for some Windows programs to hold configuration settings (again, mostly for older programs).

The registry is still around, and it is used much more than it was in Windows 3.*x*. In addition to software extension information, it also contains software configuration information and hardware configuration information. Generally speaking, most of the Windows 95 settings that were previously stored in INI files are now stored in the Registry.

Let's discuss the Windows 95 configuration files and the tools used to edit them.

Windows 95 Configuration Concepts

The two major types of configuration files are the INI files and the Registry. The INI files are still used in Windows 95, but as previously mentioned, they have a lesser responsibility. Since they are edited the same as they are under Windows 3.x, we won't discuss them here.

The Registry, on the other hand, is used almost exclusively for holding configuration settings. It holds them not only for applications, but also for the system itself. Additionally, it contains different settings for different users.

The Windows 95 Registry is a database that is made up of two files: USER.DAT and SYSTEM.DAT. The USER.DAT contains environmental settings for each user who logs into Windows 95. The SYSTEM.DAT contains information about the hardware configuration of the computer that Windows 95 is running on. Finally, the CONFIG.POL contains security settings about which features of Windows 95 are enabled or disabled for a particular user. This file is used to "lock down" the Windows 95 interface so a user can't change it (useful if you have a user who is constantly changing their settings and messing up their computer).

TIP   The CONFIG.POL file is edited with a utility called the Windows 95 Policy editor. It's located on the Windows 95 installation CD-ROM in the \ADMIN\APPTOOLS\POLEDIT directory.

None of these files are editable with a text editor as they aren't ASCII text files (like AUTOEXEC.BAT, CONFIG.SYS or the INI files). To edit the Windows 95 Registry, you need to use the Registry

Editor (REGEDIT.EXE). To start the editor, Click Start ➤ Run and type **REGEDIT**. Click OK and the Registry Editor will open, allowing you to view the Registry. The screen shown in Figure 5.12 shows a typical registry. On the left side of this screen you will see the areas that the Registry is broken into. Each area (called a *key*) contains different types of settings. Table 5.10 explains these six keys and their functions.

TIP   If you make changes to the Registry, you will have to reboot your computer to have them take effect. The Registry is loaded into memory at startup.

FIGURE 5.12:

A typical REGEDIT screen

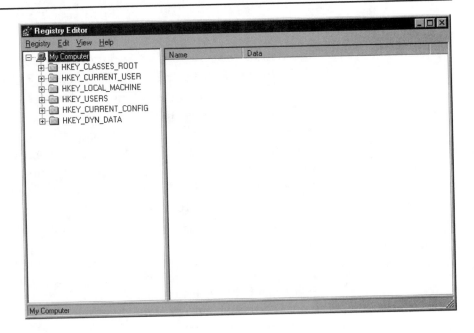

TABLE 5.10: Registry keys and their functions

Key	Description
HKEY_CLASSES_ROOT	Contains file extension associations. This tells Windows when a file with a particular extension should be opened in a particular application. Much of the data in this key is duplicated in the HKEY_LOCAL_MACHINE key
HKEY_CURRENT_USER	Contains user profile information for the person currently logged into Windows. It contains the preferences for color settings and desktop configuration. It is a subset of the HKEY_USERS key (described below)
HKEY_LOCAL_MACHINE	Contains settings and information for the hardware that is installed in the computer. When troubleshooting hardware issues, you might make changes to this section
HKEY_USERS	Contains the default user profile and the profile for the current user (HKEY_CURRENT_USER, described above)
HKEY_CURRENT_CONFIG	Contains the current hardware configuration. This key is a subset of the HKEY_LOCAL_MACHINE (described above)
HKEY_DYN_DATA	Contains the dynamic settings for any Plug-n-Play devices in your computer. This setting is kept in RAM and doesn't require a reboot when changes are made to it

Whenever you need to make changes to the Registry, open REGEDIT. The next step is to locate the subkey (the folders underneath the keys shown) that contains the setting you want to change. You can find it two ways. You can browse to it by clicking on the plus sign (+) next to a folder to display the subkeys inside. Keep clicking until you find the subkey you're looking for. This can take a while because there may be several hundred folders to browse through. The other method is much more logical. In REGEDIT, select Edit ➤ Find (Figure 5.13). Then, type in the string of characters you are looking for and click Find Next. REGEDIT will search the database until it comes across a string that matches what you typed in. If it isn't the one you are looking for, press F3 to find the next entry that contains the string you are looking for.

FIGURE 5.13:

Performing a Find in REGEDIT

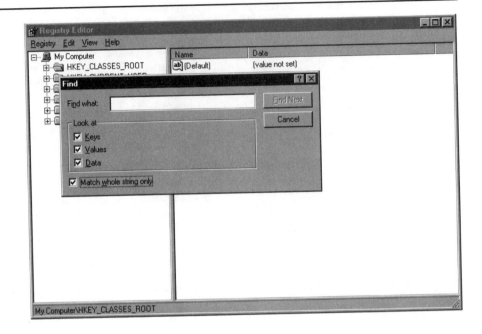

Thankfully, there aren't many times you need to go into the Registry to make changes. Most often, changes you make using the Windows 95 configuration utilities will make changes to the Registry. Let's discuss three of the tools that allow you to make these changes: the Properties menu option, the Control Panels, and the Device Manager.

And Now for the Real World...

If it's not apparent by now, the Registry is very important for correct Windows 95 operation. That's why every time Windows 95 successfully loads the Registry, it makes a backup of the two Registry files: USER.DAT and SYSTEM .DAT. These backup files are called USER.DA0 and SYSTEM.DA0, respectively and can be used to restore a good Registry over one that's

continued on next page

broken. In case of a Registry corruption, boot in Safe Mode Command Line by pressing F8 at system startup and choosing Safe Mode Command Line. Or, boot to a Windows 95 startup disk. Then, rename the Registry files from .DA0 to .DAT and reboot the computer. The Registry will be current as of the last successful boot.

The Properties Screen

You may have noticed that Windows 95 uses the right mouse button much more than Windows 3.*x*. As a matter of fact, almost everything in Windows 95 can be right-clicked (also called *alternate-clicking* or *secondary clicking*). Right-clicking brings up a quick menu (Figure 5.14). You can choose several options from this menu; one of the more important options is Properties.

FIGURE 5.14:

A typical quick menu

Every time you choose Properties you will get a different menu, depending on what you clicked. For example, if you right-clicked on the desktop and chose Properties, it would bring up the Display control panel and allow you to change the settings for the desktop color, background image and so on. If you were to instead right-click the My Computer icon and choose Properties, the System control panel would appear. This control panel allows you to view your systems configuration and change it, if necessary. (We will discuss the System control panel in the next section).

In general, if you want to change the way something operates in Windows 95, try right-clicking on it and choosing Properties. The same is true for programs under Windows 95. In word processors, you can highlight text, right click, and choose from several options, one of which may be Properties. This may bring up a screen that will allow you to choose typestyles, font sizes, and font colors as well as other settings.

Control Panel

The Control Panel folder (found under Start ➢ Settings) is used to configure most aspects of Windows 95. When you open the Control Panel, you will see a screen similar to the one in Figure 5.15. Different systems will have different control panels, but there are a few that are common between all. Table 5.11 describes a few of the most common control panels and their uses.

FIGURE 5.15:

The Windows 95 Control Panel folder

TABLE 5.11:   Common Control Panels and their uses

Control Panel	Description
Accessibility Options	Configures special needs options for Windows 95 like sticky keys (allows you to press a modifier key, then a key, in succession, without holding both down)
Add New Hardware	Used for installing and configuring new hardware (described later in this chapter)
Add/Remove Programs	Used for adding/removing Windows 95 components as well as uninstalling installed software
Date/Time	Used to change the date and time of the computer
Display	This control panel is used to configure settings that relate to the "look" of Windows 95. This includes resolution, color settings, screen savers, and desktop wallpaper
Fonts	Displays the fonts that are currently installed in the computer
Internet	This control panel is installed with the Windows 95 Plus Pack. It is used to configure Internet Explorer and Windows 95 dial up to the Internet
Joystick	If your computer has a joystick attached to it, you can use this control panel to configure it for use with Windows 95
Keyboard	Used to set keyboard settings like key repeat rate, keyboard language, and type of keyboard
Mail and Fax	If any of the mail software is installed, you will see this control panel. It is used to configure how Windows 95 uses MAPI (Mail Application Programming Interface) with various e-mail services
Modems	This control panel shows a list of the modems configured for use with Windows 95. It also is used to configure how the modem dials (i.e. dial 9 for any outside line, 1 for long distance, etc.)
Mouse	Used to configure the various settings for using a mouse with Windows 95. Settings like double-click speed, pointer size, and mouse button assignment can be done from this control panel
Multimedia	Configures how Windows 95 uses multimedia devices like sound cards and CD-ROM drives
Network	If your computer is going to be networked, refer to this control panel that configures all the networking components including Clients, Protocols, and Network Interface Cards

TABLE 5.11 (CONTINUED): Common Control Panels and their uses

Control Panel	Description
Passwords	Allows you to set and change the password you use to log into Windows. Additionally, it specifies whether or not every user on this PC will use the same desktop settings
PC Card (PCMCIA)	Displays which PC Cards are installed in this computer (if any). This control panel will let you stop a PC card so that you can remove it without causing problems with Windows 95
Power	Configures power management settings like hard disk power down delay and screen dim delay time. Most computers with APM (Advanced Power Management) will support this control panel
Printers	Allows you to configure new or existing printers. This control panel is discussed later in this chapter
Regional Settings	Lets you tell Windows what part of the country it's in. This is important because Windows 95 can change the time and date automatically for daylight savings time as well as configure Windows for the right country settings
Sounds	Allows you to assign sounds to system events like startup, shutdown and application start. (Requires a sound card to work properly)
System	Displays details about the current operating system configuration. You can determine what hardware is installed from the Device Manager tab in this control panel (discussed later in this section)

Device Manager

The *Device Manager* is a graphical view of all the hardware installed in your computer that Windows 95 can detect. You can open it by right-clicking My Computer, choosing Properties, then clicking the Device Manager tab. Or, you can open the System control panel (From Start ➢ Settings ➢ Control Panel) and choose Device Manager. In either case, you will see a screen similar to the one in Figure 5.16.

FIGURE 5.16:

An example of a
Device Manager screen

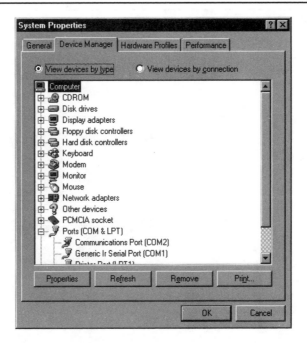

NOTE As you can see, one of the devices (COM2) has an X through it. That is because the COM2 port needed to be disabled so that the modem (which is installed to use COM2) can use it.

The device manager is used to display all the hardware that Windows 95 "knows about" and to configure the hardware settings of those devices. If you click the plus sign (+) next to a category of devices, it will "tree out" that category and allow you to see the devices in that category. If you then click on a device and click Properties, you can view the information about that device. In Figure 5.17, I have selected my network card and clicked Properties. Notice that there are three tabs: General, Driver, and Resources. Most devices will have these tabs (although some devices may only have one or two). The General tab (shown in Figure 5.17) shows general information about the device and status information. It also allows you disable this device in the current hardware profile.

NOTE For more information about hardware profiles, refer to either the Windows 95 Help file or the *Windows 95 Resource Kit* by Microsoft. Don't worry, hardware profiles aren't covered on the exam.

FIGURE 5.17:

Displaying the properties of a device in the Device Manager

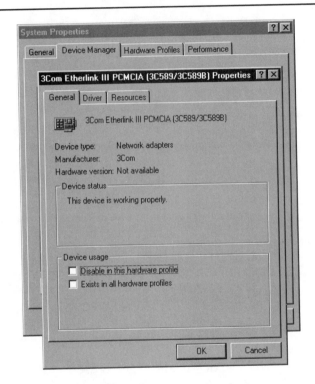

The next tab over is usually the Driver tab (Figure 5.18). This tab allows you to see the driver name for the device as well as its version, if available. You can see in the figure that no drivers have been loaded for this device. That may be true, but in this case, drivers have been loaded but aren't reported to the Device Manager. If you need to load a driver (or update a driver), click the Update Driver... button. Windows 95 will present you with a list of drivers to select from or allow you to install your own from floppy disk or CD-ROM.

FIGURE 5.18:

The Driver tab of a device in the Device Manager

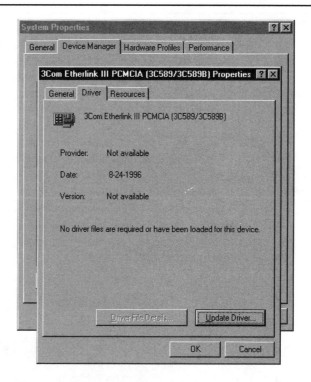

The rightmost tab is usually Resources. From this tab you can view and configure the system resources that the device is using (Figure 5.19). Most often, the check box next to Use Automatic Settings is checked, meaning that Windows 95 Plug-n-Play has determined the settings for the device and is managing it. However, if the device is not a Plug-n-Play device and needs to be configured manually, simply uncheck the Automatic Settings check box. You can then select the setting (i.e., Interrupt Request) and click the Change Setting button to pick the correct setting from a list.

TIP When you configure settings manually, Windows 95 will let you know if the setting you have chosen conflicts with another device. A sharp contrast between 95 and Windows 3.*x*! However, if you are in Safe Mode, this feature can't be used and Windows 95 will not tell you.

FIGURE 5.19:

The Resources tab of a device in the Device Manager

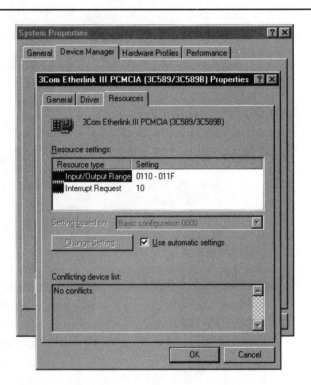

Adding New Hardware

Adding new hardware devices is very simple under Windows 95. When you start Windows 95 after installing a new hardware device, normally Windows 95 will detect the new device using Plug-n-Play and automatically install the software for it. If not, you need to run the Add New Hardware Wizard.

General Hardware Installation Using the Hardware Installation Wizard

To start adding the new device, double-click the My Computer icon. Then double-click the Control Panels folder. To start the Wizard, double-click Add New Hardware in the Control Panel window (Figure 5.20).

FIGURE 5.20:

The Control Panel window

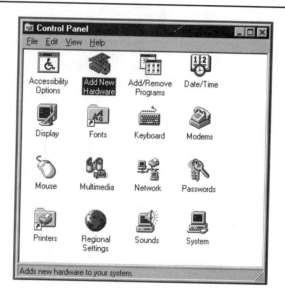

> **TIP**
> You can also bring up this window by clicking the Start menu, then the Settings submenu, then the Control Panels folder.

Once you have started the Add New Hardware Wizard, you will see a figure similar to the one in Figure 5.21. This is the introduction to the Wizard. To start the configuration of the new hardware, click Next.

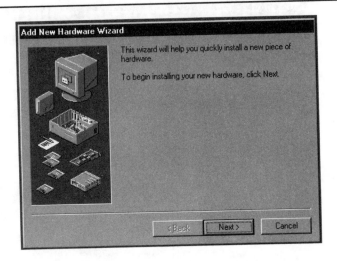

The next screen that is presented (Figure 5.22) allows you to select whether the Wizard will search for the hardware or you need to specify the type and settings of the hardware. If you choose Yes, then in the next step Windows will search for the hardware and install the drivers for it automatically. It is the easiest method (especially if the hardware is Plug-n-Play compliant) and is the least complex. If you choose No, you will have to select the type, brand, and settings for the new hardware. For our example, choose Yes (recommended) and click Next.

The next screen will tell you that Windows 95 is ready to search for the new hardware. To begin the detection, click Next again. Windows 95 will make an intensive scan of the hardware (you should notice the hard disk light will be on almost constantly and you will hear the hard disk thrashing away during the detection). During this scan, you will see a progress bar at the bottom of the screen (Figure 5.23) that indicates Windows 95's progress with the detection. You can stop the detection at any time by clicking the Cancel button.

FIGURE 5.22:

FIGURE 5.22:

Telling Windows to
search for the new
hardware

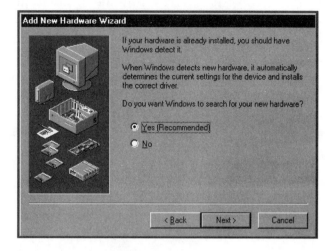

FIGURE 5.23:

Detecting new
hardware

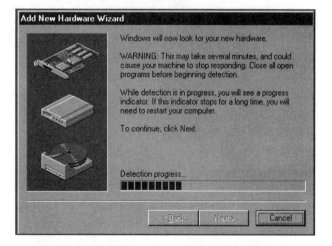

When the progress indicator gets all the way to the right, Windows 95 will tell you that it found some hardware that it can install (Figure 5.24). You can see which hardware it found by clicking the Details button. To finish the setup of the new hardware, click the Finish button. When you do this, Windows 95 will copy the drivers from the installation disks or CD for the device. Once it has done that, it may ask you for configuration information, if necessary. To finish the hardware setup, it will ask you to reboot Windows 95 so that the changes take effect and Windows can recognize (and use) the new hardware.

FIGURE 5.24:

Finishing new hardware installation

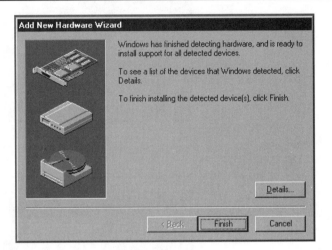

Configuring Printing Under Windows 95

One of the most common devices to add to computer system is a printer. Whether you are installing a dot-matrix printer or laser printer, the configuration is basically the same. In this section, we'll examine how to set up a Windows 95 computer to print to a locally attached printer. Setting a workstation to print to a network printer is covered in Chapter 9.

Adding a Printer

Microsoft was thoughtful enough to provide a wizard to help us install printers. The name of this wizard is the Add Printer Wizard (neat, huh?). It will guide you through the basic steps of installing a printer by asking you questions about how you would like the printer configured.

To start the Add Printer Wizard (APW for short), you must first open the Printers folder by either going to Start ≻ Settings ≻ Printers or double-clicking the Printers control panel in the Control Panel folder. Once you get to the Printers folder, you can double-click the Add Printer icon. Doing so will display a screen (like the one shown in Figure 5.25) that tells you the Wizard is going to help you install your printer "quickly and easily." Let's hope so. Click Next to begin the configuration.

FIGURE 5.25:

The Add Printer Wizard start screen

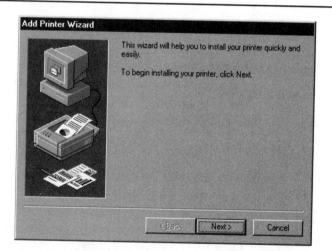

The first question the APW will ask you is where this printer is (Figure 5.26). If it is connected to the network, click in the button next to Network Printer. If the printer is connected to your PC, click Local Printer. We will discuss using network printers in Chapter 9, so for right now, click Local Printer and click Next.

FIGURE 5.26:

Choosing what the printer is hooked to

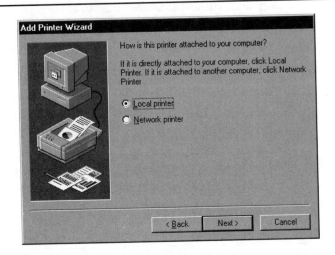

The next screen that the APW presents allows you to pick the driver for your printer by simply picking the manufacturer from the list on the left and the model from the list that appears on the right (Figure 5.27). You may need to scroll on either side since the lists can get rather long. If your printer is not listed, or if you would like to install a more current driver, you can click the Have Disk... button and APW will prompt you to insert the disk and type in the path to the directory where the driver is located. Either way, select your driver and click Next.

TIP   Make sure to select the correct driver for your model of printer. Most printing problems can be traced to a corrupt or out-of-date printer driver.

NOTE   Some printer drivers can't be installed in this method. You must run a SETUP or INSTALL from the disk to install the printing software. This program will not only install the correct printer drivers but will also set up the printer for use with Windows 95 as well. In this case, you won't have to run the APW (in fact, it won't work because you can't select the right driver).

FIGURE 5.27:

Selecting a printer
driver to install

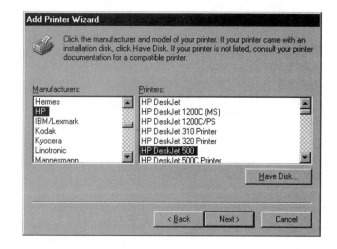

The next screen (Figure 5.28) allows you to choose which port the printer is hooked to. It will present you with a list of ports that Windows 95 knows about, including Parallel (LPT), Serial (COM), and Infrared (IR) ports and ask you to choose which port the printer is hooked to. Simply click on the port name from the list and click Next. If necessary, you can click Configure Port... to configure any special port settings the printer may require.

FIGURE 5.28:

Picking the printer port

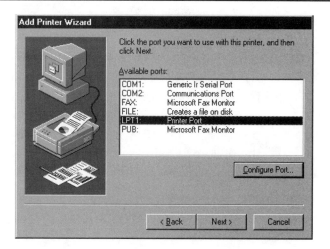

In the next step, APW asks you to give the printer a name (Figure 5.29) so that you can choose the printer by name when you select Print from any program. By default, the APW will supply the name of the print driver in this field. You can change it by simply clicking in the field and typing in a new name. Additionally, you can select whether or not you want this printer to be the default that Windows 95 selects when you don't select a specific printer when printing. If you want this printer to be the default, click the button next to Yes. If not, click No. When finished changing these settings, click Next.

FIGURE 5.29:

Naming the printer

The final step in setting up a new printer is to indicate to the APW whether or not you'd like to print a test page (Figure 5.30). If you say Yes and click Finish, Windows 95 will copy the driver and any support files, then try to print a test page. Once done printing, Windows 95 will present you with a screen asking you if the page printed correctly. If you click Yes, the APW wizard is finished and you know the printer works. If you select No, APW will

launch Windows 95 Help and bring you to the Printing Troubleshooting page. If you don't want to print a test page, select No
(from the Do You Want to Print a Test Page... screen) and APW will
simply copy the files and bring you back to the desktop.

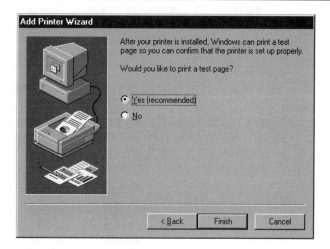

Managing an Existing Printer

If you have a printer installed on your Windows 95 computer,
there are times where you need to change the way the printer
functions. For this reason you should know how to manage an
existing printer under Windows 95. Managing a printer involves
knowing how to configure the printer object after you have used
the APW to set it up.

First of all, most of what you need to configure is centered
around the printer icon in the Printers folder that represents the
printer you want to configure. You can configure most items from

either the properties of the printer or by opening the printer by double-clicking on it.

If you right-click a printer in the printers folder and choose Properties, you will see a screen similar to the one in Figure 5.31. There may be more options, depending on the type of printer it is. Each tab is used to configure different properties. Table 5.12 lists the tabs and a description of their function.

FIGURE 5.31:

The Properties page of a printer

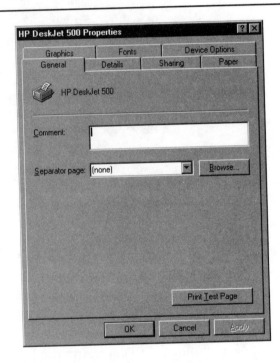

TIP   You can print a test page from this page at any time by simply clicking the Print Test Page button.

TABLE 5.12: Printer Properties tabs and functions

Tab	Description
General	This tab displays the printer's name as well as any comments you want to enter to describe the printer's functions (or eccentricities)
Details	This tab is used to configure how Windows 95 communicates with the printer. (Described in the next section)
Sharing	This tab is used to share the printer on the network the machine is connected. (Described more in detail in Chapter 9)
Paper	This tab allows you to configure what kind of paper the printer is using (size-wise) as well as its orientation when printing.
Graphics	This tab lets you configure the resolution of the printer. Lower resolutions use less toner
Fonts	You can use this tab to view the installed fonts as well as install other fonts
Device Options	This tab changes depending on what kind of printer it is. It lets you set the device-specific settings for the printer

If you select the Details tab, you will see a figure similar to the one in Figure 5.32. From here you can configure how Windows 95 communicates with the printer. For example, you can select a different port to print to for this printer. Additionally, you can install a new or updated driver from this screen. Simply click on the New Driver button. Windows will present you with a driver selection screen (similar to the one shown in Figure 5.31 earlier in this chapter).

One of the most important options on this screen is the Spool Setting button. This button allows you to configure whether or not Windows 95 will spool print jobs. If print jobs are spooled, every time you click Print in a program, the job is printed to a spool directory (usually a subdirectory of the C:\WINDOWS\SPOOL directory) by a program called SPOOL32.EXE. Then the job is sent to the printer in the background while you continue to work. If you don't want this to be the case (it is the default), click the Spool

Settings button. From the screen shown in Figure 5.33, you can choose either Spool Print Jobs... or Print Directly to Printer. Choose the appropriate option and click OK. Once you have made changes to a printer, click OK on the Properties page to save them.

FIGURE 5.32:

The Details tab of the Properties page of a Windows 95 printer

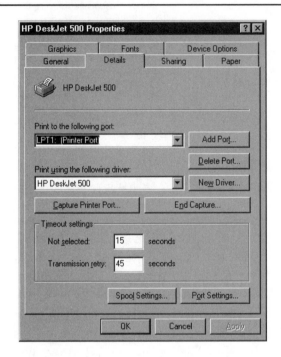

The other way to configure a printing is through the printer item in the system tray (Figure 5.34). When you print a document, a printer will appear in the system tray. You can open it so that you can manage the print jobs by double clicking on it.

FIGURE 5.33:

Changing a printer's
spool settings

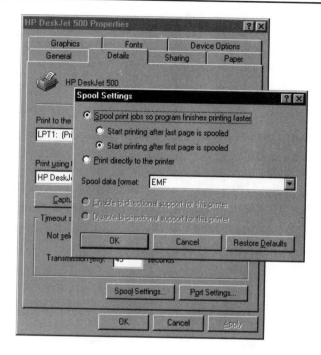

FIGURE 5.34:

The printer icon in the
system tray

When you double-click the printer, you will see the screen shown
in Figure 5.35. From here you can see any pending print jobs listed
as well as the statistics for the print job. Notice there is one print
job currently being printed. If you want to stop the printer, you can
choose Printer ➤ Pause Printing and Windows 95 will stop sending
print jobs to the printer. If you want to delete a job, click the job in
the list of jobs and hit the DEL key on your keyboard.

FIGURE 5.35:

Printer job list

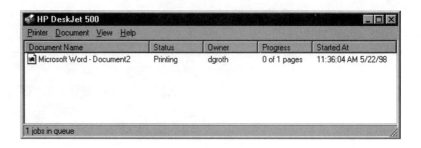

> **TIP** If you want to delete all jobs in this list, choose Purge Print Jobs from the Printer menu. All jobs that are currently spooled will be deleted.

Review Questions

1. If SMARTDRV.EXE is used, which CONFIG.SYS parameter's value should be reduced?

   A. FILES=20

   B. CACHE=10

   C. BUFFERS=50

   D. SMARTDRV=10

2. The PATH environment variable specifies what kind of directories?

   A. Directories that DOS uses

   B. Directories that COMMAND.COM searches to find programs to run

   C. Directories that COMMAND.COM searches to find files

   D. Directories that DOS searches to find files

3. Which memory driver controls access to the High Memory Area (HMA)?

   A. HIMEM.SYS

   B. EMM386.EXE

   C. SMARTDRV.EXE

   D. MEM.EXE

4. Which DOS components can be used for caching?

    A. BUFFERS=

    B. CACHE=

    C. SMARTDRIVE

    D. SMARTDRV

5. Name the three files that MS-DOS requires in order to boot.

6. Name the three files that PC-DOS requires in order to boot.

7. Which command replaces the DEVICE= command in the CONFIG.SYS but performs the same function and adds the ability to load drivers into free UMBs?

    A. LOADUMB=

    B. DEVICEUMB=

    C. LOADHIGH=

    D. DEVICEHIGH=

8. Which MS-DOS file must be loaded in order for the AUTOEXEC.BAT to execute?

    A. MSDOS.SYS

    B. COMMAND.COM

    C. IO.SYS

    D. IBMBIO.COM

9. Which MS-DOS command controls the appearance of the MS-DOS command prompt?

   A. CSET

   B. DOSPROMPT

   C. PROMPT

   D. CONFIG.SYS

10. Which CONFIG.SYS area (in a multiconfig setup) contains commands that execute regardless of the menu option chosen?

    A. :ALL

    B. [ALL]

    C. :COMMON

    D. [COMMON]

11. Which CONFIG.SYS loads device drivers into memory?

    A. DEVICE=

    B. LOAD=

    C. START=

    D. DOS=

12. Which type of DOS command is contained within COMMAND.COM?

    A. .EXE

    B. Internal

    C. External

    D. .COM

13. What DOS utility is used for disk compression?

    A. DRVSPACE

    B. DISKSPACE

    C. DUBDRIVE

    D. DBLSPACE

14. Which of the following is *not* an internal DOS command?

    A. CLS

    B. COPY

    C. MORE

    D. PAUSE

15. Which Windows 3.*x* INI file contains drivers and VXDs for Windows devices?

    A. WIN.INI

    B. SYSTEM.INI

    C. PROGMAN.INI

    D. CONTROL.INI

16. Generally speaking, the SYSTEM.INI file gets updated when you run which Windows program and make changes?

    A. CONTROL.EXE

    B. PIFEDIT.EXE

    C. SETUP.EXE

    D. PAINT.EXE

17. What does PIF stand for?

    A. Programmable Initialization File

    B. Program Information File

    C. Program Instant File

    D. Program Instruction File

18. Which Windows component is a small piece of executable code shared between many applications to reduce the size of each application that shares it?

   A. USER.EXE

   B. INI files

   C. The Registry

   D. DLL files

19. Which file(s) cannot be edited with SYSEDIT? (Choose all that apply.)

   A. AUTOEXEC.BAT

   B. CONFIG.SYS

   C. WIN.INI

   D. SYSTEM.INI

   E. PROGMAN.INI

   F. CONTROL.INI

   G. COMMAND.COM

20. Which type of font file prints fastest?

   A. Bitmap

   B. TrueType

   C. Hardware printer

   D. Screen

21. Which section of the SYSTEM.INI file contains the drivers that are loaded at system startup?

   A. [boot]

   B. [drivers]

   C. [boot.description]

   D. [386Enh]

22. Which entry do you place in WIN.INI to make an application program start automatically as a minimized application?

    A. Minimize=*filename*

    B. Run=*filename*

    C. Load=*filename*

    D. Start=*filename*

23. Which entry do you place in WIN.INI to make a program start automatically as a regular, full-screen application?

    A. Minimize=*filename*

    B. Run=*filename*

    C. Load=*filename*

    D. Start=*filename*

24. What is the extension of TrueType font files?

    A. .TTF

    B. .TT

    C. .FOT

    D. .FNT

25. Which Windows 95 component is used to add new programs to Windows 95?

    A. Device Manager

    B. Add/Remove Programs

    C. Desktop

    D. Start ➤ New Program

26. Which tool can be used to edit the Windows 95 Registry?

   A. SYSEDIT

   B. EDIT

   C. REGEDIT

   D. EDITREG

27. Which tool(s) can be used to add new hardware to Windows 95?

   A. Plug-n-Play

   B. Device Manager

   C. Add/Remove Programs

   D. Add New Hardware

28. Which tool(s) can be used to install an updated driver for a Windows 95 device?

   A. Plug-n-Play

   B. Device Manager

   C. Add/Remove Programs

   D. Add New Hardware

29. Your print jobs are taking a long time to print. Which set of steps will solve the problem?

   A. Select Start ➢ Settings ➢ Printers then right-click the printer and choose Properties. Go to the Details tab, click Spool Settings, and change Spool Print Jobs… to Print Directly to Printer.

   B. Select Start ➢ Settings ➢ Printers then right-click the printer and choose Spool Settings. Go to the Properties tab and change Spool Print Jobs… to Print Directly to Printer.

   C. Select Start ➤ Settings ➤ Printers then right-click the printer and choose Properties. Go to the Spool Settings tab and change Spool print jobs… to Print Directly to Printer.

   D. None of the above

30. You want to change which screen saver your Windows 95 computer is using. Which control panel will you use?

   A. Desktop Settings

   B. Screen Saver

   C. Background

   D. Display

31. Which program would you use to edit the registry?

   A. EDITREG.EXE

   B. EDITREG.COM

   C. REGEDIT.EXE

   D. REGEDIT.COM

32. How do you display what devices are installed in your computer?

   A. Use the Device manager in the System control panel.

   B. Use the Device manager control panel.

   C. Use the Add New Hardware control panel.

   D. Type **DISPLAY ALL DEVICES** at a command prompt.

33. What file(s) make up the Registry in Windows 95?

    A. REG.DAT

    B. USER.DAT

    C. SYSTEM.DAT

    D. SPOOL.DAT

34. Which of the following are the Windows 95 Registry's automatic backup files?

    A. USER.DAT, SYSTEM.DAT

    B. USER.DA0, SYSTEM.DA0

    C. USER.BAK, SYSTEM.BAK

    D. USER.OLD, SYSTEM.OLD

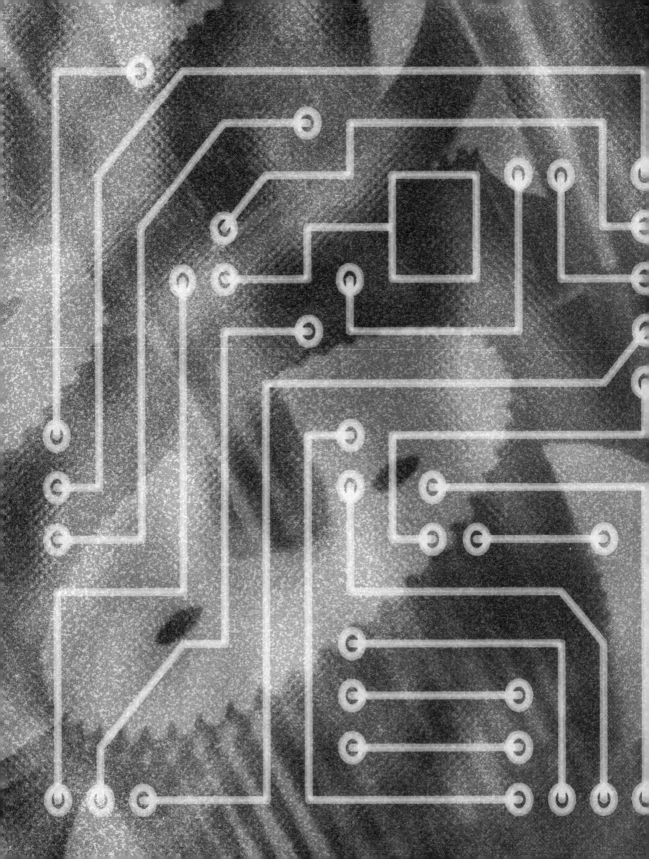

CHAPTER

SIX

6

Operating System Management

- Identify the procedures for basic disk management.

- Differentiate between types of memory.

- Identify typical memory conflict problems and how to optimize memory use.

This chapter will explore the essential methods used to fine-tune an operating system and a hard drive subsystem. The examination concepts that will be covered here include file systems used in DOS and Windows, underlying hard drive structures that are related to these files systems, and memory management concepts. Maintenance and troubleshooting are covered in Chapters 8 and 10. Some of these methods will be utility programs that the technician can run, some will be commands and drivers to be accessed from the CONFIG.SYS and AUTOEXEC.BAT files, and some will be programs or utilities that actually modify these two configuration files.

MS-DOS Management

System management under MS-DOS, often involves legacy systems, those systems that are still important enough to keep going but are in many ways antique. Control systems for equipment are one example. Systems used for packet radio are another example. If the system being worked on is actually a legacy system, the hard drive subsystem brings up special concerns that don't come up in more modern equipment. On the other hand, memory management and system optimization for DOS-based systems form the foundation of modern techniques.

Disk Management

The hard drive, while technically hardware, is critical to the functioning of the operating system because it is the storage medium where the operating system resides. DOS hard drive subsystems are frequently either MFM drives or RLL drives.

MFM hard drives are typical in older PCs. The MFM hard drive has essentially defined most other hard drives used in PCs. MFM stands for Modified Frequency Modulation, which is the electronic method used to encode information onto the hard drive platters. MFM hard drives are usually fairly small by today's standard, often being no more than 20 or 40MB in capacity.

These drives almost always have stepper motors that move the heads in set increments across the platters. This method of finding the tracks is efficient but not very accurate, and the accuracy becomes worse with temperature differences, leading to seasonal problems with many drives, causing these drives to become unreadable at times.

RLL drives became as common as MFM drives because they can contain 50 percent more information. RLL stands for Run Length Limited, a reference to a type of data compression. The RLL compression is built into the hard drive controller, and otherwise the RLL drive is basically a high quality MFM drive. The difference in the actual bits that are written to and read from the drive and the minor differences required in the controller to encode and decode these bits are what set this drive apart.

Indeed, an RLL drive can be used with an MFM controller, and in a pinch, an MFM drive can be used with an RLL controller. However, the MFM drive used with an RLL controller is unreliable.

These two drive types eventually led to the IDE type drive with embedded intelligent electronics. IDE stands for Integrated (or Intelligent) Drive (or Disk) Electronics. An IDE drive is pretty much an RLL drive with a controller onboard.

In this section, you'll learn about low level formatting, partitioning, and high level formatting for MFM, RLL, IDE, and SCSI drives. If you'd like to learn more about these types of drives, please refer to the *A+: Core Module Study Guide*.

Low Level Formatting

Low level formatting is the first step of preparing to install an operating system into a computer. Fortunately, these days hard drives are usually low level formatted at the factory, so for most technicians this is just an historical fact that may appear on an exam question.

Low level formatting is the process of getting the surface material of the hard drive platters prepared to accept information. Low level formatting creates the tracks and sectors that higher level processes look for. This formatting process destroys any information that is already present on the hard drive. For this reason, low level formatting is rarely used on IDE hard drives, which contain some special information written at the factory. SCSI hard drives will occasionally be low level formatted; on very rare occasions, an IDE drive will also be low level formatted.

For older drives, a low level formatting program is embedded into the hard drive controller interface. This interface is found on a card that is inserted into one of the bus slots. Different brands of controllers use different means to accomplish a low level format. The instructions for low level formatting are included with the literature that comes with the card. Also, you can usually find instructions on the Web sites of hard drive manufacturers. The most common method of accessing the formatting program is to use the DEBUG program that comes with DOS.

NOTE   Modern drives are usually low level formatted at the factory.

An important step of the formatting process is to set the interleave of the hard drive:

- A 1:1 (one to one) interleave places sectors with contiguous information right next to each other on the hard disk platter. If the hard drive circuitry cannot pass information quickly to the CPU, then data will be read from a sector and the hard drive will spin another complete revolution before reading the next sector.

- A 2:1 interleave places data on a platter sector, skips the next sector, and places contiguous data on a third sector. In a 2:1 interleave, the middle sector is not lost; it is coupled with another sector with at least one sector skipped in between.

Many times a 2:1 interleave is enough of a difference for the circuitry to keep up with the data flow. If not, then a 3:1 interleave might be used. You will need to be determine the interleave at the time of formatting.

Figure 6.1 shows how the sectors on a track might be laid out if there were 17 sectors per track. (MFM drives typically have 17 sectors per track.) The first three sectors of the first track are marked as they would appear with a 3:1 interleave and are labeled *logical sectors* to differentiate them from the physical sectors.

FIGURE 6.1:

Hard drive sector interleave example (3:1)

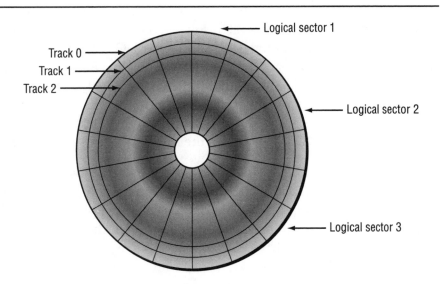

Partitioning

After the hard drive is low level formatted, it will have to be partitioned. On modern drives, this is often the first step because IDE drives are low level formatted at the factory.

Partitioning refers to establishing large allocations of hard drive space. A partition is a continuous section of sectors that are next to each other. In DOS and Windows, a partition is referred to by a drive letter, such as C: or D:. Partitioning a drive into two or more parts gives it the appearance of being two or more physical hard drives.

TIP   DOS partitions always have a drive letter assigned, but this is not universally true of FAT partitions. When Windows 95 is on a network, some network partitions may not appear with a drive letter. These partitions are referred to by a UNC (universal naming convention) name. Local drives and partitions still have drive letters associated with them.

When a drive is partitioned in DOS, there is generally a *primary partition*, which is marked active. The active partition is the location of the boot-up files for DOS or Windows. If there is more than one partition, the second and remaining DOS partitions are found inside of another partition type called an *extended partition*. An extended partition contains one or more *logical partitions*; it is the logical partitions that have drive letters associated with them. DOS only allows the creation of one extended partition on a drive.

To partition a drive, most technicians use a program called FDISK. When FDISK is executed, a screen appears that gives four or five options (see Figure 6.2). The fifth option, which allows you to select a hard drive, appears only when there is more than one physical hard drive. FDISK will only partition one hard drive at a time.

FIGURE 6.2:

The introductory screen in FDISK.EXE

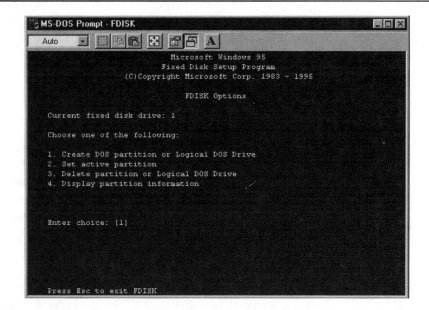

With FDISK, you can create partitions, delete partitions, mark a partition as active, or display available partitioning information. You must create a primary partition before you can create any other partitions. If space is still available on the drive, then a second, extended partition may be created. No drive letter is assigned to the extended partition. One or more logical partitions must be defined within the extended partition. No partition need be marked active on a particular drive, but one and only one partition must be marked active to be able to boot from a hard drive.

FDISK creates a start and an end to a section of hard drive space. At the beginning of that space it creates a special file called the Master Boot Record, or MBR. The MBR contains the partition information about the beginning and end of the primary and extended partitions. At the beginning of the partitions, this record is called the DOS Volume Boot Sector.

The size of a partition will determine certain aspects of a file pointer table called the *File Allocation Table*, or FAT for short. The larger the drive partition, the more space will be wasted on the drive. This problem will be described below under the topics of *High Level Formatting* and *Optimization*.

High Level Formatting

The next step in management of a hard drive is high level formatting, initiated by the FORMAT command. High level formatting should not be confused with low level formatting, although it can be just as destructive to information on the hard drive. High level formatting is, these days, normally the only formatting a technician will do. High level formatting performs several actions:

- It briefly scans the surface of the hard drive platter to find any possible bad spots, and it marks the areas surrounding a bad spot as bad sectors.

- High level formatting lays down magnetic tracks in concentric circles. These tracks are where information is eventually encoded. These tracks, in turn, are split into pieces of 512 bytes called sectors. Some space is reserved in between the sectors for error correction information, referred to CRC or Cyclic Redundancy Check information. The operating system may use CRC information to recreate data that has been partially lost from a sector.

- Additionally, high level formatting creates a File Allocation Table (FAT). This table will contain information about the location of files as they are placed onto the hard drive. The FAT has a limited number of entries. Therefore the space allocated for the partition may need to be divided into clusters of sectors, where a sector is the smallest part of a hard drive.

Optimization

Each FAT has a set number of entries, which depends on the size of the hard drive. On a very small hard drive, the FAT could theoretically be large enough to track all the sectors, but in practice this never occurs. Only high density floppy disks have FATs that track individual sectors. Sectors on hard drives will be clumped together in what is called a *cluster* or *allocation unit*. In general, as the drive or drive partition increases in size, the number of sectors per cluster increases.

A drive between 16MB and 128MB will have four sectors per cluster. A larger drive of up to 256MB will have eight sectors per cluster. In fact, every time you double the hard drive size, you double the number of sectors per cluster. Thus, drives of up to 512MB will have 16 sectors per cluster, drives of up to 1024MB will have 32 sectors per cluster, and so on. Clusters of 32 sectors are 16KB in size.

Allocation units may not be used by two different files, thus any empty space in an allocation unit (any space not filled by the file assigned to that allocation unit) is wasted. Many files almost fill the last cluster allocated to them, but many files barely use this last allocated cluster. On the average, files use half of the last cluster allocated to them.

Imagine large clusters with one cluster per file being only half-filled. If these clusters are 16KB and there are 5000 files, then roughly 40MB of hard drive space is designated but unused. My hard drive has almost 25,000 files on one partition, which translates to 200MB of wasted space.

One solution to optimizing hard drive space is to set up multiple partitions that are smaller in size and therefore use smaller clusters. It is not unusual for a 1GB drive to regain 200MB or more when split into two partitions. You should also avoid partition sizes that are just over the limit for cluster sizes. A 528MB partition has less available space on it than a 512MB partition does, simply because the clusters are large enough to waste more than the extra space on the larger partition.

Another solution is implemented in Windows 95 release B and is called FAT32. Earlier versions of the file allocation tables are known as FAT12 and FAT16 (because the size of the FAT entries are 12 bits and 16 bits respectively). FAT32 has two prominent features: support for larger hard drives and smaller clusters for larger hard drives. A 2GB drive with FAT16 has clusters of 32KB; with FAT32 the clusters sizes are 4KB.

The disadvantage of FAT32 at this time is that it is not compatible with older DOS, Windows 3.x, and Windows 95 operating systems. This means that when you boot a Windows 95 OSRB (Operating System Release B) FAT32 computer with a DOS boot floppy, you can't see the partition that is FAT32.

File Management

Once the drive has been formatted and partitioned, files will be placed onto the drive by the DOS installation process, by the user, and by various applications that the user might be running. These files tracked of in the FAT. As files are added, the FAT fills up.

Certain entries in the table are pointers to the files, and other entries are pointers to directories and sub-directories. The FAT has an overall limit, and it also has a limit of 512 entries (either files or subdirectories) in the Root directory. When a user places many files into the Root directory, the Root directory can reach this limit.

TIP   Good housekeeping practices suggest keeping files in organized sub-directories. This relieves the problem of filling up the Root directory and makes finding files easier.

Prior to DOS 5.0, when a file was erased or deleted, it was gone forever. (Well not really gone, but untouchable by the average user.) In DOS 5.0 or above, when a file is deleted, the information initially remains intact. The name of the file is changed in the FAT so that the name is unreadable by DOS. Companies such as Norton and Central Point Tools made use of this fact when they designed and marketed "undelete" programs. These utilities could see the hidden names and restore the name to a readable condition.

WARNING Microsoft thought so highly of this UNDELETE idea that they included the UNDELETE command in DOS 5.0. Along with this comes a warning. Once a FAT entry is marked as unused, any file being written to the hard drive may actually use the space that the entry originally pointed to. A file cannot always be undeleted.

Earlier versions of DOS made this newly opened space available immediately to other files being written to the hard drive. Later, this vacated space was left alone until other available space was entirely used, making deleted files more secure for the undeleting process.

WARNING The casual user may not realize that his/her deleted files can so easily be reconstructed. A computer that belongs to a company can be searched for deleted or hidden information. The technician should not generally engage in undeleting files without a good reason or without instruction from the company management.

Memory Optimization

Memory management, when I learned it, was an arcane art, similar to voodoo or magic. These days it is rather simplified by a program called MEMMAKER, which comes as part of DOS.

Memory management has a goal of freeing conventional memory for use by DOS programs that require a large amount of real mode memory. Recall that real mode memory (the memory available when the CPU is in real mode) is limited to 1MB of space. The top 384KB (the Upper Memory Area, or UMA) of this is reserved for various hardware components such as the video BIOS and memory, the system BIOS, and the BIOS of other optional hardware such as network interface cards.

Even so, there are holes (Upper Memory Blocks, or UMBs) available in the upper memory, which may be used by small DOS programs, including drivers and TSRs, and as expanded memory. Using this space efficiently is called "memory management."

Another piece of memory is available when the processor is in protected mode. This is the High Memory Area, a piece of memory separated from the extended memory beyond the 1MB address space. High memory is controlled by HIMEM.SYS, the extended memory manager that first appeared in DOS 5.0. A unique arrangement of DOS segmented memory addressing and the A20 address line, available on all Intel and Intel compatible CPUs from the 80286 and above, has made possible the use of an almost 64KB space in memory just beyond the 1MB boundary.

High Memory is available when a processor is in protected mode. When the processor is in real mode or virtual/enhanced mode, it is limited to using the first twenty address lines, A0 to A19. DOS is able to load certain parts of its kernel in that space, freeing up much needed space in conventional RAM space for other DOS programs. Once HIMEM.SYS is loaded by the CONFIG.SYS file on boot up, this area can be occupied by DOS program code with the DOS=HIGH command line, in the CONFIG.SYS.

Upper memory blocks are made available for the use of device drivers and TSRs with the EMM386 command. Unlike HIMEM.SYS, which is an extended memory manager, EMM386 is an expanded memory manager.

Remember that expanded memory resides outside of normal DOS memory address space and that pieces of expanded memory, called pages, are swapped into and out of the Upper Memory Area. A space is reserved in the UMA called a page frame. This space is 64KB wide, and 16KB pieces of expanded memory called pages can be temporarily designated addresses in this range.

These days, EMM386 does not have to be used for actual management of expanded memory, as fewer and fewer applications in use will utilize this type of memory. However EMM386 is still used to manage the UMBs that device drivers and TSRs can use.

Optimization Utilities

Optimization is the process of bringing a system to a higher level of performance. In this section, you'll learn about several optimization utilities that fall into the categories of disk management, memory management, and disk maintenance.

Disk Tricks

Speeding up access to data on a hard drive by caching is one of the oldest tricks in the book. A cache (usually pronounced "cash," sometimes pronounced "cash-ay") is a temporary storage place. In the case of hard drive caching, the temporary storage place is in RAM set aside for the purpose.

A quick comparison of the relative access speeds of RAM versus hard drive will demonstrate why caching works. RAM access is measured in nanoseconds, with a typical access speed being about 70 ns or 70 billionths of a second. On the other hand, hard drive speeds are measured in milliseconds, with a typical speed being about 10 ms, or 10 thousandths of a second. Using these numbers, RAM access speeds are almost 150 times faster than hard drive access times.

If a caching program can access information on the hard drive and place it into RAM cache and do so accurately, then the CPU can look in the much faster RAM cache for needed information and the whole system speeds up. In the early days of disk caching, my PC sped up by about 50 percent overall, from a speed rating of .9 to a rating of 1.4, simply by adding a caching utility.

Caching uses rules to predict which data will be required next and moves that data to the cache during the CPU's idle moments. Modern DOS hard drive caching is done with a program called SmartDrive. It allows for caching of data as it is read from the hard drive and also as it is written to the hard drive. The latter, when data is held in RAM before writing to the hard drive, is called "write-back cache."

WARNING Write-back caching is sometimes risky business. Occasionally, a computer will get shut off prior to the cache being written to the hard drive and the data will be lost. If the data included revisions to the FAT, whole files or directories can be lost. The computer could be shut down deliberately without knowing that the cache had not been written, or accidentally, as in a power failure. I suggest that you turn off the write-back cache. Type **smartdrive /?** for help.

RAM disks are an alternative to caching for speeding up access to a variety of information. A RAM disk is a virtual or pretend disk drive found in RAM. This space can be set aside and assigned a drive letter. The drive letter can be a floppy drive letter, such as B:, or a hard drive letter.

The RAM disk may be assigned the characteristics of a floppy drive and used as a floppy. A common use for a RAM disk is to hold temporary files. In this capacity, it acts like a hard drive with a folder or directory called TEMP.

WARNING A common problem with RAM disks is that people who are not used to working with them treat them as if they were real disks. When the computer is shut down, the contents of the RAM disk are lost.

Remember that early MFM and RLL drives require a low level format. These disks have another unusual property: they are effected by changes in temperature. Often during a change of season, the temperature of an office changes, and these hard drives will not boot. One option is to reformat the hard drive, but then data might be lost.

A program called Spin Rite was created to do a non-destructive format. The program reads the data from a sector or a cluster and holds the data in the computer's memory. Then the program reformats that data area on the drive, performing both a low level and high level format. When the formatting is finished, Spin Rite writes the data back onto the drive. Spin Rite can also test for the optimum disk interleave ratio and re-format based on that ratio. A technician with Spin Rite could revitalize a hard drive and speed it up at the same time.

Another optimizing technique is to get more room for storage on a hard drive with a disk compression utility, such as Stacker. The primary difference between an MFM drive and an RLL drive is that the RLL drive uses a data compression technique to squeeze data on the hard drive. Stacker does the same but uses software to do so. Depending on the nature of the data being squeezed, Stacker can effectively double the storage capacity of a hard drive. Its descendant, DriveSpace, is now found in Windows 95.

Another disk trick that can speed up data access is *defragmentation*, fondly referred to as "defragging." When files are erased, the hard drive space formerly occupied is then free for other files. Eventually, files will end up filling bits and pieces of hard drive space, instead of filling continuous space. A file that's broken up into bits and pieces is *fragmented*. The read-write heads of the hard drive must swing back and forth to several locations to read the entire file, and this takes extra time.

When a file is defragged, it is placed into one continuous space on the hard drive. Two common examples of defragging utilities are PC Tools COMPRESS command, and the DOS DEFRAG command (DOS 6.0 and above).

Memory Tricks

Conventional memory statistics can be viewed with the MEM program. The main number of concern for memory management is the amount of free conventional memory, which in Figure 6.3 is 585KB. Other numbers reported include upper memory, expanded memory, and extended memory usage.

FIGURE 6.3

Output from the MEMMAKER command

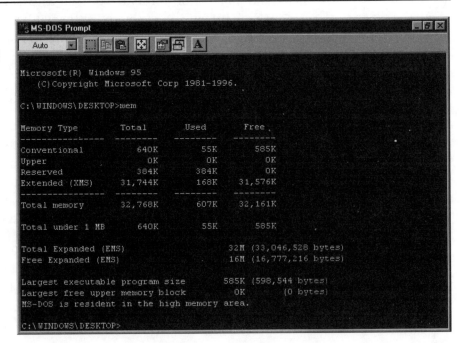

MEMMAKER is a utility that comes with DOS. Its purpose to automate the process of memory management. MEMMAKER attempts to load various drivers and TSRs found in the CONFIG.SYS and AUTOEXEC.BAT files into upper memory blocks, thus freeing up a larger contiguous space of conventional memory. It rapidly calculates hundreds or even thousands of different configurations to find the one that best fits the pieces into upper memory.

WARNING One problem that MEMMAKER usually (but not always) deals with is that some TSRs use extra memory when loading and then reduce their size. MEMMAKER will try to determine both memory requirements. It loads TSRs in upper memory first so that the space left over when the TSRs reduce their memory footprint can be allocated to a driver. MEMMAKER is not always successful at this, and a TSR may have to be loaded into the AUTOEXEC.BAT after MEMMAKER has been run.

To run MEMMAKER, make sure that HIMEM.SYS and EMM386 are loaded, that you are at a DOS command prompt, and that Windows is not running; type in **MEMMAKER**.

WARNING Some versions of MEMMAKER offer an aggressive search of the UMA for free memory. This is not recommended unless there is an extreme memory shortage. The aggressive search looks for spots within a memory range reserved for a BIOS chip, to see if there are any further free places within that range. If the aggressive search misidentifies a memory range as free, then programs could occupy space needed by a BIOS. The system might become unstable or lock up.

Other Utilities

SCANDISK and CHKDSK are DOS utilities for verifying the integrity of a hard drive. CHKDSK examines the file allocation table for errors and optionally attempts to correct those errors.

CHKDSK is an older utility that comes with almost every version of DOS still in use. To use it from the DOS command, type **CHKDSK**. If you include the /f switch (type **CHKDSK /F**), it will optionally find file fragments that have gotten damaged and fix or delete these fragments. (See Figure 6.4.)

FIGURE 6.4

A CHKDSK report

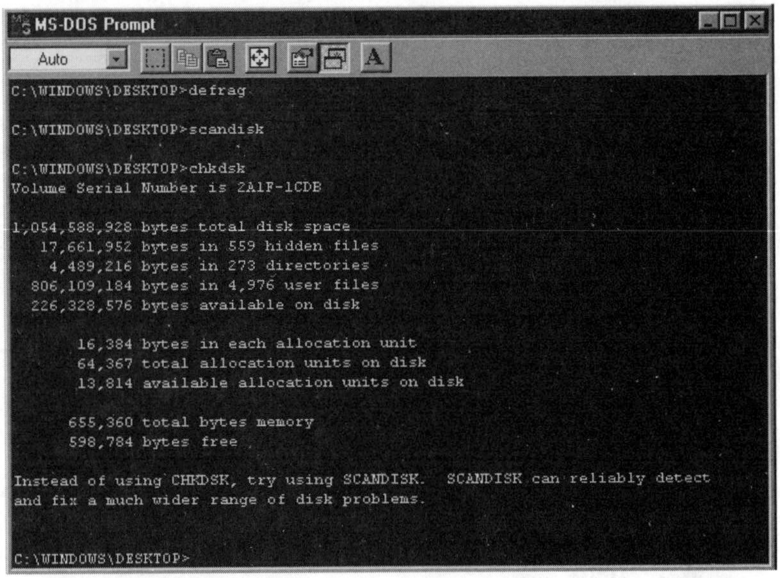

```
MS-DOS Prompt                                                    _ □ ×
Auto        ▼   [ ] ▣ ▣ ▣ ▣ ▣ ▣ A

C:\WINDOWS\DESKTOP>defrag

C:\WINDOWS\DESKTOP>scandisk

C:\WINDOWS\DESKTOP>chkdsk
Volume Serial Number is 2A1F-1CDB

1,054,588,928 bytes total disk space
   17,661,952 bytes in 559 hidden files
    4,489,216 bytes in 273 directories
  806,109,184 bytes in 4,976 user files
  226,328,576 bytes available on disk

       16,384 bytes in each allocation unit
       64,367 total allocation units on disk
       13,814 available allocation units on disk

      655,360 total bytes memory
      598,784 bytes free

Instead of using CHKDSK, try using SCANDISK.  SCANDISK can reliably detect
and fix a much wider range of disk problems.

C:\WINDOWS\DESKTOP>
```

SCANDISK is a newer utility, available both from the DOS command line and as a Windows 95 program. SCANDISK performs more extended checks of the drive, including a surface scan of the platters. It also optionally corrects the errors that it finds.

Several optimization utilities exist that are actually suites of programs. Norton Utilities and PC Tools are two of the more well-known suites. A program called Norton Disk Doctor may be used to analyze a disk's problems.

Windows 3.*x* Management

For the most part, the DOS utilities mentioned above are sufficient for many aspects of system management with regard to the DOS-based Windows 3.*x*. However, there are a few special considerations for these early versions of Windows.

Disk Management

One advantage to the use of a 386 processor (or above) is that *virtual memory* is available. Virtual memory is hard drive space that is set aside to behave as if it were real RAM:

- The advantage to virtual memory is that hard drive space is less expensive than real memory, although today's memory prices are lower than those seen in past years.

- The disadvantage is that hard drive space used as if it were real RAM is much slower than actual RAM.

With virtual memory, the contents of RAM may be placed into virtual memory, thus freeing up the RAM for other ongoing applications. The content that is placed into RAM is said to have been *swapped*, and the hard drive space that it is swapped into is referred to as a *swap file*. Windows has been designed to utilize swap files.

Windows swap files come in two types:

- A *permanent* swap file has a piece of hard drive space assigned to it at all times.

- A *temporary* swap file has hard drive space assigned when Windows 3.*x* starts up.

Two rules apply to swap files. First, the hard drive space assigned to a permanent swap file may not be fragmented. It needs to be contiguous space. Second, the swap file may not be on a drive partition that is compressed.

When a temporary swap file is used, the space that was available the last time may no longer be available because it is used up. A temporary swap file may reside in fragmented disk space, which can lead to performance degradation as the hard drive seeks in different areas for information.

A permanent swap file always has a set amount of space available, regardless of other non-Windows usage of the computer. Because this swap file is in contiguous space on the hard drive, seeking information that has been put there is more efficient than with the temporary swap file. The permanent swap file is called 386SPART.PAR.

WARNING Do not delete the permanent swap file. It looks like a large file wasting space, but it is not.

Windows Fast Disk is a set of programs that in essence speeds up disk access. The core of these programs is the 32-bit access for hard drives. 32-bit disk access allows Windows to access the hard drive directly, thus avoiding going through the DOS hard disk driver. Fast Disk 32-bit disk access is limited to use with hard drives that have WD1003 compatible controllers. These are found with most MFM, RLL, and IDE drives, but not with ESDI or SCSI drives.

In general, most disk management programs that attempt to restructure the disk drive system should not be run from Windows 3.x. It is therefore a bad idea to run a DEBUG low level format routine, to partition a drive with FDISK, or to do a high level format with the FORMAT command while Windows 3.x is running.

> **WARNING** It is very easy to get to the DOS prompt while running Windows 3.*x*, and it is also easy to forget that Windows is running in the background. If an application such as a disk management program should not be run while in Windows, it should not be run while in a Windows DOS window.

Memory Optimization

The best thing you can do for a Windows computer is add more memory. RAM prices are low, and additional RAM prevents or minimizes the computer's use of the hard drive swap file. There is a type of utility called a RAM doubler that may also be of some benefit. It uses a compression scheme similar to that used by DriveSpace. Data stored in the RAM doubled space will need to be compressed and decompressed, but this process is still quicker than swapping data to the hard drive.

EMM386 is the expanded memory manager that is generally used with DOS and Windows 3.*x*. Windows 3.1 and 3.11 have a built-in memory manager when in enhanced mode. Alternatively, a company named Quarterdeck has a product, QEMM, which is an equivalent to EMM386, with some added features. It has a Stealth feature that can gain a bit more available upper memory.

One problem with EMM386 is that it can allow certain programs to create memory conflicts. For example, when Windows 3.*x* starts up, it may load network-card drivers. If these are loaded in an area that is reserved for some other hardware or software, the system will not run properly. The statement EMMExclude= may be required in the SYSTEM.INI file in order to resolve such conflicts.

Optimization Utilities

For Windows 3.*x*, there are two choices for optimization: you can either manually fine tune the system in conjunction with some built-in utilities, or use a freeware utility like Wintune 2.0. Wintune 2.0 is available off the Internet at `http://www.winmag.com/software/wt95.htm`.

MEMMAKER is a DOS utility, but it has a Windows option in it. Make sure to run MEMMAKER and use the option to detect the Windows installation on the hard drive. MEMMAKER in a non-aggressive mode is generally good enough for the management of upper memory blocks, the high memory area, and extended memory. Unless a legacy program specifically requires expanded memory, make sure that expanded memory is turned off.

For hard drives, as a general rule, the swap file should be permanent. A temporary swap file should be selected only if hard drive space is at a premium, and the little remaining space often changes in capacity.

For Windows 3.0 or 3.1, or when using a SCSI hard drive, SMARTDRIVE (the hard drive caching program) should be turned on and should have write-back caching turned off, fast disk access should be enabled, and the hard drive should be defragmented.

Windows 95 Management

There are three types of system management possible with Windows 95: operating system, hardware, and application software. Our focus here will be on the hardware side of system management. Specifically, we will examine the aspects of hard drive and memory management that effect the overall system.

Disk Management

Several configuration settings that previously had to be manually adjusted are now automatic with Windows 95. Among the most notable of these settings are the swap file and disk drive caching.

The swap file is used for virtual memory. The swap file is hard drive space that idle pieces of programs are placed in, while other active parts of programs are kept in or swapped into main memory. Windows 95 uses a dynamic swap file that is adjusted on-the-fly. This means that if more space is needed, the OS will assign that space to the swap file.

The swap file in Windows 95 can reside on certain types of compressed drives, namely those controlled with a virtual device driver. The protected mode driver, DRVSPACE.VXD, that comes with Windows 95 is one such driver. The swap file in Windows 95 does not require a contiguous hard drive space, unlike the earlier swap files.

TIP

Locate the swap file on a drive with plenty of empty space. As a general rule, try to keep 10 percent of your drive space free for the overhead of various elements of the operating system, like the swap file.

WARNING

Do not disable the swap file. If you disable the swap file, the system is likely to become unbootable.

Disk caching in Windows 95 is no longer handled by SMART-DRIVE. Instead, Windows 95 uses a 32-bit caching program called VCACHE, originally introduced with Windows 3.11. This protected mode driver runs more efficiently than its real mode predecessor, SMARTDRIVE. It uses a more efficient set of rules for predicting the needed hard drive data. Further, it caches data from the network and from the CD-ROM; thus it is able to speed up the access to data from these devices.

The disk compression utility that comes with Windows 95 is still called DriveSpace, but unlike the earlier DriveSpace, it is now a protected mode driver with faster performance. Older drives that have been doubled in space by using DriveSpace or Double-Space should be switched to the new protected mode version. DriveSpace is automatically loaded, but not activated, when Windows 95 is installed.

Memory Optimization

According to Microsoft (see for example the *Microsoft Windows 95 Resource Kit*), memory management for conventional memory while running the Windows 95 operating system is the same as for MS-DOS 6.*x*. This applies to the management of conventional memory only, as all other memory management in Windows 95 is essentially automatic. If 16-bit DOS and 16-bit Windows 3.*x* programs are not even going to be used, then these techniques are not necessary.

To maximize available memory for real mode programs, load the extended memory manager, HIMEM.SYS, and the expanded memory manager, EMM386, in the CONFIG.SYS file. If possible, remove the real mode drivers from the AUTOEXEC.BAT file and utilize the protected mode drivers that are built into Windows 95. You should not load SMARTDRIVE, as the VCACHE disk caching that comes with Windows 95 is superior and does not detract from conventional memory.

MEMMAKER, which came with DOS 6.2*x*, is found on the Windows 95 CD in the directory OTHER\OLDDOS. MEMMAKER may be used to optimize the CONFIG.SYS and AUTOEXEC.BAT files for conventional memory.

Optimization Utilities

Today's Windows 95 is so well optimized that the third party software companies are having a hard time creating utilities. However, there is Norton Crash Guard and Norton Utilities from Symantec, as well as Wintune 97, which is available off the Internet at `http://www.winmag.com/software/wt7.htm`. Crash Guard is a set of add-in utilities that help prevent system lockups on Windows 95. Norton Utilities is a set of programs to help recover from damaging events, such as lost files; it also includes a utility to compress and decompress single files on-the-fly.

Wintune 97 is offered by Windows Magazine as freeware. It has a performance tester and a set of help files that will provide pointers on how to best optimize a system's performance.

Special Utilities for Managing Operating Systems

I would like to mention two special aids that I have found very valuable: one in the deployment of multiple workstations, and the other in repartitioning hard drives without losing data. These utilities are from companies that are ground breakers in their areas.

The first is Partition Magic. The latest version of Partition Magic can re-partition a hard drive without losing data and without the need to reformat the drive. It can change partition types from FAT12 to FAT16, or even FAT32. The partition type can be changed to NTFS, if you are working with Windows NT. More information is available at `http://www.powerquest.com`.

The other is utility is Ghost. This utility is a disk replication program. An entire hard drive or drive partition may be saved in an image file and later restored onto another hard drive. This allows the technician to set up one computer the way many will be set up and simply clone the hard drive image onto the other computers. The hard drives and/or partition sizes do not necessarily have to be the same, although of course the partition will have to be big enough to hold the cloned image. You can download a demo version of Ghost at `http://www.ghostsoft.com/dlsoft.htm`.

Review Questions

1. Which drive type should not be low level formatted by a technician?

   A. IDE

   B. MFM

   C. RLL

   D. All of the above.

2. The hard drive partition with the bootable system files is called:

   A. Logical parirition

   B. Extended partition

   C. System partition

   D. Active partition

3. A File Allocation Table is created:

   A. At the factory

   B. By FDISK

   C. By the interleave program

   D. During a high level format, using the FORMAT command

4. Deleted files may be recovered by:

   A. UNERASE

   B. UNDELETE

   C. RECOVER

   D. UNDO

5. Which application reorganizes files on a disk in order to optimize disk drive performance?

   A. SCANDISK

   B. FDISK

   C. OPTIMIZE

   D. DEFRAG

6. On a DOS based system, memory is conveniently optimized:

   A. Using HIMEM.SYS

   B. Manually changing entries in CONFIG.SYS

   C. With a hard drive cache

   D. Using MEMMAKER

7. A problem with RAM disks is:

   A. They often break

   B. Data is lost when the computer is shut down

   C. They need frequent reformatting

   D. They have slow access times

8. In Windows 3.*x*, the best choice of swap file is a:

   A. High speed trade file

   B. Compressed swap file

   C. Permanent swap file

   D. Temporary swap file

9. In Windows 95, the swap file:

    A. Must be on an uncompressed drive

    B. May be on a compressed drive controlled by DRVSPACE.VXD

    C. Requires a contiguous hard drive space

    D. May be disabled without effect

10. Windows 95 handles hard disk caching with:

    A. SMARTDRIVE

    B. DEFRAG

    C. VCACHE

    D. FAT-CACHE

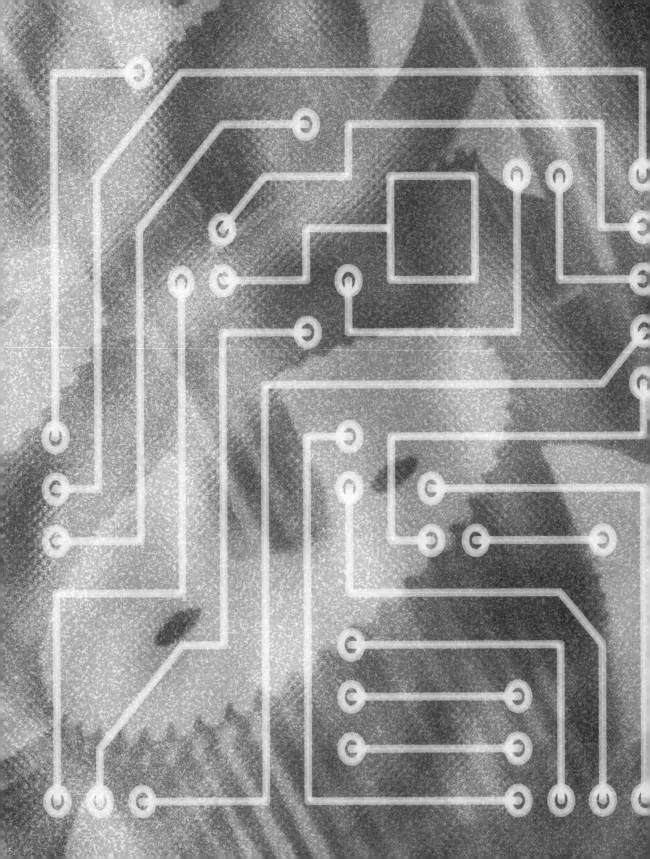

CHAPTER

SEVEN

7

Installing and Running Applications

- Identify the procedures for installing and launching typical Windows and non-Windows applications.

In this chapter, I'll discuss installing, configuring, launching, and uninstalling applications in DOS, Windows 3.*x*, and Windows 95.

There are two basic methods used to install applications onto a computer:

- First, an application may be copied onto the computer.
- Second, and most common, an application may have its own installation routine.

The difference is, for the most part, related to the complexity of the program. In general, DOS programs are copied to a computer and Windows programs include a setup program (because Windows programs are usually more complex than DOS programs).

However, there *are* Windows programs that can simply be copied to the computer and run. For example, a simple Windows game called Comet Busters can be copied onto the computer's hard drive without any problem or further configuration. Similarly, there are DOS applications with setup or install programs included. An example would be WordPerfect for DOS, which has a complex installation routine used for its setup.

With the issue of complexity comes configuration. For a large and complex DOS program, you will need to configure a variety of drivers. Likewise, a large and complex Windows program may have many pieces with options to load or install.

Even in DOS, there are several ways to launch a program. Unless a shell program, such as PC Shell, has been loaded, all of these ways involve naming the DOS program executable, either directly on a command line or indirectly through a batch file. Likewise, there are a number of ways to launch an application from within Windows 3.*x* and Windows 95.

The two final issues I'll discuss in this chapter are:

- Configuring the operating system environmental variables to optimize the running of a DOS program within Windows
- The uninstall process for various DOS and Windows programs

Using Applications in DOS

Two methods apply to installing programs onto a DOS computer. Many older DOS programs can simply be copied. Newer, more complex DOS programs will have to be installed with a setup routine specific to that application.

Installing an Application by Copying

Many years ago, DOS applications were simple executable .COM or .EXE files that could be run from a floppy. Copying these files to the hard drive was a common practice (if the computer had a hard drive) because programs run faster from a hard drive than they do from a floppy drive. As programs became larger, with many pieces and added-in drivers, it became more than just practical to copy the files to the hard drive. It became necessary.

In Figure 7.1, we see a list of files on a floppy disk and copied to a directory on the hard drive. Two of these files are DOS executables, INTERLNK.EXE and INTERSVR.EXE. (These files are required to establish an interlink connection between two computers.)

FIGURE 7.1:

Copying DOS
Program Files

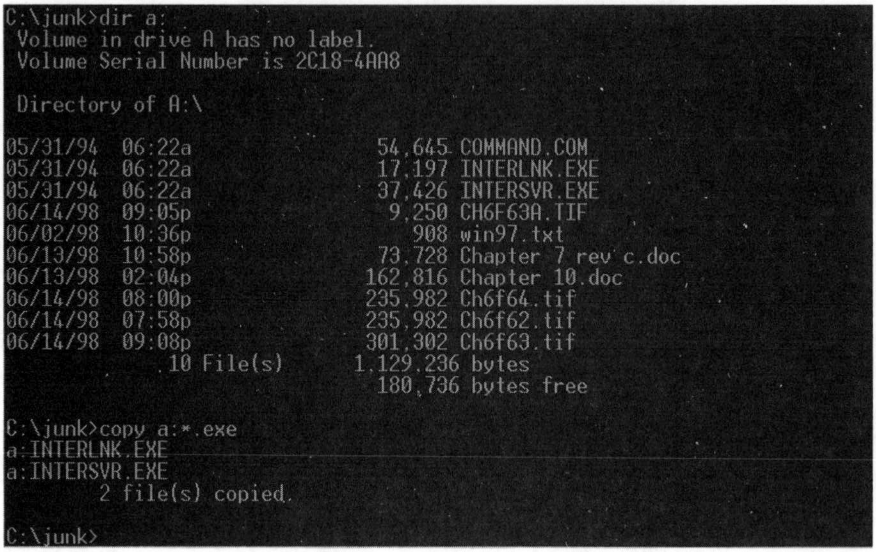

```
C:\junk>dir a:
 Volume in drive A has no label.
 Volume Serial Number is 2C18-4AA8

 Directory of A:\

05/31/94  06:22a              54,645 COMMAND.COM
05/31/94  06:22a              17,197 INTERLNK.EXE
05/31/94  06:22a              37,426 INTERSVR.EXE
06/14/98  09:05p               9,250 CH6F63A.TIF
06/02/98  10:36p                 908 win97.txt
06/13/98  10:58p              73,728 Chapter 7 rev c.doc
06/13/98  02:04p             162,816 Chapter 10.doc
06/14/98  08:00p             235,982 Ch6f64.tif
06/14/98  07:58p             235,982 Ch6f62.tif
06/14/98  09:08p             301,302 Ch6f63.tif
              10 File(s)      1,129,236 bytes
                               180,736 bytes free

C:\junk>copy a:*.exe
a:INTERLNK.EXE
a:INTERSVR.EXE
        2 file(s) copied.

C:\junk>
```

Installing an Application with a Setup Routine

More complex DOS programs need to be installed to work properly. One example is PC Tools from Central Point Software. PC Shell is a DOS shell with a bit of a graphical look and feel that can be used for file management. It's made up of a collection of files that fit onto several floppies but can work together only on a larger drive. Some of the utilities included in this suite can be run from the floppy, but others require the presence of overlay files and device drivers that span more than one floppy disk.

Although PC Tools (in its early versions, at least) *can* be copied onto the hard drive, it comes with an installation program that aids in the copying process by locating or creating a subdirectory for the files to be copied to. The install program also prompts you to insert each floppy disk as it is needed.

More complex programs require a more intricate installation procedure, usually meaning that you'll have to make decisions throughout the setup process. DOS programs generally use device drivers that are specific to that program, so when you load WordPerfect for DOS, you'll need to select a printer, even though you may have already selected the printer for Lotus 1-2-3. Likewise, you may have to select a display driver for fitting more text or typed data on a screen.

As shown in Figure 7.2, early installation routines primarily copy files and offer a few options on how to configure the files and computer after the application had been installed. Notice that this screen is a little bit graphical but not to the extent that modern Windows screens are. This PC Tools installation screen is actually built-up out of DOS ASCII characters.

FIGURE 7.2:

Installing PC Tools
Version 6

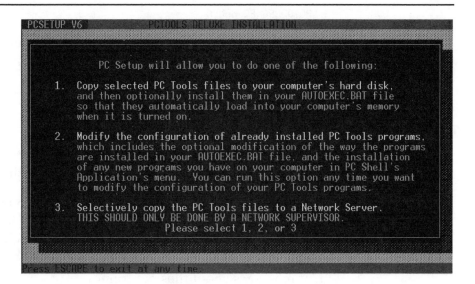

NOTE   If you have questions about installing a DOS-based programs in a DOS environment, refer to the user guide that comes with the software.

Launching an Application

Launching an application in DOS usually means typing in its name or the name of its main executable file at a DOS command prompt. For example, you could start the Central Point Software program PC Shell by typing **pcshell** at the DOS command prompt. Generally, programs are put into their own subdirectories, so a path must exist pointing to that subdirectory or the user must have changed to that subdirectory.

Alternatives include typing the complete path at the command prompt along with the startup command or launching the application with a batch file that has the complete path as part of the startup command. For example, an AUTOEXEC.BAT file could include the following command line in order to start the PC Tools shell when the computer starts up:

```
C:\PCTOOLS6\PCSHELL6
```

The PC Shell utility provides file list and directory tree windows similar to Windows *Program Manager* or Windows *Explorer*.

Uninstalling an Application

With DOS programs, the uninstall process is the reverse of copying: you simply erase all the files associated with the program.

Of course, sometimes an installation will have made modifications to the CONFIG.SYS and AUTOEXEC.BAT files. Depending on the nature of these configuration modifications, there may be no side effects to the removal of a program, or there may be some error messages about files not found.

Rarely are these configuration changes harmful if left in, although many times the changes will leave extra and unneeded drivers loaded or memory configurations that are not optimized for the applications left on the hard drive. If you edit the CONFIG.SYS and the AUTOEXEC.BAT files, remarking out suspicious statements, it will usually fix things up.

Using Applications in Windows 3.*x*

In Windows 3.*x*, as with DOS, two methods of installation are used depending on the nature of the program being installed:

- Copying will work with many DOS programs and some Windows 3.*x* programs.

- Setup routines will be needed for the more complex applications.

Installing DOS and Windows Applications by Copying

A major advantage of Windows over DOS is the shared use of device drivers and program overlays or program extensions, mostly found in .DLL files. This system means that many simple Windows programs can be copied into a directory on the hard drive and run from there. These programs access the Windows configuration settings and native drivers.

Some Windows programs can even be copied onto a floppy disk and run off of the disk. One such example is NOTEPAD.EXE. As a simple exercise, try copying NOTEPAD.EXE to a floppy disk and executing it. Notepad will use whatever printers and display you have set up for use by other Windows applications.

As part of the process of installing DOS programs into a Windows environment or operating system, you need to specify certain resources (such as video settings and memory requirements) so that the program will run properly. Under Windows 3.*x*, such resource specifications are found in a Program Information File (PIF).

A PIF Editor can be used to change the specifications in the PIF, in case the default PIF settings don't work correctly. (Most programs work fine with the default settings.) You can start the PIF Editor using the PIF Editor icon, located in either the Accessories Group or the Main Group.

NOTE The details of which PIF settings to change are too varied to discuss here, however the *Windows User Guide*, which comes with Windows 3.x or with the user's computer, has instructions for this task.

There are two main types of PIFs:

- The default PIF that is used for a DOS application when no other PIF is associated with the program. This type works with most DOS programs.

- A PIF specifically customized for an application. Some programs will come with a PIF on the assumption that the program might be used in a Windows environment. The other source of a customized PIF is when the program installer creates a new PIF, using the PIF editor.

Installing DOS and Windows Applications with Installation Routines

The installation routine for installing a DOS program should be run from the DOS command prompt and not from within Windows 3.x. The setup routine for most DOS programs that are meant to be compatible with Windows 3.x will either accept the default PIF, mentioned above, or will install a PIF customized for the application.

There are often three types of installations available, sometimes even four with complex Windows applications. These are *typical installation, custom installation, minimal installation*, and *run from a CD-ROM.*

Windows Program Typical Installation

The first type of installation is what is called a typical installation. This includes the installation of those pieces of the application that its authors felt would be used by ordinary or typical users.

Windows Program Custom Installation

Most Windows programs are assembled out of lots and lots of pieces. For some Windows programs, many of these pieces are optional, and the setup procedure may let the installer pick and choose which parts of the application are going to be installed. This type of install is referred to as a custom installation.

The custom installation is of the most interest to the technician as installer. In the custom installation, the pieces that are optional are listed so that each piece may be selected or deselected. Selected program parts are then installed onto the computer. A custom *installation* also gives the installer the choice of where to install the program and often where to install individual parts of the program.

TIP

If you use a custom installation option, you can find out which parts are considered "typical" by the authors of the application. The typical choices are generally displayed as being selected, rather than deselected, at that point in the installation where options can be picked. You don't need to make custom changes simply because you picked the custom option.

Alternative Installation Options: Minimal and Run from CD

These alternatives usually have no configuration options to worry about. These are simple picked from the installation options, and the setup routines do the rest.

The minimal installation, allows the basic application to run without any added options. Minimal installation is often a good choice for laptop and notebook computers that have limited hard drive space.

The run from CD option doesn't really install anything besides configuration and launching files; the application executable code is then read and run from the CD. This option requires even less hard drive space than the minimal installation does; however it requires that a CD-ROM drive be present, which is often not the case on a notebook computer, and it assumes that the CD itself is present, which is often not the case in an institutional setting such as a school.

Installing a Windows Application by Moving It

You can install an application using a hybrid of the setup routine and copying methods. First, you must be installing the application by whatever normal means is associated with that program. Then, you must transfer the program and its various configuration files to another location.

A program that has its own INI files and does not use any other Windows INI files can be moved by copying. For example, I have successfully moved copies of CorelDRAW by copying all the files in the Corel directory and then modifying the INI files that have file paths in them to reflect the new paths. Depending on the complexity of the application to be moved, this may not be a wise option. Also notice that the original installation of the program used the application's setup routine.

Launching Programs in Windows 3.*x*

Starting up programs in Windows 3.*x* involves finding the appropriate program icon and double-clicking. When you install Windows 3.*x*, part of its setup routine examines the existing DOS applications on the hard drive and creates icons for these programs.

Another way to start programs in Windows 3.*x* is to use the RUN command found on the FILE pull down menu. The RUN command uses a pop-up dialog box in which you can enter a command name, with or without a path.

One last method is to enter a command name at the command prompt of a DOS shell. You can start a DOS shell by selecting the DOS Prompt icon and double-clicking or by selecting the RUN dialog box and typing in **command**. Once you start the DOS shell, it will look very much like a standard DOS screen—but Windows 3.*x* will still be running in the background. Any Windows program can thus be started from the command prompt.

Uninstalling Programs in Windows 3.*x*

The brute force method of deleting files is the common practice for uninstalling DOS and Windows programs in Windows 3.*x*. This method often leaves many drivers and DLLs intact. They *usually* don't affect other programs, but they *might* cause conflicts. And they certainly take up valuable hard drive space.

Because of this problem, some technicians believe that a hard drive should be reformatted every once in a while and that all the applications should then be reinstalled. This problem also led to the development of the uninstall routines found in Windows 95.

Using Applications in Windows 95

The typical configuration files needed for a DOS/Windows 3.*x* combination include the CONFIG.SYS, AUTOEXEC.BAT, WINDOWS .INI, SYSTEM.INI and various other INI files. In Windows 95, the *Registry* is a central location for most configuration information. Other places hold some of the information, but only for reasons of backwards compatibility with older DOS and Windows programs.

The use of a registry has an impact on installing programs. Older Windows applications will install their usual way in Windows 95, which includes setting up INI files. Newer Windows 95 programs (meaning most, but not all, Windows 32-bit programs) will make changes to the Registry reflecting their configuration settings. These changes can be tracked by special software to make uninstalling much easier.

INI Files

INI is short for initialization. INI files contain information to aid in the initial configuration of a program as it starts up. INI files are generally but not always created by 16-bit Windows applications. A few 32-bit applications also create INI files. Listing 7.1 is an example of a brief INI file that my 32-bit Netscape program produced.

NOTE   Not all 16-bit Windows applications create INI files, and not all INI files are created by 16-bit applications.

| Listing 7.1: | **NETSCAPE.INI, A 32-bit Windows Application INI File** |

```
[MailComposeToolBar-Summary]
Bars=4
ScreenCX=800
ScreenCY=600
[Settings]
PreviewPages=2
[MailComposeToolBar-Bar0]
BarID=33333
[MailComposeToolBar-Bar1]
BarID=470
[MailComposeToolBar-Bar2]
BarID=2013
[MailComposeToolBar-Bar3]
BarID=59393
```

Simple programs with no real configuration may have no INI files associated with them or perhaps just a single INI file. A simple game, for example, may have an INI file that remembers certain game settings from the last time the game was played. Such settings might include a list of the highest scores and whether sound is turned on or off. Figure 7.3 shows WINMINE.INI, the INI file for the windows game Minesweeper.

INI files are created in several different ways:

- Upon installation, a default INI file might be created. This file will hold the normal or default settings for the program. (Or, it could instead contain the initial settings you configured during a custom installation.)

- Occasionally, a default INI is not created, but an INI file is created after the first time you run the program. In this event, the INI will simply contain settings for the last run instance of the application. Programs that create custom INI files often create more than one. The different INI files, in this case, are used to configure different pieces of the application.

FIGURE 7.3:

Minesweeper's INI File, WINMINE.INI

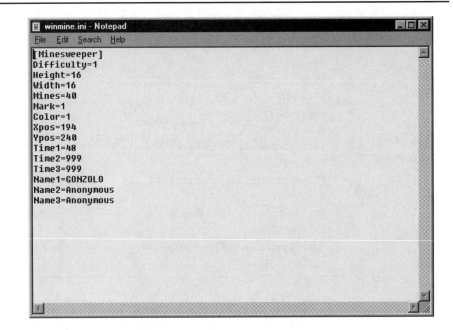

The INI files have a structure that involves groups of logical connected settings. This group of settings is called a *section* and is denoted by labels in square brackets, [and]. The settings in each group are called *entries*. An entry has two parts—an entry name and its value—separated by an equal sign. Both of these INI elements can be observed in Listing 7.1.

INI files are usually altered when the user changes a program's settings from its menus and when the user exits the program. Occasionally, a technician might be required to alter an INI setting manually, either for troubleshooting purposes or if the program or Windows fails to change the setting properly.

Registry Files

The Registry is the modern Windows 95 version of the INI file. Of course, it is much more. My library includes several large books devoted to the Registry. A technician can think of the Registry as a substitute for the many tens or even hundreds of INI files that occur with older versions of Windows and with older Windows programs.

The Registry contains information about configuration settings for the Windows 95 operating system, information about how various programs and applications work, and special information about the user. In Windows 95, the Registry actually consists of two files: the USER.DAT and the SYSTEM.DAT. A registry editor called *REGEDIT* is used to edit the Registry.

The Registry is backed up in two files with similar names to those mentioned above: USER.DA0 and SYSTEM.DA0. (The last character is a number zero, not the letter O.) The registry files are stored in the Windows folder. If the original Registry files become damaged, corrupted, or inadvertently changed, you can restore the system by booting up from a floppy disk and renaming the .DA0 files to .DAT. The boot floppy can be the clean-boot floppy that every technician should have, or it may be made in advance on another computer.

On computers in public areas that are prone to changes in the Registry files, a simple restoration routine involves writing a DOS batch file. On boot up, this batch file takes copies of the .DAT files and writes these to the Windows folder. This batch file will run automatically when pointed to from the AUTOEXEC.BAT.

Installing DOS and Windows Applications by Copying

DOS and Windows 16-bit applications may be copied in the Windows 95 environment as described above for the Windows 3.*x* and DOS environments. It is virtually impossible to copy a 32-bit program that makes changes to the Registry.

Installing Applications with Installation Routines

In this section, I will go through a step-by-step procedure for installing a typical application, Microsoft Office 97. Office 97 is a suite or a collection of program applications that are commonly used in a business office setting. The applications include Word 97 (a word processor), Excel 97 (a spreadsheet), Access 97 (a database manager), and PowerPoint 97 (a presentation graphics program), along with some auxiliary and supplemental utilities.

The Maintenance Install

If you run the Office 97 setup program after Office 97 has already been installed, a *maintenance install* will be performed. One of the first steps in the setup process is checking for installed components to Office 97. If the setup program finds components, then it assumes that Office 97 is installed and gives the technician an opportunity to install or remove components or to reinstall damaged or missing files.

Installing for the First Time

In this example, I will discuss running the installation program when Office 97 has not yet been installed.

> **WARNING** You should always ensure that you, as the responsible installer, have a legal copy of the installation CD with the CD-KEY number. Microsoft Office 97 is copyrighted and licensed software, and illegal copies should not be installed.

Special installation floppies can be generate from special installation CDs, but are not otherwise available, so a CD is required. To install Office 97:

1. Insert the CD in the CD-ROM drive.

   - If autorun is set, the install will start automatically. (*Autorun* is a setting that automatically starts an install or other startup program found on a CD, when the CD is inserted into the CD-ROM drive.)

   - Otherwise, use Explorer (Figure 7.4) or My Computer (Figure 7.5) to find SETUP.EXE on the CD, and execute it by double clicking.

> **NOTE** Take a look at the other folders that are on the CD. For example, the VALUPACK directory contains extra templates for easily creating special document styles.

FIGURE 7.4:

The Office CD, viewed in Internet Explorer

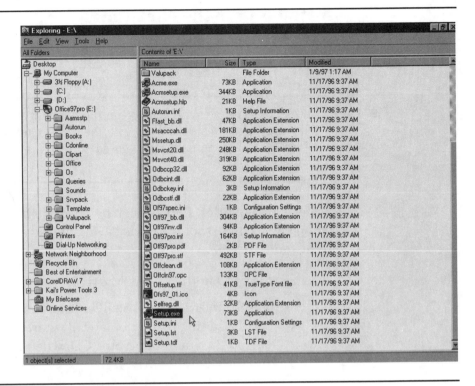

FIGURE 7.5:

The Office CD, viewed in My Computer

> **TIP**
>
> Another way to start the install process is to use the Start ➤ Run command and run *x*:\SETUP.EXE, where *x* is equal to the drive letter of the CD-ROM as shown in Figure 7.6. Use whichever method you, as the installing technician, prefer. My preference is to use Explorer to find the SETUP.EXE file.

FIGURE 7.6:

Start Menu method of launching a setup routine

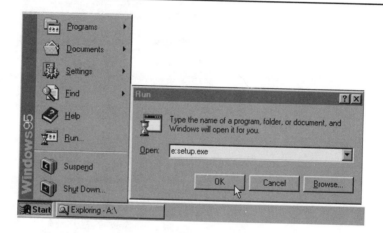

2. Setup will show the licensing screen in Figure 7.7. You should read the licensing agreement or point it out to your customer. Most licensing screens have an Accept button or an I Agree button that you click to agree to the license.

3. At this point, you may enter a user name and an organization or business name (Figure 7.8). These names will be used by Office to automate the entry of information into documents.

4. The setup process then shows a CD Key number screen (Figure 7.9). Find your CD Key number, generally included on the insert label to the CD case, and enter it.

FIGURE 7.7:

Microsoft Office
Installation License
Agreement

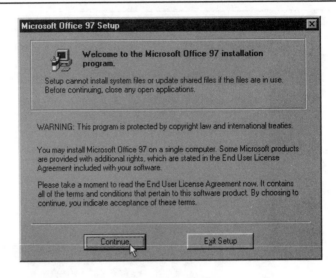

FIGURE 7.8:

Enter the user's name
and the organization's
name here.

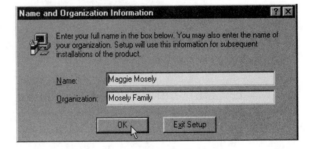

5. The installation program will generate a product identification number and display it on a product number screen. Write the number down, in case you need it in the future, and click OK.

6. In the screen shown in Figure 7.10, select the directory where Office will be installed. This directory is usually but not always C:\PROGRAM FILES\MICROSOFT OFFICE. If you wish to change the installation folder, select the Change Folder button and enter the new location.

FIGURE 7.9:

Entering the CD Key

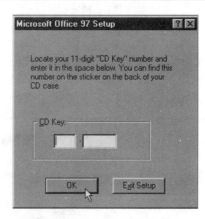

FIGURE 7.10:

Selecting the
Installation Folder

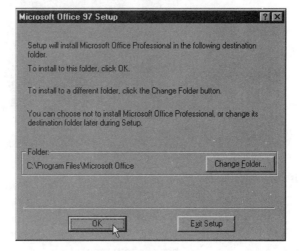

7. The Office install will provide an Installation Option screen with three choices: Typical, Custom, and Run from CD-ROM. This screen is shown in Figure 7.11

Windows Program Typical Installation The casual user will generally select Typical. The custom installation provides many options to select from and average users will often not understand what the choices mean.

Windows Program Custom Installation The technical installer will usually pick Custom, in order to have more control over the installation (Figure 7.11). If you select this option, an option list will become available for you to choose from (Figure 7.12).

FIGURE 7.11:

Office Installation
Option Screen

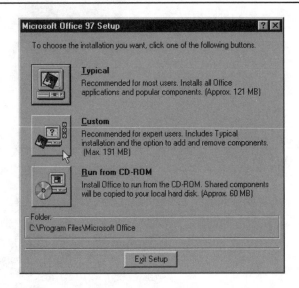

<TIP> One reason to select Custom is to discover what options Microsoft considers to be typical. When Custom is chosen, the options that are checked off are the same options that are installed by default using the Typical choice. If space is at a premium, another reason to choose Custom is so you can choose components to optimize the space required.

FIGURE 7.12:

Choosing Components
to Install in a Custom
Installation

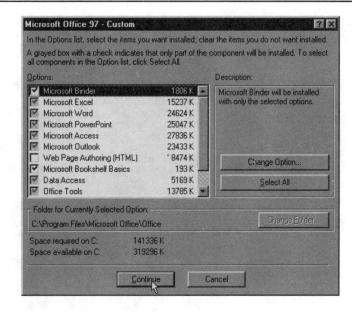

8. An important option for many users is the Office Tools Short-cut Bar. Most often, this option is not included in the Typical list of selected options. Change the option screen to include Office Shortcut Bar as shown in Figure 7.13.

9. After various options have been selected or deselected, the installation will proceed automatically. The final screen, shown in Figure 7.14, will tell you that the installation is finished. You can click the button for Online Registration to register the software with Microsoft, if you want to receive updates and new product information. You can only do this, however, if you have an Internet connection.

FIGURE 7.13:

Turning on the Office
Shortcut Bar

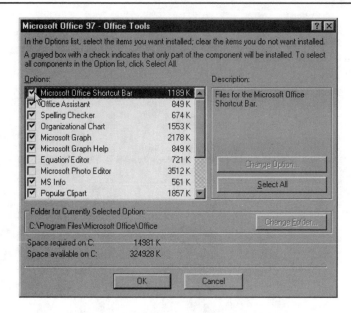

FIGURE 7.14:

The final Office 97
Setup screen

In summary, for most applications, just make sure that there
is a legal copy of the application to be installed, load the media

(whether CD or floppy disk) into the computer, find the SETUP .EXE or INSTALL.EXE command, and run it. Follow instructions on the various screens and refer to the user guide or manual for additional instructions.

TIP   This section showed the installation of one application from Microsoft. Luckily, most applications from Microsoft install in basically the same manner. To get the exact details on how to install a particular piece of software, be sure read the instructions that come with it.

Launching Programs in Windows 95

A separate PIF editor for customizing DOS applications does not exist in Windows 95. Instead, you can use the Properties box to set video settings, memory requirements, and so forth. To access the Properties box, right-click the DOS application executable (the file used to start running the DOS program) and select Properties from the pop-up menu. Or, select and right click a Windows 95 Shortcut to a DOS program. A Properties screen similar to those seen in Figure 7.15 will appear. In the middle section of this screen, you will notice a line referring to the MS-DOS name, and in one case, that name ends with the PIF extension.

TIP   If a DOS program needs to be brought up in different ways (at times with screen output showing but with its window closed on exit at other times), then different shortcuts can be created, and the shortcut properties adjusted for the different needs.

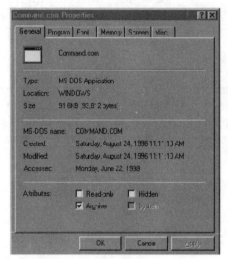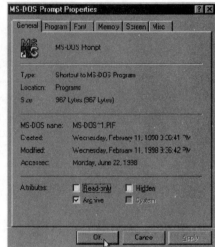

This Properties screen is the PIF editor and more. The shortcut or link file pointing to the DOS program file is the equivalent of the PIF file found in Windows 3.*x*. The only settings that can be changed on this first screen are the Attributes: Read-only, Hidden, Archive, and System.

The second tab brings us to a screen that offers some more significant choices (see Figure 7.16). It is here that we see which program an icon brings up and what its working directory is. The Close on Exit check box is very important. If a DOS program is executed and the results need to be seen, then this box should not be checked. On the other hand, if it is a batch file or other program that simply needs to be run without observable results, then this box should remain checked.

FIGURE 7.16:

The PIF or Properties
screen: Program
Settings

FIGURE 7.16:

The PIF or Properties
screen: Program
Settings

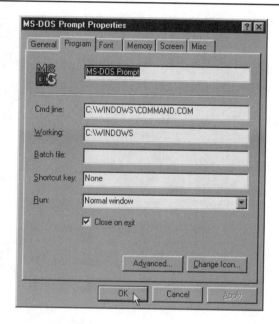

This discussion of PIF files for DOS applications has bordered
on the topic of shortcuts. Figure 7.17 shows the properties screens
for a Windows 95 32-bit application, namely Microsoft Excel, and
the same properties screen for its shortcut file. Because these programs are 32-bit Windows programs, they interact directly with
the Windows 95 operating system and need very little in the way
of customization. Hence, these properties screens have fewer tabs
across the top.

NOTE   You might notice that the Microsoft Excel shortcut file shown in Figure 7.17 has an extension of LNK rather than the PIF extension used
for the DOS application shortcut. This is clearly a reminder to the technician that the shortcut is not the same as the real program but is
rather a pointer to that program.

FIGURE 7.17:

Properties of a Windows 95 application and its associated shortcut

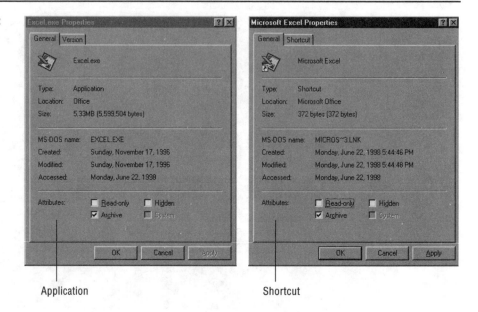

Application   Shortcut

Actually launching the application from within Windows 95 is very much like launching a program in the older Windows 3.*x*, with some added options:

- It is common to find the icon associated with a program and double-click that icon. But, as we have just seen, Windows 95 also uses shortcuts, which are pointers to a program. Shortcuts also have icons and these shortcut icons may be used to start an application.

- The method of using a Run dialog box also works, although bringing up that dialog box is most often done on the Start menu. To use this method, click on the Start button and then click on the Run option. Type in the name of a program in the dialog box, with or without path as needed.

- Programs also may be started from a DOS command shell, which may in turn be started from the Run dialog box by typing in **COMMAND** or from a DOS icon. As in Windows 3.*x*, Windows programs can be started this way.

- Another method of launching programs is from inside an Explorer window or a My Computer window. Bring up Explorer from the Start menu or desktop shortcut, or bring up the My Computer window. Open directories or folders until you have the correct location for the program to be started. Once the executable is located, simply double-click its name or icon, depending on how the files are displayed.

- Finally, most programs will have an entry on the Start ➤ Programs menu.

Uninstalling Programs in Windows 95

Uninstalling applications can be more important than installing them, or at least more complicated. When applications are installed in Windows 95, often a number of DLLs are also installed, sometimes duplicating one another or copying over one another. An uninstall process could actually remove a DLL being used by other programs, and an install process could actually copy over a newer DLL, rendering already installed programs non-functional.

For this reason, several programs have been developed that track the pieces of applications as they are installed. These programs make the uninstall process a procedure that can be automated.

Windows 95 has a built-in uninstall procedure. It is simple, though not necessarily foolproof:

1. Use whichever technique you are comfortable with to select the Control Panel. I generally use Start ➤ Settings ➤ Control Panel. Once in the Control Panel, select Add/Remove Programs. You will see a screen similar to the one shown in Figure 7.18.

FIGURE 7.18:

The Add/Remove
Program Screen

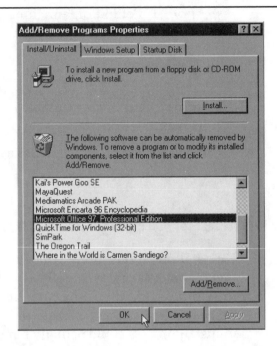

2. In the Add/Remove Program screen, select the program that
   you wish to remove and click the Add/Remove button.

3. This procedure will, like many Windows 95 procedures, allow
   you one last chance to change your mind about removing a
   program: a screen will appear asking you if you are sure you
   want to remove the program. If you are sure, click Yes.

The program will be uninstalled, if possible. All the files that
Windows 95 thinks that belong to that program will be deleted
and most of the Registry settings will be erased. This method
works most of the time for most applications.

NOTE　In the case of Office 97, which we explored above, the removal procedure involves the maintenance install program. The maintenance program will allow you to add or remove various Office 97 components by simply marking or unmarking the appropriate check box.

Review Questions

1. Pick the two basic methods for installing applications:

    A. Copying files onto a hard drive

    B. Copying program files onto a floppy disk

    C. Editing the Registry

    D. Running a setup routine

2. Windows programs:

    A. Are more complex than DOS programs

    B. Can be run under DOS

    C. Always make changes to the Registry

    D. Are always easy to uninstall

3. Launching programs may be accomplished by:

    A. Entering the path and command name at a DOS prompt

    B. Double-clicking on a program icon

    C. Entering a command name in the RUN dialog box

    D. All of the above

4. Uninstalling a DOS application involves:

    A. Removing DLLs

    B. Erasing program files

    C. Using the Add/Remove Programs option

    D. Formatting the hard drive

5. The Windows 95 Registry is:

   A. Edited with Notepad

   B. Made up of the USER.DAT and the PROGMAN.DAT files

   C. Edited with REGEDT32.EXE

   D. Made up of the USER.DAT and the SYSTEM.DAT FILES

6. The Registry:

   A. Takes the place of all of the INI files

   B. Holds most of the configuration settings for Windows 95

   C. Was first introduced with DOS 6.22

   D. Has no importance for Windows 95

7. 16-bit Windows programs:

   A. All create INI files.

   B. Never create INI files. The registry takes care of that.

   C. May use default PIFs.

   D. Usually have an INI file associated with them.

8. Which installation method gives the installer the most flexibility?

   A. Run from CD

   B. Typical

   C. Flexible

   D. Custom

9. When installing programs, it is always important to:

   A. Have a screwdriver ready

   B. Have a legally licensed copy of the program

   C. Have plenty of floppy disks on hand

   D. Reformat the hard drive

10. When you pick a custom installation of a Windows program:

    A. You lose the choice to do a typical installation.

    B. You need more hard drive space.

    C. You won't be able to use the CD drive.

    D. You will be able to see the options that are typically selected.

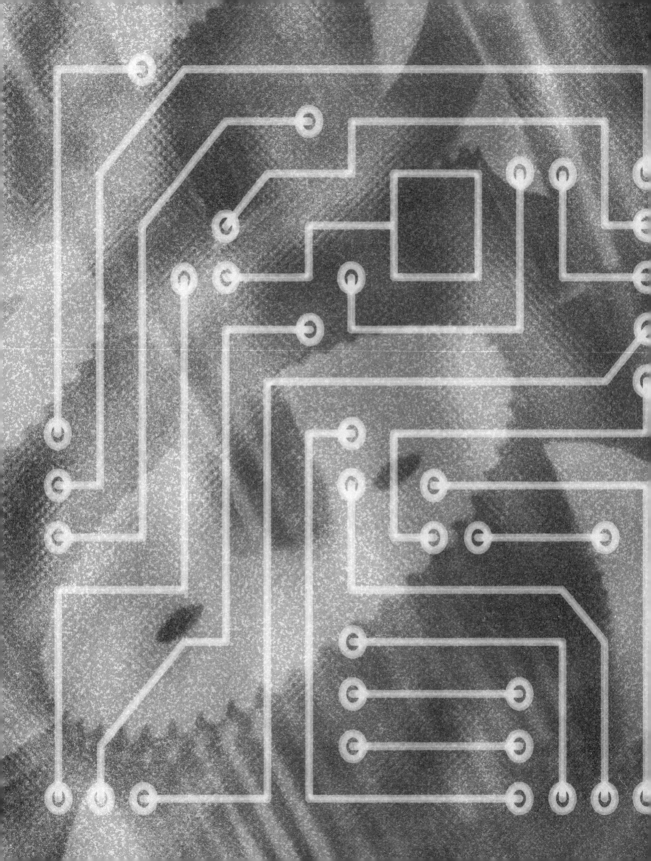

CHAPTER
EIGHT

8

Preventative Maintenance

■ Identify the basic system boot sequences, and alternative ways to boot the system software, including the steps to create an emergency boot disk with utilities installed.

■ Identify concepts relating to viruses and virus types—their danger, their symptoms, sources of viruses, how they infect, how to protect against them, and how to identify and remove them.

Because of their very nature, computers can and do fail. *Preventative maintenance* involves performing certain practices on a computer so that the computer will function reliably and not fail as often.

Thankfully, Microsoft has included a few pieces of software with their operating systems that allow us to perform preventative maintenance fairly easily. No fuss, no muss. The three preventative maintenance procedures we're going to discuss in this chapter are:

- Backing up your data
- Guarding against virus attacks
- Creating and using an emergency disk

With these procedures, you should be able to recover most of the common problems.

Backing Up Your Data

A *backup* is a duplicate copy of all the files and software on your hard disk. This copy is usually stored in a safe place (like a safe) in case of a system failure. When a system failure occurs, the backup can be copied back onto the system, restoring the system to the state it was in at the time of the last backup. This process of restoring the system is known as a *restore*.

Most backups are done the same way: select what you want to backup, then select where you want to backup to, then finally begin the backup. The files and directories you want to backup (and, subsequently, the drive they are stored on) are called the *source*. The device that you are backing up to is called the *target*. Once you have selected these items, some backup software will let you save these selections in a file known as a *backup set* so that you can reselect them later for restore by simply retrieving the backup set file from the backup media.

Backup Devices

There are several pieces of backup hardware that are currently available. You can backup your information to magnetic tape, Digital Audio Tape (DAT), Digital Linear Tape (DLT), Optical disk, removable hard disk, and many other removable media. The key here is that all of these media can be removed from the drive and stored in a safe place.

It's a common misconception that if you back up your data to a second, non-removable, hard disk in your computer your data is safe. But what happens if your computer is in a fire? What happens is that you lose your data. On the other hand, if the backup media are stored in a fireproof safe, you can purchase a new computer (assuming you have insurance), restore the data from the backup, and be back working in a short time.

Of all the backup media that are available, the most popular is magnetic tape (including reel-to-reel, DAT, DLT, and any backup system that uses a magnetic tape in a cartridge). There are a few reasons it is the most popular:

- First, it's inexpensive. Magnetic tape costs around $.01 to $.02 per MB (around $30 to $40 to back up 2GB), and the price is going down.

- Second, magnetic tapes are small and each holds several hundred MB of data.

- Finally, it's reliable. Magnetic tape is a proven technology that has been around for several years and will continue to expand in capacity and speed in the future.

Backup Types

There are four major types of backup that most backup software will use when backing up files. The four types are Full, Differential, Incremental, and Custom. Each type differs in the amount that it backs up, the time it takes to perform the backup, and the time it takes to restore the system to its pre-backup condition.

Full Backup

A Full backup, as its name suggests, backs up everything on the entire disk at once. It simply copies everything from the disk being backed up to the backup device. The backup takes a long time to perform (relative to the other types of backup), but the advantage is that the backup (and, subsequently, the restore) will use only one tape (assuming the tape capacity is large enough to handle backing up the hard disk in one shot).

Full backups are most often performed on systems that require that there be very little down time. Insurance computer systems are one such example. Their administrators will perform a Full backup every night so that if there is a failure, the system can be brought up quickly and the data will be as current as the time of the last backup.

Differential

A Differential backup backs up the files on a disk that have changed since the last Full backup, regardless of whether a Differential or Incremental backup has been done since the last Full backup. The Full backup is done usually once a week (i.e., on Friday) and copies all the files from the disk to the backup device. The Differential backup is done every day.

The size of a Differential backup increases every day following the Full backup. For example, if you do a Full backup on Friday night, then start your Differential backups on Monday, the Monday Differential tape will only have a small amount of information on it. When you get to Thursday, the Thursday tape will have all of the information on the disk that has changed since last Friday (including Monday, Tuesday, Wednesday, and Thursday's information).

The advantage to a differential backup style is that during the week, the backups don't take very long (although the time it takes to back up increases as the week goes on). In addition, you don't have to buy many backup tapes or media. You can use the same backup media you use for the Differential backup (not the one for the Full backup) over and over again each day.

When you restore from a Differential backup, you will need two tapes: the Full backup from the previous week and the current Differential backup. You will need to restore the Full backup first, then restore the Differential backup to restore the changes made since the last Full backup.

Incremental

What kind of backup strategy would you use with a terabyte (1024 gigabytes) of data? A Full backup every day would be impractical because it would take too long and use several tapes. A Differential backup would use even more tapes. Given these limitations, an Incremental backup would be the best choice.

The Incremental backup works similarly to the Differential backup but uses fewer tapes in a large backup situation. An Incremental backup does a Full backup once a week, then the backup software backs up all the files that have changed since the *previous* backup (not necessarily the last *Full* backup). Each day the backup software backs up a different amount of data, depending on the amount of data that was created that day.

The upside to the Incremental backup is that only the files that have changed that day will be backed up. If only three files changed today, then only three files will be backed up. Incremental backups tend to be very quick. Additionally, there is very little wasted effort because you aren't backing up files that haven't changed since you last backed them up. The downside to Incremental backups is the number of tapes needed for a restore. To restore from an incremental backup, you need the last Full backup tape and all the Incremental backup tapes from the day of the failure back to the day of the last Full backup.

Custom

The last type of backup that is performed is the Custom backup. A custom backup is any combination of the above three types. A custom backup involves selecting the files you want backed up as well as when you want them backed up. Most backup software programs have the ability to perform this type of backup. An example of a time when you might need to perform a custom backup is the end of the year. Accountants will need to back up the previous year's accounting data before finishing the year's accounting, just in case they make any mistakes and need to restore and start over.

And Now for the Real World...

There are some computer systems that can't afford any "down time" (i.e., banking, flight control, and certain high-volume sales systems). These systems back up all the data in real time and are called "high-availability data solutions." They will use various techniques to ensure that as soon as the data is written to disk, another copy is written to a second disk. If the system goes down, the backup system takes over automatically.

As you can imagine, these systems are usually impractical for home users, but they are found quite commonly in the network world on servers.

Backing Up in MS-DOS: Using MSBACKUP.EXE

Because of the importance of backing up your data, there are many different backup programs to choose from. Microsoft has ensured that you will have one to use by including one with each of its major operating systems: DOS, Windows 3.*x* and Windows 95 (a backup utility is also included with Windows NT).

NOTE   We will assume that you will be backing up to floppy for these examples, but it should be noted that most computers can be fitted with tape drives that can be used by some of these programs (the Windows 95 Backup, for example). If you have a tape drive in your computer and want to use the following guidelines to back up your data, just ignore the steps where you need to swap disks.

The MS-DOS backup program MSBACKUP is a very simple, very powerful program. It can be run in either command line mode or with a menu-driven interface. In either mode it can copy files to any DOS device (including floppy drives and redirected network drives—tape drives aren't supported). It can perform any of the types of backups including Full, Incremental, and Differential (Custom is an option if you select specific files to back up).

MSBACKUP uses special settings files called .SET files to store the settings for how it should run. The default SET file is called DEFAULT.SET and if unmodified by the user will allow a user to back their entire hard drive by simply starting the backup program and pressing B for Backup and S for Start Backup.

To start MSBACKUP, simply type **C:\>MSBACKUP** at the DOS command line and press Enter. MSBACKUP will start and present you with a menu giving you five choices: Backup, Restore, Compare, Configure, or Quit. Because the A+ Exam doesn't have too many questions about this menu, we'll just give a summary of each of these options.

NOTE If you have never run MSBACKUP before, it will present you with a screen that asks you to configure it. You will need to enter some settings and test MSBACKUP to make sure that backups are reliable.

Configure

Because MS Backup is a DOS program, you may need to configure the hardware it's using. When you select the Configure button from the main menu, you will be presented with a screen where you can configure the video settings (like what resolution and which colors you want to use), mouse settings (important if you want the mouse to work properly in this program), and which backup devices MS Backup is going to use (not really necessarily if you are backing up to floppy).

The final option on this screen is the Compatibility test. This test ensures that your system is able to backup files reliably. The test is automated (you must specify which drive you are using to back up to), but you will need to have a disk available so that it can do a test backup. Click the button to perform this compatibility test. If it finishes with no errors, you can begin your backup

---

NOTE You cannot perform a backup until you run a compatibility test!

Backup

To use the Backup option:

1. Click the Backup button (assuming your mouse is set up to work under DOS) or type **B**. When you select this option, a menu will appear.

2. At the top of this menu, you will see a file name under "Setup File." This is the name of the .SET file that MSBACKUP gets its settings from. If you have saved previously configured settings, choose this option and pick the .SET file that contains the details of how backup should run. Otherwise, leave this option set to DEFAULT.SET.

3. You can then click the Backup From box and choose which files you want to back up. Click the drive(s) that you want to back up or use the Select Files button underneath this window to pick specific files you want to back up. Remember that the more you choose to back up, the longer the backup will take and the more media (disks) you will use.

4. Choose the drop-down list under Backup To to pick which drive letter you want to back the files up to. If you pick a floppy disk drive (A: or B: in most systems), MSBACKUP will copy as many files as it can to the disk, then ask for a new, blank disk when it is full.

TIP

As you remove disks or other backup media that are full from a drive, label them immediately. That way you won't lose them or get them out of order.

5. After you have chosen where you are backing up to, you should choose whether to do a Full, Differential, or Incremental backup. (Custom backups simply involve changing the settings for any of the other types.) The default type is Full, but you can change this option by clicking on the drop-down menu and selecting Differential or Incremental.

6. When you have finished setting up the backup, you can click Start Backup. During the backup, MS Backup will display how long the backup will take, how many disks it will take, and how much data is being backed up. When the backup is complete, it will display a screen telling you all the statistics about the backup that was performed, including any files

that were skipped and the speed (in KB per minute) at which the backup took place.

Compare

Once you have performed a backup, you should use the Compare option on the MS Backup main menu to compare the files you just backed up to the originals that are currently on the disk. This option, when selected, will allow you to perform one of two operations:

- You can check the integrity of the current backup.

- You can check to see how many files have changed on your computer since the backup was performed.

The second of these two operations is useful before performing an Incremental or Differential backup because it will give you an idea of how many files have changed and thus of how many will be backed up during either an Incremental or Differential.

Restore

Hopefully, you will never need to restore. If you have to restore, that usually means there was a disk failure of some kind and you've lost some (or all) of your data. Before you can restore, you must have DOS, as well as the MS Backup program installed on the computer. Then, follow these steps:

1. Run MS Backup and select Main ➢ Restore.

2. Place the first disk of your backup into the A: drive (or place the backup tape you want to restore from into the tape drive).

3. Choose the location you want to restore from by clicking Restore From: and choosing the drive letter of the disk you are restoring from.

4. Select Restore To ➤ Original Locations so that the files will be restored along with the directories they came from.

5. Next, you *must* choose which files to restore (you can't proceed with the restore otherwise):

   - To restore the entire backup of the drive, just make sure that [-C-] All Files is selected in the Restore Files window.

   - If you want to restore a particular file or files, choose Select Files and pick the file(s) you want to restore.

6. When you are finished with your selections, click the Start Restore button to begin the restoration. During the restoration, MS Backup will ask you for several disks, in the same order it did when you performed the backup. Insert each disk when MS Backup asks for it.

When the restore is finished, you will see a status screen informing you of how long it took and how many files were restored.

Quit

Select this option when you have finished performing your backup, configure, or restore. When selected, this option will exit the program and leave you at a DOS prompt.

Backing Up in Windows 3.*x*: Using MWBACKUP.EXE

Now that we have discussed the MSBACKUP program for DOS, we need to discuss the available, built-in backup for Windows 3.*x*. There is a Windows version of MSBACKUP.EXE that comes with MS-DOS. It is called MWBACKUP.EXE, and it runs basically the same as the MS-DOS version, except all screens now have the

Windows "look and feel" to them. Additionally, the main menu has been replaced by a menu bar at the top of the Microsoft Backup window. The four buttons are the same choices you have with the DOS version and they perform the same functions.

Using the Microsoft Backup for Windows is basically the same as using the DOS version. This is mainly because they are based on the same backup engine. Generally speaking, you can follow the same steps to backup with MS Backup for Windows that you did with MSBACKUP.EXE for DOS. The only difference is that you will see Windows windows and menus instead of DOS windows and menus.

Backing Up in Windows 95: Using Backup for Windows 95

The third backup utility we're going to discuss is Microsoft Backup for Windows 95. It is basically the old Microsoft Backup, with a new interface and a few new features. It can support backing up to both floppies and other types of backup devices (like tape drives). However, the types of tape drives it can use are somewhat limited. Table 8.1 lists the tape drives that are compatible with Windows 95 and the ones that aren't.

TABLE 8.1: Windows 95 Backup tape drive compatibility chart

Tape Drive	Compatible
Archive (any)	No
QIC 40	Yes
QIC 80	Yes
QIC 3010	Yes
QIC 40, 80, and 3010	Yes

TABLE 8.1 (CONTINUED): Windows 95 Backup tape drive compatibility chart

Tape Drive	Compatible
Irwin (any)	No
Mountain (any)	No
QIC Wide	No
Qic 3020	No
SCSI tape drives (any)	No
Summit (any)	No
Travan (any)	No
Wangtek (QIC 40, 80, and 3010)	Yes

As you can see, basically only a QIC 40, 80, or 3010 tape drive will really work properly with Backup for Windows 95 (as well as any floppy drive).

Installing Windows 95 Backup

In Windows 95, Backup can sometimes be found under Start ➢ Programs ➢ Accessories ➢ System Tools. I say "sometimes" because it is not installed by default. You must specifically install it (either after Windows 95 has been installed or during a custom install) in order to use it.

To install Backup after Windows 95 has been installed, follow these steps:

1. Proceed to the Windows 95 Control Panel under Start ➢ Settings ➢ Control Panel.

2. Select Add/Remove Programs and choose the Windows Setup tab (Figure 8.1).

3. Click the checkbox next to Disk Tools. Doing so will tell the Windows 95 Setup program that you want to install the disk tools (including Backup).

4. To finish the installation, click OK.

Windows will copy the files from the installation location (either floppy or CD-ROM) and update the System Tools program group with an icon for Backup.

FIGURE 8.1:

Installing Windows 95 Backup using Add/ Remove Programs

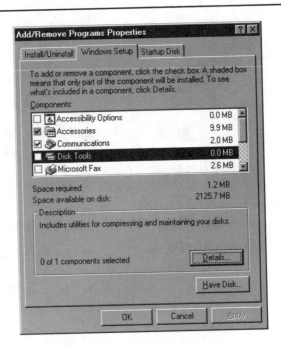

Starting Backup

To start the Windows 95 Backup, choose Start ➤ Programs ➤ Accessories ➤ System Tools ➤ Backup. The first time you run Backup, you will see a screen similar to the one shown in Figure 8.2. As you can see, this window explains, in a very broad sense, how to use

Backup to back up your files. If you haven't used backup before, you might want to click on the Help button. This will bring up a Windows Help screen that will allow you to browse and search for help on how to use Backup. Once you have read the help file, or if you already know how to use Backup, you can click OK.

FIGURE 8.2:

You will see this screen the first time you run Backup.

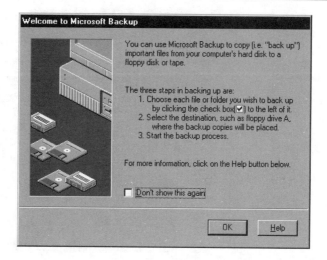

Welcome to Microsoft Backup

You can use Microsoft Backup to copy (i.e. "back up") important files from your computer's hard disk to a floppy disk or tape.

The three steps in backing up are:
1. Choose each file or folder you wish to back up by clicking the check box[✔] to the left of it.
2. Select the destination, such as floppy drive A, where the backup copies will be placed.
3. Start the backup process.

For more information, click on the Help button below.

☐ Don't show this again

OK   Help

TIP

If you don't want to see this screen again, check the box next to Don't Show This Again.

This nice thing about the Windows 95 Backup program is that it automatically makes a backup set for you, to get you started. This backup set is a full backup of the hard disk, including the registry files (which some backup programs can't back up). After you click OK to the screen in Figure 8.2, Backup will present you with the screen shown in Figure 8.3, which tells you it has made this backup set and what you can use it for.

WARNING Do not use this backup set (called Full System Backup) to base your Incremental or Differential backups on. They may not work correctly if based on this particular backup set.

FIGURE 8.3:

Backup automatically creates a backup set called Full System Backup for you the first time you run it.

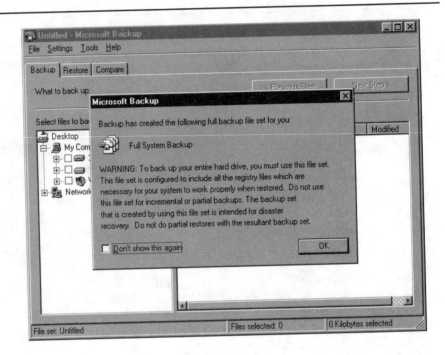

To start using Backup, mark the check box (if you don't want to see this warning again) and click OK.

Layout of Backup

Backup is a rather simple yet powerful program. There are two panes in the main window (Figure 8.4). These two panes work very similarly to the Windows Explorer program. If you double click on an item in the right pane, it will open and allow you to see what's inside. You can also use the right pane and click on the + signs next to items to "tree them out" and show the directory structure. These two panes allow you to select items to be backed up or restored depending on which tab is selected above. In Figure 8.4, the Backup tab is forward, meaning that selections you make will be for files and directories to be backed up.

FIGURE 8.4:

The Windows 95 Backup main window

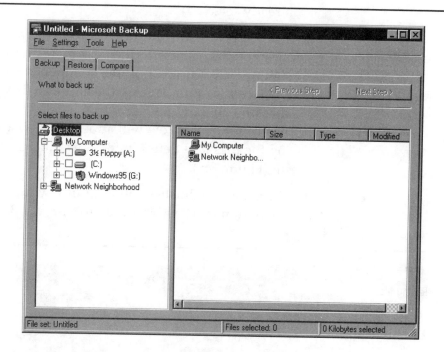

In addition to the two panes, you will notice that there are menus at the top of the screen. The most important of these menus is Help. If you don't understand how to do something in Backup, press the F1 key or choose Help ➤ Help Topics. Doing so will open the Windows 95 Help topics for Backup.

Backing Up Files

Backing up files in Windows 95 Backup works very similarly to the Windows MWBACKUP.EXE program. First you select what you want to backup, then where to want to backup those files and directories to, and then you initiate the backup:

1. To start the backup process, select the Backup tab (if it's not already selected).

2. Then select the directories you want to back up by clicking the check boxes next to them (you may need to click the + sign next to a directory if the subdirectory you want is inside it). If you want to back up the entire C: drive, simply click the check box next to the drive icon labeled "C." When you make a selection, a window will appear that shows you it is counting the files and determining how much space they will take up (Figure 8.5).

3. Once Backup finishes counting files, you will be able to click the button marked Next Step to start the Backup Wizard.

FIGURE 8.5:

Selecting files to backup

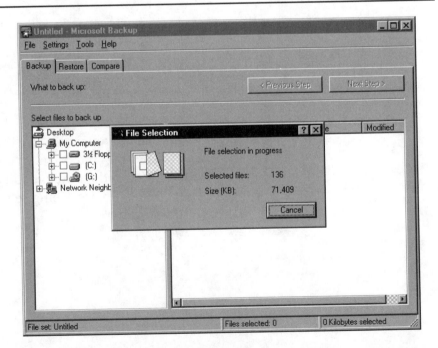

TIP If you make an icon on your desktop for Backup and you have a pre-configured backup set (.SET file), you can start the backup by dragging the .SET file onto the Backup icon.

4. The next step in the backup process involves selecting where you want to back the files up to (Figure 8.6).

- If you have a compatible tape drive installed, it will show up in the list on the left. You can then select it as the target device and click Start Backup to begin the backup.

- If you don't have a tape drive (or don't want to use it), you can select one of the floppy drives as the target device by clicking on its name. The name of the device will appear under Selected device or location as the device that has been specified as the target. In either case, select the device you want to back up to and click Start Backup to continue.

FIGURE 8.6:

Selecting a backup target device

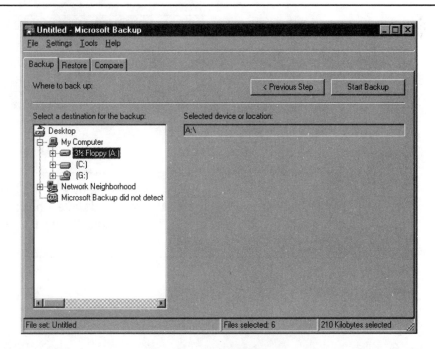

5. Now that you have selected what you want to back up, chosen the target backup device, and begun the backup, Backup will ask you want you want to call the backup set (Figure 8.7). Type in a name that describes what you are backing up. You can use any character except \, /, :, or > in the backup set name. For example, if you are backing up the entire C: drive, you might call the backup C: drive Full Backup. To start the backup, type the name of the backup set, then click OK.

FIGURE 8.7:

Entering a backup set name

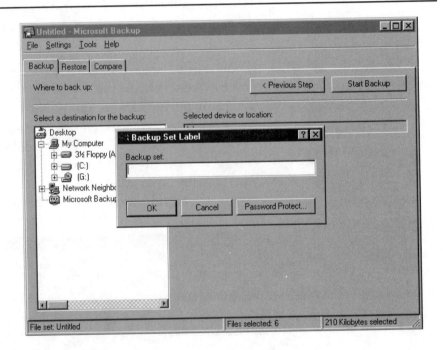

| TIP | You can protect sensitive backup data by entering a password for the backup set. Simply click the Password protect button to enter a password. This password will be required during the restore process in order to restore the data. |

6. As soon as you click OK, Backup will present you with a screen similar to the one shown in Figure 8.8. As you can see, this screen shows you how many files it is backing up, how much space they occupy, and how far along the backup is. When the backup is finished, it will present you with a screen telling you that the backup is finished (Figure 8.9). Click OK to acknowledge this screen, and you will see the backup statistics screen that shows you how many files were backed up, how much data (in KB) was backed up, and how long it took. Click OK and you are finished with the backup.

FIGURE 8.8:

Backup progress screen

FIGURE 8.9:

The Backup Finished window

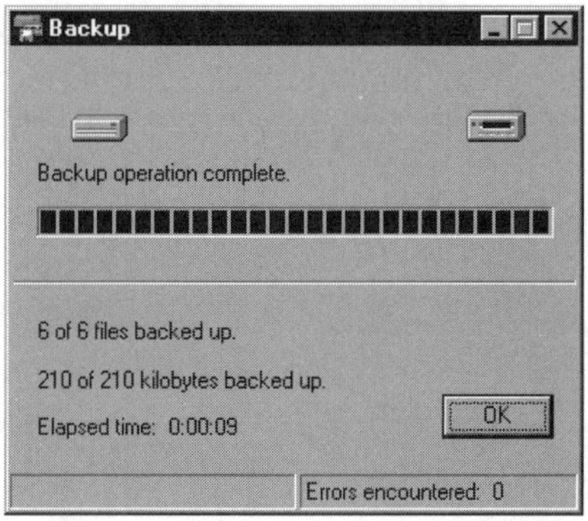

Restoring Files

It's amazing: There are some customers I've done work for who have had a computer company come in, set up their backup system for them, and only show them how to change tapes! When the customers have a problem, they feel helpless and don't know if their backup is any good until the computer company comes in and does their restore for them.

In order to ensure that your backups are good, you should perform a test restore every once in a while. If you used the Windows 95 backup program to back up your files, you will need to know to use it to restore, as well:

1. To begin a restore, run Backup and insert the first disk (or tape) of the backup into the drive.

2. Once Backup is up and running, you must click on the Restore tab to start the restore process.

3. In the screen that appears (Figure 8.10), you will see a list of the possible backup devices on the left. From this list, you must select the device you want to restore from by clicking on it.

4. Once you select a backup device, a list of the backup sets on that device will appear in the right hand window. To continue, you must select the backup set that contains the files you want to restore and click Next Step.

5. If there is a password on the backup set, Backup will prompt for it. You must enter the correct password before Backup will let you continue with the restore.

FIGURE 8.10:

The Windows 95
Backup Restore
window

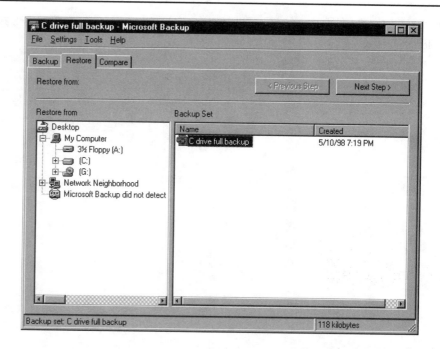

FIGURE 8.10:

The Windows 95
Backup Restore
window

6. The next step in the restore is to select the files and directories you want to restore. The screen shown in Figure 8.11 works the same as the file selection screen for backing up files earlier in the chapter: simply place a check mark next to the file(s) you want to restore and click Start Restore. On the other hand, if you want to restore the whole backup set, click the check box next to the name of the backup set in this window. All files from the backup set will be restored with this selection.

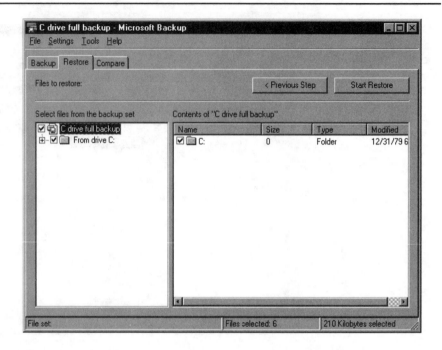

Once you have clicked Start Restore, Backup will review the
backup set and count how many files there are to restore. It will
then display a status window (very similar to the backup progress
window in Figure 8.8) that will show how far along the backup is.
(See Figure 8.12.) This screen will display how many files have
been restored (out of the total number of files to be restored), how
long you have been restoring files, and how much data has been
restored (in KB).

FIGURE 8.12:

Restore progress
screen

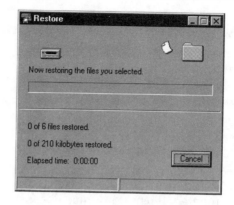

When Backup finishes restoring all the files you have selected, it will present you with a summary of the restore (Figure 8.13) detailing how much data was restored and how long it took. Click OK to complete the restore and return to the Backup main screen.

FIGURE 8.13:

Restore summary
screen

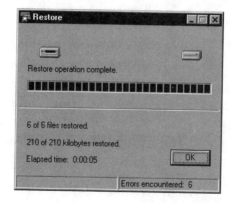

And Now for the Real World...

In most situations, the backup software that comes with most operating systems is adequate. However, you can buy backup software that has more features than the included software. Some of those features include data compression, backup scheduling, and greater hardware device support.

For home computers, the Microsoft backup products are more than adequate. However, for business users, I would recommend looking at products like Norton Backup or Central Point backup. The features they add will make a computer administrator much happier in the end.

Guarding Against Virus Attacks

A computer *virus* is a small, deviously genius program that replicates itself to other computers, generally causing the computers to behave abnormally. Generally speaking, a virus's main function is to reproduce. A virus attaches itself to files on a hard disk and modifies the files. When these files are accessed by a program, the virus can "infect" the program with its own code. The program may then, in turn, replicate the virus code to other files and other programs. In this manner, a virus may infect an entire computer.

When an infected file is transferred to another computer (via disk or modem download), the process begins on the other computer. Because of the frequency of downloads from the Internet, viruses can run rampant if left unchecked. For this reason, anti-virus programs were developed. They check files and programs for any program code that shouldn't be there and either eradicate it or prevent the virus from replicating. An anti-virus program is generally run in the background on a computer and examines all the file activity on that computer. When it detects a suspicious activity, it will notify the user of a potential problem and ask them what to do about it. Some anti-virus programs can also make intelligent decisions about what to do as well. The process of installing an anti-virus program on a computer is known as *inoculating* the computer against a virus.

NOTE For a listing of most of the viruses that are currently out there, refer to Symantec's Anti-Virus Research Center (SARC) at `http://www` `.symantec.com/avcenter/index.html`.

But Where Do I Stick the Needle?

You may notice that a lot of the language surrounding computer viruses sounds like language we use to discuss human illness. The moniker "virus" was given to these programs because a computer virus functions much like a human virus, and the term helped to anthropomorphize the computer a bit. Somehow, if people can think of a computer as getting "sick," it breaks down the computer phobia that many people have.

There are two real categories of viruses, benign and malicious. The benign viruses don't do much besides replicate themselves and exist. They may cause the occasional problem, but it is usually an unintentional side effect. Malicious viruses, on the other hand, are designed to destroy things. Once a malicious virus (i.e., the Michelangelo virus) infects your machine, you can usually kiss the contents of your hard drive goodbye.

Anti-Virus Software

Wouldn't it be nice if Microsoft included an anti-virus program with their operating systems? They did, but only with MS-DOS. MS-DOS 6.22 comes with anti-virus software that lets you detect viruses on your computer as well as clean any infected files. This software is called Microsoft Anti-Virus and has been included with DOS since version 6.0. The same program contains files to allow it to work with Windows.

Using Microsoft Anti-Virus for DOS

To use Microsoft Anti-Virus for DOS:

1. Type **C:\>MSAV** at the MS-DOS command line. From the main menu on the screen that appears, you can check for viruses on any disk drive as well as remove them if any are present. In the lower-right corner of this screen, you can see which drive you are currently scanning for viruses.

2. From the main menu, you have five options: Detect, Detect & Clean, Select New Drive, Options, and Exit. Choose Select New Drive. This option allows you to pick which drive you want to scan. You can select from any of the disk drives you have installed in your system.

TIP   You don't necessarily have to scan the drive letters for CD-ROM drives. CD-ROMs are read-only so viruses can't be transferred to them from your machine. On the other hand, you may want to scan them anyway because viruses can be burned onto CDs if the machine doing the burning has a virus.

---

3. Back at the Main menu, you have two options if you want to see if you have a virus on your computer. You can use the Detect option or the Detect & Clean option. Choose either one

and MS Anti-Virus will check the entire disk to find any viruses that it knows about.

- If it detects a virus and you have Detect & Clean selected, it will present you with a screen that allows you to choose whether or not you want MS Anti-Virus to try and clean the virus from the disk or to ignore it (Figure 8.14).

- If MS Anti-Virus finds a virus and you have Detect selected, the program will simply tell you which files are afflicted.

FIGURE 8.14:

MS Anti-Virus finds a virus

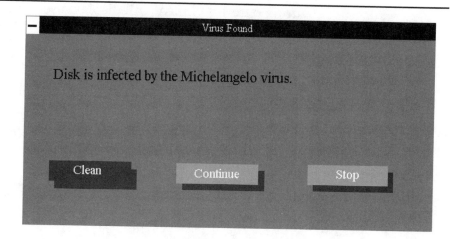

4. When it has finished scanning the disk, MSAV will present you with a list of the disks it has scanned, the file types it has scanned, the number of viruses found on the disks, and the number of files cleaned. If it hasn't found any viruses, select OK to return to the main menu. Then select Exit to quit MSAV. If it did find a virus or two, select OK and return to the main menu, then re-run the Detect & Clean process just to make sure the virus is gone.

There are two options left on the main menu to discuss: Options and Exit. Both are pretty much self-explanatory. The Options menu allows you to change how aggressively MSAV checks for viruses. The Exit menu completely exits you from the MSAV program.

Using Microsoft Anti-Virus for Windows

If you want to use Microsoft Anti-Virus from Windows, simply open the Microsoft Tools program group and double-click the Microsoft Anti-Virus icon. In the window that appears, select which disk (or disks) you want to scan from the list at the left side, then click the Detect button or the Detect & Clean button to start the scanning for viruses.

During detection MSAV will display a screen showing which files it's scanning and the progress. If it finds a file infected with a virus, it will display a warning and give you the same options it does under MS-DOS.

Finally, once MSAV is finished running, it will present you with a status screen that gives you a list of the number of files it scanned, the number that were infected, and the time it took the scan (similar to the status screen for the DOS version).

And Now for the Real World...

There are several commercial anti-virus programs available. One of the best and most widely used is Symantec Anti-Virus (SAM). It has a memory resident component to constantly look for viruses, as well as an executable component for scanning for viruses. SAM is available for Macintosh, Windows 3.x, Windows 95, Windows NT, UNIX and a few other platforms.

There are also programs like Norton Anti-Virus and Central Point Anti-Virus available if the Symantec product isn't your bag. And you can always just use the ones that come with DOS and Windows (unless you have Windows 95, which doesn't come with one).

Creating and Using an Emergency Disk

What happens when your Windows 95 computer has a problem? Often times, if the Registry is corrupt, the Windows 95 interface won't come up—not even in safe mode. Windows 95 comes with a utility that allows you to create a disk that can be used to fix Windows 95. This disk is often called the Windows 95 Emergency Repair Disk (also called the Start-Up Disk). It contains enough of Windows 95 to boot the computer. The disk also contains files and utilities to examine (and possibly fix) the machine, utilities like FDISK, SCANDISK, EDIT, ATTRIB, REGEDIT, FORMAT, DEBUG, CHKDSK, and UNINSTAL.EXE.

To create an Emergency Repair Disk select Start ➤ Settings ➤ Control Panel, double-click on Add/Remove Programs, and click on the Startup Disk tab (see Figure 8.15). When you are ready to create a startup disk, insert a blank floppy disk in your A: drive and click the Create Disk icon. Windows 95 will format the disk and make it bootable (see Figure 8.16). It will then copy the aforementioned utilities to it so that you can use them to fix Windows 95.

When Windows 95 finishes copying files to the disk, remove the disk from the drive, label it "Windows 95 Emergency Repair Disk," and put it in a safe place so that you can get to it easily if there is ever a problem.

FIGURE 8.15:

The Startup Disk tab
of the Add/Remove
Programs control panel

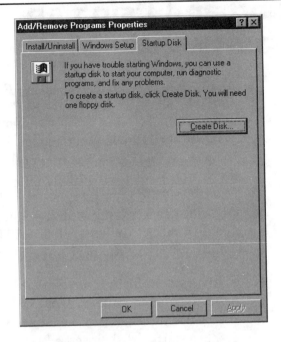

FIGURE 8.16:

Creating a new
startup disk

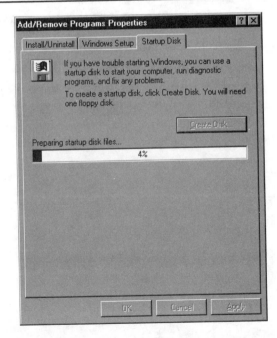

Review Questions

1. Which type of backup copies all files that have changed since the last full backup, regardless if they have been backed up since then?

   A. Full

   B. Incremental

   C. Differential

   D. Custom

2. A computer virus is:

   A. A small program

   B. A small living organism

   C. Something that makes you sick

   D. A type of cheese

3. One of the main functions of all viruses is to:

   A. Party

   B. Reproduce

   C. Destroy files

   D. Make strange things happen to your computer

4. Backing up is important because you need to have something to do when you're not working on your computer.

   A. True

   B. False

5. If you backed up 60MB of data, how many tapes are required to restore from a full backup (generally speaking)?

   A. 4

   B. 2

   C. 7

   D. 1

6. What is the name of the executable for Microsoft Backup for DOS?

   A. MSBKUP.EXE

   B. MSBACKUP.EXE

   C. BACKUP.EXE

   D. MWBACKUP.EXE

7. What is the name of the executable for Microsoft Backup for Windows 3.x?

   A. MSBKUP.EXE

   B. MSBACKUP.EXE

   C. BACKUP.EXE

   D. MWBACKUP.EXE

8. You can use a Travan tape drive with Windows 95 Backup.

   A. True

   B. False

9. What would you type at a DOS command line to start the Microsoft Anti-Virus?

    A. AV

    B. MSANTIVI

    C. MSAV

    D. ANTIVIRU

10. Which control panel can be used to create a Startup Disk?

    A. System

    B. Add new hardware

    C. Add/Remove programs

    D. Startup

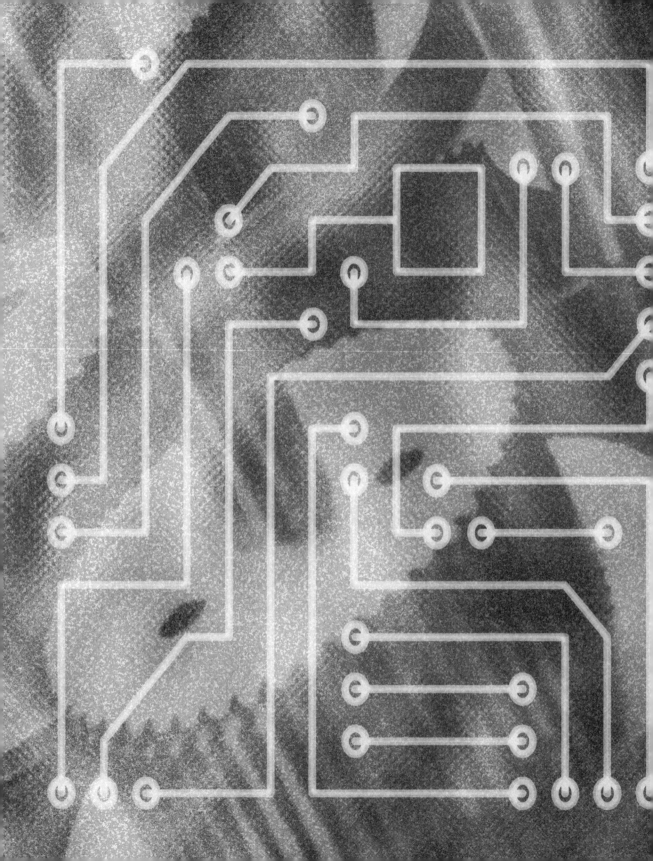

CHAPTER

NINE

Networking

■ Identify the networking capabilities of DOS and Windows including procedures for connecting to the network.

■ Identify concepts and capabilities relating to the Internet and basic procedures for setting up a system for Internet access.

It seems that everywhere you look today, someone is talking about the Internet. Just look at the preponderance of Web site addresses on radio and television commercials today. The Web has become a "hot button" that advertising companies love to exploit. But, very few people realize what the Internet actually is. Some people think it's a public thoroughfare for information (hence the moniker "information superhighway"). Others believe it to be some kind of new high-tech toy. In reality, however, the *Internet* is just a mesh of interconnected private networks that spans the globe. To understand the Internet, you really must understand the underlying infrastructure: networks.

Simply put, a *network* is several devices (not just computers) connected together for the purpose of sharing resources, such as printers or disk space. Previous versions of the A+ Certification by CompTIA lacked any information about networks. The current exam, however, includes information about basic networking concepts, the Internet, and setting up computers to access both regular business networks and the Internet. In this chapter we will discuss these topics as they relate to MS-DOS, Windows 3.*x* and Windows 95.

NOTE   For detailed information about networks, protocols, networking hardware, and clients, refer to the first book in the A+ series from Sybex: the *A+: Core Module Study Guide*.

The Networking Giants

No doubt about it, the software industry is one of the largest in the world today. In the United States alone, it is a multi-billion dollar a year industry. The majority of the money, however, is made in networking software. Networking software is written to be used by several people at once and perform a variety of functions like e-mail, collaboration, and business management. Every company can use these types of networking software and reap the benefits.

In the networking software business, there are quite a few major players (like Novell, Microsoft, IBM, and Seagate). However, there are clearly two leaders in the game: Novell out of Provo, UT and Microsoft out of Redmond, WA. Each company produces several software products for networks, but in the following sections, we are going to focus on the different ways DOS, Windows 3.x and Windows 95 connect to the Networking Operating Systems (NOSes) made by these two companies. Novell has developed an NOS called Netware (currently at version 4.11, with version 5 due out in Summer of 1998). At this time, Netware has the largest market share of any NOS. However, Microsoft's Windows NT (currently at version 4, with 5 due sometime in late 1999) is selling more copies every day and seems to be the "hot ticket" for NOSes because of its ease of use for the inexperienced administrator and its familiar Windows interface.

MS-DOS and Windows 3.x Networking

When MS-DOS was developed, it was designed to be a simple, stand-alone, operating system. To that end, it doesn't contain any network software, except SHARE.EXE. SHARE.EXE was designed as an add-on to popular networking software that would allow two users to be editing the same file at the same time on a network. Without SHARE.EXE, when a second user tries to open a file that the first user has opened, they get an error message. With SHARE.EXE installed, when the second user tries to open the file, they receive a message saying that the file is being used by someone else and offering to provide a copy of that file.

SHARE.EXE could also come in handy with Windows programs. In the past, you were only able to run one copy of a Windows program per machine. With SHARE.EXE loaded, you can run more than one copy of, say, Microsoft Word.

Another side of networking with MS-DOS and Windows is client software for Novell and Microsoft networks. *Client software* will allow a computer to connect to a server and access the network resources hosted by that server. Most client software for DOS and Windows 3.*x* falls into the category of redirection software. This software redirects requests bound for local resources out to network resources (Figure 9.1). For example, with network client software installed, you can point a DOS drive letter to some disk space on the network. When you save a file to that drive letter, you are really saving that file to a server. But, as far as DOS is concerned, it is accessing a local drive letter.

FIGURE 9.1:

Network client software redirects local requests to the network

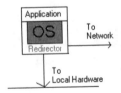

Finally, it should be noted that Windows 3.11 has an add-on called Windows for Workgroups. This add-on allows a machine running DOS and Windows 3.11 to participate in a peer-to-peer network and share its files and any local printers with the rest of the network. This involves installing the Windows for Workgroups add-on and the networking software specific to your network card.

Windows 95 Networking

When Windows 95 was released in late 1995, it wasn't the first Microsoft operating system to contain built-in networking. Both the Windows NT operating system and, to a lesser extent, Windows for Workgroups already did. However, Windows 95 is the first Microsoft operating system with built-in networking that is easy for the average user to use and configure.

Network Control Panel

You can see the configuration of Windows 95 networking centers on the Network control panel in Figure 9.2. From this interface, you can configure clients, protocols, network interface cards (NICs) and the network services you want this machine to perform. To access the Network control panel, select Start ➢ Settings ➢ Control Panel and double-click Network in the Control Panel window that appears. Windows 95 will display the network control panel. Alternatively, if you already have some networking components installed, you can simply right-click the Network Neighborhood icon on your desktop and choose Properties from the pop-up menu.

A Windows 95 workstation can support multiple simultaneous network types. For example, a user can log in to both Novell and Microsoft networks, assuming they have both network clients installed and configured correctly. The Primary Network Logon drop-down list shown in Figure 9.2 determines which network type you will log on to first. If there are none, this list will only give you one option, Windows Logon.

The list above the Primary Network Logon drop-down list shows which network components are currently installed on this machine. In the screen shown in Figure 9.2, you will see that the Novell Intranetware Client is currently installed (it is also

FIGURE 9.2:

The Windows 95 Network control panel

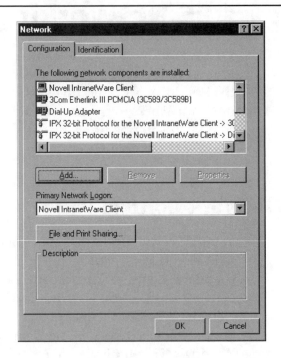

the primary network logon). You may also notice that there is a scroll bar on the right hand side. The scroll bar allows you to see all the clients, network adapters, protocols, and services that might be installed.

Let's suppose you wanted to add the Microsoft Client for Microsoft Networks to this machine for the purpose of connecting to Microsoft servers (including Windows NT, Windows 95, and Windows for Workgroups). To do so, follow these steps:

1. Click the Add button towards the bottom of the Network control panel. This will display the screen shown in Figure 9.3.

2. In this screen you can choose what type of item you are going to install. For our example, the Microsoft Client is a Client, so click Client and click Add.

FIGURE 9.3:

Choosing a networking
component type

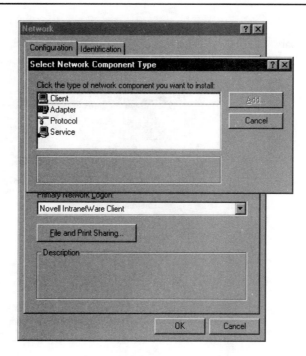

3. You will see a screen similar to the one in Figure 9.4. This
   screen is the standard "Pick your component" screen that
   Windows 95 uses. On the left, select the company whose software (or driver) you want to install. When you have selected a
   manufacturer, a list of the software that Windows 95 can
   install from that company appears on the right.

NOTE   Only software written by Microsoft appears in this list. The Windows
95 CD doesn't include any software from any other vendor. The software you do see was written by Microsoft to allow Windows 95 to
use the hardware from various vendors.

FIGURE 9.4:

Selecting the software you want to install

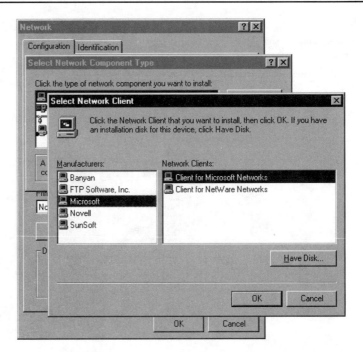

4. Because you are installing a Microsoft Client for Microsoft networks, you need to click on Microsoft in the left pane and then click on Microsoft Client for Microsoft Networks when it appears in the right pane.

5. To begin the installation, click OK. Windows 95 will bring you back to the main Network control panel screen (shown earlier in Figure 9.2).

6. Now that you have the Microsoft client installed, you will be able to select it as the primary logon in the Primary Network Logon drop-down list.

7. In most cases, you will need to configure the client before you reboot so that when you reboot you'll be able to log on to a Microsoft network. To configure any item in the Network control panel, simply click the item and click the Properties

button. If you click on Microsoft Client for Microsoft Networks and click properties, you will see a screen similar to the one in Figure 9.5. From here you can configure how your workstation logs on to the network by entering the appropriate information (which you can get from your network administrator). In my case, I have to log on to a Windows NT domain called CT_TRAINING, so I'll put a check in the box next to Log On to Windows NT Domain and type in **CT_TRAINING** in the box.

FIGURE 9.5:

Configuring the Client for Microsoft Networks to log on to a domain

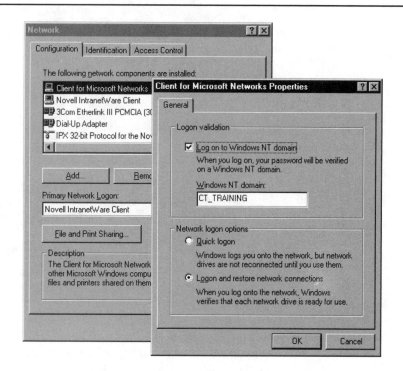

NOTE   For more information on configuring a workstation to talk to a specific network, refer to that manufacturer's education courses or printed documentation. There are usually instructions for which Windows 95 clients to set up and how to configure them. Since the A+ test only tests you on the network software basics, that's all we'll cover here.

8. When you have finished installing the Microsoft Client for Microsoft Networks, your network control panel will have that entry in the list of network components currently installed. (Compare Figure 9.6 with Figure 9.2, noticing the differences between the two Network control panels.) Click OK to close the control panel.

FIGURE 9.6:

Microsoft Client for Microsoft Networks now installed

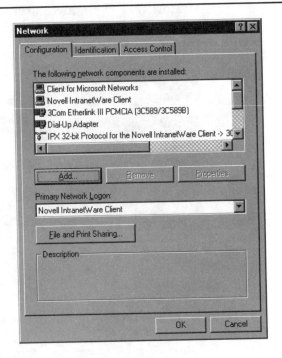

9. Windows 95 will copy some files (possibly asking for a disk or CD, unless the .CAB files are located on the hard drive somewhere) and ask you to reboot so that the settings can take place. Go ahead and click OK on the dialog box that pops up so that Windows can reboot.

10. Once Windows 95 has rebooted, you will be able to use resources from any Microsoft-based network (assuming you have been given access to those resources). If you have

checked the Log On to Windows NT Domain, you will see a screen similar to the one in Figure 9.7. Type in your user name and password (given to you by the domain's administrator) and click OK to log on.

FIGURE 9.7:

Logging on to a
Windows NT network

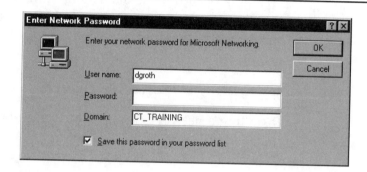

TIP

If you have problems logging on to a network, try logging on as a different user. If you can't log on, and the other user can, the problem may be related to the settings associated with your user. The problem then is the responsibility of the network administrator.

Setting Up Windows 95 to Share Files and Printers

As I have already mentioned, it is possible to set up Windows 95 to share files and printers with other Windows 95 users on the same network. You will do this if you want other people on the network to use your files or print to your printer. By doing this, you will be making what is known as a *peer-to-peer network*, where each computer acts as both a workstation and a server.

For you to be able to do this, you'll need a few prerequisites: First of all, you must have a network card installed in both computers and have those network cards hooked to the same network. Second, you must have a client and protocol loaded. Third, the file and print sharing must be turned on and configured properly. Finally, you must share something on the host machine so that the client machine can use it. Let's discuss these three requirements in detail.

Installing a Network Card

Installing a network card is a fairly simple task if you have installed any expansion card before, as a network interface card (NIC) is just a special type of expansion card. To install an NIC:

1. First move jumpers or flip DIP switches on the expansion card to set it to the correct IRQ/DMA/IO port settings as per the factory instructions (if the card uses a software set program, you can ignore this step).

2. Next, power off the PC, remove the case and insert the expansion card into an open slot.

3. Secure the expansion card with the screw provided.

4. Put the case back on the computer and power it up (you can run software configuration at this step, if necessary). If there are conflicts, change any parameters so that the NIC doesn't conflict with any existing hardware.

TIP Sometimes older NICs can conflict with newer Plug-n-Play (PnP) hardware. Additionally, some newer NICs with PnP capability don't like some kinds of networking software. To resolve a PnP conflict of the latter type, disable PnP on the NIC either with a jumper or with the software setup program.

5. The final step in installing an NIC is to install a driver for the NIC for the type of operating system that you have. Windows 95, however, should auto-detect the NIC and install the driver automatically. If not, run the Add New Hardware wizard by double-clicking Add New Hardware in the control panels folder.

After installing an NIC, you must hook the card up to the network using the specific patch cable supplied by your network administrator. You will need to attach the patch cable to the connector on the NIC and to a port in the wall, thus connecting your PC to the rest of the network.

NOTE   Sometimes installing an NIC card will install a client and protocol, so some of the next steps won't be necessary.

Installing a Client and Protocol

Turning on file and print sharing is simple, once you have a network card installed and configured properly. All you need to do is install the other components for networking and enable the Microsoft File and Print Service for Microsoft Networks. The other components that you will need are the Microsoft Client for Microsoft Networks (discussed earlier) and a common communications protocol.

A *communications protocol* is a specific set of rules governing communications between two entities on a network. Both entities must be speaking the same protocol in order to communicate. One of the most common protocols used on LANs today is the Internetwork Packet Exchange or IPX for short. It was developed by Novell for use with their Netware operating system. It is one of the more efficient protocols used for small file transfers today.

WARNING Communicating between two PCs using IPX can cause some problems with the rest of your network if you're not careful. You may want to consult your network administrator before doing this.

To add the IPX protocol:

1. Choose Add from the Network control panel, pick Protocol from the list of components, and choose Microsoft from the list of vendors on the left side of the screen that pops up (Figure 9.8).

FIGURE 9.8:

Selecting the IPX/SPX-compatible Protocol

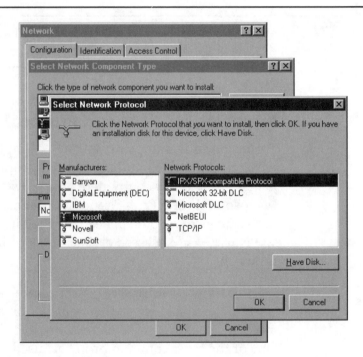

2. Choose IPX/SPX-compatible Protocol on the right-hand side, and click OK.

3. Click OK to close the Network control panel and install the IPX protocol.

4. Of course, Windows 95 will ask you to reboot to finalize the settings. Go ahead and reboot to finalize the installation.

Now that you have the network card installed and configured, as well as the client and protocol installed, it is time to start the file and printer sharing services. This is also done through the Network control panel. To start the services, follow these steps:

1. Open the Network control panel and click on the File and Print Sharing button. You will see a screen that will allow you to pick which services you want to share (see Figure 9.9).

2. Click the box next to the top option (I Want to Be Able to Give Others Access to My Files) if you want to share files on your machine with someone else on the network. If you want others to be able to print to a printer hooked to your machine, click the box next to the bottom option (I Want to Be Able to Give Others Access to My Printers). When each option is enabled, a check mark will appear in the appropriate box. To disable an option, simply click in the box again and the check mark will disappear.

3. Once you have enabled File and Printer sharing, the service called File and Printer Sharing for Microsoft Networks will appear in the list of installed network components. In addition to specifying what you are going to share, you must specify how security is going to be handled. There are two options: Share-Level access control and User-Level access control. Share Level access control means that you supply a username, password, and security settings for each resource that you share. User-level means that there is a central database of users (usually administrated by the network administrator) that Windows 95 can use to specify security settings for each shared resource. Most of the time, Share Level access control is fine. There are only a few cases where user-level is needed (like in a

network where the administrator has said you will do it this
way). To specify these settings, choose the "Access Control" tab
from the Network control panel (Figure 9.10) and choose the
appropriate option.

Enabling file and
printer sharing

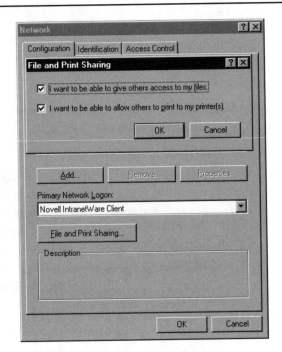

4. Click OK to save all of these new settings.

5. Windows 95 will copy some files and ask you to reboot (big
   surprise, huh?). Reboot your computer to start sharing files
   and printers.

FIGURE 9.10:

Specifying the Access
Control method

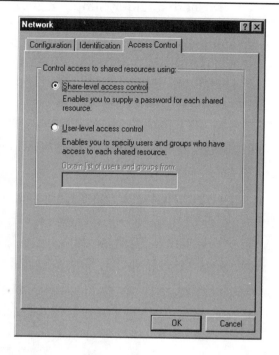

Sharing Folders

Hypothetically, let's say you have a folder on your machine called
REPORTS that contains reports that everyone should be able to
see. To allow everyone to see them, you will need to enable file
sharing (as previously discussed) and share that folder. The sharing can be done through either the Desktop or the Windows
Explorer program.

Basically, any folder can be shared (including the root of the
C: drive), as long as you can see it. Additionally, when you
share a folder, the person you share it with will be able to see
not only the folder you've shared but also any folders inside
that folder. So don't share a folder that contains a folder you
don't want anyone to see!

To share a folder, simply right click on it and choose Sharing... from the menu that pops up. This option will bring up the Properties window of that folder with the Sharing tab in front (Figure 9.11). You can do basically the same thing by right-clicking on a folder and choosing Properties and then clicking on the Sharing tab.

FIGURE 9.11:

The Sharing tab of the Properties window

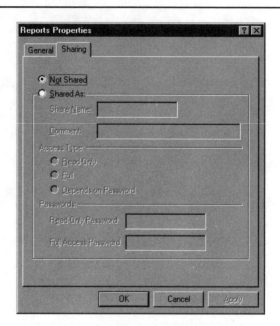

To start the share, click the Shared As radio button. A couple of fields will become visible (Figure 9.12). The first field is Share Name. The name you enter here will be used to access this folder. It should be something that accurately represents what you are sharing. In addition, you can enter a description of the share in the Comment field.

FIGURE 9.12:

Enabling a share

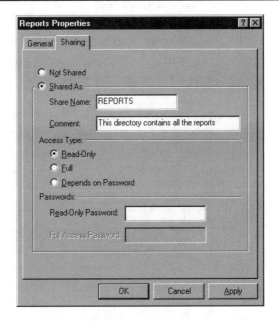

Finally, you must specify the access rights and password(s) for the share. There are three options for access rights when using the share-level security scheme. To select either of the following options, click the radio button next to each option:

Read-Only With this option selected, anyone accessing the share will only be able to open and read the files inside the folder and any subfolders. You must specify a password that users can use to access the share in read-only mode.

Full Access In full access mode, everyone accessing the share has the ability to do anything to the files in the folder as well as any subfolders. This includes being able to delete those files. You must specify a password that the users will use to access this share.

Depends on Password This option is probably the best option of the the three. With this option, users can use one password to access the share in read-only mode and use a different password to access it in full access mode. You can give everyone the read-only password so they can view the files and give the full access password only to users who need to change the files.

Once you have specified the share name, comments, and access rights, click OK to share the directory. Notice that the REPORTS directory now has a hand underneath it, indicating that it's being shared (Figure 9.13).

FIGURE 9.13:

REPORTS folder now shared

Sharing Printers

Sharing printers works very similarly to sharing folders. First of all, you must have the printer correctly set up to printer on the machine that will be "hosting" it. Secondly, you need to right-click on a Printer in the PRINTERS folder and click Sharing. The printer properties screen in Figure 9.14 will appear with the Sharing tab selected to allow you to share the printer.

FIGURE 9.14:

The Sharing tab of a printer

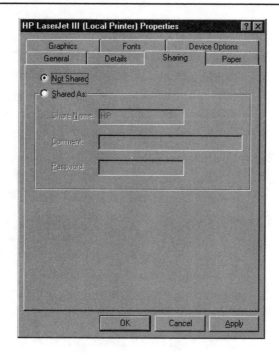

To share the printer, simply click Share As and specify a name for the share (Figure 9.15). The name will default to a truncated version of the printer name you gave it when you installed it. When I set up my workstation for my new laser printer, I called it HP LaserJet III (the local name) because that's what it was. Notice in Figure 9.14 that Windows 95 truncated this name to HP. The name you give this share (called the *share name*) should be something that everyone will recognize when they see it on the network and that accurately describes the printer. I'm going to call it DavesHP so people will know that it's next to my workstation and that it's an HP printer.

FIGURE 9.15:

Sharing a printer

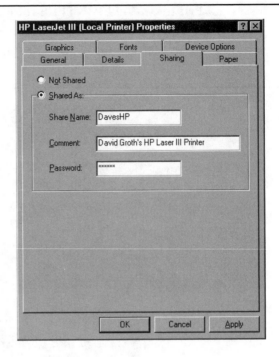

In addition to specifying the name of the printer share, you can enter a comment that describes the printer accurately. Finally, you should specify a password that users must enter in order to install this printer on their workstations (they won't have to enter it every time they print).

To finish sharing the printer, click OK. Windows 95 will prompt you for the password again, just to verify that you know what it is and that you didn't misspell it. Retype the password in the box that appears and click OK, and the share will be active. Notice that the printer in the PRINTERS folder in Figure 9.16 has a hand under it, indicating that it is shared.

FIGURE 9.16:

The printer is now shared

Using a Shared Folder

Now that we have shared a folder and printer, we need to discuss how to get access to them. For this, we'll turn to the Network Neighborhood icon. When you double-click this item, it lets you browse the network for resources. Figure 9.17 shows an example of a Network Neighborhood browse window. As you can see, there are several entities on our network. The little icons that look like computers are just that, computers on the network. However, there isn't a different icon for a Novell server, an NT server, or a Windows 95 machine sharing out part of its hard disk. They all look the same to Windows 95. The one that looks like a tree is in fact an NDS Tree for a Novell network.

Through this screen you can double-click any computer to see the resources that are hosted by that computer.

TIP   If you do know the name of the computer that hosts the resource you are looking for, you can use the Find command. Just go to Start ➤ Find ➤ Computer and type in the name of the computer preceded by two backslashes (the beginning of a UNC path).

FIGURE 9.17:

A sample Network Neighborhood window

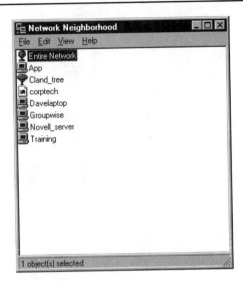

Using a shared folder is just like using any other folder on your computer, with one or two exceptions. First of all, the folder exists on the network, so you have to be connected to the network in order use it. Also, for some programs to work properly, you must map a local drive letter to the network folder. This is because the Windows 95 reference to a share on the network uses the Universal Naming Convention path (or UNC path). The UNC path uses the format *machine name**share**path*\. So, a directory called JULY98 underneath a share called REPORTS on a machine called DAVELAPTOP would be written as \\DAVELAPTOP\REPORTS\JULY98.

NOTE　　If any item has a space in the name, be careful. Some DOS utilities can't interpret spaces.

To connect to a network folder share, simply double-click the computer that's hosting it to view the list of shares (Figure 9.18). Notice that both the folder and printer I shared in the previous examples are there. Because we want to use the folder share, we can just double-click it to see its contents (and copy files to and from if necessary). Or, we can map a drive letter so that all our applications will be able to use it.

FIGURE 9.18:

Viewing the resources
a computer is hosting

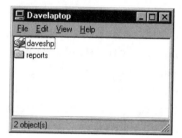

Now that we see all the resources the computer is hosting, we can map a drive letter to it by right clicking on the folder (REPORTS in this case) and choosing Map Network Drive. This will cause the screen shown in Figure 9.19 to appear. You must pick a drive letter (preferably one that is not being used) and click OK to map the drive. Remember that most Windows applications can use UNC paths and don't need drive mappings. We do this for any DOS or old Windows 3.x applications we might be running.

FIGURE 9.19:

Mapping a drive letter
to a network share

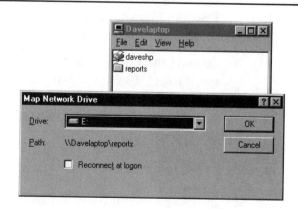

Now that you have a drive mapped, you can use the files and directories in the share that you mapped to.

Using a Shared Printer

Now that we've discussed the way of using a shared folder, we can discuss the way to set up a workstation to print to a shared printer. Both situations are somewhat similar because in both cases, you are accessing a resource that has been shared on the host computer. Additionally, in both cases you are pointing a local resource (in this case a printer icon) to a network resource (a shared printer).

To set up the printer on your workstation, you most likely will use the Point and Print option for Windows 95 printing. This option allows you to click and drag a printer to the PRINTERS folder and run the Point and Print wizard, which will set up the printer icon and set up the right drivers on your machine. Follow these steps:

1. Browse to the computer that hosts the printer you want to set up and double-click the computer name so you can see the printer you want to install.

2. Open up the PRINTERS folder under Start ➤ Settings ➤ Printers. Arrange these windows so you can see both at the same time (Figure 9.20).

3. To start the Point-and-Print wizard, drag the printer you want to set up from the list of resources the computer is hosting to the Printers window. As soon as you release the mouse button, you will see the wizard start, and it will display the window shown in Figure 9.21.

4. The wizard will ask you a series of questions that will help you to configure the printer. The first question it will ask you is "Do you print from MS-DOS–based programs?" The reasoning behind this question is similar to the reason we map drive

FIGURE 9.20:

Preparing for the Point-
and-Print process

FIGURE 9.20:

Preparing for the Point-
and-Print process

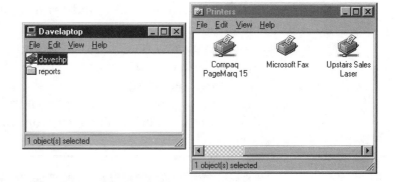

letters. Most older DOS programs (and to a lesser extent, Windows programs) don't understand the UNC path syntax for access to a shared resource. Instead they understand a name for a local hardware resource (like LPT1: for the first local parallel port). So, we must point a local printer port name out to the network in a process known as capturing. If you need to capture a printer port, answer "Yes" to this question, otherwise leave it set to the default ("No"). For our example, click Yes and click Next to move to the next step of the wizard.

FIGURE 9.21:

Starting the Point-and-
Print wizard

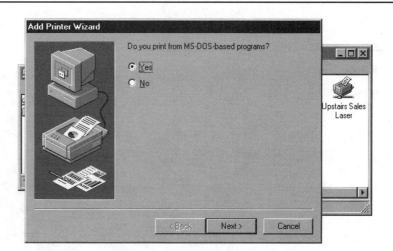

5. The next step in the Point-and-Print wizard is to capture the printer port, assuming you chose Yes in the previous step. If you did, you will see the screen in Figure 9.22. This screen allows you to capture a printer port so that DOS programs can print to the network printer. Click the Capture Printer Port... button to bring up the screen (shown in Figure 9.23) that allows you to choose which local port you want to capture.

FIGURE 9.22:

Capturing a
Printer port

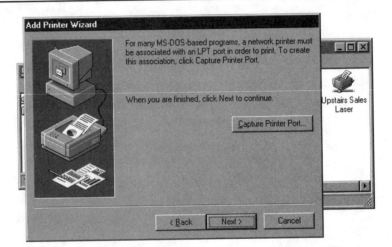

FIGURE 9.23:

Picking which local
port to capture

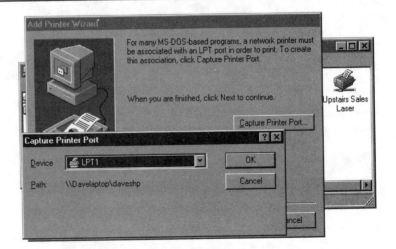

6. From the drop down list shown, choose the local port you want to capture (any port from LPT1 to LPT9). Remember two things about capturing ports:

    - The port doesn't physically have to be installed in your computer in order to be captured. The capture process just associates a port name with a shared printer.

    - If the port you capture *is* installed in your computer and you capture it, all print jobs sent to that port name will be sent to the network printer, not out the local port (which is the way it is supposed to work). If you have a printer attached to that port, you would not be able to print to it.

7. Pick the LPT port you want to capture and click OK to accept the choice and return to the Capture screen. Then, click Next to continue running the wizard.

8. The next step is to give the printer instance a name. With network printers, you should give them a name that reflects what kind of printer it is and which machine is hosting it. In this case, I labeled it HP LaserJet III (the default name of the driver), but I could have named it Laser on Bob's PC. Whatever name makes sense to you, type in the name that you want to call the printer in the screen that the wizard presents (Figure 9.24). You also have the choice as to whether or not you want the printer to be the default printer that gets used by all Windows applications.

From here on, printer installation is exactly the same as installing a local printer. I covered this in Chapter 5, so I won't discuss it further here.

FIGURE 9.24:

Naming the printer

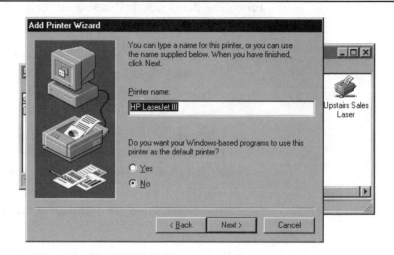

Networking and the Internet

One of the most oft-performed procedures by today's technicians is setting up a computer to connect to the Internet. The Internet is no longer just a buzzword, it's a reality. It has been estimated that over fifty percent of the homes in America have computers and that over fifty percent of those computers are connected to the Internet. It's is no wonder that most computers come with software to connect them to the Internet.

Internet Concepts

Before we can discuss connecting Windows 95 to the Internet, we need to discuss the Internet itself. There are some common terms and concepts every technician must understand about the Internet. First of all, the Internet is really just a bunch of private networks connected together using public telephone lines. These private networks are the access points to the Internet and are run by companies called Internet Service Providers (ISPs). They will sell you a connection to the Internet for a monthly service charge (kind of like your cable bill or phone bill). Your computer talks to the ISP using the public phone lines as well.

Types of Connections

There are several designations and types of public phone lines that range in speeds from 56Kbps to several Megabits per second (Mbps) that your computer might use to talk to an ISP. Remember that these same types of phone lines connect the ISPs to each other to form the Internet. Table 9.1 details a few of the more common phone line types and speeds.

TABLE 9.1: Common phone line types and speeds

Designation	Speed Range	Description
POTS	2400 bps to 115Kbps	Plain old telephone system—your regular analog phone line
ISDN	64Kbps to 1.554 Mbps	Digital Phone line—popular for home office internet connection
Frame Relay	56Kbps to 1.554 Mbps	Cheap, simple connection where you share bandwith with several other people
56K Point-to-point	56Kbps	A direct connection between two points at a guaranteed bandwidth
T1	1.554 Mbps	A direct connection between two points at a guaranteed bandwidth
T3	44 Mbps	A direct connection between two points at a guaranteed bandwidth. Extremely fast
DSL	256Kbps to ?	New digital phone technology using existing phone wire
ATM	155Mbps	Fiber optic ring network. Extremely fast

The majority of home Internet connections use POTS (Plain Old Telephone System) and a modem. Most ISPs connect together using phone lines of T1 speeds (1.554 Mbps) or faster. Certain ISPs that make up the backbone of the Internet use technologies like SONET that can get the data moving at Gigabit speeds.

Connection Protocols

Network entities need to use the same protocols to communicate. Because the Internet is a network, everyone on it needs to be running the same protocol in order to communicate. The protocol that they run is TCP/IP. TCP/IP is actually a suite of several protocols that work together. The two biggest of them are the Transmission Control Protocol (TCP) and the Internet Protocol (IP), which is where TCP/IP gets its name from. Currently, anyone who connects to the Internet must be running TCP/IP in one form or another.

There are two types of TCP/IP that run for dial-up (POTS) connections: Serial Line Internet Protocol (SLIP) and Point-to-Point Protocol (PPP). Both work to get you on the Internet, but PPP is more commonly used because it is more easily configured.

Internet Software

You will need a couple of pieces of software installed on your Windows 95 machine in order to use the Internet. The first, and probably the most important, is a Web browser. This piece of software will allow you to view Web pages from the Internet. The two browsers with the largest market share are Netscape Navigator and Microsoft Internet Explorer (also known as IE). They both work equally well at browsing the Internet. Figure 9.25 shows a picture of Netscape and Figure 9.26 shows a picture of Internet Explorer.

FIGURE 9.25:

The main browsing window of Netscape Navigator (version 3.0)

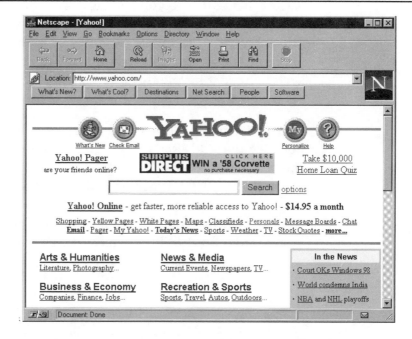

FIGURE 9.26:

The main browsing window of Microsoft Internet Explorer (version 3.0)

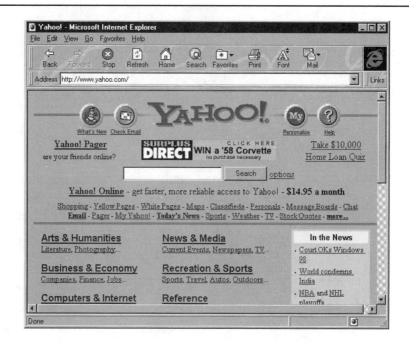

The other software you need is dialer software that will automatically dial up your ISP when you start browsing the Internet. This software comes with Windows 95 in the form of a component called Dial-Up Networking (DUN). If it's not installed, you need to have it installed before you start configuring your Internet connection.

To install Dial-Up Networking after Windows 95 is installed, simply open the Add/Remove Programs control panel and click the check box next to Dial-Up Networking in the Communications group (Figure 9.27). When you click OK, Setup will copy the files for Dial-Up Networking and ask you to reboot your machine. After the reboot, you will see the Dial-Up Networking program group under Start ➤ Programs ➤ Accessories ➤ Dial-Up Networking (Figure 9.28).

FIGURE 9.27:

Installing Dial-Up Networking

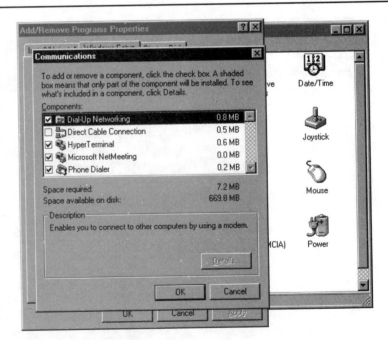

FIGURE 9.28:

Accessing Dial-Up
Networking

Windows 95 Internet Configuration

If you want to connect your Windows 95 machine to the Internet,
the first step is to get an account with an Internet service provider.
They will give you a sheet with all the information you need to
connect your machine. In some cases, they will give you a disk
with a pre-configured dialer and browser so all you have to do is
install the software and you'll be ready to connect to the Internet.
In most cases, to connect Windows 95 to the Internet, we simply
need to make a Dial-Up Networking connection.

Creating a DUN Connection

To create a new DUN connection, open the Dial-Up Networking folder under Start ➤ Programs ➤ Accessories. This will open a window that shows all the DUN connections that are configured. You must create a new one to connect to the Internet. To do this, double-click the item in this folder called Make New Connection. This will bring up the screen shown in Figure 9.29. From this screen, you can give the connection a name. As with other names in Windows 95, use one that reflects what it is (in this case, a connection to the Internet). So, call your connection to the Internet, "Internet." Additionally, this screen will allow you to select which modem you want to use to dial this connection (if you only have one configured in Windows 95, it will default to that one).

FIGURE 9.29:

Making a new connection and naming it

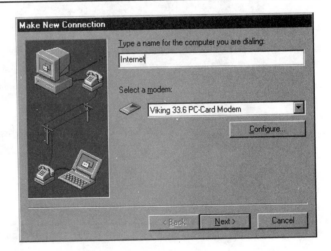

The next step is to enter the phone number of the system you are dialing (Figure 9.30). Your ISP will supply you with a phone number to dial (in this example, it's 555-0432). Simply type in the area code and phone number of your ISP and click Next to continue. Windows 95 will determine if it's a long-distance number automatically during dialing and either add or omit the 1 plus the area code.

> **NOTE**   If you live in another country, select your country under Country Code to change how Windows 95 interprets phone number syntax.

FIGURE 9.30:

Entering the ISP's
phone number

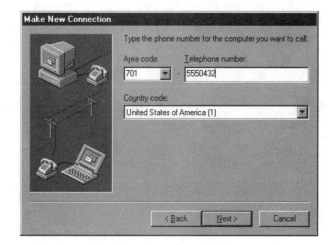

Finally, we are presented with the final screen that tells us we are basically done setting up the connection (Figure 9.31). All we have to do is click the Finish button to finish creating the connection.

FIGURE 9.31:

Finishing creating the
connection

Configuring the Properties of a DUN Connection

Now that you have a DUN connection, you need to configure the settings specific to your Internet connection. To do this, simply right-click the connection in the Dial-Up Networking folder (Figure 9.32). From the menu that appears, you can choose to use the connection to connect (the Connect option), or choose the Properties option to configure it. Because you aren't ready to connect yet, choose the Properties item from the menu.

FIGURE 9.32:

Choosing the DUN connection to configure

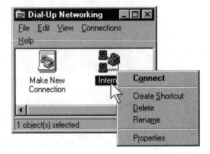

You should now see a screen similar to the one in Figure 9.33. From this screen you can configure the same properties that you did during the Connection Setup wizard (i.e., telephone number, connection name, and modem). This screen now has two more tabs that we can use to configure the other properties (like protocol settings).

If you click the Server Types tab, you will see the settings for the type of server you are dialing in to (Figure 9.34). For an Internet connection, this is usually set to PPP:Windows 95, Windows NT 3.5, Internet unless your ISP instructs you otherwise. Notice also that there are check boxes for several other settings, including which protocol(s) this dial-up connection will use. TCP/IP must be selected in order for an Internet connection to work. Set these settings according to your ISP's instruction and click OK to accept the settings.

FIGURE 9.33:

Properties of the Internet DUN connection.

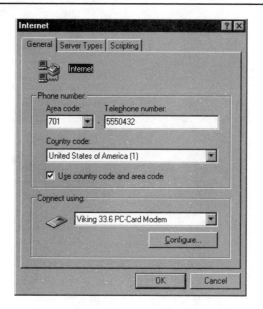

NOTE   The Scripting tab is used if your ISP doesn't support any type of automatic username and password authentication protocol like PAP or CHAP (if in doubt, ask your ISP). This tab allows you to specify a file that will automatically enter your username and password. The Windows 95 help file documents how to use this feature.

FIGURE 9.34:

Configuring the Server
Types parameter

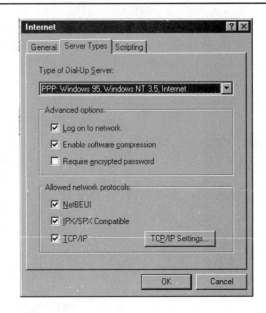

The other area to configure DUN parameters is in the Connect
screen of the Internet connection. To access this area, double-click
the connection. You will see a screen similar to the one in Figure 9.35. In this screen, you enter the username and password
that your ISP has assigned you. Additionally, double-check the
phone number you entered to make sure it's correct. Once you've
finished configuring the phone number, you're ready to connect
to the Internet.

TIP   If you want to save the password so you don't have to type it in every
time, click the check box next to Save Password. Be careful, though. If
you save your password, anyone can get onto the Internet as you from
your computer without having to enter a password.

FIGURE 9.35:

The Connect screen

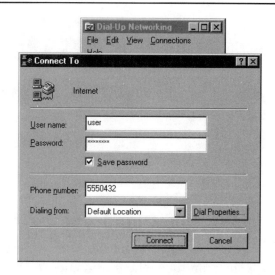

| TIP | If you need to setup the connection to automatically dial a number for an external line, dial the number as a long-distance call, or to enter a string to disable call waiting (i.e. *70 or 1170). |

Connecting to the Internet

Connecting to the Internet is simple, once you get the connection configured. Simply double-click the connection, enter the password (unless you chose the Save Password button previously), and click Connect. A window will appear that allows you to follow the status of the connection (Figure 9.36). You should hear the modem dial, then connect. When it connects, the status screen will say, Verifying Username and Password, and then Connected. Once you are connected, the status screen will go away, and you will get an icon on the taskbar (as shown at left). At this point, you are connected to your ISP and you can fire up your favorite Web browser and start surfin'.

FIGURE 9.36:

Connection status
screen

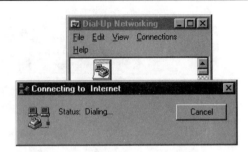

Disconnecting from the Internet

To disconnect from the Internet, simply right-click the connection
icon on the taskbar and choose Disconnect. That's all there is to it.

Review Questions

1. Which service must be installed in order to share files on a Windows 95 workstation?

    A. Networks

    B. 3Com

    C. File and Print Sharing for Microsoft Networks

    D. Windows 95

2. In Windows 95 where do you configure which networking components are installed?

    A. Network Control Panel

    B. Windows 95 Setup

    C. Add/Remove Programs

    D. Add New Hardware

3. Which protocol must be configured on your Windows 95 machine in order to connect to the Internet?

    A. IPX/SPX

    B. TCP/IP

    C. NetBEUI

    D. Asynchronous

4. Which of the following is the fastest Internet connection?

    A. ISDN

    B. PPP over POTS

    C. T1

    D. T3

5. With a computer named SERVER1 and a shared directory named DOCUMENT, which is the correct UNC path syntax?

    A. \\SERVER1\DOCUMENT

    B. /SERVER1/DOCUMENT

    C. \\DOCUMENT\SERVER1

    D. Document/Server1

6. You have a Plug-n-Play network card, but all other ISA cards in your computer are non-PnP cards. You want to avoid problems, where possible. What can you do?

    A. Configure the PnP cards to "manual configuration" (i.e., non-PnP mode)

    B. Don't use the PnP network card. Get a new, non-PnP card

    C. Set all ISA cards to the same interrupt

    D. Set all ISA cards to Software Configure

7. A Web browser allows you to access what part of the Internet?

    A. NNTP

    B. Routers

    C. WWW

    D. Gopher

8. A set of rules that governs network communications is called:

    A. The Internet

    B. A Communications Protocol

    C. The TCP/IP law

    D. IPX

9. How do you share a folder once file and printer sharing has been enabled on your Windows 95 workstation?

    A. Right-click My Computer, choose Sharing, click Enable, and click OK.

    B. Right-click Network Neighborhood, choose Properties, click Add, choose the folder you want to share, and click OK.

    C. Right-click the folder you want to share, choose Sharing, click Shared As, and click OK.

    D. Right-click the Desktop, choose Sharing, click Shared As, and click OK.

10. The Internet is owned by the government.

    A. True

    B. False

11. Which of the following is an acronym for the phone line that most people have in their houses?

    A. ISDN

    B. T1

    C. T3

    D. POTS

12. SHARE.EXE provides which functionality for DOS?

    A. Allows file and printer sharing

    B. Provides file and record-locking functions

    C. Makes DOS into a multi-user OS

    D. Puts DOS on the network

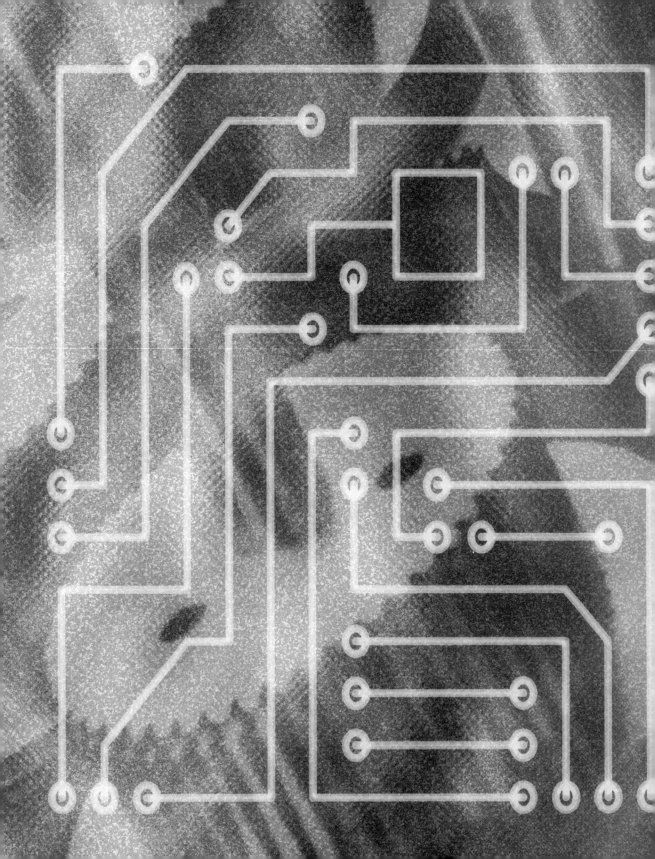

CHAPTER

TEN

10

Troubleshooting Operating Systems and Applications

■ Recognize and interpret the meaning of common error codes and startup messages from the boot sequence, and identify steps to correct the problems.

■ Recognize Windows-specific printing problems and identify the procedures for correcting them.

■ Recognize common problems and determine how to resolve them.

Troubleshooting involves asking a lot of questions of yourself and of other people. Beginners (and yes, I was a beginner once upon a time) like the trial and error method of fixing things, but in the long run, a methodological approach will work better. The reason that beginners often choose a trial and error approach is that they don't yet have a good enough background to analyze the problem.

> **NOTE**   Analysis is the act of breaking down a structure or system into its component parts and their relationships.

More than occasionally, a technician will unwittingly create new problems in an attempt to fix a real problem. For example, if a program will not run and displays an Out of Memory error, it might seem logical to add more memory.

But certain types of memory currently on the market will not work in a 486 computer—what happens if the memory the technician installs is the wrong type for the computer? Now there are two problems.

And what if the computer with the mismatched memory actually starts up but eventually locks up because of the memory problem? The lock ups could create an interruption in writing information to the hard drive, and a program could become corrupted. That would make three problems total.

Once the technician has sorted out all the problems, it's time to actually repair whatever went wrong. In the above example, it is quite likely that the source of the original Out of Memory error was really some corrupted program code. Many times, a Windows program with some damage to one or more components will cause exactly that error to be displayed.

A Step-by-Step Guide to Troubleshooting

In a computer system, there are at least four main parts to be considered, each of which is in turn made up of many pieces:

- First, there is a collection of hardware pieces that are integrated into a working system. As you know, the hardware can be quite complex, what with motherboards, hard drives, video cards, etc. Software can be equally perplexing.

- Second, there is an operating system that in turn is dependent on the hardware. Remember that the DOS and Windows operating systems have kernels, internal commands and external commands, which may interact with the hardware in different ways.

- Third, there is an application or a software program that is supposed to do something. Programs such as Microsoft Word and Excel are now bundled with a great many features.

- Finally, there is a computer user, ready to take the computer system to its limits (and beyond). A technician can often forget that the customer user is a very complex and important part of the puzzle.

Effective troubleshooting will require some experience just for the background required to analyze the problem at hand, but there are also some other logical steps that need to be remembered. Ask yourself the question, "Is there a problem?" Perhaps it is as simple as a customer expecting too much from the computer. If there is a problem, is it just one problem?

Step 1: Talk to the Customer

Talking to the user is an important first step. Your first contact with the computer that has a problem will usually be through the customer, either directly or by way of a work order that contains the user's complaint. Often, the complaint will be something straight forward, such as "There's a disk stuck in the floppy drive." At other times, the problem will be complex and the customer will not have mentioned everything that has been going wrong.

The act of diagnosis starts with the art of customer relations. Go to the customer with an attitude of trust: *believe* what the customer is saying. At the same time, go to the customer with an attitude of hidden skepticism, meaning *don't* believe that the customer has told you everything. This attitude of hidden skepticism is not the same as distrust. Most customers are not going to lie, but they may inadvertently forget to give some crucial detail.

NOTE For example, a customer once complained that his CD drive didn't work. What he failed to say was that it had never worked and that he had installed it himself. It turned out that he had mounted it with screws that were too long and that these prevented the tray from ejecting properly.

Step 2: Gather Information

The user can give you vital information. The most important question is "what changed?" Problems don't usually come out of nowhere. Was a new piece of hardware or software added? Did the user drop some equipment? Was there a power outage or a storm? These are the types of questions that you can ask a user in trying to find out what is different.

If nothing changed, at least outwardly, then what was going on at the time of failure? Can the problem be reproduced? Can the problem be worked around? The point here is to ask as many questions as you need to in order to pinpoint the trouble.

Step 3: Eliminate Possibilities

Once the problem or problems have been clearly identified, your next step will be to isolate possible causes. If the problem cannot be clearly identified, then further tests will be necessary. A common technique for hardware and software problems alike is to strip the system down to barebone basics. In a hardware situation, this could mean removing all interface cards, except those absolutely required for the system to operate. In a software situation, this may mean booting up with the CONFIG.SYS and AUTOEXEC.BAT files disabled.

Generally, then, you can gradually rebuild the system toward the point where it started. When you reintroduce a component and the problem reappears, then you know that component is the one causing the problem.

Step 4: Document Your Work

One last point needs to be made in this brief introduction to troubleshooting: you should document your work. If the process of elimination or the process of questioning the user goes beyond two or three crucial elements, start writing it down. Nothing is more infuriating than knowing you did something to make the system work but not being able to remember what it was.

Troubleshooting in MS-DOS

A familiarity with DOS is important, even in today's world of Windows 95. The key versions of DOS to be aware of are 3.3, 4.01, 5.0, and 6.*x*. DOS 5.0 and 6.*x* are similar, with many differences being either bells and whistles or bundled utilities.

Most problems with DOS itself will be difficulties with drivers, TSRs (terminate and stay resident programs), and memory management. DOS itself is fairly stable. Some problems will involve IRQ (interrupt request) and DMA (direct memory access) conflicts, hard drive glitches, stubborn printers, or ill-behaved applications.

Configuration Errors and General Software Practices

When you are faced with fundamental software problems, there are two strategies that will generally help you:

- The clean boot
- Editing the CONFIG.SYS and AUTOEXEC.BAT files

The Clean Boot

A *clean boot* into DOS means a boot into the operating system with no CONFIG.SYS or AUTOEXEC.BAT file. Depending on the status of the system and the version of DOS being used, you can choose from several methods:

- The tried and true method is a boot off of a clean boot floppy disk. You should use this method only on a computer known to be free of viruses.

- In cases where you are able to boot but you have problems later, try temporarily renaming the CONFIG.SYS and AUTOEXEC.BAT files and rebooting. The files will not be activated at boot up time.

- A similar method consists of editing the CONFIG.SYS and AUTOEXEC.BAT files so that various lines are remarked out. (I'll tell you more about how to edit these files later in the chapter.)

- Finally, with versions 6.*x* of DOS, you can press the F5 or F8 keys at the time the message Starting MS-DOS appears on the screen.

  Pressing the F5 key will boot the computer without the CONFIG.SYS and AUTOEXEC.BAT files, just as if these files didn't exist.

  Pressing the F8 key will give you the option to step through the CONFIG.SYS and AUTOEXEC.BAT files one line at a time so that you can eliminate suspected offending commands.

In general after a clean boot, you should try removing non-essential device drivers and TSRs. These could include printers, scanners, and others. FASTOPEN and disk caching commands such as SMARTDRIVE should also be removed.

Occasionally, you may need to increase the environment space. The environment is a memory space set aside to hold environmental variables, such as the style of prompt used, TEMP directories, etc. You can check what is in the environment by typing **SET** at a command line prompt. If any lines are truncated or the listing shown does not have all the variables in it that you might expect, you should increase the environment space.

TIP   To increase the environment space, place the following line in the CONFIG.SYS: SHELL=COMMAND.COM /P /E:2048

Editing CONFIG.SYS and AUTOEXEC.BAT

Much of what is referred to above requires editing the CONFIG .SYS and AUTOEXEC.BAT files. These files are straight ASCII text and should not be edited with a word processor, such as Word or WordPerfect, unless they are saved in ASCII text format. Later versions of DOS come with an ASCII editor called EDIT. An editor called EDLIN (which is short for edit line) came with earlier versions. EDLIN is difficult to use if you have never used it. Faced with that choice, you might try editing in a word processor, making sure to save the output as text or ASCII text.

If you are faced with a stubborn editing situation and need just a bare minimum CONFIG.SYS or AUTOEXEC.BAT file, you can do the following:

1. Rename the original file. Make sure the new name is one that you or another technician can recognize, like AUTOEXEC.OLD.

2. Create a new AUTOEXEC.BAT file by typing **COPY CON AUTOEXEC.BAT** and pressing Enter. This allows you to enter short and simple lines into a brand new file, one line at a time.

3. Use the F6 key to exit and save the new file.

In troubleshooting, the usual thing to do while editing a file is to remark out the line that you think is causing the problem. Type **REM** and a space at the start of the line. REM is short for remark or reminder, and it deactivates a line in a batch file or in the CONFIG.SYS file.

Two problems in the DOS environment are as follows:

- When a hardware interrupt occurs, whatever the CPU is handling at the moment gets placed to the side in what is referred to as a *stack*. An Internal Stack Overflow occurs when there is not enough memory set aside to handle a hardware interrupt situation. You can increase available stacks by adding a stacks=x,y in the CONFIG.SYS file. The variables x and y represent numbers that may be selected according to software requirements. Consult the software or DOS documentation.

- The Bad or Missing Command Interpreter error message occurs when the COMMAND.COM file is not found. The Command Interpreter's location defaults to the root of the C: drive, if it is not otherwise specified. This error will occur if the Command Interpreter COMMAND.COM is erased or otherwise corrupted or replaced after the computer is booted. COMMAND.COM may be replaced by booting up with a floppy disk that has the correct version of DOS and copying the COMMAND.COM to the right spot on the hard drive.

WARNING The COMMAND.COM has a pointer to it, set in the environment space, specifically because it may be erased from memory by programs that need some extra memory space. It should be re-loaded after that program terminates. Occasionally, it won't get reloaded; this can even be a common event in certain network situation.

Checking the Memory

Memory is a scarce resource in DOS based systems. DOS programs need contiguous memory space within the first megabyte of RAM. Small programs such as device drivers and TSRs may be loaded into small RAM areas in upper memory with the help of memory managers, including HIMEM.SYS and EMM386.EXE. If a

DOS application claims to need more memory, verify that this will work and then attempt to manage memory resources to allow more RAM to be available to the application.

To check on the available memory, use the MEM command. By itself, it will show the total of conventional memory available, as well as that conventional memory that has been used. With a /d or /c switch following it (i.e., MEM /d) it will show the distribution of the used memory. This screen tends to be lengthy, so type in **mem /d /p** or **mem /c /p**, and it will scroll one screen at a time.

Another check on available memory is the MSD command found in later versions of DOS and found in Windows. MSD stands for Microsoft Diagnostics. A graphic representation of the memory usage is available.

To verify that a program will work with additional conventional memory freed up, simply remark out of the CONFIG.SYS and the AUTOEXEC.BAT files any unneeded drivers that might use memory and try the application again.

Memory management used to be a chore that only experienced technicians would attempt. Now it is made easy with the command MEMMAKER. MEMMAKER shuffles around different memory configurations looking for the best possible combination.

Problems with Drivers

Drivers are small background programs that usually translate between a piece of hardware and the main program of an application. The main conflict that I have seen connected with drivers occurs when they are loaded into an upper memory block that is associated with an I/O device, particularly network interface cards.

Network interface cards often have a memory buffer with a real address in the upper memory area. If that address is allocated to a driver and then the network card is activated, a conflict occurs. The network card and the driver will fail, and the technician will become extremely frustrated.

The other problem that drivers cause is a shortage of conventional memory. The solution is good memory management, usually through placing the driver or drivers into upper memory blocks.

Problems with TSRs

A TSR is a *Terminate and Stay Resident* program. A good example is a utility called *Sidekick*. The program is launched like any other program, it is named on a command line. Unlike most other programs, Sidekick loads a small portion of itself into memory. When a *hot-key* combination is pressed, such as Shift+F10, then the main utility loads and allows various functions to be performed.

In our example, Sidekick 2.0 for DOS provides five utilities: a calendar planner, an address book, modem and communications capabilities, a notepad, and four different styles of calculator.

Sidekick also frequently interferes with other programs that are running. Many older TSRs were similar because they tend to allocate memory that other programs either need or already possess.

The easiest way to troubleshoot TSRs is to remove them and put them back in one at a time. If the TSR is loaded from the AUTOEXEC.BAT, then the startup line that refers to the TSR should be remarked out. Otherwise, removing a TSR is as simple as rebooting the computer.

IRQ, DMA, and I/O Address Conflicts

Hardware conflicts, namely IRQ and DMA channel conflicts and I/O address conflicts, are not quite a part of DOS troubleshooting, however these resources are often set or configured in the CONFIG.SYS and AUTOEXEC.BAT portions of booting up the computer.

Available and used IRQs may be determined using MSD or a variety of third-party diagnostic programs such as Norton Utilities or PC Doctor. The most common conflict is when a mouse is attached to COM1 and an internal modem is set to COM3. Both of these com ports, by convention, use IRQ 4. A common solution, if COM2 is not in use, is to reset the modem to COM4, using IRQ 3.

DMA conflicts often occur in the configuration of a non-standard CD-ROM drive or a sound card. Because DMA channels are rarely used by any device and these are usually set in software, a DMA conflict can be rectified simply by playing with the DMA configuration settings.

Much less common are I/O address conflicts. Standard ISA bus I/O addresses range from 000h to 3FFh, for a total of 1024 addresses. Most I/O devices actually use a range of addresses, so although a printer port might be thought of as residing at 378h, it actually uses the range from 378h to 37Ah. Even while using multiple addresses out of the 1024 available, there are usually more than enough.

Most devices have customary port addresses assigned, so conflicts are rare. If two or more of a similar device were installed, an I/O conflict might occur. Occasionally, a network interface card might use a standard I/O address. These situations are usually easy to spot, and alternative addresses can be selected.

Hard Drive Problems and Settings

A hard drive problem is a hardware problem with a great impact on the operating system. Sometimes these are hard to spot, but any error message indicating a problem writing to the hard drive should be taken seriously. For example, Data Error Reading/Writing Drive C: generally indicates that a hard drive failure has occurred. At this point, the technician should run the CHKDSK /f command or the SCANDISK command.

CHKDSK /f is used to check for FAT and other errors, as well as missing file fragments. The /f switch stands for fix it. SCANDISK will also perform an integrity test of the hard drive called a *surface scan*. This test checks each sector on the hard drive for read or write errors and optionally attempts to correct the errors.

In common with later operating environments, DOS has some hard drive configuration settings to worry about. For example, SmartDrive is installed with write-back caching turned on. As described earlier, this can lead to accidental loss of data. Smart-Drive and other caching programs should be set to write-through caching.

The other caching setting to be concerned with is how much memory is allocated to the hard drive cache. If extended memory is available, then most or all of it may be allocated to SmartDrive. This is for a DOS only environment, remembering that DOS itself does not use extended memory.

Printer Diagnosis

The most common printer problem is the printer that won't print. The *second* most common printer problem is the printer that prints gobbledygook or meaningless output. Printer ports and serial ports can become electronically stuck so that they don't function. A technician may try rebooting the computer to cure a printing problem, but if the boot is not a *cold boot*, then the ports may not reset. (In a cold boot, you actually turn the computer off and back on again.)

The next step is to try to print from the DOS command line. I like to use the COPY and DIR commands with a pipe to the printer port. A pipe redirects the output of a command and looks like this:

```
COPY AUTOEXEC.BAT > LPT1
```

(or some other file may be copied), or

```
DIR > LPT1
```

(Check the length of the directory listing on the screen prior to sending the directory output to the printer. It may be too short or too long.)

If these simple DOS printing tricks prove that the printer is working, then the next step is to isolate which program has a problem. If DOS can print to the hardware port, then the problem is most likely in an application's printer device driver. The same is true for garbage printouts, which usually arise from the wrong printer driver being selected.

Setup Problems

Setup problems are rare in the process of installing DOS. With versions prior to 4.0, the installer simply formatted the drive with an /s switch, placing the boot files onto the hard drive automatically. All other files were simply copied, generally to a DOS directory.

DOS 4.0 and 4.01 introduced a problem with drives larger than 32MB. The solution: place the SHARE.EXE command line into the AUTOEXEC.BAT.

The most significant problem that I have seen with installing DOS occurs with the DOS 6.*x* versions. These versions came as upgrades and as new install versions. If you perform the setup using an upgrade version on a new disk, an error will occur. The legal solution is to get a new version.

Assuming that the upgrade version is a legal copy, for example if the older version was erased when a drive was reformatted, then the solution is to place the boot files onto the hard drive. This is done with the /s switch on the format command or by using the SYS.COM command from a floppy boot disk.

Application Troubleshooting

Most application troubleshooting falls under one of the above topics, however there are exceptions. Viruses may effect the performance of an application. If a virus is suspected, then a virus checker and disinfectant is required. If you have access to the Internet, you should try the f-prot, which is one very popular shareware virus checker that is available. The f-prot is frequently updated to include the very latest of viruses.

Other utilities, such as Norton Utilities, are particularly useful, if you believe that the program executable files have become damaged. (Norton Utilities can also often rescue a damaged floppy or hard drive.) For more information about viruses, see Chapter 8.

And Now for the Real World...

Appearance may be deceiving, even in the simplistic DOS environment. For example, a client called me one time with an accounting program problem. Their Real World accounting had run fine for years. The computer was an 80286 AT clone with DOS 4.01 and a 40MB hard drive.

continued on next page

I inquired about what happened just prior to the problem, and they responded that they had resized the database in anticipation of needing more room for accounting entries. This put the allocated space on the drive at just over 32MB. DOS 4.01 requires SHARE to be loaded if the drive is over 32MB, otherwise FAT entries for files beyond the first 32MB area are written at the beginning of the FAT, overwriting other entries.

Within thirty minutes, we had restored the system from backup tapes, put SHARE into the AUTOEXEC.BAT, and then resized the database. What appeared to be an accounting program problem was really a DOS problem.

Troubleshooting in Windows 3.*x*

Windows 3.1 and 3.11 are fairly stable. (The best troubleshooting advice for Windows 3.0 is to upgrade to Windows 3.1 or 3.11!) However, when problems do occur, they can be especially frustrating.

Problems fall into several categories:

- Installation difficulties
- Configuration errors
- Out of memory errors and GPFs (general protection faults)
- Printing problems
- Other miscellaneous troubles

Configuration Errors and General Software Practices

As with DOS, there are two basic troubleshooting strategies in this area:

- The clean boot

- Editing the critical system files, such CONFIG.SYS, AUTOEXEC.BAT, WIN.INI, and SYSTEM.INI files

There's No Such Thing As a Windows 3.*x* Clean Boot

With Windows, there is no such thing as a clean boot. This is because many of the DOS configuration settings required to run Windows are located in the CONFIG.SYS and the AUTOEXEC.BAT files. The minimum required files to be loaded at boot up include any disk compression drivers and the HIMEM.SYS command.

If you are using DOS 5.0 or earlier, then you should make a boot floppy, either ahead of time or on another computer. An alternative is to edit the CONFIG.SYS and AUTOEXEC.BAT files so that only these disk and memory drivers are loaded. If you are using DOS 6.*x*, then pressing the F8 key at start up will offer you the chance to select or omit any driver or command in these files.

As a general rule, you should back up CONFIG.SYS, AUTOEXEC .BAT, WIN.INI, and SYSTEM.INI prior to any troubleshooting or modifications. You can copy these files into a special directory or save them with slightly different names.

To edit these files, use the DOS EDIT command to invoke the DOS ASCII editor or, while in Windows 3.*x*, use the SYSEDIT command. To use the SYSEDIT editor, go to the File pull down menu (in Program Manager or in File Manager), and select Run. Enter **SYSEDIT** into the Run dialog box. SYSEDIT will open editing windows for CONFIG.SYS, AUTOEXEC.BAT, WIN.INI, and SYSTEM.INI. If you are using Windows for Workgroups 3.11, you will also see editing windows for the PROTOCOL.INI and MSMAIL.INI files.

General Protection Faults

GPFs (general protection faults) occur when a program attempts to use memory that is already allocated. The term "protection" refers to the fact that protected mode memory is being used. If the allocated memory is being used for temporary holding of data, then little damage will occur. When the allocated memory is part of the Windows program, then Windows will lock up, and the system will need to be restarted.

If the GPF error message provides enough detail, you may find a starting point for troubleshooting these errors. KRNL386.EXE GPFs usually occur as a result of poor memory management. Follow the guidelines for DOS troubleshooting to maximize the amount of conventional memory available. Also, look below for more on Windows memory management.

When the error involves the GDI.EXE or the USER.EXE executables, then the Windows setup and configuration should be checked. The GDI and the USER.EXE are tightly linked to display configuration and to input/output devices.

Application GPFs will usually occur when an application is ill-behaved, often with beta versions or software in an early version or when software is corrupted or installed improperly. For example, much of program code is stored in DLL files, which are often shared by different applications. A new DLL installed by an application setup routine may cause an old application to misbehave because the DLL code is different. In this circumstance, you could try to reinstall the old application.

Dr. Watson

Finally, Dr. Watson is a diagnostic program that comes with Windows. To use it, load DRWATSON.EXE while Windows is running. It will create a log file that may track errors in the way that applications are behaving.

Memory

Most memory errors in Windows 3.x are caused by GPFs, as described above. A GPF occurs when a program is not compatible with Windows 3.x, has become damaged or corrupted, or has a conflict with another program or the DLLs that another program has installed.

Other memory errors can occur, and so the standard DOS memory management techniques are important. Use MEMMAKER to optimize the available conventional memory.

You should realize that a portion of Windows 3.x uses conventional memory, so those DOS programs that had enough memory to run in the DOS environment may not have room to run while Windows 3.x is started. This does not change when going from Windows to a DOS prompt or DOS shell because Windows is still running. Optimizing the DOS memory management is crucial to running DOS applications while in Windows. For more information about memory, see Chapter 6.

If You Are Using Windows 3.x on a Network

A common memory configuration problem develops when Windows 3.x computers are used on a network. Many network cards use an Upper Memory address space for their onboard memory buffers. If the card is initialized while still in DOS, then the memory space that is used by the NIC (network interface card) will be excluded from use by Windows.

However, if that memory address space is designated for use by MEMMAKER and the NIC is not initialized until Windows is started, then network access errors can occur. To solve this problem, enter **X=*memory range*** (where *memory range* is the start and ending memory address the NIC uses) on the line in the CONFIG.SYS that loads the EMM386.EXE driver. This practice will prevent Windows from accessing a particular address space for drivers.

If Windows 3.*x* Won't Relinquish Memory When It's Done Using It

Out of memory errors may occur when system resources have been used up. Some resources, such as breakpoints, are used by the Windows system and not relinquished when the system is done using them. This system leads to problems that can be resolved by rebooting the computer or restarting Windows. The problems, however, reoccur after Windows has been running for a period of time. For this type of error, add this line to the [386Enh] section of the SYSTEM.INI file:

```
MaxBPS=768
```

Raise the numeric value if the problems persist.

Problems with Drivers

Most problems with drivers in a 16-bit Windows environment are actually DOS driver problems. If you have a problem with a driver, check Microsoft's Web site (`http://www.microsoft.com`) or the hardware manufacturer's Web site for a list of updated drivers. Also check to see if duplicate drivers exist, and delete the older drivers.

IRQ, DMA, and I/O Conflicts

Windows 3.*x* is remarkably free of DMA and I/O conflicts. These conflicts are almost always based in the underlying DOS system that Windows 3.*x* runs on top of.

Occasionally, com ports will have conflicting IRQs. The com ports are commonly used for modems and mice and are sometimes used for plotters, printers, and other output devices. Com port conflicts are diagnosed for Windows 3.*x* in much the same way as for DOS. MSD is a good starting point for isolating which IRQs are used and which are available.

However, the Windows settings, kept in the SYSTEM.INI file, are known to cause problems with the use of com ports. In particular, if com ports 1, 2, and 4 exist, Windows 3.*x* will treat COM 4 as if it were COM 3. You can adjust the com ports settings in the Windows control panel so that what Windows calls COM 3 can use the COM 4 settings.

Hard Drive Problems and Settings

Two features are available in Windows 3.1 and 3.11 that allow for increased performance but can also lead to problems: FastDisk (also known as 32-bit hard disk access) and virtual memory. These features are available only when Windows is run in the enhanced mode on a 386 or greater computer.

Virtual memory is hard drive space that is used as if it were real RAM. Of course, it has a much slower access time than real memory, but it is also less expensive than RAM and can be used to hold portions of an application's code that are not being directly accessed.

Virtual memory uses a portion of the hard drive set aside as a swap file. It may be temporary, meaning that Windows establishes this space at time of start up. Or it may be permanent, meaning that the space is allocated prior to Windows starting up. A permanent swap file must exist in contiguous memory space on an uncompressed hard drive partition.

One problem with using a permanent swap file is that it takes up hard drive space you might want for user files. If the hard drive becomes filled up, you can try reducing the size of the permanent swap file or changing to a temporary swap file. Either of these actions will lead to more hard drive space for files and less available memory for applications.

TIP The problem with temporary swap files is that the needed memory space may not always be available. If you choose to have a permanent swap file, you guarantee that the swap file is large enough to accomplish the desired purpose.

FastDisk 32-bit access speeds up access to the hard drive by alleviating a chore that Windows otherwise has. To access the hard drive, Windows must ordinarily switch from protected mode to real mode and back. This action allows Windows to use the BIOS routines that allow writing to and reading of the hard drive. The FastDisk drive is a 32-bit protected mode driver that bypasses the system BIOS and writes directly to the hard drive without switching the CPU to real mode.

FastDisk works only with hard drives that conform to the WD1003 specification. These drive types include most MFM, RLL, IDE, and ESDI hard disks. Check with the manufacturer's documentation to be sure.

Printer Diagnosis

The first step in diagnosing printer problems in Windows 3.x is to test the printer port while in DOS, as discussed earlier in this chapter. If the printer works in DOS using the standard LPT driver that is built into DOS, then the problem must be with Windows.

Most Windows printer difficulties are attributable to wrong drivers or printer settings that are in error. First, check the printer settings for the printer being used and try printing again. You can also use a similar printer driver or reload the original printer driver. Most, but not all, dot matrix printers will work with an Epson FX or LQ driver. Likewise, most laser printers will work with an HP LaserJet IIp driver.

Setup Problems

Installation of Windows 3.x can fail during the DOS portion of the install, during the Windows portion of the install, or after the install when Windows may fail to start up.

- During the DOS portion of the install, a hardware detection phase occurs. This is not as extensive or accurate as the detection that occurs with Windows 95, but it can cause the installation to fail. Restart the installation with SETUP /I. Doing so forces the system to install without hardware detection. You can then enter the hardware into the Windows configuration manually.

- Similar hardware detection problems can cause installation problems during the Windows phase of installation. If you get to this phase and have difficulties, select the custom option for installing, and manually enter the hardware configuration. Further, double check to make sure the version of DOS is 3.1 or higher. Stop or close any TSRs and remark out the TSRs in the AUTOEXEC.BAT. Reboot, then reinstall Windows.

- After Windows has been installed, if it fails to start up, you should check for conflicting TSRs and try reinstalling using SETUP /I.

Application Troubleshooting

Application failures, other than GPFs, seldom occur. When these do occur, they are usually related to other factors, such as driver and DLL conflicts; so application troubleshooting should start with those areas, as described above.

Getting back to the basic troubleshooting techniques will help. Ask the following questions: What has changed? Has a program been added that may have installed its own DLLs, that might be older versions or simply conflicting versions? Have any Windows drivers been added, deleted, or changed?

When a Windows application does fail, and it does not involve a GPF, then you may want to manually terminate the application. To do so, press Ctrl+Alt+Delete. At this point, you can do one of the following:

- Escape back to the application if you change your mind about terminating it.

- Go forward and terminate the program.

And if both of these choices fail, you can reboot the computer.

Troubleshooting in Windows 95

Troubleshooting in Windows 95 is different from troubleshooting in DOS and Windows 3.*x* because most memory management and driver issues are controlled automatically by Windows 95. Also, Windows 95 is a Plug-n-Play operating system, which means that many resources are allocated on-the-fly during boot up so that these resources need not be configured manually.

Typically, problems may occur during installation of Windows 95, during or because of modification of the operating system or computer hardware, with communications through serial ports and with printers.

While many of the specific traditional troubleshooting techniques we've discussed so far are not used with Windows 95, the same general strategy applies:

1. Talk to the customer.

2. Gather information.

3. Eliminate possibilities.

4. Document your work.

In addition to performing a thorough analysis, check to see if the problem occurs frequently enough to be listed in the online Help or special files on the Windows 95 CD installation disk. (Look for .TXT files such as README.TXT.)

Configuration Errors and General Software Practices

The most important troubleshooting methods are still the same in Windows 95:

- Back up critical system files, including CONFIG.SYS, AUTOEXEC.BAT, WIN.INI, SYSTEM.INI, USER.DAT, and SYSTEM.DAT.

- Edit these files as necessary.

- Perform a clean boot from the hard drive or from a floppy.

Backing Up and Editing Critical Files

You should back up critical system files prior to any troubleshooting or modifications. You can copy them into a special directory or copy them with slightly different names. Use the Windows 95 Explorer to create a new folder and make copies of these four files in the new folder.

To edit CONFIG.SYS, AUTOEXEC.BAT, WIN.INI, and SYSTEM .INI, you may use NOTEPAD, which is an ASCII editor or you may choose to use the SYSEDIT command. To use the SYSEDIT editor, go to the Start menu, and select Run. Enter **SYSEDIT** into the Run dialog box. SYSEDIT will open editing windows for CONFIG.SYS, AUTOEXEC.BAT, WIN.INI, and SYSTEM.INI.

The Windows 95 Registry is a central location for configuration information. This data is stored in two files called SYSTEM.DAT and USER.DAT. Backups of these files are automatically generated every time that Windows 95 sucessfully shuts down. The backups are called SYSTEM.DA0 and USER.DA0. These backups may be used to restore the registry, but remember that the backups change at every shut down, so make your own backups of these critical files prior to making major registry changes.

To edit the USER.DAT and the SYSTEM.DAT, you must use a utility called REGEDIT. You can start REGEIT by selecting Start ➤ Run, typing **REGEDIT**, and pressing Enter.

WARNING Editing the Registry is an advanced topic, beyond the scope of this book. You shouldn't edit the Registry unless you know for sure what you are doing. You could inadvertently make changes that would prevent the system or some system components from working.

Performing a Clean Boot

To perform a clean boot on a computer that starts to boot up into Windows 95 but doesn't quite make it, press the F8 key when the message Starting Windows 95 appears on the screen. Depending on the exact configuration of the computer, a list of various choices will appear in a menu. Normal and Safe Mode are the two most often picked, although others may be useful.

NOTE *Safe Mode* allows only the basic system drivers to be loaded, so any new drivers that have been added are bypassed. This gives the technician a chance to see which drivers might be in conflict or not applicable to the computer and optionally to turn off certain drivers. A variety of Safe Mode options may appear, including Safe Mode with Network Support, Safe Mode Command Prompt Only (which brings up a DOS prompt screen), and Step-by-Step Confirmation, which allows the technician to select certain drivers throughout the boot up process.

To do a clean boot with a floppy disk, use a Windows 95 startup disk. During the initial setup procedure, you will have an opportunity to have Windows make a startup disk. This disk can be made later from Control Panel. Choose the Add/Remove Programs icon and click the Startup Disk option.

Memory

Troubleshooting memory is not often needed for Windows 95, as its built in memory management is more than sufficient. Memory problems are usually limited to GPFs and insufficient memory. With memory selling for about $2 per megabyte, it's pretty easy to simply increase the RAM on the motherboard.

Drivers

Drivers and DLLs can cause the same kinds of conflicts that we examined in Windows 3.*x*. Those troubleshooting techniques apply here. You should avoid duplicate drivers and DLLs and make sure that your drivers and DLLs are up to date.

TSRs

TSRs are a poor man's substitute for multitasking in a DOS environment. As a rule, if a TSR does not work right, replace it with a Windows version of the program, preferably a 32-bit version if available. Occasionally, the new version will not have a feature found in the DOS program. If the DOS version does not work, the user will have to choose between running the program in a DOS environment and running the Windows 95 operating system.

IRQ, DMA, and I/O Conflicts

Windows 95 uses Device Manager to identify and change these hardware resources' device allocation. To open up Device Manager:

1. Open Control Panel by selecting Start ➤ Settings ➤ Control Panel.

2. Once the Control Panel is open, double-click System. The System Properties box will appear.

3. Select the Device Manager tab and click the Properties button. The Device Manager window will appear.

4. To check for the resources that have been used, select the resource you want more information about. Click on the Properties box. A properties window will appear. Finally, select the Resources tab. Windows 95 will show any resource conflicts in this resource window.

If the device or devices that are in conflict are also Plug-n-Play devices, then the Device Manager can be used to change the settings on one or both devices, to eliminate the conflict.

Hard Drive Problems

Hard drive problems with Windows 95 usually include lack of free space, file fragmentation, and disk corruption. Swap files exist, but it is generally best to let Windows 95 automatically handle virtual memory.

Several old DOS style utilities still exist and are best executed from a Safe Mode DOS prompt. CHKDSK can be used to check the file structures for lost file fragments and optionally fix these problems. SCANDISK can also be used for the same purpose and to optionally perform an integrity check of the hard drive itself.

From within the Windows 95 GUI, the drive may be defragmented. You can access the defragmentation utility by right-clicking the hard drive icon in My Computer, clicking Properties, and selecting Tools. Defragmenting a drive will allow quicker access to files, because it will put all the pieces of a file together.

A lack of hard drive space is usually and best corrected by cleaning out the old and unused files. One alternative is to install a bigger hard drive. Another alternative is to use disk compression on the drive.

Printer Diagnosis

If a printer is not printing at all, then you should start with the DOS troubleshooting method. First reboot the computer in Safe Mode DOS Prompt. Then copy a file or a directory listing to the printer port. If the file or directory listing doesn't print, the cause is most likely a hardware failure or loose cable. If it *does* print, then you can assume the printing problems are associated with the Windows printer drivers.

One common source of printer driver errors is corruption of the driver. If a printer doesn't work, you can delete the printer from the printer settings window and reinstall it. If this method fails, the problem may be that related printer files were not replaced. Delete all printers from the computer and reinstall them. If this second method fails, then the printer driver is not compatible with Windows 95 or with the printer, and you will need to obtain an updated driver.

A quick way to test the printer functionality is to use the Print Test Page option. Always select this option when you're setting up a new printer. To print a test page for a printer that's already set up, look for the option on the Properties menu for the particular printer.

TIP   After the test page is sent to the printer, the computer will ask if it printed correctly. I always answer Yes because I don't care for the troubleshooting wizard that appears if I answer No. For the first few times, you'll probably want to answer No and use the wizard, but after you have troubleshooted a few printer problems, you may prefer to bypass the wizard.

Setup Problems

When you install Windows 95, the setup procedure will automatically detect various pieces of hardware. Plug-n-Play hardware is easily detected because it is designed to be recognized. Other hardware is detected based on characteristic signatures found in extension BIOS chips and other controller chips.

Occasionally, a piece of hardware cannot be detected properly. When this occurs, the Windows 95 installation process may halt and the computer may lock up. In this situation, the setup routine tracks the steps that have been completed successfully in a file called DETCRASH.LOG. This way the setup procedure can know which step failed.

After a setup failure, you should restart the computer using the Safe Recovery option and redo the installation. When the setup routine gets to the step that failed, as noted in the DETCRASH .LOG, it will skip that step and hopefully avoid another lock up. This is normally the only special consideration for installing Windows 95.

NOTE   As a note to network installers, I have found that making adjustments to the network card settings, including protocol additions and configuration settings, is best done after the initial installation of Windows 95. A mistake in changing the network card settings can force you to start the setup over again.

Application Troubleshooting

Troubleshooting applications in Windows 95 varies with each application. However I can offer some general guidelines:

- First, wait a few moments if an application doesn't seem to start. Some computers and some programs take longer than others. Be patient.

- Second, pay attention to error messages. These are usually your best indicator of what is going wrong.

- If things seems to be headed in the wrong direction while running the program, trying pressing Escape or Ctrl+C. Both of these will stop certain types of programs.

- Try rebooting the computer. Many problems just go away after a reboot.

  Cold boot If the problem has to do with a communications port, such as a serial port or a printer port, do a total power off reboot.

  Warm boot Many application problems can be reset by doing a warm boot, using the Ctrl+Alt+Delete key combination.

- Many technicians simply resort to reinstalling the troublesome application.

Reinstalling Windows 95 is not nearly as effective as reinstalling Windows 3.*x*, but many installers learn that lesson the hard way. A Windows 95 reinstallation often fails to actually reinstall many files that are already on the computer, such as DLLs and drivers. If the problems arise from corrupted program files that don't get reinstalled, then the problems won't go away.

Likewise, many Windows 95 programs, when reinstalled, do not write over all of the already installed files. If a program has problems and reinstallation is attempted, then the program should be totally uninstalled first. I have even had to make this drastic step with program setups that claim to reinstall over damaged files.

Microsoft installations will add a 0 byte file to every folder that they create. This file, MSCREATE.DIR, is used as a marker when and if the application is uninstalled. To the uninstall procedure, this marker means that the folder was created by the application setup and that it is safe to remove the folder if all other files have been removed. Microsoft uninstall procedures do not remove text, data, and document files.

Review Questions

1. A clean boot is:

   A. The same as a cold boot

   B. The same as a warm boot

   C. Accomplished by pressing Ctrl+Alt+Del

   D. A boot with no drivers loaded or with minimal drivers loaded

2. An important step in troubleshooting is:

   A. Backing up critical system files

   B. Talking to the customer about the computer's problems

   C. Documenting all of your work

   D. All of the above

3. When gathering information, it is important to:

   A. Determine when the computer was last used.

   B. Determine the last changes made to the computer

   C. Tell the customer to use surge power protection

   D. Check in with the office

4. Which of the following is true about IRQ conflicts?

   A. They most often involve com ports.

   B. They most often involve sound cards.

   C. They almost never occur.

   D. They are the same as DMA conflicts.

5. Which of the following is true about DOS memory management?

    A. It can be done manually.

    B. It is often done with MEMMAKER.

    C. It is built-in and needs no further action.

    D. Both A and B

6. With Windows 3.*x*, editing system files:

    A. Can be done with SYSEDIT

    B. Can be done with any text editor

    C. Includes CONFIG.SYS, AUTOEXEC.BAT, WIN.INI, and SYSTEM.INI

    D. All of the above

7. Which of the following is true about GPF?

    A. It stands for General Provision Finding.

    B. It stands for General Protection Fault.

    C. It occurs when the same memory is allocated to two different programs.

    D. Both B and C

8. The two files that make up the Windows 95 Registry are:

    A. USER.DA0 and SYSTEM.DA0

    B. USER.DAT and SYSTEM.DAT

    C. WIN.INI and SYSTEM.INI

    D. None of the above

9. When installing Windows 95, an error log is created. This log is called:

    A. ERRORLOG.TXT

    B. ERROR.LOG

    C. DETCRASH.LOG

    D. DETCRASH.TXT

10. Which key, when pressed at startup, will prevent Windows 95 from starting and leave you at a command prompt?

    A. F5

    B. F7

    C. F9

    D. F10

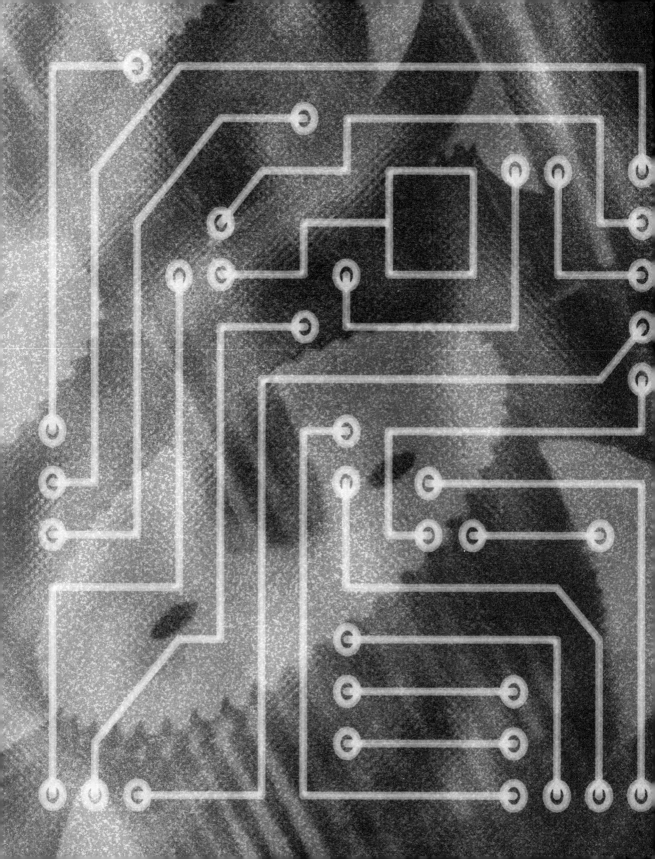

APPENDIX

A

Answers to Review Questions

Chapter 2 Answers

1. Which of the following is not a standard feature of DOS?

    A. Network support

    B. Running programs

    C. Managing files

    D. Managing disks

    Answer: A

2. Which of the following is a program?

    A. Windows 3.1

    B. WordPerfect 5.1

    C. FORMAT.EXE

    D. All of the above

    Answer: D

3. Which of the following filenames is invalid in DOS?

    A. myfile.txt

    B. my file.txt

    C. myfile

    D. MYFILE.TXT

    Answer: B

4. Which is a disk-related service provided by DOS?

    A. Creating and deleting partitions on hard drives

    B. Compressing files to increase the number of files stored on a drive

    C. Copying and backing up disks

    D. All of the above

    Answer: D

5. Which utility allows you to view memory usage?

    A. MEM

    B. MEMORY

    C. TIME

    D. FORMAT

    Answer: A

6. Which utility allows you to view the system's processor type?

    A. MEM

    B. MSD

    C. FDISK

    D. PROC

    Answer: B

7. Which of the following actually talks to a computer's hardware?

    A. The ROM BIOS

    B. The DOS System Files

    C. COMMAND.COM

    D. The processor

    Answer: A

8. What is the Basic Input/Output System also known as?

    A. RAM

    B. ROM

    C. COMMAND.COM

    D. BIOS

    Answer: D

9. Which is not a function of COMMAND.COM?

    A. Providing a consistant user interface to all DOS system files

    B. Presenting the results of a command to the user

    C. Receiving input from the user

    D. Formatting requests so they can be sent directly to the processor

    Answer: D

10. Which DOS attribute is used by backup programs?

    A. Read-only

    B. Archive

    C. Hidden

    D. System

    Answer: B

11. Which DOS command allows you to see the syntax of the DATE command?

    A. DATE /?

    B. DATE ?

    C. HELP /DATE

    D. HELP /DATE /SYNTAX

    Answer: A

12. To run a Windows-based program in DOS without the Windows interface you have to:

 A. Use the DOS Shell to run the program.

 B. Configure DOS to support a mouse.

 C. Run the Windows program as the only program on the machine.

 D. Windows programs do not run under DOS alone.

 Answer: D

13. Which of the following is not an important function of Windows?

 A. Running applications

 B. Preparing hard disks for use

 C. Managing files and directories

 D. Managing printing

 Answer: B

14. Which of the following is not included within the Program Manager?

 A. Icon

 B. Group

 C. Desktop

 D. Menu

 Answer: C

15. Which of these best describes an Icon?

   A. Any Windows-based program file

   B. The graphical configuration file needed to run all Windows apps

   C. The graphical shortcut to a file

   D. A graphical application

   Answer: C

16. Which of these is used to close a window?

   A. Restore button

   B. Title bar

   C. Minimize button

   D. Control box

   Answer: D

17. Which of the following is not a mouse function?

   A. Double-click

   B. Skip

   C. Drag

   D. Click

   Answer: B

18. Which is not configurable through an Icon's properties window?

   A. Its Label

   B. Its Working directory

   C. Its Group

   D. Its Icon graphic

   Answer: C

19. Where can you *not* find Icons?

    A. On the Desktop

    B. On the Program Manager workspace

    C. In a Group

    D. In the Control Panel

    Answer: B

20. Which DOS wildcard is used in File Manager to represent any number of characters in a string?

    A. *

    B. %

    C. @

    D. ?

    Answer: A

21. In which area do Windows and Windows for Workgroups differ the most?

    A. File management

    B. Network support

    C. Local printing

    D. Virtual Memory settings

    Answer: B

22. The Control Panel is used to configure:

    A. System settings

    B. DOS settings

    C. Applications

    D. I/O drivers

    Answer: A

23. A set of colors that define the appearance of Windows elements is a:

A. Scheme

B. Group

C. Palette

D. Rainbow

Answer: A

24. Which of the following is not an option under Windows Setup in Windows 3.1?

A. Display

B. Keyboard

C. Mouse

D. Network

Answer: D

25. Selecting the Exclusive in Foreground option in the 386 Enhanced Control Panel affects the foreground application by:

A. Slowing it down

B. Speeding it up

C. Assigning it specific memory

D. Assigning it specific hard disk space

Answer: B

26. Which of the following input devices is used to represent a Boolean (on or off) option?

    A. A check box

    B. A spinner box

    C. A drop-down menu

    D. An icon

    Answer: A

27. Which of the following Control Panels is used to password protect a Windows 3.*x* workstation?

    A. Colors

    B. Keyboard

    C. Enhanced

    D. Desktop

    Answer: D

28. You can install Windows 95 on a 386DX.

    A. True

    B. False

    Answer: A

29. Which Windows 95 interface component contains the Settings submenu?

    A. Desktop control panel

    B. Right-click menu

    C. Start menu

    D. Network control panel

    Answer: C

30. You can change the size of the Taskbar.

    A. True

    B. False

    Answer: A

31. To turn off a Windows 95 machine you should:

    A. Exit Windows, then turn off the machine

    B. Run SHUTDOWN.EXE

    C. Just turn it off

    D. Choose Shut Down from the start menu and shut the computer off when Windows 95 says it's okay.

    Answer: D

32. Which command is used to find files on a Windows 95 machine?

    A. Program Manager

    B. Find under the Start menu

    C. FINDFILE.EXE

    D. You can't find files on a Windows 95 machine.

    Answer: B

33. How do you access the Control Panel in Windows 95?

    A. Select Start menu ➢ Settings ➢ Control Panel.

    B. Select Start menu ➢ Control Panel.

    C. Select Start menu ➢ Programs ➢ Control Panel.

    D. Right-click My Computer and select Control Panel.

    Answer: A

34. You can't search the help system in Windows 95.

    A. True

    B. False

    Answer: B

Chapter 3 Answers

  1. Which of the following files is not needed under Windows 95?

    A. USER.DAT

    B. IO.SYS

    C. MSDOS.SYS

    D. AUTOEXEC.BAT

    Answer: C

  2. Which of the following components starts a Windows 3.x session?

    A. WIN.CNF

    B. WIN.COM

    C. KRNL286.EXE

    D. KRNL386.EXE

    Answer: B

3. Which technology allows Windows 95 to use up to 2 tera-bytes of drive space?

   A. FAT32

   B. IDE

   C. Enhanced IDE (EIDE)

   D. SmartDisk

   Answer: A

4. Which Windows 3.*x* component is responsible for drawing windows and scroll bars?

   A. USER.EXE

   B. GDI.EXE

   C. KRNL286.EXE

   D. WINDOW.EXE

   Answer: B

5. Which of the following files is the command interpreter for MS-DOS?

   A. COMMAND.COM

   B. COMMAND.EXE

   C. MSDOS.SYS

   D. KRNL386.EXE

   Answer: A

6. Generally speaking, you can run Windows 3.*x* programs under Windows 95.

   A. True

   B. False

   Answer: A

7. Which key could you press at the "Starting Windows 95 . . ." screen to boot directly to an old operating system instead of starting Windows 95?

   A. F1

   B. F2

   C. F4

   D. F5

   Answer: C

8. One of the disadvantages of the FAT32 file system is:

   A. It isn't compatible with Windows NT or earlier versions of Windows 95 (before service release B).

   B. It is slower than other types of file systems.

   C. It is expensive.

   D. It can't be used on computers with a National Semi-conductor 80753 pre-processor integrator.

   Answer: A

9. Which Windows 3.*x* core component controls display of windows, icons, and menus?

   A. KRNL286.EXE

   B. KRNL386.EXE

   C. GDI.EXE

   D. None of the above

   Answer: C

10. If you save a file called MYLONGFILENAME.DOC under Windows 95, what does it look like in a directory listing in a DOS window?

    A. MYLONGFILENAME.DOC

    B. MYLONG~1.DOC

    C. MYLONG~1.FIL

    D. MYLONGFI.DOC

    Answer: B

11. Place the following MS-DOS files in order by placing a number next to them to indicate their loading order (i.e., 1=first, 2=second, and so on)

    _____ MSDOS.SYS

    _____ CONFIG.SYS

    _____ IO.SYS

    _____ AUTOEXEC.BAT

    _____ COMMAND.COM

    Answer: 2, 3, 1, 5, 4

Chapter 4 Answers

1. Which program is used to install DOS?

   A. INSTALL.EXE

   B. INSTALL.BAT

   C. SETUP.EXE

   D. STEPUP.EXE

   Answer: C

2. Which utility (or utilities) can be used to determine the amount of disk space on a machine that already has a version of DOS installed? (Choose all that apply.)

   A. DIR

   B. CHKDSK

   C. SPACE /DISK

   D. DISK /SPACE

   Answer: A, B

3. When upgrading DOS, Setup renames the AUTOEXEC.BAT to what?

   A. AUTOEXEC.BAK

   B. AUTOEXEC.001

   C. AUTOEXEC.OLD

   D. AUTOEXED.DAT

   Answer: C

4. DOS can be installed on IBM-compatible computers. True or false?

   A. True

   B. False

   Answer: A

5. How many disks are required to do a regular DOS installation?

   A. 1

   B. 2

   C. 3

   D. 4

   Answer: C

6. If you are upgrading from MS-DOS 6.20 to 6.22, how many disks (not counting uninstall disks) will you use to do the upgrade?

   A. 1

   B. 2

   C. 3

   D. 4

   Answer: A

7. It is necessary to back up the entire hard disk before doing a DOS upgrade. True or false?

   A. True

   B. False

   Answer: B

8. Prior to installing DOS onto a hard disk for the first time, you must do which of the following?

    A. FDISK and FORMAT the disk.

    B. Delete any unnecessary files.

    C. Back up the entire disk.

    D. Turn off the computer, then turn it back on.

    Answer: A

9. When you are installing DOS 6, you have to install to one of your floppy drives.

    A. True

    B. False

    Answer: B

10. Which function key, when pressed, will halt Setup and leave you at a DOS command prompt?

    A. F1

    B. F3

    C. F5

    D. F7

    Answer: B

11. Which function key will display help in the Setup program?

    A. F1

    B. F3

    C. F5

    D. F7

    Answer: A

12. A computer with an AMD K5 processor (an Intel-compatible CPU) can run MS-DOS.

    A. True

    B. False

    Answer: A

13. To install Windows 3.*x* to a computer, you can copy the files to your hard disk from the A: drive and then start Windows by typing WIN at the C:> prompt. True or false?

    A. True

    B. False

    Answer: B

14. Which of the following Windows 3.*x* Custom Setup steps is *not* included in the Express Setup?

    A. DOS File Copy

    B. Windows File Copy

    C. Printer Setup

    D. Specify Windows Directory

    Answer: D

15. If you don't want to install Notepad, which Windows 3.*x* installation method do you use? (Choose all that apply.)

    A. Easy Setup

    B. Difficult Setup

    C. Custom Setup

    D. Express Setup

    Answer: C

16. What is the name of the Windows 3.*x* installation program?

    A. SETUP.EXE

    B. INSTALL.EXE

    C. INSTALL.BAT

    D. Setup.BAT

    Answer: A

17. If you want the simplest possible installation, in which Windows 3.*x* Setup makes all the choices for you, which Setup method do you use? (Choose all that apply.)

    A. Easy Setup

    B. Difficult Setup

    C. Custom Setup

    D. Express Setup

    Answer: D

18. Which Windows 3.*x* Setup switch is used to decompress the Windows compressed files onto a network drive?

    A. /A

    B. /B

    C. /C

    D. /N

    Answer: A

19. Which Intel processor must your computer have (at minimum) in order to install Windows 3.*x*?

    A. 8086

    B. 8088

    C. 80286

    D. 80386

    Answer: C

20. Which Windows 3.*x* Setup switch is used to ignore the hardware detection?

    A. /A

    B. /B

    C. /C

    D. /I

    Answer: D

21. How much memory (minimum) does Windows 3.*x* require to run in 386 Enhanced mode?

    A. 512 KB

    B. 640 KB

    C. 1024 KB

    D. 2048 KB

    Answer: D

22. Which key, when pressed, will stop Setup in either Windows 3.*x* or Windows 95 and exit you to DOS?

    A. F1

    B. F3

    C. F5

    D. F7

    Answer: B

23. Which Windows 3.*x* Setup mode allows you to verify which type of computer you are installing Windows 3.*x* on?

    A. Easy Setup

    B. Difficult Setup

    C. Custom Setup

    D. Express Setup

    Answer: C

24. Which Windows 3.*x* Setup mode allows Setup to automatically configure the swap file type and size? (Choose all that apply.)

    A. Easy Setup

    B. Difficult Setup

    C. Custom Setup

    D. Express Setup

    Answer: D

25. During an Windows 3.*x* Express Setup, if you have just completed inserting Disk 2 in the DOS portion of the Setup, the next step you have to do is:

    A. Enter user information.

    B. Run the Windows Tutorial.

    C. Select Express Setup.

    D. Select Windows components to install.

    Answer: A

26. When choosing a printer in a Windows 3.*x* Custom Setup, you notice that your printer type isn't listed. What option do you choose to install your printer?

    A. Generic/Text Only

    B. Install Unlisted or Updated Printer

    C. HP LaserJet III

    D. Install New Printer

    Answer: B

27. Which Windows 3.*x* operating mode is used for older hardware and slower performance machines?

    A. 386 Enhanced Mode

    B. Real Mode

    C. Standard Mode

    D. Slow Mode

    Answer: C

28. The Windows 95 Setup type that is most like the Windows 3.*x* Express setup is:

    A. Typical

    B. Laptop

    C. Minimum

    D. Custom

    Answer: A

29. Which of the following Windows 95 Installation steps is *not* done during the course of a normal Custom installation:

    A. Copy system files

    B. Save old system files

    C. Select the Windows installation directory

    D. Install the Exchange client

    Answer: B

30. How much RAM does Windows 95 require?

    A. 2MB

    B. 4MB

    C. 6MB

    D. 8MB

    Answer: B

31. Which processor is required in your computer in order to install Windows 95?

   A. 286

   B. 386SX

   C. 386DX

   D. 486DX

   E. Pentium

   Answer: C

32. Which software component(s) must be installed in order to use Microsoft Fax to send and receive faxes with a fax modem? (Choose all that apply.)

   A: Microsoft Fax

   B. WinFax Pro

   C. Exchange Client

   D. Fax-o-la

   Answer: A, C

33. You must install at least a basic installation of DOS before installing Windows 95.

   A. True

   B. False

   Answer: A

34. True or false: the Windows 95 installation has a DOS portion.

   A. True

   B. False

   Answer: B

35. Which Windows 95 component is an online service, similar to AOL or CompuServe?

    A. The Microsoft Channel

    B. The Microsoft BBS

    C. The Microsoft News Network

    D. The Microsoft Network

    Answer: D

36. How many times do you have to reboot to install Windows 95?

    A. 1

    B. 2

    C. 3

    D. 4

    Answer: B

37. You have just finished entering your name and company information. What is the next step in installing Windows 95?

    A. Copy system files.

    B. Set up Microsoft Exchange.

    C. Select Components to Copy.

    D. Enter the product identification number.

    Answer: D

38. What is the name of the Windows 95 installation executable?

    A. INSTALL.BAT

    B. SETUP.BAT

    C. SETUP.EXE

    D. INSTALL.EXE

    Answer: C

39. After upgrading Windows 3.*x* to Windows 95 (and installing 95 to a directory called C:\WIN95) you can no longer run Windows 3.*x* on that computer.

    A. True

    B. False

    Answer: B

40. Which of the following is *not* a Windows 95 installation type?

    A. Express

    B. Custom

    C. Laptop

    D. Minimum

    Answer: A

41. The Custom installation allows you to choose which Windows 95 components you want to install.

    A. True

    B. False

    Answer: A

42. You can configure networking software during an installation of Windows 95.

    A. True

    B. False

    Answer: A

43. If you don't agree with the Microsoft License Agreement, Setup will let you install Windows 95 anyway.

    A. True

    B. False

    Answer: B

44. In a Typical installation of Windows 95, you have the option of picking which Windows 95 components you want to install.

    A. True

    B. False

    Answer: B

45. The last step in installing Windows 95 is:

    A. Configuring Microsoft Exchange

    B. Copying system files

    C. Setting the time, date, and time zone

    D. Entering the Product Identification Number

    Answer: C

46. Which of the following Setup switches will cause Setup to forgo the initial disk scan?

    A. /id

    B. /is

    C. /i

    D. /noscan

    Answer: A

Chapter 5 Answers

1. If SMARTDRV.EXE is used, which CONFIG.SYS parameter's value should be reduced?

   A. FILES=20

   B. CACHE=10

   C. BUFFERS=50

   D. SMARTDRV=10

   Answer: C

2. The PATH environment variable specifies what kind of directories?

   A. Directories that DOS uses

   B. Directories that COMMAND.COM searches to find programs to run

   C. Directories that COMMAND.COM searches to find files

   D. Directories that DOS searches to find files

   Answer: B

3. Which memory driver controls access to the High Memory Area (HMA)?

   A. HIMEM.SYS

   B. EMM386.EXE

   C. SMARTDRV.EXE

   D. MEM.EXE

   Answer: A

4. Which DOS components can be used for caching?

   A. BUFFERS=

   B. CACHE=

   C. SMARTDRIVE

   D. SMARTDRV

   Answer: A, D

5. Name the three files that MS-DOS requires in order to boot.

   Answer: MSDOS.SYS, IO.SYS, and COMMAND.COM

6. Name the three files that PC-DOS requires in order to boot.

   Answer: IBMBIO.COM, IBMDOS.COM, and
   COMMAND.COM

7. Which command replaces the DEVICE= command in the
   CONFIG.SYS but performs the same function and adds the
   ability to load drivers into free UMBs?

   A. LOADUMB=

   B. DEVICEUMB=

   C. LOADHIGH=

   D. DEVICEHIGH=

   Answer: D

8. Which MS-DOS file must be loaded in order for the
   AUTOEXEC.BAT to execute?

   A. MSDOS.SYS

   B. COMMAND.COM

   C. IO.SYS

   D. IBMBIO.COM

   Answer: B

9. Which MS-DOS command controls the appearance of the MS-DOS command prompt?

   A. CSET

   B. DOSPROMPT

   C. PROMPT

   D. CONFIG.SYS

   Answer: C

10. Which CONFIG.SYS area (in a multiconfig setup) contains commands that execute regardless of the menu option chosen?

    A. :ALL

    B. [ALL]

    C. :COMMON

    D. [COMMON]

    Answer: D

11. Which CONFIG.SYS loads device drivers into memory?

    A. DEVICE=

    B. LOAD=

    C. START=

    D. DOS=

    Answer: A

12. Which type of DOS command is contained within COMMAND.COM?

    A. .EXE

    B. Internal

    C. External

    D. .COM

    Answer: B

13. What DOS utility is used for disk compression?

    A. DRVSPACE

    B. DISKSPACE

    C. DUBDRIVE

    D. DBLSPACE

    Answer: A

14. Which of the following is *not* an internal DOS command?

    A. CLS

    B. COPY

    C. MORE

    D. PAUSE

    Answer: C

15. Which Windows 3.*x* INI file contains drivers and VXDs for Windows devices?

    A. WIN.INI

    B. SYSTEM.INI

    C. PROGMAN.INI

    D. CONTROL.INI

    Answer: B

16. Generally speaking, the SYSTEM.INI file gets updated when you run which Windows program and make changes?

    A. CONTROL.EXE

    B PIFEDIT.EXE

    C. SETUP.EXE

    D. PAINT.EXE

    Answer: C

17. What does PIF stand for?

   A. Programmable Initialization File

   B. Program Information File

   C. Program Instant File

   D. Program Instruction File

   Answer: B

18. Which Windows component is a small piece of executable code shared between many applications to reduce the size of each application that shares it?

   A. USER.EXE

   B. INI files

   C. The Registry

   D. DLL files

   Answer: D

19. Which file(s) cannot be edited with SYSEDIT? (Choose all that apply.)

   A. AUTOEXEC.BAT

   B. CONFIG.SYS

   C. WIN.INI

   D. SYSTEM.INI

   E. PROGMAN.INI

   F. CONTROL.INI

   G. COMMAND.COM

   Answer: E, F, G

20. Which type of font file prints fastest?

    A. Bitmap

    B. TrueType

    C. Hardware printer

    D. Screen

    Answer: C

21. Which section of the SYSTEM.INI file contains the drivers that are loaded at system startup?

    A. [boot]

    B. [drivers]

    C. [boot.description]

    D. [386Enh]

    Answer: A

22. Which entry do you place in WIN.INI to make an application program start automatically as a minimized application?

    A. Minimize=*filename*

    B. Run=*filename*

    C. Load=*filename*

    D. Start=*filename*

    Answer: C

23. Which entry do you place in WIN.INI to make a program start automatically as a regular, full-screen application?

    A. Minimize=*filename*

    B. Run=*filename*

    C. Load=*filename*

    D. Start=*filename*

    Answer: B

24. What is the extension of TrueType font files?

    A. .TTF

    B. .TT

    C. .FOT

    D. .FNT

    Answer: A, C

25. Which Windows 95 component is used to add new programs to Windows 95?

    A. Device Manager

    B. Add/Remove Programs

    C. Desktop

    D. Start ➢ New Program

    Answer: B

26. Which tool can be used to edit the Windows 95 Registry?

    A. SYSEDIT

    B. EDIT

    C. REGEDIT

    D. EDITREG

    Answer: C

27. Which tool(s) can be used to add new hardware to Windows 95?

    A. Plug-n-Play

    B. Device Manager

    C. Add/Remove Programs

    D. Add New Hardware

    Answer: A, D

28. Which tool(s) can be used to install an updated driver for a Windows 95 device?

    A. Plug-n-Play

    B. Device Manager

    C. Add/Remove Programs

    D. Add New Hardware

    Answer: B

29. Your print jobs are taking a long time to print. Which set of steps will solve the problem?

    A. Select Start ➢ Settings ➢ Printers then right-click the printer and choose Properties. Go to the Details tab, click Spool Settings, and change Spool Print Jobs... to Print Directly to Printer.

    B. Select Start ➢ Settings ➢ Printers then right-click the printer and choose Spool Settings. Go to the Properties tab and change Spool Print Jobs... to Print Directly to Printer.

C. Select Start ➤ Settings ➤ Printers then right-click the printer and choose Properties. Go to the Spool Settings tab and change Spool print jobs… to Print Directly to Printer.

D. None of the above

Answer: A

30. You want to change which screen saver your Windows 95 computer is using. Which control panel will you use?

   A. Desktop Settings

   B. Screen Saver

   C. Background

   D. Display

   Answer: D

31. Which program would you use to edit the registry?

   A. EDITREG.EXE

   B. EDITREG.COM

   C. REGEDIT.EXE

   D. REGEDIT.COM

   Answer: C

32. How do you display what devices are installed in your computer?

   A. Use the Device manager in the System control panel.

   B. Use the Device manager control panel.

   C. Use the Add New Hardware control panel.

   D. Type **DISPLAY ALL DEVICES** at a command prompt.

   Answer: A

33. What file(s) make up the Registry in Windows 95?

    A. REG.DAT

    B. USER.DAT

    C. SYSTEM.DAT

    D. SPOOL.DAT

    Answer: B, C

34. Which of the following are the Windows 95 Registry's automatic backup files?

    A. USER.DAT, SYSTEM.DAT

    B. USER.DA0, SYSTEM.DA0

    C. USER.BAK, SYSTEM.BAK

    D. USER.OLD, SYSTEM.OLD

    Answer: B

Chapter 6 Answers

1. Which drive type should not be low level formatted by a technician?

   A. IDE

   B. MFM

   C. RLL

   D. All of the above.

   Answer: A

2. The hard drive partition with the bootable system files is called:

   A. Logical parirition

   B. Extended partition

   C. System partition

   D. Active partition

   Answer: D

3. A File Allocation Table is created:

   A. At the factory

   B. By FDISK

   C. By the interleave program

   D. During a high level format, using the FORMAT command

   Answer: D

4. Deleted files may be recovered by:

    A. UNERASE

    B. UNDELETE

    C. RECOVER

    D. UNDO

    Answer: B

5. Which application reorganizes files on a disk in order to optimize disk drive performance?

    A. SCANDISK

    B. FDISK

    C. OPTIMIZE

    D. DEFRAG

    Answer: D

6. On a DOS based system, memory is conveniently optimized:

    A. Using HIMEM.SYS

    B. Manually changing entries in CONFIG.SYS

    C. With a hard drive cache

    D. Using MEMMAKER

    Answer: D

7. A problem with RAM disks is:

    A. They often break

    B. Data is lost when the computer is shut down

    C. They need frequent reformatting

    D. They have slow access times

    Answer: B

8. In Windows 3.*x*, the best choice of swap file is a:

    A. High speed trade file

    B. Compressed swap file

    C. Permanent swap file

    D. Temporary swap file

    Answer: C

9. In Windows 95, the swap file:

    A. Must be on an uncompressed drive

    B. May be on a compressed drive controlled by DRVSPACE.VXD

    C. Requires a contiguous hard drive space

    D. May be disabled without effect

    Answer: B

10. Windows 95 handles hard disk caching with:

    A. SMARTDRIVE

    B. DEFRAG

    C. VCACHE

    D. FAT-CACHE

    Answer: C

Chapter 7 Answers

1. Pick the two basic methods for installing applications:

    A. Copying files onto a hard drive

    B. Copying program files onto a floppy disk

    C. Editing the Registry

    D. Running a setup routine

    Answer: A, D

2. Windows programs:

    A. Can be run under DOS

    B. Are easier to install than DOS programs

    C. Always make changes to the Registry

    D. Are always easy to uninstall

    Answer: A

3. Launching programs may be accomplished by:

    A. Entering the path and command name at a DOS prompt

    B. Double-clicking on a program icon

    C. Entering a command name in the RUN dialog box

    D. All of the above

    Answer: D

4. Uninstalling a DOS application involves:

    A. Removing DLLs

    B. Erasing program files

    C. Using the Add/Remove Programs option

    D. Formatting the hard drive

    Answer: B

5. The Windows 95 Registry is:

    A. Edited with Notepad

    B. Made up of the USER.DAT and the PROGMAN.DAT files

    C. Edited with REGEDT32.EXE

    D. Made up of the USER.DAT and the SYSTEM.DAT FILES

    Answer: D

6. The Registry:

    A. Takes the place of all of the INI files

    B. Holds most of the configuration settings for Windows 95

    C. Was first introduced with DOS 6.22

    D. Has no importance for Windows 95

    Answer: B

7. 16-bit Windows programs:

    A. All create INI files.

    B. Never create INI files. The registry takes care of that.

    C. May use default PIFs.

    D. Usually have an INI file associated with them.

    Answer: D

8. Which installation method gives the installer the most flexibility?

    A. Run from CD

    B. Typical

    C. Flexible

    D. Custom

    Answer: D

9. When installing programs, it is always important to:

   A. Have a screwdriver ready

   B. Have a legally licensed copy of the program

   C. Have plenty of floppy disks on hand

   D. Reformat the hard drive

   Answer: B

10. When you pick a custom installation of a Windows program:

    A. You lose the choice to do a typical installation.

    B. You need more hard drive space.

    C. You won't be able to use the CD drive.

    D. You will be able to see the options that are typically selected.

    Answer: D

Chapter 8 Answers

1. Which type of backup copies all files that have changed since the last full backup, regardless if they have been backed up since then?

   A. Full

   B. Incremental

   C. Differential

   D. Custom

   Answer: C

2. A computer virus is:

   A. A small program

   B. A small living organism

   C. Something that makes you sick

   D. A type of cheese

   Answer: A

3. One of the main functions of all viruses is to:

   A. Party

   B. Reproduce

   C. Destroy files

   D. Make strange things happen to your computer

   Answer: B

4. Backing up is important because you need to have something to do when you're not working on your computer.

   A. True

   B. False

   Answer: B

5. If you backed up 60MB of data, how many tapes are required to restore from a full backup (generally speaking)?

   A. 4

   B. 2

   C. 7

   D. 1

   Answer: D

6. What is the name of the executable for Microsoft Backup for DOS?

    A. MSBKUP.EXE

    B. MSBACKUP.EXE

    C. BACKUP.EXE

    D. MWBACKUP.EXE

    Answer: B

7. What is the name of the executable for Microsoft Backup for Windows 3.*x*?

    A. MSBKUP.EXE

    B. MSBACKUP.EXE

    C. BACKUP.EXE

    D. MWBACKUP.EXE

    Answer: D

8. You can use a Travan tape drive with Windows 95 Backup.

    A. True

    B. False

    Answer: B

9. What would you type at a DOS command line to start the Microsoft Anti-Virus?

    A. AV

    B. MSANTIVI

    C. MSAV

    D. ANTIVIRU

    Answer: C

10. Which control panel can be used to create a Startup Disk?

A. System

B. Add new hardware

C. Add/Remove programs

D. Startup

Answer: C

Chapter 9 Answers

1. Which service must be installed in order to share files on a Windows 95 workstation?

A. Networks

B. 3Com

C. File and Print Sharing for Microsoft Networks

D. Windows 95

Answer: C

2. In Windows 95 where do you configure which networking components are installed?

A. Network Control Panel

B. Windows 95 Setup

C. Add/Remove Programs

D. Add New Hardware

Answer: A

3. Which protocol must be configured on your Windows 95 machine in order to connect to the Internet?

    A. IPX/SPX

    B. TCP/IP

    C. NetBEUI

    D. Asynchronous

    Answer: B

4. Which of the following is the fastest Internet connection?

    A. ISDN

    B. PPP over POTS

    C. T1

    D. T3

    Answer: D

5. With a computer named SERVER1 and a shared directory named DOCUMENT, which is the correct UNC path syntax?

    A. \\SERVER1\DOCUMENT

    B. /Server1/Document

    C. \\DOCUMENT\SERVER1

    D. Document/Server1

    Answer: A

6. You have a Plug-n-Play network card, but all other ISA cards in your computer are non-PnP cards. You want to avoid problems, where possible. What can you do?

   A. Configure the PnP cards to "manual configuration" (i.e., non-PnP mode)

   B. Don't use the PnP network card. Get a new, non-PnP card

   C. Set all ISA cards to the same interrupt

   D. Set all ISA cards to Software Configure

   Answer: A

7. A Web browser allows you to access what part of the Internet?

   A. NNTP

   B. Routers

   C. WWW

   D. Gopher

   Answer: C

8. A set of rules that governs network communications is called:

   A. The Internet

   B. A Communications Protocol

   C. The TCP/IP law

   D. IPX

   Answer: B

9. How do you share a folder once file and printer sharing has been enabled on your Windows 95 workstation?

   A. Right-click My Computer, choose Sharing, click Enable, and click OK.

   B. Right-click Network Neighborhood, choose Properties, click Add, choose the folder you want to share, and click OK.

   C. Right-click the folder you want to share, choose Sharing, click Shared As, and click OK.

   D. Right-click the Desktop, choose Sharing, click Shared As, and click OK.

   Answer: C

10. The Internet is owned by the government.

    A. True

    B. False

    Answer: B

11. Which of the following is an acronym for the phone line that most people have in their houses?

    A. ISDN

    B. T1

    C. T3

    D. POTS

    Answer: D

12. SHARE.EXE provides which functionality for DOS?

   A. Allows file and printer sharing

   B. Provides file and record-locking functions

   C. Makes DOS into a multi-user OS

   D. Puts DOS on the network

   Answer: B

Chapter 10 Answers

1. A clean boot is:

   A. The same as a cold boot

   B. The same as a warm boot

   C. Accomplished by pressing Ctrl+Alt+Del

   D. A boot with no drivers loaded or with minimal drivers loaded

   Answer: D

2. An important step in troubleshooting is:

   A. Backing up critical system files

   B. Talking to the customer about the computer's problems

   C. Documenting all of your work

   D. All of the above

   Answer: D

3. When gathering information, it is important to:

   A. Determine when the computer was last used.

   B. Determine the last changes made to the computer

   C. Tell the customer to use surge power protection

   D. Check in with the office

   Answer: B

4. Which of the following is true about IRQ conflicts?

   A. They most often involve com ports.

   B. They most often involve sound cards.

   C. They almost never occur.

   D. They are the same as DMA conflicts.

   Answer: A

5. Which of the following is true about DOS memory management?

   A. It can be done manually.

   B. It is often done with MEMMAKER.

   C. It is built-in and needs no further action.

   D. Both A and B

   Answer: D

6. With Windows 3.*x*, editing system files:

   A. Can be done with SYSEDIT

   B. Can be done with any text editor

   C. Includes CONFIG.SYS, AUTOEXEC.BAT, WIN.INI, and SYSTEM.INI

   D. All of the above

   Answer: D

7. Which of the following is true about GPF?

   A. It stands for General Provision Finding.

   B. It stands for General Protection Fault.

   C. It occurs when the same memory is allocated to two different programs.

   D. Both B and C

   Answer: D

8. The two files that make up the Windows 95 Registry are:

   A. USER.DA0 and SYSTEM.DA0

   B. USER.DAT and SYSTEM.DAT

   C. WIN.INI and SYSTEM.INI

   D. None of the above

   Answer: B

9. When installing Windows 95, an error log is created. This log is called:

   A. ERRORLOG.TXT

   B. ERROR.LOG

   C. DETCRASH.LOG

   D. DETCRASH.TXT

   Answer: C

10. Which key, when pressed at startup, will prevent Windows 95 from starting and leave you at a command prompt?

    A. F5

    B. F7

    C. F9

    D. F10

    Answer: A

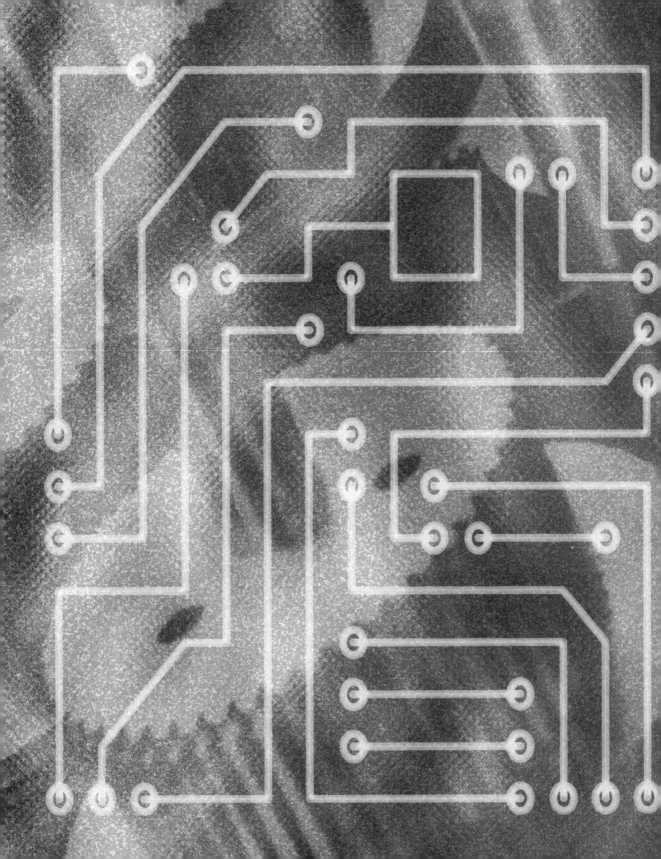

APPENDIX

B

Computer Service Information Web Site Directory

Within this appendix are several tables of URLs for service information that can be found on the Internet (specifically, on the World Wide Web). Most of the URLs listed point to the companies' support websites. Where a support page was unavailable, we give the URL of the company's home page, where you can at least get an idea of how to contact the company for questions about their products or services.

In this appendix, we offer URLs for the following selected websites:

- Computer hardware vendors
- Computer software vendors
- Third-party technical support

Computer Hardware

Table B.1 is a listing of the service and support websites of some of the most popular computer hardware vendors. While this is not a comprehensive list, it includes most of the important manufacturers that have useful websites as of this writing.

TABLE B.1:   Major hardware vendor support sites

Company	Address
3Dfx	http://www.3dfx.com/download/
Acer	http://www.aceramerica.com/aac/support/index.htm
Advanced Logic Research (ALR)	http://www.alr.com/service/service.htm
Apple	http://support.info.apple.com/tso/tsohome/tso-home.html
AST	http://www.ast.com/support/support.htm
ATI	http://support.atitech.ca/

TABLE B.1 (CONTINUED): Major hardware vendor support sites

Company	Address
Boca Research	http://www.bocaresearch.com/support/
Creative Labs (Soundblaster multimedia equipment)	http://www-nt-ok.creaf.com/wwwnew/tech/support/support.html
CTX	http://www.ctxintl.com/techsup.htm
Diamond Multimedia	http://207.1.65.7/vweb/
Digital Equipment Corp.	http://www.dec.com/info/services/mcs/mcs_hardware.htm
DTK	http://www.dtkcomputer.com/tech.html
Epson	http://www.epson.com/connects/
ESS Technology	http://www.esstech.com/
Fujitsu	http://www.8fujitsu.com/
Gateway 2000	http://www.gw2k.com/corp/support/cs_techdocs/
Hayes	http://www.hayes.com/support/index.htm
Hewlett-Packard (HP)	http://hpcc923.external.hp.com/wcso-support/Services/services.html
IBM	http://www.ibm.com/Support/
Leading Edge	http://www.primenet.com/~fwagner/le/
Logitech	http://support.logitech.com/support.nsf/support?OpenView
Matrox	http://www.matrox.com/mgaweb/techsupp/ftp.htm
Media Vision	http://www.svtus.com/new/new.html
Micron	http://www.micronpc.com/support/support.html
Midwest Micro	http://www.mwmicro.com/support/
Multi-Tech	http://www.multitech.com/servsupp.htp
NCR	http://www.ncr.com/support/
NEC	http://www.nec.com/support.html

TABLE B.1 (CONTINUED): Major hardware vendor support sites

Company	Address
Okidata	http://www.okidata.com/services/
Packard Bell	http://support.packardbell.com/
Panasonic	http://www.panasonic.com/host/support/index.html
PNY Technologies	http://www.pny.com/Tech/index.stm
Power Computing	http://support.powercc.com/service.html
Practical Peripherals	http://www.practinet.com/support.htm
Quantum	http://support.quantum.com/
S3	http://www.s3.com/bbs/0main/topindex.htm
Samsung	http://www.sec.samsung.co.kr/Support/support.html
Seagate	http://www.seagate.com/support/supporttop.shtml
Sony	http://www.ita.sel.sony.com/support/
SUN Microsystems	http://www.sun.com/service/
Supermac	http://www.supermac.com/service/index.html
Toshiba	http://www.toshiba.com/tais/csd/support/
US Robotics	http://infodeli.3com.com/
Viking Components	http://www.vikingmem.com/support/index.html
VisionTek	http://www.visiontek.com/htdocs/services/support.html
Western Digital	http://www.wdc.com/support/
Zenith Data Systems	http://support.zds.com/default.asp

Computer Software

In addition to hardware vendors, we have compiled a list of some of the major software vendors (Table B.2). Again, it's not a comprehensive list, but should be useful for getting you the information you need.

TABLE B.2:   Major software vendor support sites

Company	Address
Adobe	http://www.adobe.com/supportservice/main.html
Caldera	http://www.caldera.com/tech-ref/
Claris	http://www.claris.com/support/support.html
Corel	http://www.corel.com/support/index.htm
Lotus	http://www.support.lotus.com/
Microsoft	http://www.microsoft.com/support/
Netscape	http://home.netscape.com/comprod/products/support_programs/index.html
Novell	http://support.novell.com/

Other Technical Support Information

Of course, there are all sorts of sources for technical support information besides the websites of the vendors. In this table (Table B.3), we provide the URLs for some useful websites that are run not by vendors, but by informed third parties.

TABLE B.3:   Other technical support sites

Description	Address
HealthyPC.com *Offers computing advice columns,* *and software patch downloads*	`http://www.zdnet.com/hpc/`
HelpMeNow.com *A free technical support forum* *and chat area*	`http://www.HelpMeNow.com/`
CMP Techweb *An e-zine for all aspects of the technical* *support industry. Check out the encyclo-* *pedia for a definition of almost any* *technical term.*	`http://www.techweb.com/`
PC Week *The magazine's website. Great for* *information on PC developments.* *Also, you can download the Ziff-Davis* *benchmarking utilities.*	`http://www.pcweek.com/`
Help Desk Institute *Great source of help desk resources*	`http://www.HelpDeskInst.com/`
The Computer Technology Industry Association *Information on computer resources* *as well as information on the* *A+ certification*	`http://www.comptia.org/`
Ask a Geek *('nuf said?)*	`http://www.flash.net/~cge/java/ask.htm`
Software.net *A vendor directory that lists vendors* *offering technical support information*	`http://www.software.net/directory.htm`
Software Support Professionals Association *Provides support professionals a place to* *chat and exchange support information*	`http://www.sspa-online.com/`
The Technical Support Nightmare *A humorous look at technical support*	`http://www.geocities.com/SiliconValley/` `Vista/9426/`
Scott's page o' Computer Literacy *Another technical support humor page*	`http://www.center-net.com/8888/`

TABLE B.3 (CONTINUED): Other technical support sites

Description	Address
Association of Support Professionals *Another professional support organization*	http://www.asponline.com/
SupportHelp.com *A database of technical support websites, addresses, phone numbers, and other support resources*	http://www.supporthelp.com/

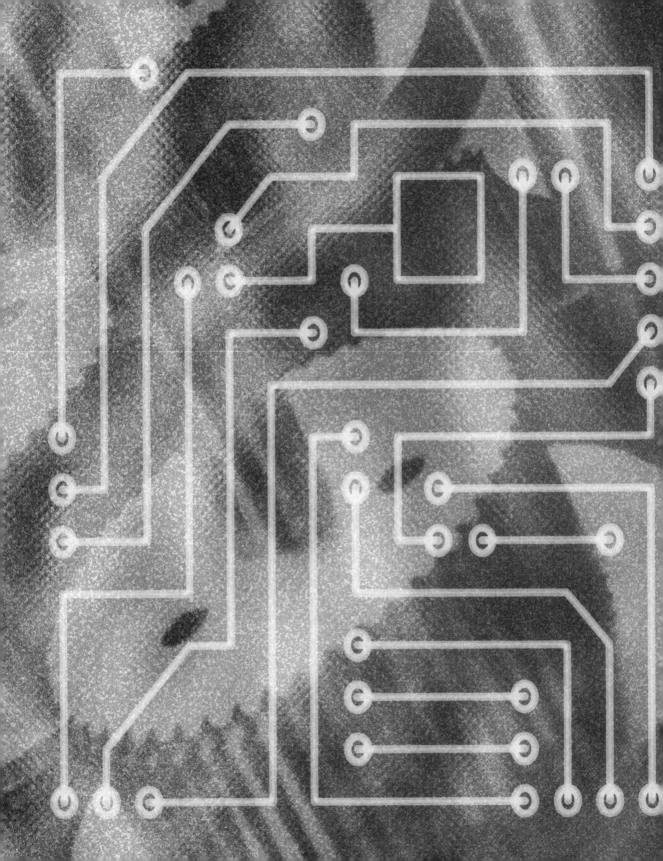

APPENDIX

C

DOS/Windows Glossary

A

active partition The DOS partition that will be read at startup and will be expected to have the necessary system files on it to boot the computer.

Add/remove windows components Windows 95 option that brings up a window that allows you to change which optional components are installed on the system.

Alpha release The release of software that is intended only for testing within the software company itself and may not include all the features in the eventual release.

archive Attribute used to mark files that have been modified since they were last backed up. It is set with the DOS ATTRIB command.

ATTRIB Command used to alter a file's attributes.

attribute Unique properties of a DOS file that are altered using an external DOS command called ATTRIB.

B

BACKUP Program that is used to back up a small amount of data on a floppy disk.

batch file File with a .BAT extension that contains other DOS commands. Simply by typing the name of the batch file and pressing ENTER, DOS will process all of the batch file commands, one at a time, without need for any additional user input.

Beta release The release of a piece of software that is given to a select group of testers. The software has 95 percent of its functionality and usually only needs a few bug fixes to be a full, released version of software

BIOS (Basic Input/Output System) The ROM-based software on a motherboard that acts as a kind of "interpreter" between an operating system and a computer's hardware.

Boolean Logic A type of math where the operators are represented by English words (i.e., AND, NOT, BUT, OR). The result of any Boolean equation is usually TRUE or FALSE. This type of logic is often used in DOS batch files to allow for some branching.

boot disk A diskette that allows the technician to load a limited version of DOS and then do troubleshooting and configuration tasks on the PC.

booting Term used for starting up a computer and loading the operating system into memory.

BUFFERS CONFIG.SYS command that determines the number of buffers DOS creates so that it can store cache information in RAM before it stores it on disk.

(

cache "hit" Indicates that the requested information was found in the cache.

cache miss Indicates that the system did not find required data in the cache, which necessitated a disk read.

CALL Batch file command that executes the commands in another batch file and returns control back to the batch file that "CALLed" it.

Central Point Backup The disk backup program that is included with PC-DOS.

CHDIR (CD) Internal command that is used to change the current or default directory.

CHKDSK.EXE Program that provides information about the size of the disk as well as how many bytes are left on the disk.

"Cold boot" The process of rebooting the computer by turning off and on the power switch.

COMMAND.COM Takes commands issued by the user through text strings or click actions and translates them back into calls that can be understood by the lower layers of DOS. It is the vital command interpreter for DOS. See also *Command interpreter*.

Command Interpreter The primary vehicle used by DOS that allows the user to communicate with the computer and vice-versa.

CONTROL.INI File that contains all the colors, patterns, and color schemes that Windows can use.

control panel The Windows component that allows a user to customize the look and operation of Windows.

command-line execution parameters Parameters that are passed to the batch file or program from its command line.

conditional statement A statement (usually in a program or batch file) that performs an operation based on some condition (usually a Boolean logic statement like IF <some condition> IS TRUE THEN <do operation>).

CONFIG.SYS The DOS system file that controls hardware configuration and general system environment parameters.

contiguous memory Memory occurring in a single, continuous block.

COPY Internal DOS command that is used to copy files from location to location.

current path Refers to the order in which COMMAND.COM searches specified subdirectories for programs typed in and entered at the command prompt.

D

DBR (DOS Boot Record) The area on a hard disk that contains the MS-DOS system files. This area contains MS-DOS startup files and configuration files.

DEL Internal command contained within COMMAND.COM that is used to delete files from a disk.

Desktop Contains the visible elements of Windows and defines the limits of graphic environment.

Desktop Control Panel Windows panel that is used to configure the system so it is more easily usable. This control panel contains the settings for the background color and pattern as well as screen saver settings.

DEVICE= Command found in the DOS CONFIG.SYS that tells DOS which driver to find and load into memory at boot time.

device fonts Windows fonts that print the fastest because the printer has the routines to "draw" those fonts inside the printer.

DEVICEHIGH= Command that is used to load the device drivers into Upper Memory Blocks, thereby freeing up space in conventional memory.

differential backup Backs up files that have changed since the last full backup.

DIR (directory) An internal command contained within COMMAND.COM. DIR is the principal means by which you examine the contents of your computer's storage media.

disk-caching program A program that reads the most commonly accessed data from disk and keeps it in memory for faster access.

DOS Environment Variables Variables that specify global things like the PATH that DOS searches to find executables.

DoubleSpace DOS Program that allows for doubling of disk space through disk compression.

Dynamic Link Library (DLL) files Windows component files that contain small pieces of executable code that are shared between multiple Windows programs. They are used to eliminate redundant programming in certain Windows applications.

E

EDIT Command in MS-DOS that invokes the MS-DOS Editor, which is used to create new text files or modify existing text files.

EMM386.EXE Reserved memory manager that emulates Expanded Memory in the Extended Memory area (XMS) and provides DOS with the ability to utilize upper memory blocks to load programs and device drivers.

ERASE See *DEL*.

Extended Memory (XMS) Memory above 1,024KB that is used by Windows and Windows-based programs. This type of memory cannot be accessed unless the HIMEM.SYS memory manager is loaded in the DOS CONFIG.SYS with a line like DEVICE=HIMEM.SYS.

Extended partition The type of DOS partition that can be created after the primary partition. It is the only other partition allowed on a disk once the primary partition has been made using FDISK.

Extensions Defines the file's type and function. Extensions are the 1, 2, or 3 characters that appear after the dot in a DOS filename.

external commands Commands that are not contained within COMMAND .COM. They are represented by a .COM or .EXE extension.

F

FAT (File Allocation Table) A special file located on a DOS-formatted disk that specifies where each DOS file is located on the disk.

FDISK.EXE The DOS utility that is used to partition hard disks for use with DOS

File manager Windows utility that allows the user to accomplish a number of important file-related tasks from a single interface (e.g., copying files, making directories, moving files, and deleting files and directories).

FILES= CONFIG.SYS command that describes how many file handles DOS can keep track of at one time.

font files Windows files that specify the different typefaces that can be used to display letters.

FORMAT.COM External DOS command that prepares the partition to store information using the FAT system as required by DOS.

formatting The act of preparing a disk for DOS and creating the DOS File Allocation Table (FAT) so the DOS can place and retrieve files on the disk.

fragmentation A disk storage problem that exists after several smaller files have been deleted from a hard disk. The deletion of files leaves the disk with areas of free disk space scattered throughout the disk. The fact that these areas of disk space are located so far apart on the disk causes slower performance because the disk read/write heads have to move all around the disk's surface to find the pieces of one file.

full backup A method of backup that backs up all the files on a disk.

G

GDI.EXE Windows core component that is responsible for drawing icons and windows in Windows 3.x.

General Protection Fault A Windows error that typically occurs when a Windows program tries to access memory currently in use by another program.

GOTO Batch file command that allows a batch file execution to "branch." The execution of a batch file starts at the top of the file and executes one line at a time until it reaches the end. However, if you need a batch file to be written in one order and then executed in another, you can use GOTO to specify the order of the commands.

group icons A type of Windows icon that groups Windows program icons together in the Program Manager.

H

hidden attribute Attribute of DOS used to keep files from being seen in a normal directory search.

HIMEM.SYS The DOS memory manager which enables Extended Memory above 1,024KB on your system.

I

IBM-compatible A computer that has a processor that is compatible with the original IBM PC 8088.

Icons On-screen graphics that act as doors through which programs are started and therefore used to spawn windows. They are shortcuts that allow a user to open a program or a utility without knowing where that program is or how it needs to be configured.

incremental backup Backs up every file that has changed since the last full or incremental backup.

INI files Text files that are used to store program settings.

internal command Commands contained within COMMAND.COM.

Internal DOS commands commands like DEL and DIR that are part of COMMAND.COM.

IO.SYS Hidden, read-only system file that manages the input/output routines of your computer. IO.SYS deals with the basic issues of data communication between various hardware devices such as the hard disk, printers, floppy disk drives, etc.

K

kernel file Windows core component that is responsible for managing Windows resources and running applications.

M

MBR (Master Boot Record) File that contains information on how the hard disk is divided into partitions.

MKDIR (MD) Internal command for "Make Directory," DOS command used to create new directories.

MSBACKUP A DOS program that allows the user to make backup copies of all the programs and data stored on the hard disk. This program is menu-driven and allows the user to set up options that can be used each time you back up the hard drive.

MEM.EXE DOS command that allows you to examine the total and used memory on the system.

Multitasking A feature of an operating system that allows more than one program to run simultaneously.

MSD (Microsoft Diagnostics) Program that allows the user to examine many different aspects of a system's hardware and software setup.

MSDOS.SYS The hidden, read-only system file for MS-DOS that handles program and file management.

P

partitioning The carving out of disk space that DOS can use.

Path The location of the file on the disk. It is composed of the logical drive letter the file is on and any directories the file is contained with in.

Personal NetWare Peer-to-peer network operating system developed by Novell, Inc. It allows computers to function as both servers and workstations on small networks.

PIF editor A Windows program used to create Program Information Files (PIFs).

primary partition The first partition created on a disk.

printable screen font The regular fonts used to display text on the screen that are translated and downloaded to the printer when printed.

printer font Files that contain the instructions that the printer needs to print a particular typeface.

Print Manager Windows program used to install printers for use with Windows.

Program Groups See *group icons*.

PROGMAN.INI The INI file that contains the configuration settings for the Windows Program Manager.

Program Information Files (PIFs) File that tells Windows how to handle DOS programs that are trying to run in the Windows environment.

Program Manager The primary interface to Windows that allows you to organize and execute numerous programs by double-clicking on an icon in a single graphical window.

Program Manager Group (GRP) Files Files in the Windows directories that store information about which application icons are contained in which group icons.

PROMPT DOS Command that is used to modify the appearance of the command line prompt .

R

RAM disk An area of memory that has been set aside and assigned a drive letter.

Raster fonts Fonts that are designed pixel-by-pixel; each size family is stored as a separate file.

Read-Only Attribute of DOS that prevents a file from being modified, deleted, or overwritten.

Registry Centralized database that contains environmental settings for some Windows 3.*x* and Windows 95 programs.

REMARK (REM) Batch file command that is placed into a batch file before a command or set of commands to detail their use. Can also be used to prevent a comment from executing since any line beginning with this command will be ignored by COMMAND.COM while the batch file is executing.

RENAME (REN) Internal DOS command used to change the name of a file.

Reserved Memory Area The area in the DOS memory map that resides between 640KB and 1,024KB. Typically contains the EMS Page Frame as well as any ROMs for expansion devices and video display circuitry.

ROM (Read Only Memory) A type of computer memory that is retains its data permanently, even when power is removed. Once the data is written to this type of memory, it cannot be changed.

S

screen saver Program originally designed to prevent damage to a computer monitor from being left on too long. These programs usually include moving graphics so that no one pixel is left on all the time. Screen savers detect computer inactivity and activate after a certain period.

scheduling option Windows option that determines how much of the system's resources are dedicated to foreground applications.

Sections Breaks up the .INI file into logical groupings of settings.

SETUP.EXE Program that is configured to run a setup automatically when the computer is booted to this disk.

SMARTDRV.EXE (SmartDrive) A disk-caching program used to improve Windows and DOS performance on a DOS-based system.

soft font Font that comes on a disk and is downloaded via a special utility to the printer's memory or hard disk.

SYSEDIT A Windows utility that can be used to edit the CONFIG.SYS, AUTOEXEC.BAT, WIN.INI, and SYSTEM.INI simultaneously.

SYSTEM.INI File that contains Windows hardware configuration settings.

Swapfile The file on the hard drive which acts as virtual RAM for Windows.

Switches Command line options for some DOS commands that determine how simply a DOS command will be executed or what special features will be invoked. Switches are sometimes bracketed and therefore optional.

System attribute Attribute of DOS that is used to tell the OS that this file is needed by the OS and should not be deleted. Marks a file as part of the operating system and will also prevent the file from deletion.

T

Timeout Specifies in seconds how long Multiconfig will wait for you to select one of the configurations.

TREE Command that allows you to examine your file structure and see the directories and subdirectories that have been created.

Troubleshooting The process of identifying a computer problem so that it can be fixed.

U

UMBs (upper memory blocks) The blocks of free memory in the upper memory area between 640KB and 1,024KB.

unattended backup Backs up files to the destination you specify at the time you specify.

Upgrade Inexpensive way to purchase a new version of any software product.

upper memory area See *Reserved Memory Area*.

USER.EXE Windows core component that allows a user to interact with Windows. It is the component responsible for interpreting keystrokes and mouse movements and sending the appropriate commands to the other core components.

W

Warm boot Refers to pressing Ctl+Alt+Del to reboot the computer. This type of booting doesn't require the computer to perform all of the harware and memory checks that a cold boot does.

wild card characters Characters such as * or ? used in place of letters or words. They are used when you want to do a particular operation with several files at once.

Windows Provide the space in which a particular program or utility can function.

Windows Desktop See *Desktop*.

Windows Program Manager File that contains all of the program icons, group icons, and menus used for organizing, starting, and running programs.

WIN.INI Files that contains Windows environmental settings that control the general function and appearance.

WINSOCK A DLL that is responsible for providing Windows applications with the ability to communicate via TCP/IP (communication over the Internet).

X

XCOPY Command used to copy entire subdirectories or the entire contents of disk.

INDEX

Note to the Reader: Throughout this index **boldface** page numbers indicate primary discussions of a topic. *Italic* page numbers indicate illustrations.

E

F

O

P

Q

R

S

U

A+ TEST PREPARATION
FROM THE EXPERTS

Sybex presents the most comprehensive study guides for CompTIA's 1998 A+ exams for PC technicians.

COVERS THE 1998 A+

A+: Core Module STUDY GUIDE

SECOND EDITION

David Groth

Everything You Need to Know to Prepare for the A+ Core Module Exam

Full Coverage of Each A+ Core Module Objective

Detailed Information On:
- Configuration
- Installation and Upgrading
- Diagnosis
- Repair
- Preventive Maintenance
- Interaction with Customers
- Safety

ISBN 0-7821-2344-9
800 pp. 7½" x 9" $49.99
Hardcover July 1998

COVERS THE 1998 A+

A+: DOS/Windows STUDY GUIDE

SECOND EDITION

David Groth

Everything You Need to Know to Prepare for the A+ DOS/Windows Objective

Full Coverage of Each A+ DOS/Windows Objective

Detailed Information On:
- Installation and Configuration
- Batch Files
- DOS Commands
- Windows Components
- Adding New Hardware and Software
- System Optimization
- Troubleshooting

ISBN 0-7821-2351-1
688 pp. 7½" x 9" $49.99
Hardcover July 1998

COVERS THE 1998 A+

A+: Certification Kit

SECOND EDITION

ISBN 0-7821-2380-5
1,488 pp. 7½" x 9" $84.98
Hardcover 2-volume boxed set
August 1998

A+ Exam Notes: CORE MODULE

David Groth

The Quick Way to Brush Up Your Knowledge
Full Coverage of Each Objective

Detailed Information On:
- Configuration
- Installation and Upgrading
- Diagnosis
- Repair
- Preventive Maintenance
- Interaction with Customers
- Safety

ISBN 0-7821-2345-7
304 pp. 5⅞" x 8¼" $19.99
Softcover August 1998

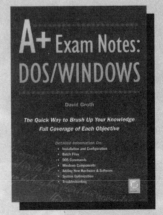

A+ Exam Notes: DOS/WINDOWS

David Groth

The Quick Way to Brush Up Your Knowledge
Full Coverage of Each Objective

Detailed Information On:
- Installation and Configuration
- Batch Files
- DOS Commands
- Windows Components
- Adding New Hardware & Software
- System Optimization
- Troubleshooting

ISBN 0-7821-2346-5
304 pp. 5⅞" x 8¼" $19.99
Softcover August 1998

SYB

www.sybex.c